RUSTIC A[...]
FOR HOM[...]

Rustic Adornments for Homes of Taste was first published in 1856 as a guide to home improvements for the middle-classes. James Shirley Hibberd gives many examples of how the natural beauty of the home can be enhanced and suggestions for decorations, from advice on the marine aquarium and the aviary to flower and fern window arrangements and hints on garden landscaping.

This edition is reprinted with the original line-drawings and an Introduction by L. John Sales, Chief Gardens Adviser to the National Trust since 1974, and author of *West Country Gardens*.

The cover shows 'A Summer's Afternoon' by George Mote

RUSTIC ADORNMENTS
FOR HOMES OF TASTE

AND RECREATIONS FOR TOWN
FOLK IN THE STUDY AND
IMITATION OF NATURE

BY SHIRLEY HIBBERD

Author of *Brambles and Bay Leaves* and *The Town Garden*

Introduction by John Sales

'Things such as these are ever harbingers
To trains of peaceful images'

KEATS

CENTURY
IN ASSOCIATION WITH THE NATIONAL TRUST
LONDON MELBOURNE AUCKLAND JOHANNESBURG

First published in 1856

This edition first published in 1987 by Century in association with the National Trust for Places of Historic Interest or Natural Beauty, 36 Queen Anne's Gate, London SW1H 9AS

Century Hutchinson Ltd, Brookmount House, 62–65 Chandos Place, London WC2N 4NW

Century Hutchinson Australia Pty Ltd
PO Box 496, 16–22 Church Street, Hawthorn, Victoria 3122, Australia

Century Hutchinson New Zealand Limited
PO Box 40–086, Glenfield, Auckland 10, New Zealand

Century Hutchinson South Africa (Pty) Ltd
PO Box 337, Berglvei, 2012 South Africa

ISBN 0 7126 1760 4

Published in association with The National Trust, this series is devoted to reprinting books on artistic, architectural, social and cultural heritage of Britain. The imprint will cover buildings and monuments, arts and crafts, gardening and landscape in a variety of literary forms including histories, biographies and letters.

The Century Classics also includes the Travellers, Seafarers and Lives and Letters series.

Printed and bound in Great Britain by
Richard Clay Ltd, Bungay, Suffolk

INTRODUCTION

James Shirley Hibberd was born in Stepney in 1825. This is not merely a biographical note, it is also a key to Shirley Hibberd's attitude to gardens, and his approach to writing about them. When he was born into a maritime family, Stepney was a village on the eastern outskirts of London. The years in which he grew to manhood saw an explosion of the population of London, and suburbs were thrown out from the City, engulfing many villages. One was Stepney, which became part of the East End, another was Stoke Newington, where Shirley Hibberd set out in his garden in Lordship Terrace to study the problems of urban and suburban horticulture.

Stoke Newington and neighbouring Hackney and Islington were in the mid-nineteenth century middle-class suburbs, inhabited by clerks who worked in the City and could either walk in or take the omnibus and the railway. It was for this prosperous new middle class of Victorian England, occupiers of modest suburban villas whose status was determined by material considerations – locality, houses, number of servants, furnishings, garden – that Shirley Hibberd wrote *Rustic Adornments for Homes of Taste* in 1856. The need to display beauty, refinement and 'taste' was high in the priorities of the time. Shirley Hibberd provided reassurance by propounding the idea that Taste is definable and constant, and that ethics and morality are keys to the recognition of the Beautiful. He recommended the study of art and nature as a means of refining morality; simple hobbies of the rustic kind 'that breathe purity and quiet and peace'.

Mrs Loudon's *Gardening for Ladies*, written in 1841 had, for the first time perhaps, stimulated an interest in gardens and gardening among middle-class married women whose domestic staff provided them with enough leisure to indulge their hobbies. In *Rustic Adornments* Shirley Hibberd sugggested a whole range of possibilities for creative and interesting pursuits inside and out-side the 'Home of Taste' fish tanks, bird houses, plant cases, garden ornaments – toys, as he called them, for providing instructive recreation and endless entertainment. His many references to their suitability for ladies makes clear his aim to bring them 'within reach of a Lady's delicate fingers'.

Although by no means the beginning of his prolific output, *Rustic Adornments* was the first of Shirley Hibberd's major works. Through his journalism and his books he became, along with William Robinson, the best known and most influential of the second generation of nineteenth-century gardening writers. For Shirly Hibberd and his contemporaries the over-riding theme of Victorian garden literature, the superiority of art over nature, had been established by the previous generation. The eighteenth-century ideal of 'nature' had been first overturned by Humphry Repton who declared that 'Gardens are works of art rather than of nature'. This philosophy was proclaimed more persistently by John Claudius Loudon who also advanced the science and practice of horticulture through his *Encyclopaedia of Gardening* and the *Gardener's Magazine*. In Hibberd's first book he could confidently state, without fear of contradiction, that 'a garden is an *artificial* contrivance, it is not a piece of ground scooped out of a wood, but in some sense a continuation of the house. Since it is a creation of art, not a patch of wild nature . . . it should everywhere show the evidence of artistic taste. . . .' In line with the established philosophy of High Victorian garden-ing he saw the 'principles of taste' as '. . . the subordination of every detail to the production of a *complete* effect, in which every contrast helps to conserve the harmony of the whole. . . .'

Alongside this revolution in taste came ever accelerating innovation in horticultural technique. Although the invention of the principle must be credited to Allen Alexander Maconochie the Wardian Case had been first described by Nathaniel Bagshaw Ward in 1829. This sealed glass case, providing a micro-climate for plants, made the long-distance importation of live specimens a practical and an economic proposition: one plant lived for a year on a long and complex journey from New Zealand to Kew. Such was the improvement in transporting exotic plants that the nurseryman George Loddiges could say that instead of receiving one live plant in twenty, to lose one in twenty was now regarded as a misfortune.

The principle of the Wardian Case was extended as a means of cultivating plants never before grown in the home by protecting plants not only from the rigours of the Victorian parlour, but also from the smoky atmosphere of Britain's industrial cities. These cases were usually ornate, glazed structures that adorned the drawing rooms of the time and have now re-appeared in every garden centre under the guise of terrariums. Like their present-day counterparts, these elaborate ornaments owed much of their success to being provided with some means of ventilation and access. They did not, as Shirley Hibberd pointed out, conform to the original principle of a closed glass case in which the atmosphere is constantly saturated.

Horticultural expertise blossomed following the publication of John Lindley's *Theory of Horticulture* in 1840 and by 1883 Shirley Hibberd was able to reflect that in fifty years he had 'seen horticulture developed from an empirical mystery to an art founded on the truths of nature and the achievements of science'.

Other developments included the end of glass tax and the invention of the sheet glass process in 1847, which released a flood of new ideas for greenhouses and brought them within the financial reach of the middle classes. Classic experiments on fertilisers and manures were begun at Rothamstead in Hertfordshire in the 1840s and even earlier than that William Barron was using his patent tree transplanter to make possible instant maturity in gardens by moving trees up to forty feet in height.

This development of the science and technology of horti-culture was, of course, only part of the rapid progress of inno-vation and experiment arising out of the industrial revolution and the economic expansion that accompanied it. The Great Exhibition of 1851 had given encouragement to industrial and stylistic invention, and national prosperity was increasing apace. Such was the mood of confidence and optimism that Shirley Hibberd could allude to the 'culminating point in our civilization' and to say with reference to the objects he rec-ommended that 'Our rooms sparkle with the products of art and our gardens with the curiosities of nature'.

Rustic Adornments also reflects his background as a naturalist, his highly imaginative purpose being to bring the study and imitation of nature into the town, the garden and even into the house. He made no attempt to discriminate between the alien and the native. This characteristically Victorian approach of acquiring in a catholic way plants and animals, British and foreign, for their intrinsic interest and beauty alone, allied nature study more closely with gardening than is normal today. Current attitudes towards nature conservation tend quite understandably to emphasise the conservation of habitat and the modern tendency to regard alien animals and plants as potential enemies of nature conservation would no doubt have been quite astonishing to Hibberd and his contemporaries. The range of his suggestions was ambitious and one wonders for example how long sea and river fish would have survived without the benefit of modern techniques. Clearly there was a degree of mortality, at least among the birds, for he writes disarmingly of the caged siskin that it may 'Die of plethora, through excess of health'! There are pangs of conscience too in his comments on cages for Larks being generally too small 'in character approaching a condemned cell, from the bars of which we expect to hear groans and curses'.

Rustic Adornments proved to be an enormous success, going into several reprints. As a result over the years Shirley Hibberd expanded several of the chapters into books in their own right. All his works can be read with profit but *The Fern Garden* 1869, *New and Rare Beautiful Leaved Plants* 1870, *The Amateur's Flower Garden* 1871 and *The Ivy* 1872 were particularly influential. From 1858 he edited *Floral World*, a magazine for owners of small gardens and people of modest income. Although he later edited the *Gardener's Magazine* and later still the newly-launched *Amateur Gardening*, it was *Floral World* through which he developed his ideas in print and to which he contributed in such measure.

His idea of gardening was rooted firmly in the 'Gardenesque', a term first coined by Loudon for the display of plants as individuals. By the middle of the century it had come to mean a mixed or irregular style something between the formal and the naturalistic, an attempt at 'the blending of art with nature'. Hibberd's own garden in Stoke Newington was a model for his readers being 280 ft long and 36–8 ft wide. It was laid out according to his precept of a graded transition from formality near the house to informality further out with paths and borders set out in the serpentine curves of the gardenesque, emphasised by neat and repetitive edging. There was a modest greenhouse with tiered staging adjoining the house, a summer house and a bee house. His rockery consisted or a rock arch and he always advocated copying ruins even on the small scale rather than attempting any kind of realism in rock work. He advised against the over-use of formal parterres and bedding in small gardens which he said 'reduced (them) to the conditon of manufacturies'. But he was keen on Pelargoniums and popularised 'Floral Pyramids' of his favourite plant, rubble-covered cones 6–8ft high, thickly planted; also 'Pincushion Beds' into which apparently any kind of plant could be stuck! In his younger days his opinions on colour were pragmatic but his views crystallised later around the popular theory of Michel-Eugène Chevreul who ruled that complementary (contrasting) colours always suited one another ie red/green, orange/sky blue, etc. More suited to the modern taste was his early advocacy of one dominant colour in any scheme, which he regarded as 'nature's method' and which was later taken up by Gertrude Jekyll and the twentieth-century artist-gardeners.

He popularised foliage plants and, against the current trend, always insisted that borders of hardy herbaceous plants were a necessity in gardens, bedding being merely an embellishment. In this way he laid the groundwork for William Robinson's rebellion against the bedding system and paved the way for Gertrude Jekyll.

Above all, perhaps, it is the independence and integrity of Hibberd's writing that leaves a lasting impression. Always based upon personal experience and observation, his books are full of practical common-sense. In some respects he was a typical Victorian, expressing his always decided opinions robustly and sometimes waspishly. But he usually gave credit where he thought it due, and he avoided the invective of writers like William Robinson. Indeed, part of his charm lay in his apt turn of phrase and his elegant language. In other respects he was very un-Victorian, being not only a teetotaller and a vegetarian, but also refusing to discourage birds or other plagues that might visit his garden. He was the dominant influence in gardens during the 1860s. With his help, after more than 100 years, the special qualities of Victorian gardening are at last being recognised and understood. How fitting it is that Shirley Hibberd's most influential book is being reprinted in the same year that the National Trust has acquired Biddulph Grange in Staffordshire, the most influential garden of the same decade.

JOHN SALES
1987

PREFACE.

WHATEVER serves to heighten the enjoyments of home, and add fresh graces to the domestic hearth, must be worthy of encouragement and culture. The last twenty years have been marked by such a progress in domestic æsthetics as to be worthy of designation as a new era in social life. The improvements in the structure of houses and the sanitary government of towns, have been accompanied by the quick march of the popular mind in the appreciation of beauty, and the promotion of every means of intellectual and moral refinement. If we have arrived at the culminating point in our civilization, we may yet feel some assurance that as long as luxury takes such innocent shapes as it now begins to delight in, our descent towards the horizon is certainly far off. But we cannot hope that the culminating point has yet been attained—we are surely still in the ascent towards it, and our course is becoming steadier and our light purer as we rise.

An eminent author has called this the Age of Veneer, and another dignifies it with the title of the Age of Fustian. I shall take the privilege afforded me in this Preface to call it the Age of Toys. We have nearly exhausted the means of morbid excitement, and are growing simpler, because purer in our tastes. Our rooms sparkle with the products of art, and our gardens with the curiosities of nature. Our conversation shapes itself to ennobling themes, and our pleasures take a tone from our improving moral sentiments, and acquire a poetic grace that reflects again upon both head and heart. The mark of our progress is seen in our love for toys, plant-cases, bird and bee-houses, fish-tanks, and garden ornaments, —they are the beads in our Rosary of homage to the Spirit of Beauty.

Happily in this country the Home of Taste is not a merely ideal creation; our domestic life is a guarantee of our national greatness, and as long as we shall continue to surround that life with emblems and suggestions of higher things, so long will the highest

teachings of knowledge, elegance, and virtue be attainable at the
fireside. Our pleasures and pursuits have as powerful an influence
on our national character as the precepts of sages at our seats of
learning; and the simple toys that afford recreation for our hours
of leisure may prove worthy advocates of morality and religion.
In the contemplation of the wonders of nature, and the cultivation
of domestic elegances, the intellect and moral nature must advance
towards perfection, just as Ingomar and all his bandit savages are
humanized by the presence among them of the chaste Parthenia.
Such is the ministry of the Toys that embellish the Home of
Taste, and to aid that ministry will, I hope, prove to be the
tendency of the present work.

Though many of the recreations treated of in the following pages
are those which pertain more exclusively to country life, I have
endeavoured to help the townsman in his participation of them,
and trust my humble labours may aid in what has already been
accomplished for the promotion of rustic life in towns—the realization, as far as possible, of the much-sought *Rus in urbe.*

S. H.

Tottenham, Feb. 1st. 1856.

PREFACE TO SECOND EDITION.

THIS Second Edition contains many subjects not included in the
First. A considerable portion of the work has been re-written, so
as to include many new inventions and improvements: many new
engravings, and about one hundred and fifty pages of letter-press
have been added; and the whole has undergone a careful revision
and re-arrangement. Except where authorities are quoted, I take
upon myself the responsibility of every description given, this
work being an epitome of my own practice, in the several
departments of which it treats.

S. H.

Tottenham, June 10th. 1857.

CONTENTS.

THE MARINE AQUARIUM.

THE FRESH-WATER AQUARIUM.

THE WARDIAN CASE.

THE WALTONIAN CASE.

FLORAL ORNAMENTS FOR THE TABLE AND THE WINDOW.

THE AVIARY.

THE APIARY.

THE PLEASURE GARDEN.

THE FLOWER GARDEN.

GARDEN AQUARIUM AND WATER SCENERY.

THE ROCKERY AND WILDERNESS.

THE FERNERY.

EMBELLISHMENTS OF THE GARDEN.

THE HOME OF TASTE.

Home! in that word how many hopes are hidden,
How many hours of joy serene and fair,
How many golden visions rise unbidden,
And blend their hues into a rainbow there!
Round home what images of beauty cluster,
Links which unite the living with the dead.
Glimpses of scenes of most surpassing lustre,
Echoes of melody whose voice is fled.

J. W. FLETCHER.

A MONG the emblems of our nationality, not one is more strongly cherished by us than OUR HOME. We pride ourselves on the strength and healthiness of our domestic life, and we challenge the world to produce an example of a people more fondly attached to their native soil, or in whom the fireside affections have a broader development, or a higher aim. We cherish the chimney corner where we first were blest by parental kisses, and through "the aisles of memory" its ruddy glow shines on our grey hairs, and warms our hearts as we hurry to the grave. At any period of life there is, with the majority of us, no dearer object of recollection than remembered scenes of the Home wherein we first lisped "Our Father," and no more hopeful subject of speculation and conjecture than the Home we have or are yet building up, in which to teach that same simple prayer to children of our own.

It is because we are truly a domestic people, dearly attached to our land of green pastures, and shrubby hedgerows, and grey old woods, that we remain calm amid the strife that besets the states around us, proud of our ancient liberties, our progressing intelligence, and our ever-expanding material resources. Those resources daily multiply the means of exalting our social life, and invention keeps pace with the demands of an improving civilization; so that while

> "The thoughts of men are widened by
> The progress of the suns,"

the facilities for calm and healthy enjoyment increase with the growth of more elevated desires. The "Home of Taste" is one of the latest fruits of the high tone to which social life has attained in this country of late years, and its complete development may not be so far off, but that the present generation may witness the union of Nature and Art in the ministration of human sympathies within doors.

We know already that the luxuries of refinement are no longer monopolized by the great, that the merchant is not rendered sordid by commerce, but that he can delight in the strength of Angelo and the grace of Raphael; the ledger does not dwarf the trader's soul below the appreci-

ation of Titian's lights or Rembrandt's shadows; and the persevering plodder, who from four to six does battle with armies of statistics, can retire to his suburban villa to rejoice as a happy soul in the midst of his family, or fondle his tame birds with the affection of a child. The fact is, that the aboriginal nature can never be drummed out of us, let visionaries say what they may; through all circumstances of life, let the whirl of excitement be never so rapid, or the stupor of despondency never so profound, that which ministers to our delicate perceptions of beauty, grace, and truth, serves at once as rest, and solace, and refreshment. Therefore we build up Homes of Taste wherein to find anchorage when life becomes a hurricane, and where, secure from the jar and dust that prevail without, we may cherish the affections that lie deepest in our nature, and from which spring the noblest and most enduring results.

A Home of Taste is a tasteful home, wherein everything is a reflection of refined thoughts and chaste desires. It is a school of the heart, in which human sympathies teach profounder lessons than are found in books, and the ornaments of walls and windows suggest a thousand modes of being cheaply happy. In such a home Beauty presides over the education of the sentiments, and while the intellect is ripened by the many means which exist for the acquisition of knowledge, the moral nature is refined by those silent appeals of Nature and of Art, which are the foundation of Taste. If Taste is an application to nature of the same faculty which in morals enables us to distinguish between right and wrong, then the Beautiful is the highest form, or rather the embodiment of the purest ethics; and to be in constant communication with it, drawing our inspirations from its most palpable phenomena, is to place our spiritual natures under the guidance of a goddess who cannot lead them wrong. No matter in what form the cultivation of Taste may manifest itself, in paintings and sculptures; in the analysis of scenery, in the grouping of flowers, in the embellishment

of the window or the mantel, in the cultivation of criticism, and the appreciation of what is true and beautiful in Art generally, refinement of manners, kindliness of feelings, and a deeper devotion of religion will be its sure attendants. We cannot come into the presence of any work of high-class art without at the instant experiencing motions that increase our happiness, nor can we take interest in the simplest pursuit of a leisure hour, without at once passing into an atmosphere of higher moral purity than we are compelled to breathe at other times, amid

"The weariness, the fever, and the fret,"

that, without such an antidote, harden the heart by degrees, and allow the inner life to be but half developed. Such "enchantments are medicinal, they sober and heal us. They are plain pleasures, kindly and native to us."

But the Home of Taste is not necessarily the result of a lavish expenditure—the most humble may command it. Though the several Rustic Adornments treated of in this work admit of extension, commensurate with the most liberal outlay, there is not one but is in some measure attainable by those who have but little leisure and most narrow means, and some indeed may be, and have been cultivated most successfully by those who could not aspire even to the ordinary luxuries of middle life. If the poor man cannot have his picture gallery, he can still gratify his love of art by embellishing his walls with copies of works of great masters, brought within his reach by the multiplying skill of the copyist and the engraver; if he cannot have a library, paneled with palm branches, and containing a collection of Aldines on vellum, and Caxtons worth twelve thousand guineas, he can still command elegant editions of the greatest historians, philosophers, and poets, to whom God ever gave the gift of expression. In the Rustic Adornment of the home, it does not require a princely fortune to set up a

vase of flowers, or an Aquarium, or a stand of bees that
shall sing to their master all day long, and entrap every
spare moment of leisure he may be able to afford to "shepherd them." He who lays out his garden in accordance
with correct principles of taste, may find in it as much
amusement, and as genuine a solace from the cark and care
of life, as if it were a domain of thousands of acres—perhaps
more so, for it is his own work, it represents his own idea,
it is a part of himself, and hence redolent of heart-ease.

It is an error common to writers to believe that the special
subject on which the pen is engaged is of pre-eminent importance, and perhaps I may be yielding to this common weakness
when I suggest that the Rustic Adornments of the household
embrace the highest of its attractions apart from the love
which lights the walls within. The pleasures of the garden,
the tending and taming of household pets, the culture of
choice plants in the greenhouse and the window, seem to
me much more remunerative, both intellectually and morally,
than even the study of the higher departments of art,
because they keep us nearer to nature, and compel us to
be students of the great out-door world, whence our noblest
inspirations and most humanizing teachings are drawn. "It
seems as if the day was not wholly profane, in which we
have given heed to some natural object."

It would be an anomaly to find a student of nature
addicted to the vices that cast so many dark shadows on our
social life; nor do I remember among the sad annals of
criminal history, one instance of a naturalist who became a
criminal, or of a single gardener who has been hanged. But
not to apply so severe a test, is it not true that the most
genial natures are of the most homely sort, attached to the
fireside; cultivators of rustic taste in some form or other;
given to simple hobbies that keep the attention fixed on
things that breathe purity, and quiet, and peace; they are
healthy folks, healthy in mind as well as in body, and to
clear perceptions add the impulses of generous hearts.

In a certain sense the Home is the outside of a man; it is an external vesture, and a visible embodiment of his mental character. The man of intellect and taste will impress on everything about him an air of usefulness or elegance, and will make the best of the roughest materials that fate may cast in his path. Architecture—the highest of the domestic arts—springs out of the common desire of the mind to dwell in a fair exterior, and in this, as in other of the useful arts, elegance, comfort, and convenience usually go hand in hand; and while deformity is invariably more expensive in every sense than grace, so the well-built and tastefully-adorned mansion more readily meets our domestic requirements, and in accordance with our station, affords proper scope for embellishment within and without. Sir Henry Wotton says, "Architecture can want no commendation where there are noble men and noble minds;" and it is not to be doubted that if ordinary residences were constructed in accordance with correct principles of taste, the dwellers in them would attain a higher status in mind and morals, for the character is powerfully impressed for good or evil by what surrounds it permanently. Why should the eye be compelled to gaze on ugly lines and awkward angles, false proportions and' abominations intended as ornaments, when symmetry is at all times cheap, and accuracy of form the most useful and convenient? If builders were not blockheads we should read art-lessons in the streets, instead of perpetually deploring the daily violation, in bricks and mortar, of every law which should control domestic architecture.

Lord Bacon gives the text on this point when he says, "Every man's proper mansion, house, and home, being the theater of his hospitality, the seate of his selfe-fruition, the comfortablest part of his own life, the noblest of his sonne's inheritance, a kind of private princedom; nay, to the possessors thereof, an epitome of the whole world, may well deserve, by these attributes, according to the degree of

the master, to be decently and delightfully adorned."

Wealth is certainly a blessing when it is made the instrument of increasing human happiness, and in the gratification of a love of rural elegance money is certainly a powerful instrument. Still the Home of Taste is within the reach of all, the spiritual life may give a radiance to a cottage, while the noblest productions of genius may even contribute to the gloom of the mansion, where moral and religious worth are strangers. Whatsoever we look upon reflects our own mood, we see ourselves perpetually, as if all Nature and Art were but repetitions of a mirror.

> "Our sleeping visions, waking dreams,
> Receive their shape and hue from what
> Surrounds our life."

Where the counsels of wisdom preside over parental love, where those "whom God has united" remain in unity under the bonds of a beautiful affection, than which

> "All other pleasures are not worth its pains;"

where woman appears in her true gentleness, and the children grow up in the love of parents and the fear of God, there is a Home of Taste, a Home of Virtue, of Mental Discipline, a Home of Moral Worth, and Domestic Affection, and Religious Aspiration. "Round it all the Muses sing;" everything within takes the semblance of the souls that preside over it; the simplest things acquire grace and meaning; vulgarity, meanness, and vice dare not cross the threshold—ennui cannot find its way there, petulance is smiled out of countenance, and temper is rebuked by little ruddy faces and curly heads of hair, and eyes that sparkle with enjoyment. There are pictures and vases, and stands of living flowers, that fill the mind with a sense of the exhaustlessness of form and colour; there are household

pets that daily teach us we may rule by love and not by
fear; there are gatherings of all kinds from the world of
art and the world of nature that demand attention, and
call for the exercise of skill, every one of which represents
an idea, and sets us thinking; while every labour they
require brings its high reward in the gratification of the
desire which possesses us. But above all there is the ripe
domestic life which forms the true centre of this circle of
adornments, heightened by them in its ever-growing appreciation of what is good in man and beautiful in nature.
Who then would not have a Home of Taste? If you have
it already, dear reader, prize it, and continually strive to
make it more and more perfect; if not, "Reform your *pleasure*
bills," and see how you can snatch a little time and a little
money from pursuits that are unprofitable to bestow in
the embellishment—perhaps in the creation of a little terrestrial paradise—

"Domestic happiness, thou only bliss
Of Paradise, that hast survived the fall!

*　　　*　　　*　　　*　　　*

Thou art the nurse of virtue, in thine arms
She smiles, appearing, as in truth she is,
Heaven-born, and destined to the skies again.
Thou art not known where pleasure is adored,
That reeling goddess, with the zoneless waist
And wandering eyes, still leaning on the arm
Of novelty, her fickle, frail support;
For thou art meek and constant, hating change,
And finding in the calm of truth-tried love
Joys, that her stormy raptures never yield."
　　　　　　　　　　　　COWPER.

THE MARINE AQUARIUM

"A sounding grotto, vaulted, vast,
O'erstudded with a thousand, thousand pearls,
And crimson-mouthed shells with stubborn curls
Of every shape and size, even to the bulk
In which whales harbour close, to brood and sulk
Against an endless storm. Moreover, too,
Fish—semblances of green and azure hue,
Ready to snort their streams."   KEATS.

CHAPTER I.

THE sale of a large edition of this Work in the short space of five months, at the end of which period my publishers suggested the preparation of a second, justifies the faith I had in the healthiness of public taste; for the love of birds, trees, and flowers, and other "little things that live and grow," must be pretty strong and pretty general, to cause the exhaustion of a large edition of an expensive work in so short a space of time. I now submit a new and a greatly improved edition, commencing, as before, with the Aquarium, which, for its novelty, its scientific attractions, and its charming elegance, deservedly takes the first place among the Adornments of the House.

The Aquarium is now an established household ornament; it graces the drawing-room of the elegant home, embellishes the conservatory and the greenhouse; is a welcome and highly-prized addition to the student's resources in the acquisition of knowledge; it extends the sphere of domestic education for the young, enlivens the solitary hours of the invalid, and gives delight to everybody.

Considered as a domestic ornament it is insurpassable, and, while in its humblest form it presents a constant succession of beautiful and novel objects, so to all the accessories of artistic decoration, it adds the charm of life in some of its most beautiful and strange developments. The merest glimpse of water is always refreshing to the eye; its clear, cool aspect, the mingling of many colours and forms; the peculiar growth of aquatic plants, and the still more curious forms and movements of aquatic animals, combine to form an assemblage of delightful and ever-changing pictures. The Naiads need no longer dwell in forests lone, dipping their white feet in streams haunted only by the robin and the humble bee, but may sport in gay drawing-rooms, in homely parlours, in the study of the recluse, or the chamber of the valetudinarian. No longer need they fear winter storms and March hurricanes, but shall henceforth have homes within sheltered walls, impervious to frost, and shadowed by curtains, where love whispers, and young children play.

To the naturalist the Aquarium opens up new studies of the choicest wonders of the deep sea. Those departments of zoology which have for their regard the creatures of mid-ocean, or even of the pebbled shore, have hitherto made the slowest and least satisfactory progress of any;

now they are to experience a "sea-change," for the dredge
brings up the

"Pale glistening pearls, and rainbow-coloured shells;"

and by the preservation of the creatures in their own element, and under circumstances almost as natural as that
in which they were produced, we may study their habits
and economy even to the minutest particulars.

We used to study the tenants of the sea by means of
wretched specimens, shrivelled up in spirits, or crushed flat
between the pages of books. Occasional festoons of sea-weed
suspended from the ceiling, or set out upon the mantel, so as
to absorb every stray wisp of smoke; a few corals and
madrepores, and occasionally a queer-looking stuffed fish,
the shape distorted and the colour gone, have long marked
the extent of the means for the domestic study of "deep
sea wonders;" while the ill-arranged specimens in the British
Museum have, for years, been little better than such collections as superannuated sailors delight in, for awakening
or directing public attention to a class of creatures having
so few analogies to those of terrestrial origin.

The Aquarium exemplifies, in an instructive manner, the
great system of compensation which, in nature, preserves
the balance of equilibrium in animal and vegetable life.
Indeed the recent adoption of this plan of studying the
characteristics of creatures hitherto placed beyond our reach,
except when dead and mutilated, has arisen out of the experiments of philosophers as to the nature of that duality
of forces which renders the two great departments of
organized existences essential to each other, not merely for
ordinary sustenance, but for the continuance of refined
chemical operations essential to their respective organisms.
Researches into the chemistry of animal and vegetable
bodies, and especially of the effects they severally produce,
by respiration, on the medium surrounding them, have
resulted in the conclusion that animals and vegetables

supply each other with the gases most essential to existence; what the one exhales as effete and obnoxious, the
other absorbs for the highest uses of vitality. Animals take
oxygen from the medium in which they live, and in return
exhale carbonic acid. Vegetables also absorb oxygen gas, and
give out carbon; but they also absorb the latter in greater
quantity than they exhale it, and during their season of
greatest activity throw off more oxygen than they take up
at other times. Herein is the first element in the management of an Aquarium, which, to be successful, must contain
a sufficient number of plants to supply the animals with
atmospheric air for respiration.

Lavoisier was the first who, upon philosophical grounds,
established the fact of this balance of influences. De
Saussure, in 1780, proved that plants had a tendency to
improve the atmosphere, by robbing it of the gases most
baneful to animal life; and Priestly, by means of well-
devised experiments, ascertained that when atmospheric air
had become vitiated by combustion and animal respiration,
plants had the power of restoring it to a normal condition,
so as to be again capable of supporting flame, and the
breathing of animals. Inglehouse and Ellis contributed to
this inquiry, and modern chemistry establishes the fact,
that though vegetables absorb oxygen, they do, by the
decomposition of carbonic acid into its elements—oxygen
and carbon—yield a large quantity of the first element to
the atmosphere, while retaining the second for the construction of their tissues.

In the philosophical examination of this subject, the
report of Professor Daubeny to the British Association,
in 1833, is perhaps the most conclusive and elaborate of
any of the contributions of modern chemists. He regarded
light as operating upon the green parts of plants in such
a way as to enable them to assimilate carbon and evolve
oxygen; and concluded that as a very small portion of a
tree or shrub generates a considerable quantity of oxygen,

there were no reasons to doubt that the influence of the vegetable might serve as a complete compensation for that of the animal kingdom.

The formation of a Marine Aquarium was first accomplished by Dr. Johnston, one of our most successful students of marine life. In his "History of British Sponges," published in 1842, he describes the formation of a little Marine Aquarium in a glass jar, containing only six ounces of sea-water, stocked with living corallines, minute confervæ, ulva, several little mussels, annelides, rissoæ, and a star-fish. The jar was placed upon a table, seldom disturbed, and after eight weeks, the water, still unchanged, had lost little of its capability for the support of animal life; some of the animals were still active, and the coralline was still growing.

Further experiments were made by Mr. Robert Warington, who reported upon them to the Chemical Society, in March 1850. Two small gold fish were placed in a glass receiver of about twelve gallons capacity, covered with muslin to exclude dust. The vessel was half filled with spring-water, with a bottom of sand and mud, and some loose fragments of limestone and sandstone, so arranged as to form shelter and shade. A small specimen of *Valisneria spiralis* was, at the same time, planted in the mud and kept in place by a stone. "Everything went on well for a time, till it was found that the natural decay of the older leaves of the plant began to produce turbidity in the water, and a confervoid growth accumulated on the sides of the vessel, and on the surface of the water; to meet this emergency, Mr. Warington introduced a few pond snails, which greedily fed on the decaying vegetable matter and slimy mucus growth, so as quickly to restore the whole to a healthy state."

Here was a complete circle of compensating processes. The plants grew and increased by offsets, and at the same time exhaled sufficient oxygen to preserve the health and beauty of the fishes. The snails ate up the mucus, and

bred rapidly: their eggs and young supplied the fishes with food. Thus the three tenants of the globe maintained each other as in any well-ordered human community; and the water preserved its purity unchanged, and the compensating powers of animals and vegetables were established.

The first Marine Vivarium established in London, was constructed by Mrs. Thynne, who made the experiment of bringing some living madrepores from Torquay to London, for the purpose of study and the entertainment of friends; this was in the autumn of 1846. A stone jar was filled with sea-water; the madrepores were fixed on a large sponge by means of a needle and thread. They arrived in London safely, and were placed in two glass bowls, and the water changed every other day. But the six gallons of water brought by Mrs. Thynne, was now exhausted, and must be used again. She here devised means to freshen it for second use. "I thought of having it aerated by pouring it backwards and forwards before an open window, for half or three-quarters of an hour between each time of using it. This was doubtless a fatiguing operation; but I had a little handmaid, who, besides being rather anxious to oblige me, thought it rather an amusement."

Thus the madrepores were supplied with air by means of the agitation of the water, into which they were to be placed, and at the expiration of three months a fresh supply of sea-water was obtained, and all went on well. This success led Mrs. Thynne to further experiments, her narrative of which is so instructive that it seems advisable to quote her own words. She says—

"In the spring of 1847, I wished to try whether I could adjust the balance between animal and vegetable life, and sent for shells and small pieces of rock, to which living sea-weed was attached. On these shells, etc., were sure to be many zoophytes and other animals, so that I obtained a very various and curious collection of marine creatures. I had a quantity of microscopic corallines, which multiplied

very fast; serpulæ, that rapidly elongated their stony cases; some nereis, ophiuræ, and a great many beautiful little things for which I could find no name. On one piece of rock was the first germ of a living sponge. I watched the shooting forth of its spicula with the greatest interest. It was very fine, and grew to the size of a hazel nut, coming to maturity in about six weeks. In the course of the next winter, from want of motion in the water, it had become so covered with dust that I did not know whether it were alive or dead; but in the following June a bright spot appeared on one side, and it threw forth a sporule which attached itself to the rock, and in about six weeks a full-grown young sponge stood beside its parent. I placed this sponge in a darkened room, and found the spicula grew most on whichever side was turned to the light. From this time I regularly placed sea-weed in my glass bowls; but as I was afraid that I might not keep the exact balance required, I still had the water refreshed by aeration. I do not know from which, or whether it was from both causes, that my little flock continued to thrive so much, but I seldom had a death."

Mr. Warington and Mr. Gosse commenced experiments with sea-water, almost simultaneously in the spring of 1852, and with such success as to establish the possibility of adjusting the balance of animal and vegetable life, so that the most delicate productions of the deep sea may be reared in small tanks, with scarcely any detriment to their health and vigour. Mr. Bowerbank, following in the steps of Mr. Ward, in the culture of fresh-water plants and fishes, gave to Mr. Mitchell, Secretary of the Zoological Society, the hint which resulted in the establishment of the interesting Vivaria at the Regent's Park Gardens, unquestionably the most curious and novel scene which those charming gardens contain. The botanist and zoologist have here presented to them, sufficiently close for microscopic examination, those productions of nature which hitherto have been most hidden, and hence least studied of all the tribes that come within their circles of research.

New species have been distinguished, the forms of those already known are now displayed in all the freshness of life and health, the habits of the creatures in all their moods manifested even more plainly than we could expect to see them, were it possible to watch them in their native deeps; beside this we can watch the growth and reproduction of animals and plants which heretofore we have been wont to make acquaintance with as isolated, mutilated, shrivelled, and dead specimens, happy if we could detect a few of their structural peculiarities after death had contracted, distorted, or destroyed the most delicate and most interesting.

> ————The minutest fish
> Will pass the very hardest gazer's wish,
> And show his little eyes' anatomy.   *Keats.*

The Vivaria at the Regent's Park Zoological Gardens was first opened to public inspection in 1853, and at once attracted popular attention for the novelty and rare beauty of the exhibition. From that day we may fairly date the establishment of the Aquarium as a popular adornment, either of a public exhibition or a private household. The knowledge of the principles involved in its construction and maintenance spread rapidly among students and *dillettanti;* exhibitions of a similar kind, though of less perfect character, were subsequently opened at various public institutions, and among others at the Crystal Palace; at the Surrey Gardens; the Royal Polytechnic Institutions; by the Zoological Society of Ireland, in Dublin; and by other public institutions at Edinburgh, Galway, and Scarborough; while on the continent, where studies of this kind are far less popular than here, several scientific societies kept pace with the times, and added Aquaria to the number of popular recreations and means of scientific study.

The Aquarium involves so many matters of minute detail,

that its present perfection is to be attributed not to its popularity, but to the persevering ardour of the many scientific men who have given their close attention to it, and who, through patient investigation, and repeated trials and disappointments, have achieved success, and through the medium of their several published experiences have secured for this choicest of in-door recreations, the appreciation of men of taste and scientific study everywhere. To the writings of Mr. Gosse, a naturalist who has traversed the globe, and who never wrote a line but what betrayed a Christian spirit united to a profound philosophical sagacity, we owe much of our extended knowledge of marine life, and of the rationale of Aquarium management; and to the student of the Aquarium I most heartily commend that gentleman's elegant and able works on the subject, and here cheerfully acknowledge that I am deeply indebted to them for information which I could scarcely have acquired by other means. Mr. Warington, an old disciple of this school; Mr. Bowerbank, Mr. Sowerby, Dr. Badham, and recently Dr. Lankester, have severally thrown light upon the subject, and to these works of high character, I humbly add my own "Book of the Aquarium,"* in which I have given the results of my experiences, during the past seven years, of which the last two have been most pleasurably devoted to its investigation.

While the literature of the subject has kept pace with its growth, the means of supplying specimens have increased also. "Demand creates supply" is an old axiom of social economy, and in Aquarian matters well exemplified. There is scarcely a town in the kingdom but has its manufacturers of tanks, and its dealers in specimens. London has nearly a hundred such, and at the head of them stand Messrs. Sanders and Woolcott, the eminent manufacturers of Doughty Street, who were the builders of the original tanks at the Regent's Park, and who now devote a considerable portion

---

* "The Book of the Aquarium and Water Cabinet." By Shirley Hibberd. London: Groombridge.

of their extensive premises to this branch of mechanism. Messrs. Treggon, of 57, Gracechurch Street, are also experienced makers, whose names should here be mentioned; they have supplied me with tanks of excellent workmanship. Among the dealers, Mr. W. Alford Lloyd, whose name has been mentioned by nearly every scientific writer on the subject, and who was a student of Aquaria long before he could have conceived any idea of trading in them, now occupies the position of representative of the Aquarian, of the United Kingdom. Since he has opened premises at 20, Portland Road, he has organised a staff of dredgers and collectors severally stationed at all the important points of our coast, so as to secure the choicest specimens of the *fauna* of many districts, and enable the student in London, or any inland town, to stock his vessels with representatives of an extensive line of shore, and with the most curious of deep-sea productions. A stock of from fifteen to twenty thousand living specimens, comprising more than two hundred genera, open to public inspection and purchase, is a suitable climax to the history of Aquarian experiments, and that Mr. Lloyd may be amply rewarded for his assiduity and high talent in this department, must be the wish of every lover of science in these days of popular aquatics.

I shall now proceed to treat, *seriatum*, the several steps to be pursued by those who enter for the first time on this delightful pursuit, but at the same time I shall not omit any matters that appear to me likely to be profitable to those who are already initiated in the mysteries of this method of out-witting Neptune. I may surely be allowed to close this chapter by insisting that the Aquarium should have a place in the home of every person of taste, for its comparative inexpensiveness equally fits it for the dwellings of those whose means are not ample, as its adaptability for costly ornament renders it worthy the attention of those whose liberal means enable them without stint to indulge a love of elegance and refinement.

CHAPTER II.

"I see the shipwrecked mariners, a bold Phœnician band,
Gathered around their sea-weed fire, upon the ocean strand;
And mark the wonder and amaze their dusky features wore,
When the first glass before them lay upon the sandy shore."
ELIZABETH PRIDEAUX.

NOTORIOUS member of an *in-*temperance society once made a hit in praise of water by asserting that "it had done wonders for navigation." Had he been "half-seas over," he might have added a word in favour of *the glass*, which occasionally enabled him to see double. Glass is certainly worthy of celebration in prose or verse; it lets light into our dwellings, gives new eyes to the purblind, glorifies the cathedral with tessellated sunbeams, "in storied windows richly dight," enables the naturalist to penetrate the profoundest mysteries of nature's invisible world, and to reach the very horizon of organized existence; neither chemistry nor horticulture could exist without it, and in either a physical or moral sense we may say of it in the words of Tennyson—

"All is dark where thou art not."

If the diving-bell—another triumph of glass—enables us to explore the sea-bottom, and

> "See things
> More dead than Morpheus imaginings:
> Old rusted anchors, helmets, breastplates large
> Of gone sea-warriors; brazen beaks and targe,
> Rudders that for a hundred years had lost
> The sway of human hand;"—

the Aquarium achieves a still greater feat in bringing the
sea-bottom,—

> "With every shape
> That skims, or dives, or sleeps, 'twixt cape and cape,"

into our very homes, that we may make a daily acquaintance
with the rarest of "deep-sea wonders."

What is the best kind of vessel for an Aquarium?—Without
doubt a properly constructed tank, of rectangular form, constructed wholly or partially of glass, with a slate bottom,
mounted on a table or a stand made for the purpose.
There are now many respectable manufacturers engaged in
the construction of tanks, and of these the Messrs. Sanders
and Woolcott, of 54, Doughty Street, London, take the
first place for the perfection to which they have now brought
the manufacture, through the extensive experience they have
acquired in fitting up the exhibitions of the leading scientific
institutions of this country and the continent, as well as
the splendid private collections of the Duke of Devonshire,
Sir Robert Peel, and other noblemen and naturalists. Messrs.
Treggon, of Jewin Street, and 57, Gracechurch Street, also
stand at the head of the London manufacturers. In Bir-
mingham the Messrs. Lloyd and Summerfield, and at
Cambridge the Messrs. Greef, are the only provincial
makers to whom I am able at present to refer.

Many readers of this Work may reside in districts where
a properly built tank cannot be readily obtained, and others
may prefer to try their own skill in the construction of one;
hence a few hints on the practical details may be acceptable.
First, as to shape and dimensions—A tank may have any

shape that a rectangular object is capable of assuming, and the size must be proportioned to the window or other position in which it is to be placed. The best form is undoubtedly that of an oblong or octagonal box, formed of plate or sheet glass, and slate, the joints bound with zinc, and cemented with Scott's cement or white-lead putty.

The simpler the outline the better, because where we have but a few broad sheets of glass, the view is less obstructed, and light—the great essential to success—can penetrate to every exposed portion of the collection. In the oblong tank here figured the dimensions are as follows:

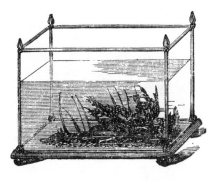

—Back and front three feet, ends one foot four inches, depth one foot six inches. The bottom is of slate, and the four sides are all of plate glass. Four turned pillars of birch wood unite the four sides, and four similar pieces bind the whole along the top edge. A tank of this kind is supplied by Messrs. Sanders and Woolcott for five guineas. For marine objects, where a great depth of water is not required, a tank of a square form would be very suitable, if made somewhat shallow, because such a vessel exposes a proportionally larger surface of water to the action of the atmosphere, and thus relieves us of the labour of frequent aeration. In the following example the dimensions are two feet four by two feet four, and only one foot deep. This however is not a very convenient form for the embellishment of a window.

In the construction of a tank it must be borne in mind that when filled with water its weight is enormous, and hence it is difficult, sometimes impossible, to move it without first removing the whole or greater portion of its contents. Strength in the joints to resist pressure from within, and strength in the table or other support on which the tank is placed, is of the first importance. The bottom is best formed of a slab of slate, and if it is intended to carry

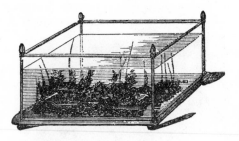

across the inside of the vessel an arch of rock-work, the ends must be of slate also. If there is no intention of building rock-work against the sides, the ends may be of glass. The slate bottom and ends must have suitable grooves to receive the sheets of glass, and the latter should be either plate of three-sixteenths thickness, or very stout crown glass. When the glass is set in the grooves, and fixed by means of white-lead putty, or best of all, Scott's cement, (obtained by post from Mr. Scott, of Newcastle,) the outside edges must be bound with zinc, or strengthened and finished by means of turned rods of birch wood, as shewn in the engravings. In every case, and whatever the dimensions of an oblong tank, where elegance of outline is required it will be attained by giving the tank the form

of the double cube, in which the length is exactly double
that of the width, the width and depth being equal. Such
an object, if cut into two equal parts, would form two
perfect cubes, and presents the most graceful outline that
straight lines and right-angles are capable of assuming. Such
is the form of the tank in Mr. Voyez's elegant design, which
forms the frontispiece to this volume. The tank there
figured measures thirty-two inches by sixteen, by sixteen.
The fountain is kept in play by means of a cistern fixed
above the level of the tank, whence a supply pipe descends,
and passing beneath the floor, enters the tank from the
wall against which it is placed, or up one of the legs of
the stand, hollowed for the purpose. The portion of the
tube which passes through the water must be of gutta-
percha; and this, perhaps, would be the best material for
the whole of the tubing, as there is then no fear of cor-
rosion. The nozzle of the fountain is of glass; the dolphin
is formed of artificial stone, and is firmly placed to the
rocks on which it rests, but so arranged as to be easily
moved away for alterations and repairs. Mr. Voyez has
chosen the fresh-water tank for illustration, on account of
the beauty of the ferns which flourish under the drip, and
add vastly to the fresh brilliancy of the scene. The Marine
Aquarium might be made after the same design, the ferns,
of course, being unfit for its embellishment.

For a conservatory, an Aquarium of a vase-like or octagonal form, either with or without a fountain, would have
a very elegant appearance. They may also be formed wholly
of slate, earthenware, or stone, though, with either of these
materials, the view must be from above the surface of the
water. Such tanks should be more shallow, in order that
objects at the bottom may be plainly visible. If surrounded
with rock-work planted with suitable plants, such tanks are
very ornamental, and well suited to the conservatory or
aviary.

Wherever there is any liability to dust or soot, the tank

must be covered over the top. The best cover is a sheet
of glass of the requisite dimensions. This may be merely
laid on, or fitted with a hinge and jointed support, so that
it may be left open, if necessary, without requiring to be
held by the hand. I do not usually have a cover of any
kind to my own tanks, but in the event of any domestic
movements, which may give rise to dust, such as sweeping,
or lighting of fires, I throw over them a light green gauze,
which is removed as soon as the dust has subsided. In
fact, if a little of the ordinary dust of a dwelling-house gets
into the tank it quickly subsides to the bottom, and as far
as I can see does no harm.

Thus much as to tanks in general. I must yet detain
the reader with a few more dry details, in order that certain particular forms of vessels may receive the attention
due to them. Among the vessels of peculiar construction
now in use for Aquaria, the *slope-back* tank of Mr. Warington deserves notice first. The object of this contrivance
is to imitate the conditions observable in Nature more
closely than an ordinary tank will allow. The peculiarity
consists in constructing a vessel, having the back and ends
of an *opaque* material, of which slate is the best, and the
front only of glass, so that as in a natural pool, light is

admitted only from *above*. Mr. Warington says, "After five
years and upwards experience, I have now adopted an Aquarium, the form of which consists in a four-sided vessel,
having the back gradually sloping upwards from the bottom
at an angle of fifty degrees. The chief peculiarity of this
tank is, that it admits light at the top only; the back and
sides are usually composed of slate."

I have a tank of this form, supplied me by Messrs. Sanders
and Woolcott, and I can safely say that so far from being
"lumbering and inelegant," as a distinguished writer has
described it, it is the very perfection of a tank, for it
admits of rock-work without the need of cement, and affords
such a peculiar and natural view of the creatures within,
as to surpass in beauty every ordinary Aquarium just as
much as the latter excels the obsolete fish-globe. The
makers have deviated from Mr. Warington's original plan
in giving the back a different angle, instead of the one
of fifty degrees. The sides and back are of slate, hence
the only view is through the plate-glass front. The lid
is formed of a sheet of stout glass, stained of a soft
sea-green, and the light admitted through this gives such
a peculiar appearance to the objects within, as more than
realizes to the eye the most glowing pictures of submarine
scenery. The lid being attached to a cord running over a
pulley, can be raised and lowered as desired, and the
objects viewed under ordinary white light, or under the
magical influence of an unearthly sea-green, which has a
strange effect upon the mind, and suggests to the imagination pictures of the stillness and sublimity that must ever
prevail far down in the silent depths among

> "The sea blooms and the oozy woods, which wear
> The sapless foliage of the ocean."

The mode in which Mr. Lloyd furnishes these tanks is
very effective in producing a picturesque effect, and what

is perhaps of more importance, it preserves the natural conditions in furtherance of Mr. Warington's intentions. The bottom is composed of a deep undulating bed of pebbles and fine shingle, and along the sloping back large blocks of rock are piled up in rugged masses, terminating in an irregular line of shore above; thus imitating the varying depths, the loose shifting bottom, and the sloping rocky beach of a portion of natural coast. When to this natural arrangement of the furniture of the vessel we add the tinted and subdued light supplied from above, we have accomplished much to increase the enchantments of the Aquarium, and to fulfil the conditions of its scientific management. Until I see some further improvement, (and that scarcely appears possible,) I shall consider the Warington tank to be a triumph of art and science.

Cylindrical vessels and vases are now largely used as substitutes for rectangular tanks, and these are not without a certain grace and elegance that commend them where cheapness is a desideratum. It is quite unnecessary now to repeat the first failings of Aquarians in the pursuit of suitable vessels; the blown tanks of Dr. Badham, costing fifteen shillings each, and Mr. Gosse's twelve-inch cylinders, costing ten shillings and fourpence, were but examples of how ingenuity may frequently be exhausted in the attempt to discover that which is already known. While manufacturers were torturing their wits, and glass-blowers were wasting their breath in producing ugly vessels at enormous prices, every glass warehouse in London contained the very thing that was needed, namely, a common gardener's propagating glass, the form of which is bell-shaped, and so regular in outline, that the refraction caused by the passage of light through such a vessel is reduced to a minimum, and the cost so trifling, that the poorest student, or most ill-paid country schoolmaster, may by its aid set up an Aquarium, and vie with the most wealthy in the success of the experiment, and the accuracy of his researches.

Mr. Hall, an experienced naturalist, of City Road, London, was the first who conceived the happy thought of turning a propagator upside down to extemporize an Aquarium; and the first Aquarium of this form was exhibited in his window, mounted on a deal box, with a hole cut in the centre to receive the knob of the bell. That simple trick of creating

a cheap and elegant tank did more to popularize the Aquarium than all the exhibitions and all the books that have been written on the subject, for it enabled thousands to enjoy a delight which had previously been confined to the wealthy few. Messrs. Claudet and Houghton, of 89, High Holborn, are makers of the most elegant and efficient form of bell-glasses yet brought into use.

Another and most elegant kind of cylindrical vessel may be formed by inverting a French shade, such as is used

to cover alabaster ornaments. If fitted into a polished-wood
frame, so constructed as to partially grasp the sides of the
vessel, and with a hollowed foot in which the base may
rest, a clear view of the interior may be obtained, and
minute specimens of animal and vegetable life, whether
marine or fluviatile, kept to advantage. Into the turned
stand which receives the base of the vessel two uprights
should be fixed, and from each of these a semicircular piece
of wood should proceed, each of them fitting partially round
the vessel, and thus grasping it, and preserving it in an
upright position, while the chief weight is borne by the
turned stand. Or, if such a vessel were required on a
larger scale, a fern shade might be inverted, and set into
a hollow on a turned stand, or even placed in the glass
dish in which the ferns are usually grown, the dish being
first filled with moss or some yielding material, to keep the
tank steady, and prevent fracture from the meeting of two
unyielding surfaces.

Lastly, an earthenware foot-bath forms a cheap and
serviceable Aquarium, especially for marine objects; glass
milk-pans do well for zoophytes and all descriptious of
ground stock; while for madrepores, the smaller *Actiniæ*,
tube worms, and for larvæ and fresh-water insects generally,
small jars of flint-glass are the best of vessels, because in
such the *balance* of vegetable and animal life may be adjusted to perfection, and the study of the minuter kinds of
aquatic life is through the portableness of the vessels
greatly facilitated.

So far the several vessels treated of are equally suitable
for either Marine or River Aquaria; the rectangular tank,
properly constructed, is the best general form of vessel, because more durable and more elegant than any other, while
there is no limit to its capacity, and no distortion by unequal
refraction. Bell-glasses are not to be obtained of greater
dimensions than twenty-one inches, while those below twelve
inches are too small to be of much general service, and

those above eighteen are liable to fracture when sudden changes of temperature happen. Hence the chief disad-vantages of cylinders are limited capacity—an eighteen-inch glass holding not more than from ten to twelve gallons—and the refraction common to *all vessels having curvilinear sides.* Half-a-dozen shillings will purchase a bell-glass, and from one to three pounds a small tank; hence on the score of cheapness propagators win the day.

A few remarks are yet necessary to complete this chapter, and since I shall have nothing to say on the subject of vessels when I come to treat of the Fresh-water Aquarium, the reader will, I hope, pardon my prolixity. I am anxious that nothing of importance shall be omitted in reference to a subject so new as this, in which experience has been gained through many disappointments and vexations.

We are indebted to that accurate observer, Mr. Warington, for valuable information on the effects of light upon certain forms of sea-weeds, and his mode of overcoming this is by passing light through variously coloured media. It can easily be understood, that plants whose natural habitat is at a considerable depth beneath the surface of the ocean, bear exposure to the full daylight very indifferently, and that some special arrangements are necessary in order to cause the solar rays to fall upon them as nearly as possible in the same manner as in the twilight recesses from which they have been removed. This is accomplished by fitting that side of the tank, which is intended to be placed next the window, with a sheet of glass stained of a soft sea-green, and the softened light, so admitted to the tank, promotes the healthy growth of the Algæ, and very materially increases the beauty of the vessel as seen from the other side. Mr. Lloyd, whose ripe experience ever takes the most practical turn, has adopted this plan of construction, and strongly recommends it for every vessel intended for the reception of marine stock. Where it is desired to stock a vessel, in which the back plate is composed of colourless glass, with marine products, a substitute for coloured glass will be found in *diaphanie;* but the paper chosen for the purpose should be of the lightest shade of sea-green, because it is less transparent than stained glass. In stocking vases, this plan of staining the side next the window, is to be strongly recommended, no less for securing a healthy vegetation than of enlivening the beauty of the collection.

Another point deserving of note is, that Marine Aquaria need a less depth of water than river collections:—For purposes of study, a number of glass dishes or milk-pans, will be found preferable to any kind of tank or vase, especially for Zoophytes, though fishes and crustaceans require more room than mere bowls would afford them. In fact, the lower forms of marine life may be kept for many months without the help of sea-weeds, if placed in shallow vessels —the absorption of oxygen, at the surface, being quite equal to their demand upon the water. Mr. Lloyd sells the Shallow Rock pools, which were originally suggested by Mr. Warington, and for the student Smith and Beck's Zoophyte Tanks, which Mr. Lloyd keeps in stock, will be found invaluable.

As to rock-work there are differences of opinion. I used it myself till I had grave doubts about its value, and what I once took a pride in, and brought to considerable artistic perfection, I now reject entirely. This is not wholly a matter of taste, for to build up rock-work, and more particularly massive arches, it is necessary to use a considerable quantity of Portland or Roman cement, and however well this may be seasoned before stocking the tank, it does appear still to give out free lime to the surrounding salt-water. I am certain that in a tank in which I had built up a very tasteful mass of rock-work, the stock was never so healthy as that in a vase which stood beside it, and which was filled with the same artificial sea-water, and in every respect had the same management. Beside this, I think the eye at last tires of gazing on the same mimic cliff—when its novelty is past it begins to look *toyish*. This struck me very forcibly whenever any young people visited me, for the rock-work took their fancy, and they called the Anemones "nasty things;" and at last, when a young lady (not young enough to be excused) told me that "the ornaments were beautiful, but there was nothing interesting in those stupid still creatures," I took a savage resolve, and abolished it for ever. I have seen some *imitations* of rock-work made in gutta percha, and no doubt to some eyes they would be attractive enough; to me they appear tawdry and nonsensical; but as my readers have a right to form their own opinions, I give the address of the maker, Mr. S. Maccarthy, 71, Newman Street, Oxford Street. A few pieces of any kind of non-metallic stone, or a stem of branching coral, may be tastefully disposed at the bottom, and will, I think, with the majority of Aquarians, have the preference over any kind of rock-work. But since many may be disposed to try their hands at the construction of an arch, I have only to suggest that either Portland or Roman cement should be used for the purpose, and that it should be first worked into a stiff paste with water, and then moulded into the form required, only a small portion of the work being attempted at any one time. It should be made thoroughly secure, and the tank well seasoned as soon as the work is completed.

The bottom of a marine tank is best formed of coarse sea-sand and pebbles, the whole well washed before being put down: in the absence of sea-sand, well-washed river-sand will serve the purpose. Upon this bed, which may be a few inches deep, place such fragments of rock as you intend to have, and the vessel is then ready to be filled.

Sea-water is easily obtainable either of the dealers in marine stock, or by means of casks direct from the sea. The cask should be a new one of fir wood, or if an old cask it should be well seasoned and cleansed before being used for the purpose, and even the *bung* should be new,

for fear of any contamination. A fee of a few shillings to
the steward of a sea-going steamer will ensure the prize,
and he should be commissioned to dip it in *mid-channel*,
shore-water and that near the embouchre of a river being
objectionable, unless you dip it yourself; when collecting,
your own judgment will then guide you as to the proximity
of land-springs.

Since the first edition of this Work was published, I
have had much experience in the use of artificial sea-waters,
and can recommend it, not only as serving the purpose to
perfection, but positively offering advantages which the
genuine article does not; for being entirely free of organic
matter, it is more easily preserved in a bright and pure
condition, is less subject to *green stain* and confervoid growths,
and may be prepared with less ease than the other can be
procured. Mr. Gosse was the first to suggest this ingenious
preparation, of which the composition is as follows:—

14   ounces (avoirdupois) table salt.

1   ounce (avoirdupois) Epsom salts.

800   grains (troy) chloride of magnesium.

160   grains (troy) chloride of potassium.

To mix these spring water is the best, and the mixture
should be diluted till the hydrometer registers 1.028, or
thereabouts; anywhere between 1.026 and 1.028 will give
a sufficiently accurate strength to the preparation.

Mr. Bolton, of 146, Holborn Bars, is manufacturer in
general to the Aquarians of the United Kingdom, and his
experience in the preparation of Marine Salts secures for
us an article on which we may depend. The original cost
of the materials is at the rate of about threepence a gallon,
and Mr. Bolton sells it ready prepared, with directions for
use, at the rate of fourpence a gallon. The most interesting
fact connected with the use of artificial water is, that though
some of the ingredients found in real sea-water are omitted,

owing to the minuteness of their quantities, yet when the preparation has been in use a few months, those same ingredients may be detected in it, communicated, of course, by the plants used in the seasoning process. It should be borne in mind by intending experimenters that a mere solution of bay salt will not do for the preservation of any kind of marine life, the salts must either be prepared by an experienced chemist, or Mr. Bolton must be resorted to for a supply. Mr. Lloyd and Mr. Bolton both supply specific gravity beads, which obviate the necessity for an hydrometer. I find that two are more useful than one. I have one obtained from Mr. Lloyd which just floats when the water is sufficiently fluid, and another obtained of Mr. Bolton, which just sinks when it is sufficiently dense—the movement of either indicates a change of density, and I act accordingly, as described further on.

A window is unquestionably the proper situation for a tank. An abundance of light promotes the growth of the plants and the health of the animals, and secures that succession of tiny globules which the vegetation on the stones at the bottom sends up, and which rises rapidly to the surface when the sun shines. This is one of the prettiest features of a well-stocked Aquarium; every stone is seen studded with little diamond points, even if its surface appears destitute of vegetation; and from some of the plants the bubbles ascend in continuous streams, reflecting the most beautiful hues as the sunlight glitters through them. These are globules of oxygen, and are produced by the plants, which decompose the water into its elements, retaining the hydrogen for their own use, and liberating the oxygen for the benefit of the animals. In a dark corner, or if not sufficiently exposed to the sun, none of this natural aeration takes place; but instead of it, the water gets exhausted of its oxygen, the plants get cankered, the animals perish, and the whole becomes rapidly a mass of obnoxious putridity.

D

On this point the chief difficulty of management arises. Occasional sunshine is beneficial, but if the water becomes tepid the animals will perish. During the fierce blaze of summer, therefore, a curtain of muslin, oiled paper, or ground glass must be interposed, by which much of the heat will be retarded, but most of the light will reach the water, and produce its beneficial effects. The mere drawing down of the window-blind will generally be found a sufficient protection against excessive sunlight.

CHAPTER III.

IT is the sea, it is the sea,
In all its vague immensity,
  Fading and darkening in the distance!
Silent, majestical, and slow,
The white ships haunt it to and fro,
With all their ghostly sails unfurled,
As phantoms from another world
  Haunt the dim confines of existence.
                LONGFELLOW'S GOLDEN LEGEND.

HE most pleasurable task in forming a Marine Aquarium is that of stocking it with specimens. Here is the sweet necessity of glorious railway and steam-boat trips through miles of waving corn-fields, green hedge-rows, and fertile flats, or along the course of the winding Thames, away out of the smoke and din, to burrow, if we will, like rabbits in the sand. The true lover of nature will collect his specimens rather than purchase them, and will learn many lessons of the minute completeness of the Great Design of Creation, as he probes among the clefts of rocks, or searches the tide-washed sand, or assists in the exhilarating work of dredging the deep water.

Any one having the least taste for natural history, may find much profitable recreation by a hunt on the coast at low tide. No doubt, since the Aquarium has become fashionable, our city folk who, when the virgin lures them with her spike of corn, hurry out of Babylon to the silver

Mediterranean shores, or even to the sands of Brighton, Weymouth, or the shadowy cliffs of Dover, there to transform themselves into mermaids and mermen; no doubt when they find themselves once again in the bright region of sea-gulls and *uglies*, they may think also of "tangle and shells," of medusas, and sea-anemones, and crabs that travel delicately on tip-toe. There are many less-gratifying amusements sought at watering-places, such as sometimes turn the balance against the benefits of bathing and invigorating sea-breezes, and cause many a pang for health shattered where it should have been renewed. If Glaucus and Arethusa will join hands to pick up shells and sea-weeds, what treasures of wonder shall they find concealed within them.

The requisites for collecting on the beach are, a geological hammer, a strong chisel tipped with steel, a neat hand-net, a large closely-woven covered basket, two stone jars, one large glass jar, or a confectioner's show glass, and two or three small phials. The vessels must be quite clean, not the least taint of any chemical ingredient, or even of stale sea-weed or water in them, if new the better; in addition to these it is well to have a pair of stout water-boots for wading into pools, or for protection against the running surf, the best specimens being found at lowest ebb, below the water-line. Lady-collectors will of course dispense with the boots, and obtain the help of the gallants in exploring the half-fathom depth.

The best season is during summer and autumn, just after new or full moon, when the tide recedes to its greatest extent, and lays bare large tracts of surface which are at other times covered by the sea. The sea-weeds that are washed on shore are useless, and it is waste of time to collect any, however tempting their appearance. We must have them in their fullness of life, fresh from the sites whereon they grow. The best hunting grounds are the ledges of rock that run out to sea, and which have the full play of the sea currents till the tide is nearly out. Be-

tween rolled boulders and in deep hollows, and indeed any
rocky shelves that are not bared till lowest ebb, and above
all the "tide pools" which abound in rocky situations. Here
will be found rich fringes of *fuci*, the lower banners of
which must be lifted up carefully, and such gems as present
themselves, whether curious weeds or animals, carefully
transferred to the jars of sea-water.

Actinia mesembryanthemum.   Dyctyota dychotoma.

You will of course get many things which you will afterwards have to throw away, but that is better than the loss
of a choice specimen. In little wet hollows will be seen
what appear to the unpracticed eye like round pieces of red
flesh, of the size of a chesnut, or larger; these are anemones,
the best of all things for a tank. A beginner will not
easily remove these, therefore the chisel and hammer must

be brought into use, and the portion of stone broken off.
A little practice, however, will enable any one to remove
an anemone by slipping the finger nail or a pewter spoon
under them.

Sometimes half a dozen of the common smooth anemone
may be obtained from one splinter; and it would be an
unusually unprofitable search that did not result in the capture of many other kinds of sea-anemones. The dark lovely
sea-grass, *(Zostera,)* will be found waving in the pools; and
by tucking up the sleeves, and working either on your knees
above the hollow, or standing in it according to its depth,
you may secure some tufts attached to portions of rock.
It is useless to tear any weed away from its hold, if you
cannot splinter off the rock on which it grows. You will
often be vexed at the snapping asunder of a specimen at
the first blow, for the weeds have no proper root, and keep
possession by a very frail tenure. Poring about the water's
edge, you will doubtless meet with many shelly substances
adhering like little grey cornucopiæ, or twisted tubes, to
such surfaces as are constantly submerged. Sometimes these
are found in little colonies under boulders and wet ledges.
These are *serpulæ,* and must be prized as worthy of preservation; these must be tenderly detached, as they adhere
only at the tip of the tube. In the quiet pools some small
fishes may be taken with the hand-net by a little dexterity.
Blennies are particularly valuable, the little shanny, *(Blennius pholis,)* and the butterfly blenny, *(B. ocellarus,)* are
both lively amusing creatures, and bear confinement in
the tank with most happy submission. The collector who
has not had some experience will be tempted to bag some
specimens of oar-weed, *(Laminaria,)* on account of their
attractive appearance: these have long puckered dark brown
fronds. They are, however, useless, for they soon perish in
confinement, and render the water turbid with their putrescence. The tangle is equally objectionable; this grows with
the oar-weed. It has broad smooth leathery fronds, of a

deeper colour than the oar-weed; the fronds start from a slender stalk, and the older specimens are seen to be split into jagged segments like fingers, hence its name of tangle.

But amongst the tangle will be found that lovely weed the *Laminaria phyllitis*, or ladies' tresses. It has delicate green waved fronds, the edges puckered like a frill, and each frond springs from a thin pinkish stalk. This must be removed with a portion of its native rock, and will form one of the best ornaments for the tank, though it will seldom flourish for any length of time.

In the deep pools will also be found the dulse or dillis, *(Rhodymenia palmata.)* This forms a conspicuous ornament in the tanks of the Zoological Society. It forms flat palmate fronds, of a rich crimson hue, running into a greenish tint towards the edges. Towards the base the fronds narrow into a kind of stalk. There is abundance of this wherever the rocks are well covered, and some specimens must be removed with care. It does not thrive well in the Aquarium, but is too elegant to be utterly cast aside. As soon as it shews symptoms of decay, by the appearance of orange-coloured spots, it must be removed.

In the quiet pools several choice plants may be found just below the surface, and amongst them some nimble fishes. To capture the latter is no easy task. The foot-fall alarms them, and away they dart in shoals. Any that can be captured with the hand-net, must be secured, and you may be lucky enough to find yourself in possession of a small collection of gobies and blennies, and by probing the sand you may take some specimens of the silvery lance, *(Ammodytes,)* which burrows on the retreat of the tide. As these turn up you will be sure to take a good stock of mollusks and anemones; the latter, if looked for, will be seen expanding their beautiful flower-cups beneath the shallow water on the sand and mud. The flat fish found in the mud and sand are useless; the brill, dab, sole, and plaice, and now and then a young thornback, may be found, but as

all these burrow, and lead a lazy life, it is folly to give
them room in the tank. Beside which they do not thrive
there, and should they die unseen, will taint the water and
perhaps destroy the whole stock before the cause of the disas-
ter is discovered. In these spots you will find that best of
plants, the sea-lettuce, *(Ulva latissima,)* which thrives so luxuriantly in the Aquarium, and forms fairy-like waving arches,
through which the lively fishes delight to dart and gambol.
It is abundant in the wet hollows, and runs up quite to
tide mark, so as to be almost uncovered at low water. It
has a delicate green hue, and is usually much crumpled
and torn at the edges. This and the grass-like Algæ, *Enter-*
omorpha compressa, should be obtained in plenty, the blocks
being carefully broken off, so as to avoid injury to the plants.
They are the best of plants for all early experiments, without them no progress can be made in preparing artificial
sea-water for Aquarian purposes. Another useful plant may
generally be found in company with these, the *Cladophora*
rupestris. It is of a darker green, consisting of many jointed
threads which grow into dense tufts. All these are difficult
to remove, and useless if broken from their site. The collector must therefore persevere until he can break off a
fragment of the rock bearing the plant uninjured, or till
the returning tide drives him back to terra-firma, a disap-
pointed fisherman.

The stony corallines should be sought for in these pools.
They will be found incrusting the stones, much in the same
way as the grey lichens coat the stones and old timber in
damp moors. This coralline, *(Corallina officinalis,)* puts out
a number of jointed purplish shelly growths, and adheres
firmly to the vertical surfaces on which it is produced, each
patch of it spreading in circular bands. The mature growth
of this coralline resembles in form minute twigs of yew-tree,
and they spread into arborescent tufts, and hang over the
edges gracefully. The young purple shoots should be chosen,
and a piece of rock well covered broken off. It suits well

for the tank, and lives a long time. White ones are useless; they are in a state of incipient decay, and soon perish.

Two other forms, allied to *Corallina officinalis*, are useful. One is the slender *Jania rubens*, a delicate hair-like coralline, somewhat resembling the small mare's tail of the hedges, the other is *Melobesia calcarea*. Both of these will be found in the same situation as the coralline just described, and must be transferred with a splinter of the rock or the seaweed base on which they grow.

Amongst the slippery bladder-weed many kinds of curious creatures will be found, some of the most singular, and others of very beautiful forms. The common winkle, and the rarer kinds of winkle, marked with yellow, black, and brown hues, are very valuable, and as we shall explain hereafter, are in some cases essential to the success of the Aquarium. A number of these may be gathered of any kinds that occur; they can afterwards be got rid of should you possess more than you want. The least useful of the tribe is the little yellow winkle, *(Littorina littoralis.)*

The well-known mollusk called top, *(Trochus,)* is very abundant in the hollows tenanted by the periwinkle, and must be welcomed as a friend. They may be known in a moment by any one, however unacquainted with marine zoology, by their neat conical shells, spirally banded, and terminating in a beautiful point, not altogether unlike the amber snail of the hedges, but less globose. These are to be sought and found, or little progress can be made in the stocking of the tank. *Trochus cinerarius, T. Zizyphinus,* and *T. umbilicatus,* are the most abundant and most useful kinds. Prawns, shrimps, sandworms, and crabs, are to be secured as they occur; they may afterwards be sorted, and the least attractive thrown away. Many useful mollusks, such as the pretty doris, one of the naked mollusks frequently found underneath water, and in appearance very similar to a grey slug; the cowry, in its porcelain and delicately-painted shell; the murex, the purple, and chitons,

are easily found in searching the rocky portions of the sea-beach. Many other curious weeds and animals will occur, and the collector must choose amongst them according to his own taste, and the instruction given farther on as to stocking and managing Aquaria.

In this, as in all other pursuits, the pleasure increases with the growth of experience, and skill once acquired, every visit to the shore will reveal new forms of beauty and wonder. The beginner will have to guard against two kinds of accident. He may wander out by means of a stretch of sand, or a group of boulders and jagged masses of rock, and when far from the mainland, be overtaken by the tide. I shall never forget having to swim for it when caught in this way, while examining a cave called the fairy's kettle, under a cliff at Tynemouth, and, in the case we are considering, the collection as well as the collector may be in danger of a ducking—possibly something worse. Haunters of the sea-side are generally pretty cautious and watchful of tide-tables, but in the abstraction of mind from surrounding circumstances which accompanies sport of all kinds, the precaution of watching for the turn of the tide may be forgotten. The other danger arises from the nature of the surface on which you tread. Sand is safe enough for the veriest cripple, but the weedy surface of a slanting block of stone, or the tuberculated crust of a well-covered boulder, may prove a slippery foot-hold, and help you into a deeper pool than you desire to fish in.

It is no pleasant matter to lose one's footing, or even sometimes to keep it when a fierce breeze blows off sea, and sends its "white horses" prancing ever the beach, soaking you if you will persevere, and frightening you if you stand aloof. The naturalist must encounter a few perils, and he does encounter them boldly, and with little regard to such a trifling matter as a grazed shin, or an impromptu bath; but it is not to be expected that all who commence the study of nature at the sea-side, will care to encounter the perils which an experienced student thinks lightly of.

The specimens must be arranged for transport as soon as the returning tide warns you to quit. You will find yourself in possession of an assemblage of objects of most opposite character, some slimy and half dead, others so lively that you have every chance of losing them, unless you exercise some caution, while others are so fragile in texture that it seems dangerous to touch them. In your basket place a layer of sea-weed, fresh gathered and dripping; common fucus is the best; on this lay your choice weeds, placing the rocky masses which have weeds attached to them, so that they cannot jar against each other, to injure those that may be near them. Cover the whole with fresh-gathered weed, taken from the dripping ledges where the sun has not shone on them. Pack the whole sufficiently tight to prevent any shaking or rubbing together, and in this manner they will preserve their vitality unimpaired for from twenty-four to thirty-six hours. A safer plan when the specimens have to be conveyed a long distance by rail, is to pack them in a tin box fitting close inside a basket, or with basket-work woven round it. The basket alone, however, will generally serve very well. Mollusks, as tops, winkles; crustaceans, as crabs and prawns; and anemones of all kinds, and *Echinodermata* may be transmitted in this way much more safely than in water. They must not be packed close, and each specimen should be surrounded with fresh wet weed. Care must be taken that none are injured by pieces of rock, and to avoid excessive pressure do not fill the vessel to the brim. Large stone jars serve well for this purpose.

The tender sorts of crustacea, sea-worms, jelly fishes, and delicate zoophytes must be placed in sea-water. Mr. Gosse's plan is unquestionably the best that can be adopted for the conveyance of these. He says, "I use wide-mouthed jars of stoneware, with water-tight screwed tops, several of which may be packed in a hamper; at other times a large twelve-. gallon zinc pail, protected by a wicker case, with a screw-

lid, of which the central part is perforated with minute
holes; at others, four small zinc cans, of square form, with
perforated tops, fitted into an open box, like case bottles
in a wine-hamper. All of these modes answer well. I know
not to which I should give the preference, except that for
fishes, the large pail is decidedly the best. If heavy stones
or oyster-shells, very rich in zoophytes and annelides, be
required, a common cabbage-net may be suspended from
the lid of the pail in mid-water; the stones or shells being
put into this net, will be kept from injuring themselves or
their neighbours, by swinging about the bottom."

Of course the transit must be quickly performed, or many
of the specimens will perish. Mail trains and special mes-
sengers must be made available, and the moment the stock
reaches its destination, the specimens should be carefully
sorted over in shallow basins of sea-water, well aerated
before the exhausted travellers are dipped out. It is advisable to pour off the whole of the water in which they
have performed their transit, but not to throw it away
too hurriedly, for if it can be aerated and brought to a
fresh condition it may be useful. The real article has this
superiority over artificial sea-water, that it contains numerous germs of plants and animals, which afterwards de-
velop themselves, and supply you with home-grown specimens. I have had several good plants presented me in
this way, and they have generally started up from a stone
that wanted covering to complete the furnishing of the tank,
though it is too often the case that these same organic
germs rapidly putrify, and cause disorganization of the liquid.
Nevertheless it is advisable to husband every drop of sea-
water, but be careful to remove your specimens from it when
they arrive home, that you may agitate it well for use, or
throw it away if too far gone in putrescence.

By sorting your specimens over in bowls, you will get
a good view of your possessions, and be enabled to judge
of the best mode of disposing of them. You will have a

superabundance of some kinds, and a scarcity of others, and sometimes you will find yourself a possessor of many rarities. Where friends can exchange specimens, the respective tanks can be kept well supplied.

Instructions for dredging would be out of place here. It is an operation for a skilled coaster, not for an amateur. Any one may poke about the sea-shore and hunt for specimens, but he who takes a haul at the dredge for deep-sea wonders, must be somewhat experienced in boating, a good swimmer, and otherwise drilled to the work. To dredge with any hope of success requires a knowledge which books cannot furnish.

After all it is most likely that a majority of those who keep Aquaria, will purchase rather than collect their stock. It is a lucky circumstance that it can be purchased, for we are not all so circumstanced that we can take train whenever the whim suits us, and erratic as crabs, suit our movements to tides, seasons, winds, and changes of the moon.

There are several skilful naturalists now engaged in preparing stock for Aquaria. These, true to the genial character of the lover of nature, are willing to give information whenever it is sought, and to aid persons in the stocking of tanks by means of good advice and suitable suggestions. William Thompson, Esq., the eminent naturalist of Weybridge, keeps a dredge constantly employed, for the purpose of supplying the Zoological Society, and is willing to supply any person desirous of setting up a Vivarium. From Weymouth to London, the cost of transit by mail train and special messenger, amounts only to a few shillings, and a moderate sized tank of about two feet by one foot, could be stocked with a beautiful variety of animals and plants, at an expense of less than forty shillings. Any one sending for specimens, or making a trip to procure them, should remember the necessity for coral rag for rock-work, and sea-sand for the bottom of the tank. They can be had along with specimens.

To Mr. Lloyd I have already more than once referred,

and have only to mention his name here in order to suggest that no one should attempt to set up an Aquarium
without first paying him a visit.   He is ready to give counsel
as well as to take money, and if the Aquarian trusts to his
own skill in securing stock, he will, nevertheless, obtain
from Mr. Lloyd many little necessaries, such as dipping tubes,
thermometers, specific gravity beads, and vessels of all kinds,
without a small supply of which there can be but little
progress in Aquarian tactics.

   To Mr. Lloyd's name I may add that of Mr. Hall, of City
Road, and Mr. Pike, of Pool Valley, Brighton.   Mr. Pike
prepares excellent and cheap collections for youth.

CHAPTER IV.

"THERE 'S beauty in the deep:—
The wave is bluer than the sky;
And though the light shine bright on high,
More softly do the sea-gems glow,
That sparkle in the depths below;
The rainbow's tints are only made,
When on the waters they are laid,
And sun and moon most sweetly shine
Upon the ocean's level brine.
There 's beauty in the deep."
BRAINARD.

THE ordinary tenants of the Aquarium are the most curious creatures in nature, and deserve more than a bare enumeration in these chapters on tanks and their inhabitants. Therefore I will appropriate a chapter in an attempt to convey some account of their history, not less for the entertainment of the reader than for the instruction of those whose eyes are already somewhat familiar with the many

"Things beauteous that grow in the sea."

The little boy who took the bellows to pieces to see where the wind lay, was really an incipient philosopher, enquiring into the causes of things, and measuring the value of his toys by the amount of study they were worthy of. The toys that we "big folks" delight in, increase in value and interest in proportion as they hide their history from superficial glances, and demand watching and investigating, before they yield up a full account of themselves. Now in this best and most exhaustless of toys, the Aquarium, or Vivarium,* there is always something new to be seen, either in the birth of new plants and animals, the growth and metamorphoses of others, the freaks, pranks, and even crimes of its inhabitants—theft, murder, and cannibalism, contributing to the fun without any shock to our moral sensibilities. And when you have seen all that your every-day eyes can detect, bring the microscope—and, lo! the very scum on the surface is a new world more wonderful than that discovered by Columbus, and more willing to make an exhibition of its inhabitants, than Hind's, or Herschel's, or Le Verrier's planets. The space which a sixpence would cover, will give you material for the study of a year. Multiply the number of such spaces over the entire area of the tank, and you have in plain figures the number of years during which you may work with your microscope, and "still find something new, something to instruct." May every genuine lover of the Aquarium live to perform the task!

Among the lively inmates of a tank, gobies take the first place. They are elegant, familiar, and playful, and will soon learn to take food from the hand. Their movements are so lively and graceful as always to attract attention; and they are so like a gang of mad school-boys just let loose for a romp, that I cannot help fancying sometimes that they possess human sympathies, so much do they seem to regard their confinement as a piece of

---

* Let Dr. Badham argue as he will, if philological evidence is in his favour, which we doubt, popular habit will overrule him, and Aquarium will be the recognised name of the tank, containing an assemblage of animals and plants. Let Vivarium do duty as of old, for the park, warren, and menagerie. Aquarius is an old friend, and why should not his water-pot "be made of hyaline?"

fun, not intended for our pleasure so much as for their own.

There are three kinds very suitable for the Aquarium, The one-spotted goby is a gay little creature, only two inches or less in length; its fins are beautifully transparent, and on the dorsal fin there is one spot of rich dark blue: this is *Gobius unipunctatus.* The two-spotted goby has on its dorsal fin two spots, which shine brilliantly, like the eye of a peacock's tail. It is called *Gobius Ruthersparri.* The black goby, (*G. niger,*) grows to the length of three inches; its form is the same as the spotted kinds, but its colour is dark, and hence its name.

When in a passive state, this fish has a transparent drab or fawn tint, with cloudy patches of brown and white; but when displaying his murderous ferocity, the colour changes to a dull indigo, with black markings. The eyes are of a lovely blue, and sparkle like gems. All these may be taken in sea-side pools, but, as they dart away on the least alarm, considerable dexterity is necessary.

When first put into the Aquarium, they hide themselves, and are but little seen for a few days, when, on throwing in a few small pieces of meat, they venture out to take it, you will probably count less than you expect. If you miss any, you scarcely need search for them—blackie has eaten them up! The black goby is most voracious, and will attack a spotted goby of his own size, conquer him, but not slay him: he swallows his victim whole, uncooked, and alive. A short time since I lost six spotted gobies in one day; they were eaten up by their black relatives. The cannibal, true to his dark propensities, seldom shows himself in the daylight, never, except when hunger presses him, makes an excursion to the surface. When thrown into the tank he darts down, searches the crannies and hollows, and then selects his den. Here, like the Scythian Anthropophagi, he lurks, waiting for a victim. By-and-bye, some innocent little fish, that would starve sooner than eat the bread of infamy, sails past. He sees no danger, and suspects none. He is a "gone coon," nevertheless; blackie makes one sharp, straight dart, like an arrow, and seizes him by the tail. The victim writhes, the cannibal exults, and, with eyes distended, gulps his prey by a series of jerks, swallows him completely, and then retires. There are no bones at the door of the den to warn other wanderers, and so he succeeds. in thinning your stock, till there is a necessity for more gobies.

The smooth blenny, the butterfly blenny, and the gattoruginous blenny are of great service; they survive in health the demise of all other tenants of a tank, when, from exhaustion of oxygen, or the presence of putrescent matter, death sets his dark seal upon your work.

The common shanny, (*Blennius Pholis*,) is taken in large numbers on all parts of our coast. The sport is usually confined to idle boys, who enjoy piscatorial half-holidays in pursuit of this pretty fellow, who is to them a sort of sea-side "tittle-bat." It seldom exceeds five inches in length, has a variety of colours, scarcely two being found alike, and bears the imprisonment of the tank with impunity. The blenny is one of the few fishes that construct a nest for their young, a circumstance which increases the interest attached to this playful and familiar tenant of the tank. The butterfly blenny, (*B. ocellarius*,) and the gattoruginous blenny, (*B. Gattorugine*,) are handsome and lively, and amuse us with their quaint gambols and clever acts of petty larceny. They interest the observer by the curious movements of their eyes, which act in unison or independent of each other. This faculty was supposed to be possessed only by the chameleon, which can glance in one direction with one eye, while the other remains motionless, or looks in another direction. It is now known that the blennies, the wrasses, the suckers, and other small fishes, have the same faculty as fully developed as the chameleon.

The grey mullet is a very sociable fish, and usually

plays about the surface of the tank, with his nose out of the water. If the water gets flat from loss of oxygen, he takes large inspirations of atmospheric air, and then withdrawing his muzzle to his own element, discharges a string of bubbles. The tank should be supplied with a goodly number of these vivacious fishes: and as they are very sociable, they are always to be seen playing in groups near the surface. A good scramble may be got up by throwing them a boiled shrimp, or the spawn of a prawn, round which they dart and play, tugging the spoil from one another, till the whole of it is eaten. Now and then they start a fight, and the battle rages fiercely at the top, though never to the shedding of blood; they are neither assassins nor cannibals.

I am very partial to pipe-fishes, not for their activity, for they are lazy dreamy creatures, but for their queer performances; they are the antipodean acrobats of the Aquarium. They sink down slowly to the sand at the bottom, and there poise themselves in perpendicular attitudes, remaining motionless for some minutes, either on the tail or on the head, after the fashion of an "India-rubber brother." Indeed they assume every possible attitude except the horizontal one, and, like the buffoons on the human stage, get laughed at for their pains. The other day I was amused to see a fine specimen of *Syngnathus acus* proceed slowly and solemnly, fluttering as he went his useless dorsal fin, and, dropping his head beside a waving frond of *Rhodymenia*, left his tail to swing over, till he brought himself to an angle of about forty degrees, where he remained for several minutes immoveable, like one of the brothers Seigrist, thrusting himself out from *La perche*. In a very small tank the pipe-fishes are rather unhappy; they want plenty of room.

The suckers are small, fat, pretty fishes, the two-spotted sort being the best for our purpose. In this fish the ventral fins are so united as to enable it to adhere to any smooth

surface, where it remains for hours, glued to a smooth stone,
or to the shell of a cockle. It is only two inches long,
and of a clear crimson colour, with a spot of deep red on
each side. If obtained adhering to a shell, as it usually is,
it is best to drop in the shell with it, rather than attempt
to remove the fish, which may be injured from its clinging
so tenaciously. It now and then shifts its position, but
does not swim about. It is apt to get out of sight for
days together, and hence the advisability of so arranging
your rock-work, if you have any, that all the arches and
hollows are visible from the front. It feeds on the microscopic growths of the tank, and hence flourishes best in
genuine sea-water, or if an artificial water, it must have
been in use some time.

But of all the fishes which may be kept in the Aquarium
the wrasses are the most brilliant and engaging. Lurking
under a dark stony ledge, the ancient wrasse, (*Labrus
maculatus*,) displays his livery of gold and green, blood-red
and olive-brown. He loves the dark cool umbrage of waving
sea-weeds, amongst which he finds the minute morsels which
constitute his innocent meal. The white under-jaw, the
iridescent eye, and the rich-mottled and many-coloured
sides shading into brown, crimson, and emerald green,
make him a conspicuous object as he lights up the sombre
depths of the submerged forest with his vivid display of
colours. He cannot be compared to a harlequin, for his
movements are solemn, and his habit quiet. The brightest-
coloured specimens are those of about six inches in length.
This fish is only to be obtained of experienced fishermen.
I have never known it to be taken near the shore.

But there is a smaller species which the amateur collector
may sometimes succeed in capturing; it is the corkwing,
(Crenilabrus Cornubicus.) This is a minute fish, not ex-
ceeding two inches in length, less beautiful in its colouring
than the one just described, but still very lovely, hardy,
and full of life. It haunts the fuci on all parts of the

British coast, and may be taken with the hand sometimes, when a number of them are entangled in the weed. It is always in motion, and puts itself into very pretty and sometimes comical attitudes, as it perseveringly hunts among the weeds for its insect prey. It is an amiable creature, and soon becomes familiar.

After the true fishes, the most important, zoologically speaking, are the crustaceans. Crabs are curious and amusing creatures, and the great variety of species astonishes those who have not made natural history their study. The common edible crab, *(Cancer pagurus,)* with which we are so familiar in a boiled form, is the least worthy of them all in a zoological aspect. It is a tame creature, which folds its hands submissively upon its breast, and yields itself to the captor without a struggle. But the *Carcinus mænas*, which scuttles sideways along the sand, is the crab to be sought for domestication. Should you meet one and capture him without getting a good nip from his fierce claws, you may deem yourself fortunate, for he offers battle boldly, and is not to be made a prisoner without a fierce struggle for liberty. When caught, and dropped into the jar, he will escape unless the inside of the vessel be very slippery; and should your tank be unwisely filled to the brim, he will cling to the zinc corner, and dropping down, make an excursion over the carpet. I had a fine one sent me lately, and instead of at once submerging him, I put him on the gravel in the garden. My cat was perched on the wall above, dozing herself into a dream about sparrow-pie, and perceiving this strange object, which had drawn itself upon its haunches, making no attempt to escape, puss, after peeping and snuffing a few moments, dropped stealthily down, and crouched up to Mr. Cancer. Presently she ventured to give him a pat with her paw, and then advanced closer, as if she relished the smell of fish. She had scarcely brought her olfactory bristles into propinquity with cancer's pedunculated eyes, than, with a sudden bound, he opened all his limbs at once, and clutched puss by the lip with one of his fierce foot-claws. There was a struggle of a moment; puss disengaged herself and darted off with a piteous howl, and cancer began dancing and scraping up the gravel in a manner which, as Mr. Pepys has it, "did give me much joy to behold." Half an hour afterwards, he was doing battle with a smaller crab of his own species, which he conquered, at the bottom of the tank. When dropped in, he goes in a tortuous course to the bottom, with a tremendous fizz, like a catharine wheel. This crab is easily taken by letting into the crevices which they haunt a line baited with a piece of meat. A mere piece of string is sufficient. Mænas grasps the bait, and holds on till you secure him. The fiddler, (*Portunus puber,*) a handsome swimming crab, may frequently be taken along with the mænas, as it haunts the same clefts. It is a creature of most murderous propensities, and will wage war against every other creature in the collection. One of the most quiet, most interesting, and most harmless of the whole cancer family is the pretty broad-claw, (*Porcellana platycheles,*) respecting which Mr. Gosse gives a most interesting account in his work entitled "The Aquarium."

The soldier and spider crabs are still more comical, both in structure and mode of life. But who ever saw a spider crab trotting along on a voyage of discovery without laughing? All our childish fables, and our admiration of Harry Longlegs dancing on the window-pane, vanish before those sprawling thread-like filaments, on which a spider crab performs locomotion. Then there is the strawberry crab, which climbs up the coral branches as a monkey climbs up trees; while of all things curious in this constellation of cancer, just now so justly in the zenith, the habit of the hermit crab in fitting up a lodging for himself, with a pretty housekeeper dozing on the threshold, is the queerest of all.

It would puzzle a novice not a little, if in a first experiment at deep-sea dredging, his boatman should turn out for him half a dozen large whelk shells, every one of them inhabited, not by whelks, but by a couple of creatures who seem to have entered into partnership in illegal distraint and possession. Yet there they are. Around the mouth of the shell is a mass of pulpy fleshy matter, disgusting at first sight, and which the novice would · drop with horror the first time his fingers touched it. Within the shell sits a little hermit crab, a sort of mongrel between crab and lobster, his eyes starting out on stalks, wondering why he

Porcellana platycheles.　　Cancer Pagurus.

should be disturbed in his home, and menacing you with his double beak and bandy legs.

The anemone, which encloses the entrance, and serves as housekeeper to the crab, is by no means an obnoxious creature, when we know her. Just as a dead clod by the way-side expands into the ruddy glory of a summer flower, under the genial influences of sun and rain, so does this dead livid-looking mass, which we at first shudder to touch, expand—as soon as it is placed in the tank—a series of elegant flower-like tentacles, which form around it a lovely fringe, every thread of which moves to and fro in search of food.

Yet delicate as this anemone appears, the crab makes egress and ingress through the mouth of the shell, we may be sure with no very tip-toe movements; he does not put carpet slippers over his sharp scratchy toes before blundering pell-mell over the quivering naked creature. But they seem to live jolly enough together, perhaps contributing in some mysterious way to each other's welfare, the idea of which would be still more pleasing did we not now and then wonder what has become of the pretty black-spotted whelk, to whom the shell originally belonged. Was he torn from his home by the allied forces, and gobbled up at the door of his own house, to make room for the invaders? The decision of the question is a deep-sea wonder.

Mr. Gosse, in his entertaining work on the "Aquarium," tells several amusing anecdotes respecting the parasite crabs, and especially of their occasional anxiety to change their apartments. An amusing incident of the kind is related as the result of an experiment made by Mr. James Salter: "I have many times found hermit crabs out of their shells, in the mingled mass of a dredge haul, and on three occasions have watched the method in which the houseless creature domiciliates himself. These were the only occasions on which I endeavoured to observe the operation; they always seemed willing enough to exhibit their housing performances. My plan of observation was simply this—I put a naked crab into a large glass jar of sea-water, with one shell, the latter of size about proportioned to the former, and I then contemplated. In each case the crab proceeded in the same way. Appearing to *see* the shell in the distance, the animal crawled up to it for the purpose of ascertaining

if the house were to let; and this circumstance he discovered,
not by sight but by *touch*. Upon reaching the shell, he
hooked two of his legs into its open mouth, and thrusting
them as far down into its cavity as possible, commenced
scrambling round the edge. He was evidently probing to
discover if there were already an inhabitant. In each case
the crab pursued this probing operation in the same direction
—commencing on the projecting side of the shell, and ending
on the receding side. Having performed this process once
round, he instantly, in the twinkling of an eye, erected
straight his tail, and whisked himself over the smooth lip
of the shell into its tube with a rapid adroitness that was
perfectly marvellous. And now in his new contrasted
position he looked so funny, such at-homeishness there was
in it; he was so different from the poor houseless vagabond
with a drivelling tail, that one had seen miserably crawling
about a moment before; he looked right up in your face,
and said, as plainly as looks can speak, 'How d'ye do?
here I am, quite at home already!' I never saw it without
laughing."

The young new-formed crab is a very different sort of
creature to the well-developed cancer. Every now and
then he changes his coat, slips out of one armour into
another, and passes through a bewildering series of changing
attire. It has long been a puzzle to philosophers how such
a creature can slip clean out of its crustaceous covering
without leaving a visible rent, and with every joint, down
to the fine-pointed claw, entire. The operation is performed
almost in an instant, and is so strange that no rationale of
the process can be given. As they grow older, they perform
the process less frequently, and perhaps cease at last to
change coats at all. One can scarcely believe that a
monster crab, containing enough meat for six hungry
sailors, in a jacket as hard as limestone, can very easily
withdraw from his calcareous breastplate and leggings.
Mr. Broderip has a specimen which was taken alive, and

on its back are oysters of six years growth. Here is proof, then, that for six years previously this individual had made no change of armour. Still we know not what he might have done if allowed to reach that primal climacteric, the seventh.

Prawns and shrimps would occupy a volume, to do them justice. Easily obtained alive, and eaten everywhere after being cooked alive, these humble creatures would stand a chance of cool treatment at the hands of the amateur, did we not here drop the hint, that for liveliness, elegance of movement, courage, and cleanliness, all varieties of shrimp and prawn are worthy of admiration, from the great lobster prawn, with its fierce pincers, down to the little shrimp, the joy of Gravesend.

Doubled up as we get them, and altogether altered in colour, by the combined effects of boiling water and red-hot poker, they convey the very remotest idea of their natural shape and character. Their natural colours are very beautiful, and a soft transparency adds much to the fasci-nating effect they produce on the eye as they dart up and down, moving rapidly their "many twinkling feet" with more grace than the bright *danseuse* of the French ballet. As they proceed they point forward their long horns, or antennæ, which glisten like silver threads. Then they curvet head over heels, and dart up and down again, either escaping from the attack of marauding fishes, which they keep at bay with the most playful menaces, or gamboling with each other for mere fun. But they do fall pretty often into hungry jaws, and the stock must be kept up by a continual supply.

Attractive as such creatures are, it is to the great family of Zoophytes we must continue to look for our supplies of specimens, and, after all the attractions of lively and tame-able creatures, what is called *ground* stock forms the staple article. Southey unintentionally sums up in a few lines the leading attractions of the Marine Aquarium.

"Here too were living flowers,
    Which like a bud comparted,
    Their purple lips contracted;
    And now in open blossom spread,
Stretched like green anthers many a seeking head.
And arborets of jointed stone were there,
And plants of fibres fine as silk-worms' thread,
    Yea, beautiful as mermaid's golden hair,
Upon the waves dispread."

These "living flowers" are sea anemones, which are found
in abundance on our coasts, or in the deep bays adjacent;
most of them thrive in confinement, and continue in health
for a length of time, varying from a few months to two or
three years, and during the whole of this time they delight
us with many changes of form—every change a new development of beauty—and in their elegant outlines, splendid
colours, and strange habits and movements, give a varying
delight that never tires, and a course of instruction that
cannot be exhausted.

SEA ANEMONES.

ALL the creatures of this kind are *Zoophytes*, that is,
"plant-like animals," members of the class *Anthozoa*, or,
"flower-life," and the order *Helianthoida*, a term which
conveys the idea of their resemblance to "blossoms of the
sun." In the "Book of the Aquarium" I have given a brief
account of their Zoological characteristics, and of their
position in the general scheme of creation. Here I will
describe a few of those which are best adapted for the
Aquarium.

Everywhere on the sea-coast the explorer may find that
commonest, but not least valuable of the family, *Actinia
mesembryanthemum*, the smooth anemone, which, when
shrunk up in the hollows of a honey-combed rock, has the
appearance of an unsightly piece of flesh of the size and
shape of a chesnut, and when closely examined, the colouring
of a dark strawberry. These may be detached from their

rocky sites by cleverly slipping the finger beneath them, or by scooping them out by a pewter spoon, and if simply packed in wet sea-weed, twenty or thirty may be placed in the same jar, one over the other. If carefully washed in sea-water as soon as they are unpacked—which should be within forty-eight hours of their capture—and dropped into the tank where you would have them fix themselves, they will in the course of a day or two take a firm hold and begin to expand. In removing this and every other anemone, it is most important not to injure even by so much as a scratch, the sucking base by which they adhere to the sea bottom; but any little accident which may occur to their jackets is of less moment; a rent or slight puncture they soon darn for themselves, but the base is most delicate, and any injury to it will be followed by the death of the specimen.

As the creatures get reconciled to their new home they will begin to shift their positions, and at last attach themselves near to the spots where originally placed; some will mount the glass sides and adhere to the vertical surface; others will cling to the stones at the bottom; and some few will, if allowed, take possession of your tufts of Enteromorpha, and do the plants some injury. When they begin to expand, a number of small tubercles, of an azure blue colour, will first be perceptible, forming a ring of beads or torquoises around the margin of the disc, and as the expansion increases a number of chesnut brown, or vermilion *tentacles* will be protruded from the disc, and these will at last expand to their utmost, and form the petals of the lovely sea-flower. When fully expanded the bright-coloured specimens are extremely beautiful, and as they remain open for many days together, they give a rich glow of colour to the collection. When partially closed, as in the engraving at page thirty-seven, they are still very beautiful, and their mottled coats have so much the appearance of strawberries that we may safely describe the Aquarium as a garden of sea-

fruits as well as sea-flowers. This anemone is the hardiest of the whole family, and will live in the foulest water, but it does not expand freely unless as carefully tended as the rest of the tribe require to be, even to preserve them.

A. Bellis, the pretty daisy anemone, is another good specimen for ordinary use. It is very accurately represented in the cut at page sixty-eight, along with its near relative *A. gemmacea*. The daisy varies greatly in colour, some are beautifully tinted with pink and white, and pale fawn colour; others display shades of green, blue, and white, but all are of elegant form, and so constantly expanded, as to be highly prized by collectors. Among the variations of form and colour to which all anemones are subject, I have just observed in one of my vessels an instance more interesting than usual; a specimen of the daisy has lately put out from the inner portion of its disc, and quite within the circle of its normal tentacles, one large, fleshy, and distinct tentacle, of a rich yellow colour, which stands quite apart on the disc near to the lips, and quite spoils the beauty of the specimen, which, in other respects, is a fine one.

The *Gem* bears a pretty close resemblance to it, but a very distinct feature of the latter consists of the rows of glands, which reach from the margin of the disc to the base of the column, and in which a number of white bead-like spots are distinctly observable. The tentacles are not nearly so numerous as in the daisy, but they are very distinct and finger-like, very pellucid, and gaily marked with tints of opal white, rose-colour, warm brown, and green, while the disc frequently exhibits a blending of colours quite prismatic in variety and splendour. It is of small size, the disc seldom expanding beyond an inch in diameter, while its height is never more than an inch and a half; indeed specimens of that size are not so frequent as those which have but half those dimensions.

A. anguicoma, the snaky-locked anemone, is not less

beautiful than any of the preceding, but its beauty is of a peculiar kind; the general colouring is between a pale fawn and a pale flesh, but very delicate; the tentacles partake of the same hue, but are pellucid, and mottled with obscure dashes of white. Sometimes stripes of white and

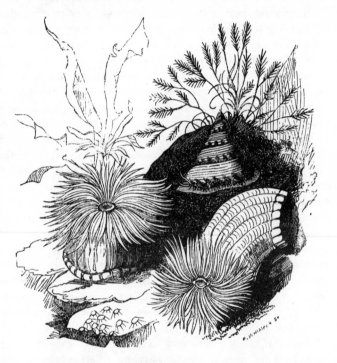

Actinia anguicoma, Trochus ziziphinus, Ulva latissima,
Bryopsis plumosa, Acorn barnacle.

buff occur, and occasionally slight touches of a warm brown, but a general pale tint is the most common. The varying form—in which it resembles *A. Dianthus*—creates an interest in this creature apart from its delicate colouring,

and snake-like tentacles, for it will occasionally start up
into a tall thin column, then shrink back again and bulge
out like a small bladder; and sometimes it leans over
from the perpendicular, and for several days continues to
expand its disc from the summit of a slender arch. The
tentacles are of great length, slender, pellucid, and very
faintly marked with white, and are very constantly expanded.

But the crowning glory of the Aquarium is the superb
plumose anemone, *A. Dianthus.* It is the monarch of
the tank, and for magnitude and splendour of colouring
throws all other anemones into the shade. Neither does
it so strictly belong to what may be termed *ground stock,*
for though it conforms to the orthodox rules of Zoophytic
life, it is so free in its actions, and exhibits so much individuality in its habits, as to appear to be endowed with
higher faculties than its more humble brethren. It seldom
remains for any length of time at the bottom of the vessel,
but slowly glides along till it meets with some perpendicular surface, such as a block of stone, or the side of
the vessel, and during the night it ascends and takes
up its position midway between the bottom and the
top of the vessel. When it has fairly settled itself, it
is not slow to exhibit its magnificent proportions and
glorious purity of colouring. Pure milk white, pale amber,
rich gold, or warm salmon colour, are its prevailing tints.

Full-grown specimens have a height of six inches, and a
diameter of one and a half when they stand upright, and
even when only four inches high their appearance is
massive and grand. When expanded the tentacles spread
over in thousands, and form huge fringing masses that
strongly resemble the petals of double carnations; they are
ever in motion, like

"Meadows fanned by heaven's life-breathing wind."

They expand outwards, droop over the column, then retract

and assume a cup-like appearance, then fall over again and
wave with a slow vibratile motion, as if

"Seeking something which they cannot find;"

and when they once more close together, the creature shows
a new caprice by suddenly shrinking down into the form
of a balloon, distended to a huge sphere, which presently
seems clasped by a cord, and the balloon is cut into two
equal halves. This zone of constriction shifts from place
to place, increasing the bulk of one sphere at the expense
of the other, until it seems as if it slipped off at the
base, when the column starts up again, rises to its full
height, and the thousands of fringes again extend and wave
to and fro as before. The slightest shock against the
sides of the vessel, or a mere breath upon the surface of
the water is at any time sufficient to alarm the beauty, and
cause it to withdraw its tentacles, but they are soon put
forth again, and are invariably in a state of expansion.

This has been described as one of the most tender of
its class, but I have long been convinced that it is
comparatively hardy, and may be preserved with very
great certainty. So long as the water is kept moderately
pure, by an occasional filtering, it lives and prospers,
occasionally moving from place to place, but almost
always expanded, and every instant assuming some new
form. It is, however, so far delicate that, if frequently
disturbed, it is sure to perish. When removed from its
native "oozy bed" it should be kept on the stone or shell
to which it is found attached, until it floats off of its own
accord, and fixes itself elsewhere. When handled it
throws out a number of white threads, which are afterwards withdrawn. Those which have very fine tentacles
are the most permanently expanded; the variety in which
the body has deep creases, and the tentacles a coarse
character, will remain closed for days together.

Actinia dianthus, Delesseria sanguinea, Callitham-nium roseum,
Griffithsia setacea.

A. crassicornis and *Anthea cereus* are species suitable only for those living near the sea-shore; they do not long survive transport to a distance, and indeed are short-lived even under the most favourable circumstances. *Serpulæ, Neries, Sabellæ, Terebella,* and *Madrepores,* afford their several points of interest to the student, and add to the graces of the collections, the *Serpulæ* being especially beautiful when their intensely brilliant trumpets and delicately-marked fans are protruded. To these may be added the *Holothuriæ,* or sea-cucumbers, and the *Echini,* or sea-urchins, which are less easily preserved than any of the foregoing, though highly remunerative when they take kindly to their in-door home. Lastly, *Edwardsia vestita,* here figured, is a new and welcome addition to the general stock of the Marine tank, for which we are indebted to the perseverance of Mr. Lloyd. It is the "clothed" anemone, and constructs for itself a tube of earthy matter—the caddis worm of the Marine Aquarium. To the anemones may be added the several species of star-fishes, of which small specimens may be kept with the greatest certainty.

The Aquarium introduces us to new scenes hitherto hidden from our view, makes us acquainted with the economy of creatures of whose very existence many of us, not altogether unlearned in the history of the world, were previously ignorant. Their habits of feeding, of moving, and burrowing; their battles, their changes of form, the display even of a strange intelligence, working its way by wonderful means to wonderful ends, impress the observer with an idea of the boundlessness, the variety, the adaptations, and resources of a world brimming with life, in all manner of strange forms and developments. Here we see them equipped and armed for battle against each other, the strong destroying the weak, yet each contributing its part to the preservation of the whole, just as in all other departments of Nature, the Great Balance of Perfection is sustained by incessant and intestine war; the struggles of

opposing elements, and powers, and beings, all working mysteriously in a manner independent of isolated circumstances—Nature, the Prodigal Mother, setting no value upon individuals, but regarding tribes and races as paramount—the whole seeming confusion tending to one great

Edwardsia vestita, Esop prawn, Enteromorpha compressa, Ulva latissima.

end—the revolution of the mighty wheel on which the creatures are painted as signs, and in which ages are but minutes, in a revolution which is itself an eternity.

In the midst of all, sits the Everlasting Wisdom, watching,

loving, and sustaining; happy we to get some glimpses of its method of working through the medium of the strange creatures, which leave the mysterious deep to throw a new radiance on our homes.

> "Each drop of water is a world containing
>   Creatures more numerous than the men of earth;
> The April shower, upon the green tree raining,
>   To fresh creations in each leaf gives birth.
> Nature, her balance everywhere regaining,
>   New breathing forms to life, leaves nothing dearth--
> Spitzbergen's ice, and Afric's sandy field,
> To Nature's living mass their tributes yield."

CHAPTER V.

————"SEAS have,
As well as earth, vines, roses, nettles, melons,
Mushrooms, pinks, gilliflowers, and many millions
Of other plants, more rare, more strange than these."
DU BARTAS.

RITERS on the Aquarium seem to have united in a compact to frown down botanical studies. It is quite true that the animals take precedence in the tank, and that the plants are chiefly used in order to effect that necessary balance on which success depends. Still I can see no reason why we should not make the best of our water-gardens, for the culture of curious and beautiful plants. At starting, we must always depend on *Enteromorpha* and *Ulva* for the preparation of the marine tank; but when the vessel has been some time stocked, a very moderate share of skill would enable any one to incorporate with its contents some of the more elegant forms of Algæ, of which there is certainly a large choice from species noted for their beautiful outlines and gay colours. If ferns convey the idea of perfect grace in the forms of terrestrial

vegetation, the perfection of colour is certainly attained by
the *Rhodosperms*, which display tints unrivalled by few
kinds of terrestrial foliage; and in their growth and structure
reveal many curious examples of vegetative adaptiveness
to the peculiar circumstances under which they are produced.

The majority of Marine Algæ flourish near the shore;
the deep sea does not appear to be productive of any great
variety of vegetation. This might be expected, seeing that
vegetable colours are only produced under the action of
light; though in tropical climates, where the intenser light
will penetrate to greater depths, and a high temperature
will promote whatever growths there may be light enough
to support, there will be exceptions to the case of temperate
latitudes.

The *Mer de Sargosse*, or Weedy Sea—now well known
as to its limits and character—was a region of mystery to
the old Spanish and Portuguese mariners, and its passage
by Columbus forms a charming episode in Horace St. John's
picturesque life of the great navigator. But Columbus was
not

> ——"The first that ever burst
> Into that silent sea;

for the Phœnicians—the fathers of marine commerce—reached
it in thirty days sail from the Mediterranean, and gave its
historical name—the Weedy Sea. There are, in fact, two
such seas in the Atlantic; one lies between 25° and 36° of
latitude, a little west of the meridian of Fayal; the other
occupies a space between 22° and 26° in the 70th. degree of
longitude, about two hundred and seventy miles east of the
Bahamas. Each of these regions bears the character of a vast
marine meadow, "sweeping in huge floating fields far as the
eye can reach." But what is most interesting in the history
of this phenomenon is the immense size of the *Fucus* which
forms the floating masses, and the immense depths at which
they are produced. Lamoroux observed stems upwards of

eight hundred feet long, not fixed to the bottom, but floating freely on the surface of the water; fronds of from two to three hundred feet are common. At the immense depth at which these are produced it is believed that all is calm, and still, and unruffled—a motionless silence, and a green twilight; and hence it seems at first sight difficult to explain in what manner the huge forests get uprooted; but Lamoroux observed that though the *fuci* adhere to rocks with great firmness before the display of fructification, yet, as soon as this took place, the plants detached themselves and rose to the surface, either to ripen their spores under the action of light, or because their term of existence had expired.

The curious modes by which the germinating principle is developed in plants which require exposure to light at the period of fructification, are very strikingly exhibited in aquatic plants, as in the *Vallisneria spiralis,* which sends up a spiral stem to the surface; the *Stratiotes aloides,* which detaches itself from the bottom, and floats during the time of its blooming. Humboldt has seen a *fucus* vegetating at a depth of one hundred and ninety-two feet, where it could receive light equal only to half of that supplied by a candle at the distance of a foot, and which, notwithstanding, was as green and glossy as a meadow in spring.

A tribe of plants which are capable of interrupting the lines of navigation, which contribute in their living state articles of food and luxury, when dried medicines and ornaments, which furnish us with soda and iodine, and other valuable chemical agencies; not forgetting their importance as manures for the land; must surely be worthy of the attention of the student, who may now class them with his window flowers, and while noting their physical economies, derive delight from their distinctive forms and colourings, and picturesque outlines, enhanced by the transforming power of the medium through which we view them.

There with its waving blade of green
    The sea-flag streams through the silent water,
And the crimson leaf of the dulse is seen
    To flush, like a banner bathed in slaughter.
There, with a slight and easy motion,
    The fan-coral sweeps through the clear deep sea,
And the yellow and scarlet tufts of ocean
    Are bending like corn on the upland lea.
And life in rare and beautiful forms,
    Is sporting amid those bowers of stone,
And is safe when the wrathful spirit of storms
    Has made the top of the waves his own.
                    Percival.

Confining our attention for the present to the plants with which a tank may be stocked by those who desire to increase its botanical attractions, and who do not mind the trouble of occasional renewal, it will be as well to have Dr. Badham's advice upon the subject.

He says, "The green weeds are in every way suited to our requirements, both on the score of their greater beauty, and also because they do not, like the red and brown kinds, render the water turbid by decomposition. The two commonest are the *Ulva latissima* (sea lettuce) and an *Enteromorpha*, which, growing together, might at first sight be confounded with it; but on looking at the latter more attentively, it will be seen that it is hollow, and tapers down all the way to the point whence it germinates, where it diminishes almost to a thread; whereas the *Ulva latissima* is a ribbon of equal breadth throughout. Either of these weeds will do, but the *Ulva* preserves the transparency of the water better than the *Enteromorpha*. Small sprigs of the more delicate red fuci may be made to inosculate very prettily with these, without communicating any perceptible tinge to the water; they should, however, be used discreetly, and to a very limited extent, or they will certainly embrown and damage its sparkling brilliancy, which it is the first object of the keeper of a Vivarium to maintain intact. The great vitality of these weeds is another ground for preference. We have known them survive the extinction of three or four sets of animals, and recover, after removal from foul water full of poisonous effluvia. Their vitality is so molecular and diffused, that when fragments become detached, the pieces, whether floating or at the bottom, look for many days afterwards, just as green and healthy as the plants from which they have been severed. Exposed, as they are, to every kind of weather all the year round, on shore, we are less surprised at finding them scarcely, if at all, affected in confinement, during the very hottest or coldest day. But hardy and tenacious of life as they are in a remarkable degree, they are not always in equal vigour. During winter, their attachments to the rock are less firm, and their growth less vigorous than in summer, and to this circumstance we attribute the development of confervoid growths, which, during the cold months, are very noticeable in both marine and fresh-water preserves; more strikingly in the first, and very strikingly in the latter."

We may now advise as to the plants which may safely be introduced, so as to insure the greatest variety of beautiful forms, with a general healthiness of the tank. Some hints have been already given as to choice of plants, and the best mode of gathering them. When obtained, some judgment is required to give them such positions in the tank as are suitable to their habit of growth, and to the disposition of their colours and forms; some thrive best in shady nooks under the dark arches, while others spring forward to the light and send their waving fronds to the surface.

Of the green weeds, *Zostera marina* and *Ulva latissima* are of great value. They are easily procurable on any of our coasts at low water; and the first usually has concealed amongst its fronds numerous specimens of *Lucernariæ* and other small animals, which will afterwards display themselves in the tank, if speedily conveyed to it without exposure to the air. *Ulva latissima,* (the sea lettuce,) is a most elegant and hardy plant, already sufficiently described; a tank is neither complete nor healthy without it; and the same may be said even more emphatically of that sheet anchor *Enteromorpha compressa. Codium tomentosum* is another green weed, which should be obtained if possible, as many of the mollusca will eat nothing else. It is not over elegant, but thrives well in confinement. When obtained fresh from the sea, it is sometimes studded with interesting little mollusks. The *Cladophoræ* are plants of simple structure, consisting of jointed threads grouped into bushes and tufts of various tints of fresh green. *C. uncialis* and *C. rupestris* are the prettiest; *C. arcta* is a strong dwarf kind, which forms little upright bushes rather stiff in outline; it is ragged and coarse in texture, but worthy of a place if there is room. They all thrive and increase with little care.

The plants of the genus *Chondrus* are very beautiful, but apt to create turbidity: at least such is my own experience. *C. crispus* is certainly the best; it is very beautiful, putting out spreading fronds, which divide into elegant rounded segments, which "glow with refulgent reflections of azure, resembling the colour of tempered steel." The *Chondrus* in a dried form is the carrageen moss of commerce, everywhere domestically known for the valuable jelly which it produces. I had a fine specimen of *C. Norvegicus* presented me some time since, but lost it in less than a month.

Punctaria latifolia is perhaps the most elegant of all the green weeds that may be readily domesticated. It resembles somewhat the well-known ladies' tresses, and sends up its fine waving fronds of pale sea-green almost to the surface of the water, forming beautiful arches of pellucid tissue, through which the fishes glide and gambol, keeping it in constant motion to and fro; it lasts a long while, and if all goes well will increase rapidly. *Bryopsis* is another genus that furnishes a few good specimens. *B. plumosa* is a very elegant but small plant, which sets at defiance all ordinary adverse circumstances, and dots the stones with its spray-like tufts most luxuriantly. It delights in crevices, and should be dropped into the deepest part of the tank. *Dictyota* is a genera that does well; these have fragile pellucid fronds, flattened and freckled, branching into angular segments, and are so frail and tender that the slightest touch injures them severely. They are by no means showy, and are not necessary in a small collection.

The red and crimson plants afford a still greater variety; the loveliness of some being unequalled in the whole vegetable kingdom. That superb plant, the *Delesseria sanguinea*, takes the first place among the crimson weeds. The *D. alata* is another species of the same genus; and of the two it is difficult to decide which is the most lovely. The first has elegant leaf-like fronds of a delightful crimson, each frond springing from a stem, and being elegantly ribbed and wrinkled, after the fashion of the leaves of land plants. The second grows in thin much-cut leaves of a very rich crimson, and is called *alata*, or winged, in consequence of its divided outline. There are several species, all of great beauty. *D. sinuosa* and *D. hypoglossum* are the best after the two just named. They all thrive in the tank, and light up its waters with lovely tintings of scarlet and crimson.

Perhaps *Ptilota* should stand next in point of beauty. There are only two species—*P. plumosa* and *P. sericea*. They are both delicately formed, the fronds being cut into fine divisions, so as to resemble, perhaps rather remotely, some of our more delicate kinds of ferns. They are of a duller red than the *Delesseria*, but the elegance of their feathery outlines has a charming effect. They may frequently be found on the clefts and ledges, covered with the fuci which the tide leaves uncovered on the coast.

Polysiphonia, Dasya, the minute *Calithamnion,* and *Ceramium* are all of similar jointed thread-like structure, and of a dull red or bluish-tinted crimson. They are easily obtained, and flourish in the tank, but are not conspicuous for extraordinary beauty. Different it is with that glorious Neried, the *Nitophyllum punctatum*, which shines amid the dark green waters, as if it were always pleased, while its growth is rapid and certain if the tank be well kept. There are six species of *Nitophyllum*, but this is the worthiest of a worthy tribe. The frond is broad, and spotted with dark crimson marks, which seem to shine through its delicate texture, as if they came through from behind; while the edges break into a number of segments and delicate puckerings, increasing and broadening from below upwards. *N. versicolor* is the next best; but the other members of the genus do not succeed so well as these two.

The two species of the genus *Phyllophora*, namely, *P. rubens* and *P. brodiæi*, are of great service, not only for the formal fingery form and bright crimson colour of their fronds, but for the immense amount of oxygen they throw off when once established, and which tends so much to the health of the animals in the tank. They are obtained, along with plants of *Delesseria*, from the rocky clefts at low water-mark; but the best specimens are those brought up by the dredge. I consider it indispensible for the reasons just described.

Rytiphlæa pinastroides, is another handsome red species which flourishes abundantly under the worst of circumstances. The same may be said of *Griffithsia*, named in honour of Mrs. Griffith, of Torquay, the most distinguished of British Algologists. This plant bears some resemblance to the small *Equisetaceæ* of the hedges—a number of thread-like and jointed growths springing from a centre. It might almost be compared to a tuft of fine grass, such as *Briza gracilis*, for instance; except that instead of being of that fresh cheering green, it is of a most delicate rose-colour. Dr. Harvey, in his "Phycologia Britannica," speaks of the ease with which this plant may be domesticated; and experiments in Aquaria bear out his statement. No sea-weed thrives better than this; but there is a difficulty in obtaining it from its natural site on the low ledges, owing to the slight hold it has upon its place of growth. Its base is so minute that the collector is pretty sure to break away several specimens before he secures one firmly attached to the rock. If ever so slightly attached, it lives and thrives; but if removed altogether it perishes.

Every one knows the *Plocamium*, which produces those crimson trees so much used by taxidermists in mounting stuffed birds in glass cases, and in the making of sea-weed landscapes. It is very brilliant in colour, and excessively ramified, but not to be strongly recommended in the formation of a marine garden. The only remaining plant of the red kind, which, in the present state of our knowledge in Aquarian matters, can be safely recommended, is the *Cystoseira ericoides*. It is not to be found in the immediate vicinity of the beach, but may be hooked up from a boat in about one fathom's depth of water, at low tide on a rocky bottom. It may then be seen forming bushes of large size, springing from the crevices of the rock, but too far from the surface to be got at by hammer and chisel. If torn away with some vigour, some of the best portions of a shrub may be brought up, and these bound to the surface of shells or stones, make ornaments of most gorgeous colouring for the Aquarium. When brought up it has a dull yellowish hue, but the moment it is submerged in its native element, all its glory returns, "the pale olive branches become invested with a most brilliant flush of iridescent light blue, not changeable in tint, though varying in intensity, according to the play of light that falls upon it."

The corallines are not to be omitted from this list of useful plants, for plants they are without doubt. *Corallina officinalis, elongata,* and *squamata,* and the elegant *Jania* of both species, *rubens* and *corniculata,* are all elegant, and contrast their light spiny stems against the more palmate forms very agreeably. They last a long while in health,

but must be removed if they show a tendency to become
white; for this, though beautiful, is the condition of death.

Of yellow weeds, the general remark must be made that
they do not succeed. The best are *Laminaria phyllitis*
and *Padina pavonia*. The first is an elegant species of
tangle, a family which has many attractive features, especially when the specimens are young. They do not suit,
however; they soon decay, and fill the water with filmy
threads of decomposing matter, which makes quick havoc
with the delicate animals.

But *L. phyllitis*, or ladies' tresses, is an exception, and
may be introduced with safety. It puts forth a number of
large waving fronds, of a yellowish green hue, the edges
puckered like frills, and the fronds bending over in elegant
pensile outlines. The *Padina pavonia*, or peacock's tail,
is as curious in structure as it is beautiful. It springs
from a point, and thence expands into a broad fan, with
an outline forming, in fine specimens, nearly three-fourths
of a circle. The fans are marked with a series of regularly
disposed concentric lines of yellow and orange, so that it
has more the appearance of a shell than a sea-weed; an
illusion strengthened by the fluted scrolls of the younger
fronds, which somewhat resemble *serpulæ*. The texture of
this alga is membraneous, the general colour of the frond
is whitish olive or drab, its surface is set over with a white
mealy powder, and the margin fringed with a line of minute
hairs set at an angle from the plane of the frond. It is
an annual, and hence only to be found in summer. Young
specimens may be obtained the first week in June, and if
transferred to the Aquarium, create considerable amusement
by their strange form and mode of growth.

The only genus of purple weeds that succeeds in a tank
is *Porphyra*. The common sloke, or laver, which most
of us know better by flavour than appearance, when growing
in *situ*, is really a very elegant plant. In texture and
surface it resembles gold-beater's skin; and when introduced

to a tank, affords a variety of colouring very acceptable as a contrast to the gay pinks and greens. All kinds of *Fuci* live well, but are too ugly to be tolerated, except for purposes of study.

From the foregoing list of genera, there are at least fifty species available for the Aquarium. Further experiments will of course increase the number of suitable plants, and we may hope that in time we shall learn how to preserve some of the many beautiful weeds which at present refuse to adapt themselves to our artificial gardens. The culture of algæ is altogether a new idea; if it proceeds at anything like the pace that floriculture has made of late years, what may we not hope to produce in our miniature oceans? Let us hope that every one keeping a tank will endeavour to increase the common stock of knowledge in such matters by judicious experiments and observations, directed to the ends of enlarging the circle of operations, and of rendering more exact our knowledge of the best proportions of vegetable and animal life, in such arrangements as that failures and accidents may become fewer, and remedies found for obviating the difficulties which at present attend this strange and seductive enterprise. Lastly, let it be borne in mind that there should be no haste in stocking a tank with botanical curiosities, the beginner must be content with the two plants so frequently named as the best for preparing and preserving the water.

The accompanying plate represents seventeen of the seaweeds just described, as best suited for the purposes of the tank. On the extreme left are two fine fronds of the elegant ladies' tresses, *(Laminaria phyllitis,)* and between them springs a small tuft of *Desseleria sanguinea.* A larger specimen of the same plant, of a paler tint and less currugated, is seen springing from the extreme right of the arch of rock-work. Behind the *Laminaria* springs a mass of sea grass, *(Zostera marina,)* and from the piece of rock to the right of the *Zostera,* where the fronds of the *Lami-*

naria terminate, spring two crimson weeds; the finely-cut specimen is *Corallina officinalis*, and the palmate and brighter-coloured weed, the *Phyllophora rubens*. The large deeply-cleft crimson plant to the right of the base of *Laminaria*, is *Nitophyllum punctatum;* at the foot of the latter grows the finely-divided *Ptilota plumosa;* the crimson patches on the stone adjoining the latter, are specimens of *Calitham-nion Rothii* and *C. spongiosum*. Immediately beneath the arch is a plant of the common dulse, or dillis, *(Rhody-menia palmata;)* and behind it springs the thread-like and much-admired *Griffithsia sectacea*. The pale green beside *Griffithsia* is *Dictyota dichotoma;* and the plant on the left hand summit of the arch, is *Dasya coccinia;* that on the right hand, *Delesseria sanguinea*. The sea-green tuft below the arch is *Cladophora uncialis;* the plant to the right of it *Chylocladia parvula;* the green sprays which spring from the stones in the right hand corner, are fronds of *Bryopsis plumosa;* above which are the large fronds of *Chondrus crispus*. Behind the latter is a crumpled frond of the sea lettuce, *(Ulva latissima;)* behind which is seen the darker tint of *Cladophora rupestris*.

CHAPTER VI.

NATURE hath tones of magic deep, and colours iris bright,
And murmurs full of earnest truth, and visions of delight;
'Tis said, "The heart that trusts in her was never yet beguiled,"
But meek and lowly thou must be, and docile as a child.
Then study her with reverence high, and she will give the key,
So shalt thou learn to comprehend the "secrets of the sea."

MARIE J. EWEN.

HE punishment of labour entailed upon our race—"by the sweat of thy brow shalt thou eat bread"—is seen in every act of our lives; nothing worth having is attainable without labour; even love, when inspired by "first sight," cannot be ripened to completeness unless at least one of the parties evinces a little perseverance in wooing. We must not expect, then, to succeed in Aquarian studies without perseverance and patience, and minor difficulties and small disappointments must not force us to the assertion that "the thing can't be done." The thing *is* done; and what one can do, can be done by everybody who will adopt similar means. In fact, though an Aquarium is a little trouble at first, failures of any kind are quite the exception, and whatever trouble is entailed upon us is in this matter of a very instructive nature.

The first point to be attended to is the proper management of artificial marine water, for that is everywhere used in place of the genuine article, except by those who live in the vicinity of the sea. The beginner must bear in mind that however bright and pure the water may be when first prepared, it nevertheless requires some preparation before any animals are introduced to it. It should be mixed and thoroughly dissolved, and the density should be 1.028. It should then be filtered into the tank, and for this purpose a bee-glass, which has a hole in the centre for the reception of a ventilator, is the best implement. If such a thing is not at hand, an *old* flower-pot does just as well, but is of course not an elegant object. Into the hole thrust a piece of clean sponge, leaving it sufficiently loose to allow the water to flow through in a thin stream. Upon the sponge throw sufficient small charcoal to half fill the vessel, and then either suspend it above the tank, or place it on a couple of strips of wood, so that the stream can flow from the sponge between them. When this apparatus is ready, place at the bottom, or in whatever situations please you best, the pieces of rock to which your *Ulva* and *Enteromorpha* are attached. The plants should be quite fresh, and the stones should have been well washed in sea-water, and, if necessary, slightly scrubbed with a brush. Then filter the water through, and throw in the specific gravity bead, that it may be kept at its proper density. If a moderate amount of daylight reaches the vessel, it will be ready to receive a few animals at the end of a week. They should not be hurriedly introduced. *Actinia mesembryanthemum* should make first entrance, then the other species which I have described as most suited for early experiments, but there should be no haste and no crowding, or the whole may be lost. It is better to work safely, and be content with half-a-dozen specimens, than

consign a number to a premature grave. I find that
madrepores and serpulæ do very well to accompany the
first batch of actiniæ. The plumose anemone should not
be placed in water that is less than a month old; and to
hasten the ripening of the prepared element, it will be
as well to throw in as much fresh weed as can be conveniently got, removing it in a few days, then replacing
the filter, and filling it continually from the top, without
emptying the tank. This enables it rapidly to imbibe those
subtle chemical elements that are communicated to it by
the sea-weeds, and the filtering removes all decomposing
taints, and at the same time charges it with abundance of
oxygen. A little real sea-water is also useful in hastening
the maturity of the artificial.

Having described the kinds of animals and plants most
suitable for Aquaria, I must now caution the beginner
against the injudicious grouping together of creatures of
dissimilar habits. Anemones may, as a rule, be kept
together. The several species agree well, and seldom or
rarely injure each other; but star-fishes and crabs are best
kept in vessels apart from them. Star-fishes are very
destructive, and readily absorb the bodies of mollusks out
of their shells. If exception is to be taken to any particular
anemone, I think the grand *Plumosa* must suffer by it; for
this noble creature gives off a flocculent exudation, which
seems injurious to other kinds. I have generally kept the
plumose anemone in company with *A. mesembryanthemum,
bellis, troglodytes,* and others, without perceiving any bad
result; but I have always been careful to remove the slimy
exuvia daily, by means of the dipping tube. Respecting
mollusks, and especially trochus and most bivalves, it should
be borne in mind that they are apt to die off rapidly, and
to cause a putrescence of a most obnoxious character,
which soon spoils the water, and causes a general havoc.
Another remark applicable to mollusks is this, that the
Eolids—members of the *Nudibranch,* or naked mollusks—

are destructive of anemones, and delight in nibbling holes in their coats, or eating off their tentacles; whereas the pretty Doris may be kept as long as it will live, in company with the most delicate creatures, without offering offence to any. The more varied the collection, the more is our interest in its examination increased; and the possessor of a single vessel, or of a tank, and a few auxiliary jars, will be naturally anxious to preserve representatives of as many tribes as possible; and this may be done, to a certain extent, by appropriating the vessels to such creatures as agree amicably in confinement. It is, indeed, possible, if a vigilant watchfulness be observed, to bring together and preserve, for a length of time, specimens of creatures that are naturally antagonistic to each other; but where crustaceans can be kept apart in one vessel, with perhaps a few fish, such as gobies and blennies—a second appropriated to anemones and madrepores—and a third to mollusks, madrepores, and tubeworms—there will be the greater certainty of success, and less supervision will be required. Crabs are very annoying to anemones, as they scratch and sprawl over the delicate creatures; and shrimps, prawns, and fishes frequently fall a prey to the barbed threads and the tentacles of the anemones; the latter also frequently take possession of the mouths of the cells of tubeworms and the shells of mollusks, and thus kill them, and cause putrid taints. Besides this, fishes, prawns, and shrimps frequently fall a prey to the searching fingers of the anemones, and hence should be kept in separate vessels.

The ninth day from the introduction of animals is considered the turning point—for better, for worse; those that survive nine or ten days usually get acclimated, and flourish, while those that fail generally begin by that time to shew symptoms of approaching death. The ninth or tenth day over, all is likely to go right.

There are two prominent affections to which both Marine and the Fresh-water Aquaria are subject, and

those are *green stain* and *confervoid growths*. The first is
most prevalent in very hot weather, the second in very
cold weather. In the Marine Aquarium green stain is to
be cured by filtering through charcoal, in the river tank
by changing the water. By green stain is meant a sudden
appearance of a green tint pervading the whole of the
water, as if some vegetable pigment had been dissolved in
it. This arises from the presence of multitudes of the
spores of algæ, and, if not attended to, increases rapidly,
and in a short time renders the water opaque. The usual
mode of remedying this has been to draw off the water
by means of a siphon, remove the animals, and cleanse
the tank, and then filter the water back. But on more
than one occasion I have done a slight injury to choice
specimens by this plan, and that induced me to adopt the
plan of simply placing the filter over the tank, and then,
by frequently filling it from the surface of the vessel, keep
up a constant dribbling, until the whole had been passed
through. This plan never fails to remove the colouring
matter; even after the lapse of an hour from setting the
filter to work there is a decided improvement, and the
whole at last comes as bright as crystal, the water more
pure than ever, and well aerated into the bargain.

To prevent confervoid growths, it is usual to include a
few common periwinkles or tops in the general stock. These
are strictly vegetable feeders, and prefer before all other
food the minute green growth that forms on the glass, and
which, if left unchecked, would in time seriously obstruct
the view. The winkles do their work well, but, not knowing
that they are there especially for that purpose, they unwit-
tingly leave little streaks and patches, and to remove these
the occasional use of a sponge is necessary. The neatest
mode of using a sponge is to attach it securely to the end
of a stick, and then ply it regularly over the inner surface
of the glass. In the marine tank confervoid growths are
by no means common, in fact, I have never but once seen

a trace of it in any of my vessels; in artificial sea-water it
is a rare occurrence.

The amount of light and the general temperature are of
the very first importance. Excess of either will be detrimental; sunshine for any length of time fatal. I am certain
that a *subdued* daylight is best for the marine tank, and
that Mr. Warington is right in making three sides of a
tank opaque. A heated room or an hour's bright sunshine
in high summer will be certain death to the delicate
anemones; they will drop from their sites, shrink up to
button covers, and all is over with them unless quickly
taken out, placed in shallow bowls, and aerated in cool
and pure sea-water. Should the tank by any accident get
heated, it may be quickly cooled by opening the window,
and wrapping over it some coarse cloths saturated with
water. The draught passing over the wet surface will cause
a rapid evaporation, and quickly reduce the temperature.
To prevent accidents of this kind, let a thermometer be
attached to the glass within. Mr. Lloyd will supply one
expressly made for the purpose; it is an elegant and
accurate instrument. But though excessive heat is injurious, excessive cold is to be guarded against. The latter
will not produce fatal effects, (a freezing temperature is of
course not referred to,) but it will cause the anemones to
"shut up shop" and retire within doors; hence to keep the
tank in its full beauty in winter-time, a fire should be kept
in the room where it is placed.

In making ablutions and purifications, any green deposit
on the rock-work must not be disturbed, nor must any
spawn be removed from the sides of the vessel; these are to
be welcomed as the germs of new plants and animals, which,
with proper attention, will soon make their appearance,
increasing your stock with healthy home-grown specimens.
From the spores of green algæ with which the stones
ought to be studded, an immense number of oxygen bubbles will be escaping; this is the life of the tank—all

goes on well when this appears profusely, and when the spores put on a downy or woolly appearance, you may consider your Aquarium as established. The weeds, if they increase, will require an occasional thinning; if they decay, they must be removed, and their place supplied by fresh ones. In winter-time the weeds will sometimes turn white, and if it is not convenient to renew them, they must be taken out, and the decayed portions trimmed off by means of a pair of scissors. The stones on which they grow should then be scrubbed with a brush, and rinsed in waste sea-water, and replaced.

In replacing the animals and plants on any occasion of emptying the tank, the stones should be looked over, to see if any are tainted with black spots. The inky patches sometimes observed on stones, sand, and shells, are the result of animal decomposition. Some of your friends have crept into corners to die, and their corrupt bodies have been generating sulphuretted hydrogen, a gas not only poisonous to animal life, but which, by a peculiar law in the chemistry of fluids, drives the oxygen out of the tank. By turning these blotches to the light, they will gradually disappear; but the quickest and most satisfactory way is to touch them with dilute sulphuric acid, taking care that the weeds are not touched at the same time. The stone must then be plunged for a few minutes into a basin of sea-water, to remove the acid, and may then be replaced.

The cause of these spots affords a further hint on management. The mollusks are, as a rule, difficult to preserve. Whelks and most bivalves die off in a hurry, and leave a stench behind them. When this happens, others of the stock are pretty sure to be cut off, unless the carcases are speedily removed, and the water and stones purified. Fish, zoophytes, and most other members of the community, are, though subject to death, by no means so liable to produce the noxious gas which issues from a dead mollusk. Pholades and barnacles produce it in large quantity, and as the latter die soon, should never be kept. Whenever a death has happened, set the filter to work, and your best friend, the charcoal, will quickly remove the taint, before it spreads and pollutes the whole.

If death spares not the humble tenants of the sea, it is not to be supposed that he will forget those in the tank;

hence there must be a watch kept for corpses; missing animals should be searched for, and if found dead, immediately removed. But there must be no undue haste in the matter, for many may be missing through having found a snug corner out of sight, where they are enjoying health and happiness.

For the removal of portions of decayed weed, the exuviæ

of anemones, and other small noxious bodies from the bottom, a glass tube of a quarter or half an inch diameter, open at both ends, will be found very useful. Place a thumb or finger on the top of the tube, and thrust it down over the object to be removed, then remove the finger, and the matter will rise in it. Lift the tube up to the surface of the water, then place the finger on again, and lift the whole away. The advantage of this plan is, that no disturbance is occasioned. A pewter spoon bent to a right angle, and attached to a stick, is very useful for lifting up objects that are too large for the dipping tube.

Some plan of artificially aerating the water must be adopted with every newly-established Aquarium. Until the plants have established themselves, there will be a deficiency of oxygen, which must be supplied by agitating the water at the surface. But aeration is at variance with the self-sustaining theory, and in an established tank there is something wrong where it is wanted; as Mr. Lloyd wisely says, "properly managed, the water and other contents of an Aquarium may be kept unchanged for periods indefinitely prolonged." For the sake of Aquarian science, I do implore the student to surmount any and every difficulty rather than own the weakness implied by changing the water. If the tank is stocked before the plants are well established, or if overstocked with a crowd of animal life, or if sulphuretted hydrogen be produced and make its presence manifest to the nose, *then* aeration may be necessary. A cup or jug may be used to dip the water from the surface, and pour it back again from a height in a thin stream; or a filter may be placed over the tank, and filled from the surface, and the water allowed to drip back; but the most efficient instrument is a common syringe. This is simply to be charged at the surface, and discharged again with some force, so as to send a stream of oxygenized water deep into the tank. The process should be repeated for a quarter of an hour at least.

At the last meeting of the British Association, Dr. Ball described an apparatus which he had used with great success in Dublin. It consisted of a tube, at the end of which was a pair of bellows; from the tube branch tubes passed into each Aquarium, so that every stroke of the bellows sent a quantity of fresh air into each tank. The amusement of pumping the air into the tanks was so great, that they had never had in the Dublin Zoological Gardens occasion to employ a man to do it, as the visitors were very fond of the occupation. On one occasion a cuttlefish had died, which they had kept for three months, and on examining into the cause it was found that the bellows were broken.

Evaporation causes the pure water to escape from the Aquarium, and hence there is a constant tendency to increase of density; in fact, if left alone, the water in the tank soon gets too salt. To prevent this, additions of pure spring or distilled water must be made from time to time, and the amount regulated by a specific gravity bubble, which it would be as well to leave at all times floating in the tank. This instrument registers the density much more accurately than the hydrometer, for it is more delicate in its determination of a balance. I find it expedient to use two bubbles of different specific gravities—one which just floats when the water is sufficiently fluid, and another which just sinks when it is sufficiently saline. The movement of either indicates at once the exact cause, and enables the Aquarian to regulate the density to perfection. In hot weather evaporation takes place rapidly, and the position of the bubbles should be noted every day.

Anemones generally do not require feeding, though the daisy and the dianthus will greedily partake small fragments of oyster and minced mutton, and some other kinds will occasionally eat of the same food; but I cannot recommend the beginner to feed anemones, for, in a well-managed tank, infusoria are sufficiently abundant to provide them

with all they require, and food not eaten soon decays, unless speedily removed. Crabs and prawns positively require feeding, and madrepores *may* be fed for amusement. Small fragments of lean raw meat should be given, or the flesh of a cooked prawn, and twenty-four hours afterwards, the undigested morsels should be removed. We should all do better in the world were it not for our abominable appetites. The want which keeps human bipeds on the stretch of invention and anxiety, besets the creatures of the deep. Your fishes must be fed. The vegetable feeders will supply themselves from the growing weeds; but the carnivorous kinds must be fed with pieces of beef, the flesh of crab and lobster, and occasionally a few prawns and shrimps. Tufts of fresh-gathered sea-weed should now and then be thrown in for the sake of the mullets and other fish that live on infusoria, which swarm out of the weed, and supply them with abundance.

Your tank is now furnished, and in working order. After the critical ninth day, you may judge fairly of your progress: but you will not arrive at this grand climacteric without the loss of a few choice things, which you must replace as opportunity occurs, and look forward to the climax of success, which is thus described by Dr. Badham:—

Then from the raised rock-work drooping streamers of emerald green *Ulvas* hang luxuriantly over the mimic abyss; the water looks bright as crystal; shells and pebbles glisten at the bottom, and sparkling bubbles are rising and bursting around. Anemones expand; observant crabs walk round on tip-toe; big bivalves lie with open doors and siphons out at full stretch; sea-urchins point their thousand blue-tipped spines in strong and equi-distant array; scarlet star-fish glide from the rocks, turn over on their backs, and move in rapid alternation the long lines of their ivory keys up and down; mysterious chitons appear and disappear behind the stones; prescient periwinkles, aware of what is required of them, lick clean the inner sides of the transpa-

rent wall, and keep it clear for observers.   The sensitive trees
of zoophytes grow perceptibly; a green efflorescence, beaded
with vescicles of air, tells that a new growth of sea-weeds
is commencing on the surface of the stone-work, hitherto
without a trace of vegetation, and all is movement within.
Here greedy gobies pulling at the opposite ends of some
wriggling lug-worm, tug and tear it backwards and forwards
through the water; here, frisking mugils disturb momenta-
rily the smooth surface of the tiny sea; and there, some
coy little fish, hid for days behind a green curtain of weeds,
now begins to shew his muzzle, and to peep timidly through
the ambush; whilst ever and anon, gently displacing the
lymph around, with wide-spread tail and many-twinkling
feet, a flapping prawn mounts hauriant to the top.   When
things are advanced to this pass, your experiment has succeeded, and you may venture to send cards of invitation
to friends, who are sure to report favourably of the
exhibition.

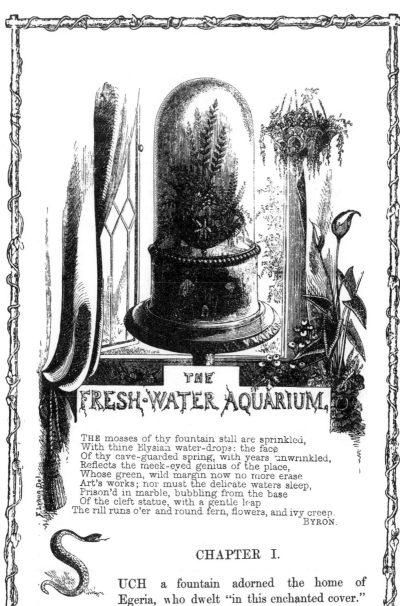

THE FRESH-WATER AQUARIUM.

THE mosses of thy fountain still are sprinkled,
With thine Elysian water-drops: the face
Of thy cave-guarded spring, with years unwrinkled,
Reflects the meek-eyed genius of the place,
Whose green, wild margin now no more erase
Art's works; nor must the delicate waters sleep,
Prison'd in marble, bubbling from the base
Of the cleft statue, with a gentle leap
The rill runs o'er and round fern, flowers, and ivy creep.
BYRON.

CHAPTER I.

UCH a fountain adorned the home of Egeria, who dwelt "in this enchanted cover." Should not beings less ethereal, yet not less pure, be freshened in the love of nature in homes "haunted by holy love, the earliest oracle" to them of affections cherished in their spring-time, secure in the fruition of domestic peace? Our homes should surely teem with poetical suggestions; where hearts beat and hands join warmly, there should be as broad a field for the exercise of imaginative fancy, and the realization of the highest precepts of morality and religion, as in any of the worlds conjured up in the dreams of poets. Egeria should hallow the winter fireside, or tend the spring flowers on the lawn; or, if she will, plant delicate "ferns, flowers, and ivy" round her mossy fountain, which bubbles and splashes under lace curtains, behind windows of stained glass, or bowers of myrtle and acacia, crystallizing her whole life into

"A beautiful thought, and softly bodied forth."

While the Marine Aquarium presents us with strange and almost unknown forms, brought from the recesses of the deep, and excels all household ornaments in its appeals to curiosity and wonder, the Fresh-water tank has its own unequalled fairy graces; its familiar forms and well-known objects, endeared to us by the tenderest associations and memories, heightened in their beauty by grouping and contrast; their interest increased by the familiar fellowship they demand and win from us.

The aspect of the Fresh-water tank is different indeed from the Marine; it excites pleasure rather than wonder; amuses more than it astonishes; but there is a rare grace in its homely display of waving banners and familiar fishes. Here are the finny favourites of our rills and lakes, the mosses of our own moors, the ferns that we have wandered miles to see waving under their native water-falls; the traditional glories of our own old English water scenes— the lilies, the arrow-heads, and, if you will, the bonny flowering rushes, over which, in the green old time, the bride walked in fragrance to the altar.

There is also, in this case, less difficulty in obtaining the necessary stock, and still less difficulty as to the supply of water, which, in a Fresh-water tank, may be kept flowing through in a constant run; or at least may be wholly changed if the least accident happens to mar its purity. A fountain, too, is more easily fitted; and few houses, now-a-days are without a cistern sufficiently elevated to keep it in constant play, vivifying and refreshing the whole; the water being already at hand, with no difficulty as to sending for, or preparing it.

What we have already said as to the construction of tanks, rock-work, and general management, applies to both kinds of Aquaria, with but few modifications. We have therefore little else to treat of here than the stock and its culture; and we have this advantage, that we are to treat of objects we are already familiar with—of plants and fishes which hold an ancient place in our list of out-door acquaintances, and hence being neither new nor strange, have only to be adapted to circumstances in a great measure natural to them in all their stages of growth.

The superiority of the flat-sided tank over the old fish globe, or the newly-constructed vessels of Dr. Badham, applies with as much force to Fresh-water as to Marine Aquaria. Every one who has kept gold fish in globes, must have regretted how rapidly they die off, spite of frequent change of water and all the tender nursing which such a vessel enables them to receive. Besides this mortality of the fishes, the distortion of them when viewed through this huge crystalline lens—for a filled globe is nothing else—makes them rather fitter subjects for laughter than admiration; and in all probability, the refraction which amuses the spectator, hastens the destruction of the fish as much as the excess of light to which they are always exposed. The tank secures a proper shade, the plants give it a more natural aspect, and assimilate it to their natural home in weedy streams and flower-covered lakes, while the

growth of vegetation supplies them with those two great requisites—air and food.

Premising that the tank has been properly constructed, the furnishing must proceed in a manner similar to that described for the Marine Aquarium, but with these exceptions:—Rock-work is less objectionable in Fresh-water tanks, because if a little free lime should dissolve out of the cement, the water may be wholly changed, and the objectionable matters got rid of. Yet it must be understood that I will not hold myself responsible for any evils that may follow through the use of rock-work, because I have already condemned it in a general sense, and here merely hint that those who like it may more safely indulge a taste for arches and caves in the fitting of a river tank than in the case of one for marine stock; and in a large vessel, a pile of rocks well managed certainly has a pleasing effect, and in some special modes of management, presently to be described, a pyramid or central pile of stones is absolutely necessary.

The bottom may be formed of loam and sand, for the growth of lilies, flowering rushes, *Alisma*, and other plants of large growth; but nothing is so clean, so bright and pleasing to the eye, as a bottom of small pebbles only, and in such a bottom almost every aquatic plant will flourish. I have abolished the use of mould in my own tanks during the last eighteen months, and am so satisfied with the result that I shall in future be very cautious how I even mention mould for such a purpose. Well-washed river pebbles laid down to the depth of from two to four inches, according to the size of the vessel, will be found better than sand or mould of any kind; and in planting it is only necessary first to place the roots of the plants on the bottom of the vessel, and then pile the stones over them so as to fix them firmly where they are to remain. If the bottom is put down first, the roots may either be thrust down into the mass with the hand, or a portion of the bottom may be

removed, and after the insertion of the roots replaced above
them. But the plan of arranging the plants first on the
bottom of the vessel is the most safe and simple; they are
thoroughly fixed by the weight of stones laid over them,
and since they depend upon water rather than soil for
nourishment they thrive and bloom freely.

River Tank, containing Gold Carp, Roach, and Minnow; Vallisneria spiralis,
Anacharis alsinastrum, and Floating Frog-bit.

For ordinary tanks and bell-glasses, almost any of the
common weeds found in brooks and ponds will be suitable;
those which have a rank growth, such as the larger kinds
of *Potamogeton* and *Ranunculus aquatilis* being the least
suitable. It is, however, an interesting fact, that the coarsest
plants soon adapt themselves to the circumstances of the

case, and native robustness being subdued by confinement,
their habit of growth becomes more delicate and refined;
Potamogeton densus, when lifted from its native oozy bed,
appears far too rank a plant for growth in a tank, but in
less than a month its character is changed, it throws out
delicate white rootlets, sheds its coarse foliage, and acquires
smaller, neater, and more delicately-veined leaves, and at
last becomes a beautiful object. The same may be said of

Callitriche, or Starwort.

Vallisneria spiralis.

many other aquatic plants, and especially of those two
favourites, *Callitriche* and *Anacharis,* which, in a few weeks,
change from the full robust green and rank growth natural
to them in the brooks, and acquire a lovely emerald tint
and a neatness of growth admirably suited to the ornamental services required of them.

Among the first botanical requisites of a river tank we
must place *Vallisneris spiralis,* the water soldier, botani-
cally known as *Stratiotes aloides;* the pretty brook star-

wort, (*Callitriche;*) and the quick-growing new water-weed, *Anacharis alsinastrum; Chara* of several species. The first of these, and the delicate *Myriophyllum spicatum*, must be obtained of the dealers; the others are common in clear brooks and rivers in every part of the country. They all grow freely when rooted among pebbles. The starwort and new river-weed may be attached to stones by means of strips of bass, and left to root in any way they please,

Stratiotes aloides, or Water Soldier.

but the *Vallisneria* must be carefully planted in a bottom of at least two inches. The water soldier is a superb thing; it will grow as well if left to float about as if rooted from the bottom, but its appearance is most beautiful when fixed in a conspicuous place. If obtained without roots, it will be necessary to trim off the decayed portions of the base, and make a clean cut across the centre. It will then throw out roots in abundance, and if moored to the bottom by means of a strip of bass and a stone, the roots will insinuate themselves into the bottom, and the crown will throw out shoots at every joint, so as in the course of a few months to furnish plants for stocking other tanks. From two crowns of *Stratiotes*, supplied me by Mr. Hall about two years since, I have raised about a hundred plants, some of them having roots of more than twelve inches in length.

Myriophyllum spicatum.

Potamogeton densus.

Of the genera of *Potamogeton*, there are three species out of fifteen highly suitable, though there is not one but may be grown in the tank to advantage. The three most suitable are *P. fluitans, crispus,* and *densus*, the latter being a very elegant plant, and a free grower. They all bloom above the surface, and increase so rapidly by off-shoots as to require frequent thinning.

Among the plants of more robust growth, suitable for

large vessels, I may name the flowering rush, (*Butomus umbellatus*,) the great water-plantain, (*Alisma plantago*,) the lovely and poetical forget-me-not, (*Myosotis palustris*,) the great arrow-head, (*Sagittaria sagittifolia*,) and the common star-fruit, (*Actinocarpus damsonium*.) I have grown each of these in vessels furnished with sand and pebbles only, and they have flowered bravely above the surface, and in some cases ripened seed; sufficiently proving that

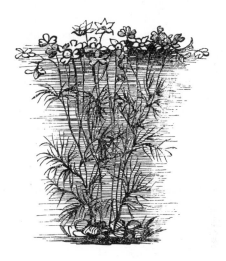

Ranunculus aquatilis.

even for plants of such huge dimensions mould is by no means requisite. These are all well-known inhabitants of our brooks and river-sides, and easily obtained either direct from their native sites, or from the dealers in Aquarium stock.

There are still some other plants of a choice kind that must not be omitted from this list, and among these the first place should be given to the water-crowfoot, (*Ranunculus aquatilis*.) This is an elegant creature of the waters,

which, unfortunately, has caused the death of many a
swimmer by entanglement with its extensive masses of
submerged roots and branches, and which, in small rivers,
frequently impedes the rower by clinging to the oars.
This forms little floating islands covered with flowers like
newly-fallen snow-flakes, and is, after the white water-lily,
the most elegant of our native aquatics. Those who have
visited Stratford-on-Avon will remember with delight as
long as they live the wonderful effect which, during the
latter part of the summer, this plant produces in the picturesque bays and inlets of the Avon; and how it seems
to hover over the quiet surface of that classic stream, like
a fairy oblation to the memory of the great poet. It is
to be met with on almost every pond and river in the
suburbs of London. There is abundance of it in the pond
at Clapham Common, in the Ravensbourne, at Rushy Green,
in all the branches of the Lea, and in the Thames, above
Fulham, and, indeed, in most of the ponds in *old* meadows
everywhere.

It has some points of interest to the botanist, which
make it all the more acceptable in a position which enables
us to study its structure and growth without wading, or
wetting the soles of our shoes. Its lower leaves are divided
into thin thread-like segments, while those on the surface
are entire and handsomely shaped. The use of these
divided leaves is to enable it to present a greater surface
to the water for the absorption of the gases which it
cannot obtain from the air above; and by the activity of
these leaves it elaborates from the water a large quantity
of oxygen, which gives it additional acceptability. It will
send down its fibres to the bottom, and bloom abundantly,
if planted early in summer. The blossoms should be clipped
off as fast as they lose their beauty, and the foliage occasionally trimmed and circumscribed. At the end of the
season it should be removed entirely.

Another native plant of great service is the water-violet,

(*Hottonia palustris.*) It is easily domesticated, and is a rare beauty. It sends down a series of elegant white thread-like rootlets, the whole of its foliage being under water. If you keep minnows and gudgeons, these will be constantly gambolling amongst its leaves, and afford much amusement. The flowers rise above the surface of the water in elegant clusters of a pale lilac or flesh-colour. Though a British plant, it is somewhat rare, and I do not know any locality near London where it is to be found, but, as it is cultivated by nurserymen, there will be little difficulty in obtaining it.

To grow the white water-lily, the stately queen of our British lakes and streams, requires great depth and extent of surface—more than an ordinary tank will afford. It is a delicate plant too, and needs a very pure air, so as to fit it only for a large tank in a conservatory, or an open-air pond; but the yellow lily, *(Nuphar lutea,)* will occupy little more than a square foot of surface, and one of these will flourish in-doors with ordinary care, and add a bold grace and reality to the mimic lake. The root must be buried in the bottom, and a stone or piece of broken flower-pot placed over it till it begins to put out its stems, when the covering may be removed. It will soon display its elegant leaves upon the surface, and should be kept as clear of weeds as possible. The other lilies that are most suitable are *Nymphea odorata minor,* and *Nymphea macrantha.*

Many aquatics which produce tufted roots, may be very neatly grown in minute flower-pots sunk into the positions the plants are to occupy, and the pots hidden with a little management of the rock-work. This plan enables us to grow them in a suitable soil, without allowing that soil to form any part of the permanent furniture of the tank. The smaller kinds of lilies do well in this way, and are easily removed, if necessary, should the tank be too cold for them in winter. Those who take interest in the culture of choice aquatic plants, may embellish their large tanks

with specimens of *Nymphæa rubra, Nampla, gigantea,* and *Amazonica,* all of them plants of large growth and superb beauty, well adapted for the embellishment of a tank in a stove. Mr. Thompson, of Ipswich, will supply seeds of these, as also of the very pretty half-hardy aquatic *Thalia dealbata. Orwirandria fenestralis* is a new and curious floating aquatic, lately introduced from Madagascar, and worthy the attention of those who delight in water-gardens.

Hydrocharis morsus-ranæ.

The last of the plants for deep water that need here be named, is the curious awlwort, *(Subularia aquatica,)* to which I, for the first time, called attention in my "Book of the Aquarium." It grows wholly submerged, and in summer produces a pretty cluster of snow-white tetraform blossoms, presenting the unique example of a flower in bloom beneath the water. It is only to be met with in clear mountain lakes in the north of England, and in Scotland and Ireland, and in elevated waters of alpine districts on the continent.

For floating plants the frog-bit *(Hydrocharis morsus-ranæ,)* takes the first place. It soon "mantles the pool" with its lily-like foliage, and increases rapidly by offsets. Starwort may also be used in the same manner, and if no other floating plants are at hand, it makes a very verdant covering. For this purpose the starwort should first be well washed, and then a number of short tops should be nipped off and thrown in. In the course of a day or two these will arrange themselves over the surface, and give a salutary shadow to the finny creatures. The flowering shoots of *Ranunculus aquatilis* may be used in the same way, and as soon as they cease to bloom may be removed. Lastly, all the species of *Lemna* and *Riccia* are useful to clothe the surface with pretty and curious forms of verdure.

Your tank stocked with plants is now ready for the lively creatures to which the plants are to act as purveyors of oxygen. Your water-garden is formed, and already presents a cheerful and instructive spectacle. It is now become a Vivarium for the finny pets which, with proper care, will soon endear themselves to their keeper, will display a thousand funny tricks for his amusement, learn to know and love the hand that feeds them, and in time become so tame as to take choice morsels from the fingers, rise to the surface at the call of a familiar voice, and through the glass sides of their prison, watch the events of the world without. From this point the real interest of the tank begins; if the vegetable world teaches us the inexhaustibleness of form and colour in nature, the animal world exhibits the workings of volition, the accomplishments of instinct—yes, and the triumphs of *reason* even in fishes. You shall soon discover that your aquatic friends have a capacity for recognising voices and features, that they are capable of affection, and of the emotions of joy, and grief, and fear; that they are as tameable as dogs, artful as foxes, amiable as doves—what more need be said in praise of keeping them in an Aquarium, where we may make close acquaintance with their beautiful forms and elegant movements; and have daily evidence of their sympathy with at least some of our human sentiments.

> A heart is there to nature true,
> Which wrath nor envy ever knew;—
> A heart that calls no creature foe,
> And ne'er designed another's woe.

CHAPTER II.

THE heart is hard in nature, and unfit
For human fellowship, as being void
Of sympathy, and therefore dead alike
To love and friendship both, that is not pleased
With sight of animals enjoying life,
Nor feels their happiness augment his own.

COWPER.

HE comfort of a reasonable joy" is certainly attendant on the care of animals, when that care is controlled by humane feelings and a desire to see the creatures happy. The Aquarium is at least one of the many aids towards the cultivation of kindness, and the enlargement of general knowledge which the Home of Taste affords. A veteran angler who has long ago mastered all the refinements of his cruel craft, will here be taught that after all he is still ignorant of even the ordinary appearances and habits of fishes. Accustomed to study how and when they take the bait, familiar with their agonies when the bait has been gorged, dead to the repugnance which the sight of suffering innocence should inspire, he will yet be moved and astonished by the contemplation, for a quarter of an hour only, of a well-stocked river tank. A century of angling experience will not afford so much knowledge as would be gained by that quarter of an hour's inspection. Here are bleak and minnows, that sport about like kittens, that play with each other, and indulge in such comical pranks as make one shudder at the idea of *hooking* such pretty creatures. Here are plump carp that glide easily about, and that become as familiar as the cat on the hearthrug; tench, that roll on their backs and submit to be tickled, and that nibble the fingers of their proprietor with a confidence with which we may well believe affection is mingled. It is rare fun at all times, and we get so enamoured of the confiding creatures, that I think it impossible for any one with a spark of genuine humanity to warm his breast, to continue an angler after once taken to the care of a tank.

Let us now consider the nature of the live stock on which we are to depend for the completion of the Vivarium. The majority of the fishes which inhabit our rivers belong to the family *Cyprinus,* of which the type is the carp. Of the true carps the best for our purpose is, first and foremost, the lovely gold carp, *(Cyprinus auratus.)* This is not the most intelligent of the family, but its exquisite beauty recommends it for any tank which is intended to be ornamental. Like most animals that have been long domesticated, this carp *sports* into many varieties of shape and colour, and in purchasing it is necessary to choose them with care, for when the sport is of that kind in which the dorsal fin is reduced to a stump, and the caudal fin is developed into the semblance of a "screw propeller," the fish is certainly more curious than beautiful. For a small and prettily-furnished vessel, such as a lady would delight in, the brilliantly-marked little Portugal gold carp would be the best. They do not attain to the huge size we are accustomed to in ordinary gold fish, but their outlines are extremely elegant, and their coats of mail have a real metallic lustre, quite different to the red and white tintings usually observable.

For beauty, the Prussian carp, *(C. gibelio,)* ranks next to the gold carp, and I think for docility and teachableness

it surpasses every other tenant of a tank. Minnows and bleak are very merry, and easily tamed, but this carp is a loving constant creature, that haunts the side of the vessel in order to watch its master or mistress, seems, indeed, to listen to all that is said, and will poise in mid-water for hours on the side next the room, in order to win attention and deserve it. The British carp, *(C. carpio,)* and the Crucian carp, *(C. carassius,)* are of similar habit to their cousin-german, but are a trifle less hardy, and not quite so attractive either in appearance or manners. As members of the general mob, they are interesting, but the Prussian carp is the gentleman of the tank, and monopolizes the attention of his keeper.

The bream, *(C. brama,)* the tench, *(C. tinca,)* the gudgeon, *(C. gobio,)* the barbel, *(C. barbus,)* and the chub, *(C. cephalus,)* are all good stock, that do well with very moderate care, and soon grow familiar in confinement. They may be kept for years, if guarded against excesses of cold or heat, and they agree well with the smaller fry if regularly fed. To bring up the rear of the hardy stock, we may include, for general purposes, young eels in small numbers, and minnows in shoals, and, for particular purposes, small specimens of the voracious jack. An Aquarium without at least half-a-dozen minnows is a sorry affair, no matter how liberally it may be stocked with gold or Prussian carp. They are like those mobs that rush pell-mell on the stage in the street scenes of pantomimes, where the beadle gets pelted by market-women, and policemen are tripped into washing-tubs, or flung into coppers as raw lobsters to come out cooked as soldiers. If you are at all fond of a row on a small scale, in which there shall be no case demanding legal interference, keep minnows and bleak in a tank, and if you do not enjoy many a laugh at their scrambling for crumbs, their fighting for worms, their leaping out for flies, and splashing back again in an excess of boisterous joyousness, then I say you are crabbed and cankered, and incapable of enjoying simple and genuine pleasures of any kind.

High summer is a trying time to fishes in confinement, but all the kinds hitherto enumerated may be preserved during the hottest season with the exercise of moderate care. But during autumn, winter, and spring, the enjoyment may be still more heightened by the introduction of the

Gudgeon, Prussian Carp, Loach, and Bream.

bleak, *(C. alburnus,)* the roach, *(C. rutilus,)* and the dace, *(C. leuciscus.)* These are delicately constituted, and it is quite impossible to preserve them during the summer months in ordinary vessels; the tank affords them no depth of retreat, no choice of ground, no escape from the tepid water to the cool hollows and umbrageous creeks which welcome them in their native streams. Were it possible to preserve them at all seasons, the enjoyments of the Aquarium would be increased a hundred-fold, for they are all elegant silvery creatures, possessed of the most amiable and playful dispositions, they glitter in many changing tints of emerald, and ruby, and gold, as they flash to and fro in the sunshine, while their general silvery brightness gives them a distinctive beauty in this general assemblage of enchanting forms and colours. As to fun, bleak are even more fond of a row than minnows, and will chase a fly or small insect of any kind, with a scrambling haste that will remind the beholder of all that has been said and sung of the far-famed Donnybrook fair.

The few other fishes that may be classed as half-hardy —reversing the ordinary meaning of the term—are perch and loach. These *may* be preserved during the summer, but there is a little risk attending it. Many of my Aquarian friends expressed surprise on finding that I kept both during the whole of the hot summer of 1856, and the fact was certainly a little surprising to myself, for the three tanks in which my fresh-water stock passed that summer, were placed on a rustic stand in the garden, where the sun shone upon them for three hours every day. But then the vessels were wrapped round with cloths saturated in water, so as to keep them cool by evaporation during the hottest weather of July, and they were so densely filled with overgrown vegetation, especially of *Hydrocharis, Stratiotes*, and large plants of *Alisma*, that the fishes had abundant shadow when the sun glared upon the vessels.

But the precautions taken to cool the vessels were not sufficient to save the lives of some favourite minnows and Prussian carp, that had already passed two years in my keeping, and had grown so tame as to know each of the household voices, and were always willing to be stroked on the head or tickled with the finger. *That* was a sad loss, and I mention it here as a warning that a screen should always be placed over vessels so exposed, though the strangest

part of the matter is that three perch and two stone loach lived through the ordeal—their preservation being, perhaps, attributable to the fact that the tank in which the carp and minnows perished stood before them, and so afforded the shelter that all needed.

As individuals, perch are bold and handsome fishes—nothing more; but the loach has more individuality than any creature in the tank. It refuses to be tamed, will not grow familiar, but leads a wild and savage life in spite of every attempt to domesticate it. But that life is vastly interesting, every motion of the creature is replete with agility and grace, and its contempt for every other fish in the vessel is a striking characteristic. It has no social qualities, but an individuality of such a peculiar kind as to entitle it to a place in every collection of fluviatile life. Nevertheless it is delicate, and towards April begins to gasp upon the surface, and in company with bleak, roach, dace, and perch, to wane before the increase of temperature. What is to be done? Why, you must consider that the creatures have done their best for six months to amuse you, and since you gain nothing by their death, give them their liberty in some neighbouring stream. This is my practice, and will continue to be, so long as I feel certain that I possess no means of preserving them when the thermometer rises to seventy degrees in the shade.

Before the sun has fairly explored the constellation of the Twins, I transfer all my delicate fishes to a can, and make a ramble to the lea. I consign them to the stream with a hearty "good-bye, and God bless you," to which they respond by frisking their tails, and then we are parted for ever, unless in the strange revolutions of the wheel of chance, any of them should find their way back to me in September. During the summer gold carp, Prussian carp, tench, bream, chub, and minnows are the staple stock, and capital stock they are as to hardiness, spite of the accident recorded of my ill-used favourites that perished in the sun.

Sticklebacks are lively and interesting, but so pugnacious in disposition that it would be dangerous to recommend them for any general collection. For small cabinet Aquaria, or for a child's tank, in which no other fishes are kept, they are admirable, for they are incessantly in action, and for elegance not to be surpassed by any of the finny tribe.

Minnow, Tench, and Perch.

With carp they are very annoying; they hunt down the quiet creatures, nibble holes in their fins, and keep up a guerilla warfare that must sooner or later end in the death of the more peaceable members of the community. They may be kept with minnows, because the minnow has a little spirit in him, and will not patiently submit to be worried.

I

In the management of the river tank, Mollusks are much more needed to keep down objectionable growths than they are in the case of marine vessels. I have very seldom witnessed confervoid growths in tanks containing sea stock, but I never saw a river tank that could be kept bright for any length of time without the use of either a cleansing sponge or an army of mollusks. The best of cleaners is the spiral-shelled *Lymnea stagnalis*, a dozen of which will restore transparency to any moderate-sized vessel in a fortnight, even if the glass be entirely coated with confervæ. But this *Lymnea* is addicted to the eating of *Vallisneria* and *Stratiotes;* and we cannot patiently bear to see our handsomest plants nibbled into shreds. Next to the *Lymnea*, the *Planorbis* family stand high as scavengers, and they have no bad habits; they are almost always on the glass scraping away to keep the view open, and hence the stock of a river tank should always include a number of them. These are also the handsomest of our fresh-water univalves; their shells are elegantly coiled round in the style of a ram's horn; and a number of them engaged in the work allotted them increases the beauty and interest of the collection.

But there is another family of water snails that should not be forgotten, and that is *Paludina*, and especially the handsome *Paludina vivipara*, so named because, though oviparous, as all mollusks are, the eggs are perfected before they appear, so that it may be said to bring forth its young alive. The shell of this snail is nearly globular in shape, and richly mottled with tintings of bronze, amber, and rich sea-green. The animal is provided with an operculum or lid, and when it retreats within its shell, this lid closes the entrance in the same way as that of the periwinkle; it may indeed be called the fresh-water winkle. With a few *Paludina vivipara, Planorbis corneus,* and *carrinatus*, a river tank may be kept perennially bright without any necessity arising for the use of the sponge;

and these are not only industrious cleaners, but they seldom or never attack the larger forms of vegetation. They are ornamental too, and highly interesting objects of study, and may be regarded as legitimate occupants of the most elegantly-furnished vessel. *Lymnea* and *Physæ* are also worthy of admittance; but since they cannot be trusted everywhere, their domestication must be a matter of individual observation with those who follow this remunerative study.

Among the bivalves, it may be broadly stated here that every variety of fresh-water mussel may be kept in tanks to advantage. The most beautiful and at the same time most easily attainable, are the swan mussel, (*Anodonta cygnea*,) and the duck mussel, (*Unio pictorum*.) If a few of these are thrown in, they will soon burrow in the stony bottom, and give you yet another lesson in the workings of instinct; you will ponder with pleasure on the strange conformation of a creature so circumstanced; you will watch them protruding their immense snow-white fleshy bodies, traversing the bottom till they find a position to suit them, and then drawing themselves down into it at an oblique angle, the pointed end of the shell being left free for purposes of feeding and respiring. As soon as they are fairly located, they begin to filter the water for you, and as long as they live—death seldom overtakes them in the tank—they will continue thus to filter it and preserve its brightness, removing from it for their own support all solvent matters that may be contributed by the decay of plants, or otherwise. This filtering process may be closely watched, and the force of the stream ejected at each expiration of filtered water, may be measured by the sudden movements of light weeds in their vicinity.

These and the water-snails complete the arrangements for a self-supporting, self-renovating system. It is the end of that grand series of compensations represented in the Aquarium, and until that is fairly established, so as to

constitute an equal balance of influences, there can be no permanent success—no unalloyed source of pleasure.

There is a large choice of creatures representing several distinct departments of organized life. Each has its special beauties, its peculiar habits, its individual claims on our attention; as Horace says in his very critical "Ars Poetica"—

> ———"Some charm when nigh,
> Others at distance more delight the eye;
> That loves the shade, this tempts a stronger light,
> And challenges the critic's piercing sight;
> That gives us pleasure for a single view,
> And this, ten times repeated, still is new."

Planorbis corneus, Paludina vivipara, Lymnea stagnalis, Unio pictorum and tumidus, and Anodon cygneus.

CHAPTER III.

"LET Art use method and good husbandry;
  Art lives on Nature's alms, is weak and poor;
  Nature herself has unexhausted store."

                                    COWLEY.

N the management of the river tank many of the rules already laid down for Marine Aquaria will be found applicable. The grand point, no matter what the size of the vessel or the nature of the stock, is to establish such a balance as that there shall never occur any necessity to change the water. If the plants decay, if animals die, if heat or any other cause destroy the brightness of the liquid, then a change of water may be necessary, but in every well-managed Marine or River Aquarium the *water is never changed.* How is this perfection to be attained?—Easily enough. In the first place let the bottom be of clean pebbles, next have none but healthy plants, and not too many of them. You may use either spring or river water; here at Tottenham we are supplied with Artesian water in *small* quantities,

and river water is only to be had by fetching it. It answers
to perfection either for river tanks or for the manufacture
of artificial sea-water; and I think if a little time were
allowed for it to soften, spring water would always be preferable for Aquaria, because of its freedom from the spores
of objectionable vegetation. When the plants have been
inserted, and the tank filled, let a few days elapse before
you introduce any live stock, and then proceed cautiously
so as not to tax too severely the supply of oxygen. Carp,
minnows, and tench do well to begin with, but for any
other kinds wait a week or two. "What is worth doing, is
worth doing well," says the proverb; and undue haste in
stocking may be followed by losses, and losses involve dis-
appointment and *cruelty*. Life should not be sacrificed, nor
should the happiness of the humblest creature be jeopardized
in building up a Home of Taste. In regard to the proportion of animal life, two fishes to every gallon of water
will be found on an average sufficient; that is, taking large
and small together indiscriminately. In a tank of twenty
gallons we should thus have room for ten small gold-fish,
a dozen minnows, four Prussian carp, four Crucian carp,
one British carp, two tench, one chub, one perch, two loach,
two gudgeons, and one bream.

In winter time, if the plants continued in good health,
as they should do with ordinary care, a few of the larger
fishes might be removed to another vessel to make room
for a shoal of bleak, which are so lively and silvery as
vastly to enhance the beauty of the scene, especially when
gamboling in company with their auriferous friends of the
carp family. Of course there is a wide field for selection;
some persons will prefer to have as many representatives
of different families as possible, while others will be content
with a number of the most showy fishes. Such matters
depend on individual taste, and must be left open as far
as I am concerned. It is only necessary to refer back to
the preceding chapter, where the comparative hardiness of

the several candidates for selection will be found stated in accordance with my own experience, for the reader to follow his or her bent in the matter. In any case keep down the stock, excess of numbers will be followed by disasters; and it is better to have but a dozen healthy and happy fishes, than fifty cripples gasping at the surface, or turning on their backs to gasp no more.

One necessity of success must not be forgotten. Light is more essential to the River Aquarium than to the Marine. Plenty of daylight and a moderate amount of sunshine is good; when the sun streams through the tank the spectacle is lovely in the extreme, and the salutary effect of it is seen in the streams of oxygen bubbles that every leaf gives out, and the increased sportiveness of the creatures, which, during its continuance, seem delirious with joy. They dart to and fro, leap out and splash back again with a delightful sound, chase each other, play at touch and bo-peep, and if a few small worms be thrown in, the bleak, minnows, carp, and stone loach engage in a scramble that will cure the most choleric observer by compelled laughter, and throw every juvenile who sees it into ecstacies.

But though sunshine is in a general sense good, excessive heat is ruinous. In high summer continued sunshine will decimate the tank, and the prettiest favourites, the most docile of pets, will be indiscriminately slaughtered. Hence a shade of some kind is needed, where a tank is exposed in a south window, or in an open spot in a garden. The window-blind is usually sufficient, but in a position where a blind cannot be fixed, a screen of calico stretched on a frame of wood can easily be fitted so as to be removed when not required. Should the tank get suddenly heated through neglect or otherwise, quickly wrap round it a large coarse cloth saturated in water, and the evaporation will soon reduce it to a more healthy temperature. I have to-day, (August 30th., 1856,) placed a thermometer in one of my tanks that stands on a bench in the garden. The

sun has shone on it for two hours, and the thermometer registers 63°. This is the tank in which tench, loach, perch, Crucian carp, and minnows weathered the fierce heat of July last, and in which not a single loss occurred. The one which stands next it bears the brunt of the sun— the stand ranging north and south—and in that occurred the loss of my pet carp, which I have so much deplored. I think if the temperature of the water rises much above sixty degrees, there is some risk, increasing of course with every increase of temperature, and to keep it to that standard should be the object of the Aquarian who is ambitious to succeed.

In winter time it would, of course, be a folly to keep tanks in the open air; for though the fishes would bear the cold well, (I have had stock exposed in pans in which water and fishes were all frozen together, and not one was lost in consequence,) there is a great probability of the vessels bursting; and hence, before frosts are to be apprehended, it would be well to transfer the whole to a sheltered place, such as a greenhouse, or to fill up windows, and keep them gay in the absence of flowering plants. Here heat may again be a cause of injury; and if a fierce fire makes the room *too* cosy, the fishes may suffer. The standard of 60° may be regarded as the maximum for all seasons.

If the room should be heated to an extraordinary degree in winter, the tank will not so readily get tepid as in summer, and by opening the window for an hour the last thing at night, it will soon be restored to a normal condition; at the same time it must be remembered that during frost, any undue exposure of the vessel to the atmosphere, may be followed by fracture. I once had a tank burst in the night through frost, and I never shall forget the spectacle which presented itself next morning; twelve gallons of water had quietly soaked through carpet and flooring; several pounds of mud had been splashed over my papers and the

furniture of the room; two huge dace that I had tended
for months, and made as tame as kittens, were dead on
the floor; and of the rest of the stock some were still
alive at the bottom of the vessel, where a little pool was
left to support them, and others that had floundered about
the carpet for hours, revived after a short time under a jet
of water.

Feeding is a very important matter; it should be performed twice or thrice a week at least; but if you want
to show off your fishes, keep them without their accustomed
meal, and when your visitors arrive have at hand a few
small red earth-worms to throw in one or two at a time,
and the fun will be worth witnessing. Bread and hard-
boiled egg are good staple foods, but flies, small spiders,
and any *soft* insects will be greedily accepted and demo-
lished in a general scramble, in which the minnows and
bleak always play the most lively parts. Food not eaten
should be immediately removed, or the water may get
tainted; and care should be exercised not to overfeed at
any one time, and not to feed too frequently. It is by
judicious feeding that the fishes are to be tamed; they soon
learn to know the hand and face of their benefactor, and
their confidence and love grow together with every act of
kindness shewn them. Give them bread from your lips
or fingers, and they will soon take it without fear, and
in time will learn, like Oliver, to "ask for more."

The triumph of success is in the establishment of a fair
balance between the animal, vegetable, and aqueous contents
of your tank; the one purifying and refreshing the other
in a charming circle of mysterious operations: not the least
advantage of the Aquarium is the perennial character of
its beauty; each season stamps its character on the little
group as definitely as on the great world without. During
summer the play of the sunlight on the green-tinted
water, the sparkling iridescence of the finny creatures,
sporting and gamboling among the thread-like roots or

matted foliage of the plants; now gliding to and fro in
search of food, now darting at each other in play, or
assembling in shoals at the surface, like mimic fleets drawn
up for battle, form an assemblage of living objects unsurpassed for beauty, and of inexhaustible interest. The very
newts slowly treading water, with crocodile feet, red eyes,
bellies splendidly variegated with orange and black, and
backs lined with a finny membrane, give to the scene a
novelty of a most curious description, and will impress
many a one with the beauty of objects hitherto associated
with feelings of repugnance and disgust.

The beauty of the scene is ever changing; it is always
bright and pure, and suggestive of pure thoughts and
pleasing images, and in every sense a fitting adornment
for a Home of Taste, more precious than all the gems,
bijouterie, and articles of *vertu* that ever were consigned
to mahogany or rosewood; because it is a thing of life, and
growth, and change, that tells a new story every hour, and
convinces us that Nature is exhaustless, but never completed; that God literally creates the universe every moment,
and that the perfection and end of all is in Him through
whom all things move, and grow, and increase in a ceaseless
round of wonder and variety.

It admits too of as much ornament as is consistent with
good taste. The framework can scarcely be too elegant,
the fishes too costly, the plants too rare. You may traverse
from the extreme of close economy to the most lavish
expenditure, and at every step it will more than repay its
cost and trouble; for, in its humblest form, it is an ornament, a recreation, a cabinet, a menagerie, a *Jardin des
plantes*, a botanico-zoological picture, in which every hour
is a new dawn, every line has life, and every colour feeling;
in short, "a thing of beauty and a joy for ever."

CHAPTER IV.

THE ripples seem right glad to reach those cresses,
And cool themselves among the emerald tresses;
The while they cool themselves, they freshness give,
And moisture, that the bowery green may live;
So keeping up an interchange of favours,
Like good men in the truth of their behaviours.

KEATS.

ITHERTO the Aquarium has been considered in its simplest forms, and fountains, ferns, and other of the high departments of Aquarium culture have been alluded to but incidentally. At this stage we may enter upon certain extensions of the original idea, and devote at least one short chapter to a few suggestions which arise out of the experience I have acquired since last addressing the public through these pages.

In the first edition of this work, I suggested that the

Fresh-water tank afforded a good opportunity for the lover of ferns to attempt the cultivation of many choice kinds in connection with it, and that suggestion has been pretty extensively carried out, with more or less success, by many ardent cultivators. Messrs. Sanders and Woolcott have so far succeeded in the combination of the fern shade and the Aquarium, that the manufacture of tanks and shades for the purpose forms now a large and distinct department of their operations, and the combination is being largely patronized by persons of wealth and leisure. But many of the readers of this work may be anxious to learn in what way to proceed to ensure success, without the necessity of heavy outlay; and I shall briefly indicate how it may be accomplished cheaply.

There are several modes of combining the Wardian Case and the tank together. A moderate-sized tank may be very readily adapted for the growth of ferns, by having the inner sides lined with a narrow border of zinc, and the centre left open. This border would comprise first a narrow shelf, running round about four inches below the top of the vessel, and at the edge of this shelf next the centre of the tank, a perpendicular edging of four inches, so that the zinc-work forms a trough or border. This trough is to be filled with peat, the ferns planted in it at proper distances from each other, and a glass dome or frame fitted over the whole. The upper frame should be fitted with a door, and the simplest way to accomplish this is to have one of the glass squares attached to hinges, so that it may be let down whenever the live stock or ferns require attention, or a breath of fresh air seems desirable. The ferns grow rapidly in the moist air by which they are surrounded, and soon fill the upper frame with their feathery verdure, so that, though there is but a border of them, the whole of the upper case appears filled.

A still more elegant way is to pile up rockwork in the

centre of the tank, and bring its summit three or four inches above the water, as shewn in Mr. Voyez's elegant frontispiece, where a fountain pipe pierces the central pile. The ferns are then comfortably tucked into the hollows left for them among the stones, and guarded against excess of moisture by means of a layer of potsherds and broken limestone under each. The fountain plays above and over them, and while its

"Crystal bubbles
Charm us at once away from all our troubles,"

it adds to the sparkling freshness of the graceful foliage, and, by keeping up *a run* in the tank, enables us to double the number of gold and silver fishes that could be safely preserved without it. In selecting ferns for this purpose, those only should be used which naturally delight in an abundance of moisture, and which are usually met with in dripping caves and under waterfalls.

The same mode of growth may be adopted without a fountain, by placing over the tank a close frame, with a door, as in the former case; or the masses of rock may be built up on each side, and an architectural fountain fitted in the centre. The manufacturers produce tanks with cases fitted expressly for this mode of culture. Messrs. Treggon, of Jewin Street, London, have among their patterns many that are admirably adapted to this combination.

If ferns of large growth are to be grouped under a fountain, the rock-work must be built up above the surface some four or six inches; a compost of sharp sand, small chips of limestone, pounded charcoal, and pieces of tile or broken flower-pots, reduced almost to dust, must be prepared and laid in masses between the rocks above the water. Care should be taken that the root-stocks are prevented reaching the water, either by the upper surfaces of the stones themselves on which the compost is placed, or by some pieces of broken flower-pots laid horizontally, with the compost on them and concealed by the superstructure, but sloping from the centre, so that the water of the fountain will readily run off into the tank; should it form pools about the roots, it may sodden and destroy the plants; small clefts are sufficient for the escape of the young fronds.

The root-stocks must be planted in the compost, and should, if possible, be chosen when they are just putting out new fronds. The old fronds had better be cut off, and the rhizoma trimmed down so as to leave but a small portion attached to the crown, and the stones built round the shooting stems so as to afford them no more room than they will require, and so that most of the falling water will run off direct to the tank over the rock-work, without penetrating to the root-stocks below. The latter will get as much as the most water-loving ferns require, in spite of all precautions to prevent the water flowing freely to their roots.

When the root-stocks are planted, it will be well to stuff the crevices with moss, through which the fronds will easily protrude. The moss will prevent any undue exhaustion should the sun shine powerfully upon the tank, or should the fountain only play occasionally.

Another plan of fitting a rectangular tank with ferns is to have the lower portion formed in the ordinary way, but of less depth than usual, and then in this to build up a large mass of rock-work so as to form an arch *above and apart* from the water. This rock-work may either be wholly composed of cement, with suitable hollows for the insertion of the plants and the compost, or a number of blocks of granite or any other rough and picturesque stone, may be cemented together firmly and tastefully. Over the whole of the arch, ferns, lichens, lycopodiums, choice bog plants, epiphetes, and moisture-loving creepers may be grown, and a magnificent scene produced of fishes

gamboling in the open water, and under the dark shadow
of the arch which spans the centre, while above creep,
and twine, and wave the chastest and brightest of vegetable creations, revelling in the moisture, and rejoicing
in the partial shade that the glass enclosure secures for
them. Mr. Voyez's design for a Fern Aquarium of such
a construction is partly modelled after a fine example in
the collection of Messrs. Sanders and Woolcott, but the
framework—a splendid specimen of Aquarian ornamentation
—has been added as a hint to those who think a tank of
this kind worthy of a costly table.

There is yet another mode of combining the two elegances, and that is by means of a common fern-shade,
the dish of which forms the Aquarium, and the shade
above a cover for the ferns. My first attempt at this
combination was made by means of a sixteen-inch fern-
shade. I explored almost every glass warehouse in London,
as well as the several bazaars, to find a fluted pillar with a
spreading summit to fit in the centre for the reception of
the ferns, and failing to find anything to my taste, I stole
a green glass flower-vase of my wife's, and proceeded as
follows:—I placed the vase in the centre, and piled pebbles
round it to keep it steady, and spread a continuous
bed of similar pebbles over the bottom of the Aquarium
dish.   The vase stood fifteen inches high, had a firm
spreading base and a fluted-lipped summit that spread over
to a breadth of six inches. Into the vase I then dropped
a handful of broken flower-pots, then a little old mortar,
and then filled it up with a compost of peat, silver-sand,
and pounded charcoal. I then planted in it the brittle
bladder fern, (*Cystopteris fragilis,*) the pretty *Trichomanes
Tunbridgense*, and the adder's tongue, (*Ophioglossum vul-
gatum.)* Around the roots I placed two pretty *Lycopods*,
namely, *Lepidopterum* and *Willldenowii*. The dish was
stocked with *Hydrocaris morsus ranæ*, small tufts of *Myriophyllum spicatum*, *Stratiotes*, *Chara*, and the only fishes

were six small picked specimens of *Cyprinus auratus*—the prettiest gold-fish I had ever seen.

This did well, but there was one objection to the whole affair, and that objection I have seen repeated in every fern-shade Aquarium I have hitherto inspected, whether on the smallest or largest scale. The evaporation is of course immense at all times, and it is confined; when the sun shines on the vessel, the evaporation is increased, and such a condensation takes place on the upper shade as for a time prohibits a view of the lovely scene within. Since we do not light a candle to place it under a bushel, this objection is almost fatal. In a case made with a door a temporary remedy is to be found in occasionally syringing the inner sides of the glass so as to carry down the moisture in a stream. Another partial remedy is to open the door during the warmest period of the day, and allow the vapour to escape: but these are only partial remedies.

Still, in fairness, it must be stated that the opaque condition of the glass is not permanent. If the tank can be kept at nearly the same temperature as the air that surrounds it, the condensation is very trifling; hence in the morning and evening the glass is generally pretty bright, and the scene may be contemplated with pleasure; it is the *difference* in temperature between the water within and the glass surrounding it, and the air without that causes the evil, and to prevent it, sunshine must be as much as possible excluded. A sheet of perforated glass of the kind now used for ventilating purposes might usefully be inserted in the top of a rectangular frame, to facilitate the escape of moisture; but in an ordinary fern-shade such a remedy is not available. A double case, with a space of an inch or more between them, would very much obviate the inconvenience, by surrounding the inner glass with a stratum of air of the same or nearly the same temperature as that prevailing within.

But the fountain carries the day in the combination of

the Fernery and the Aquarium, though in spite of the evil I have so lengthily dwelt upon, the combination is worth effecting, and the view will be open and undimmed sufficiently often to remunerate whoever has the patience or the means to carry out the scheme in its full integrity.

Since the above was written, I have seen an article in No. 405 of that able journal the "Cottage Gardener," in which there is an account of a fern-shade Aquarium, constructed by Mr. H. Baines, of the Yorkshire Philosophical Society. It consists of the ordinary glass vase and dish, the latter made slightly tinged with blue; in the centre of the Aquarium dish is inserted a pedestal of glass, and on this is placed a blue glass dish or tazza, made to fit on the top of the pedestal, as in the engraving at the head of this article. The bottom dish is covered with a layer of soil, (in my opinion unnecessary,) and this is covered with pebbles. The dish on the pedestal is also filled with soil, (peaty of course,) and planted with plants suitable to a Ward's Case. The Aquarium is then stocked and filled, and the bell-glass fitted into the rim of the Aquarium.

The following selection is adopted by Mr. Baines:—

Fishes—Small Gold Fish, Minnows, and Sticklebacks.

Mollusks—Succinea putris, Planorbis corneus, carinatus, and marginatus, Cyclas rürcola and cornea.

Insects—Several species of Colymbetes, Hygrotes, Hadaticus, and Gyrinus.

Water plants—Vallisneria spiralis, Aponogeton distachyon, Nymphæa odorata minor, and Nymphæa macrantha.

For the Wardian Case—Adiantum capillus-veneris, Lastræa dilatata Schofieldi, a beautiful small Yorkshire variety, Asplenium viride and trichomanes, Asplenium fontanum, etc.

Lycopods—Willdenowii, umbrosum, stoloniferum, mutabile, densum, and lepidopterum.

LIST OF SELECT PLANTS
FOR GROWTH IN FRESH-WATER AQUARIA.

Acorus calamus,	Sweet Rush.
Alisma plantago,	Water Plantain.
Alisma natans,	White.
Alisma ranunculoides.	
Anacharis alsinastrum,	Canadian Water-weed.
Aponogeton distachyon,	Cape Pond-weed.
Butomus umbellatus,	Flowering Rush.
Caltha palustris,	Marsh Marigold.
Callitriche autumnalis,	Water Chickweed.
Callitriche Verna.	
Ceratophyllum demersum.	
Chara vulgaris.	
Fontinalis antipyretica,	Fresh-water Alga.
Hottonia palustris,	Water Violet.
Hydrocharis morsus ranæ,	Floating Frog-bit.
Hydrocotyle vulgaris,	Water Navel-wort.
Isolepes licustrus,	Pile-wort.
Lemna gibba,	Duckweed.
Lemna polyrhiza.	
Lemna major.	
Lemna minor.	
Lobelia Dortmanna,	Dortmann's Lobelia.
Lymnacharis Humboldtii.	
Limosella aquatica.	
Littorella lacustris.	
Menyanthes trifoliata,	Bog-bean.
Myosotis scorpeoides,	Forget-me-not.
Myriophillum spicatum,	Water-mill foil.
Nasturtium officinale,	Water-cress.
Nelumbium speciosum,	Sacred Bean.
Nettela flexelis.	
Nuphar advena,	Large Water-lily.
Nuphar pumila,	Small Water-lily.
Nymphæa alba,	White.
Nymphæa odorata,	Sweet-scented.
Nymphæa cerulea,	Blue.

Nymphæa dentata,	Red.
Oenanthe fistulosa,	Drop-wort.
Ouvirandria fenestralis,	Madagascar Skeleton-weed.
Pappyris antequarian,	Paper-plant.
Pistea stratiotes,	Egyptian House-leek.
Polygonum amphibium.	
Pontederia angustifolia,	Bladder plant.
Pontederia cordata,	Pond-weed.
Potamogeton crispus,	Tench-weed.
Potamogeton densus.	
Potamogeton lucens.	
Potamogeton perfoliatus.	
Potamogeton pusillus.	
Potamogeton fluitans.	
Potamogeton gramenium.	
Potamogeton latifolius.	
Ranunculus aquatilis,	Water Crow-foot.
Ranunculus hederaceus.	
Sagittaria sagittifolia,	Arrow-head.
Stratiotes aloides,	Water-soldier.
Utricularia major.	
Utricularia minor.	
Villarsia nymphæoides,	Fringe Water-lily.
Valisneria spiralis,	
Veronica beccabunga,	Water Pimpernel.

LIST OF FERNS FOR AQUARIA.

		1ft.	0in.
Adiantum capillis-veneris,	True Maidenhair,	1ft.	0in.
Athyrium Filix-fœmina,	Beautiful Lady-Fern,	4	0
Ceratopteris thalictroides,	Water Brake,	1	0
Cystopteris Alpina,	alpine Bladder-Fern,	0	8
Cystopteris fragilis,	Brittle Bladder-Fern,	1	6
Lastrea spinulosa,	Withering's Fern,	3	6
Ophioglossum vulgatum,	Adder's Tongue,	0	4
Polypodium dryopteris,	Oak Fern,	1	6
Polypodium phegopteris,	Beech Fern,	2	0
Scolopendrium vulgare,	Common Hart's Tongue,	1	6
Trichomanes Tunbridgense,	Tunbridge Filmy Fern,	0	4

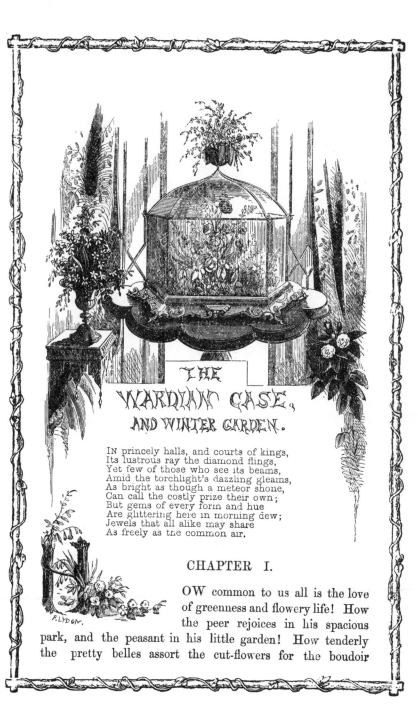

THE WARDIAN CASE, AND WINTER GARDEN.

IN princely halls, and courts of kings,
Its lustrous ray the diamond flings,
Yet few of those who see its beams,
Amid the torchlight's dazzling gleams,
As bright as though a meteor shone,
Can call the costly prize their own;
But gems of every form and hue
Are glittering here in morning dew;
Jewels that all alike may share
As freely as the common air.

CHAPTER I.

OW common to us all is the love
of greenness and flowery life! How
the peer rejoices in his spacious
park, and the peasant in his little garden! How tenderly
the pretty belles assort the cut-flowers for the boudoir

F. LYDON.

table, and watch over the pets of the greenhouse! How doatingly does the dear old granny in her white cap cherish the huge geraniums, that make her alms-house window a bower of greenery and bloom! What do we sigh for at the first blush of spring, but for the blink of greenness it brings with it; and which dots the hedgerows, and sprinkles the gardens, and carpets the meads afresh in the first glorious verdure of the year? How we rejoice in the unfolding of the buds, and the daily increase of the leafiness that shall glorify the year as the vegetative power, awakening at its appointed time,

> ———Wanders o'er the verdant earth
> In various hues, but chiefly thee, gay green!
> Thou, smiling Nature's universal robe!
> United light and shade! where the sight dwells
> With growing strength and ever-new delight.

It is very common but very precious; it is the cheapest of colours out of doors, but it is beyond all price in its value to the soul; for while it suggests the bounty of the Creator, who has appointed seed-time and harvest, it also suggests an analogy between material and spiritual things; that which is meant for all is freely given to all, and, like the Gospel, the verdure of the fields is scattered abroad for universal acceptance "without money and without price." If the love of country takes deep possession of the hearts of those who live in the land of the daisies, and within hearing of the bubbling of milk in the farm-house pail, it burns yet more fervently in the breasts of those who "in populous cities pent, breathe noisome air;" and every townsman, even if he does not own it, is beset with a perpetual hunger for the sight of something green. We cannot live without it; even when pressed by the imperious demands of city life, whatever is left of the original unstained human nature, will assert its existence by the creation of a deep longing for the sight, the smell, the touch of a green leaf or a ruddy flower.

"They alway must be with us, or we die."

Hence our towns eat up all the floral loveliness that the
adjacent nurseries can supply; hence the limits of the
towns are never to be determined, for they creep, creep
towards the country, and the smoke-dried citizen takes
revenge on commerce by wooing nature on his lawn, in
his shrubbery, among his fruitful rows of kail and peas,
or in quiet rambles through dewy arcades when the daily
cares cease, and he is once more for a few hours free to
live and to enjoy.

"The soul clings to the grass and the water-brooks;"

and every blade that glitters on the lawn, every flower
that nods to us from the highway, every leafy pet that
calls for our care in the garden, on the window-sill, or in
the conservatory, is a sort of minister to the moral nature,
that reads us a homily, and compels us to cherish thoughts
of purity and images of peace.

If flowers are so universally loved, and accepted everywhere as necessities of the moral life, whatever can be
done to render their culture easy, and to bring them to
perfection in the vicinity or within the household, must
be regarded as a benefaction. The citizen may refresh
himself with the sight of a meadow by travelling to it, he
may even here and there see in the centre of the town a
few old trees peering above the black roofs, and which, from
their forms rather than their colours, are distinguishable
from chimneys, and he may, with great care, preserve a
gaiety in his narrow garden in the midst of darkness and
smoke; but to have real verdure in the freshness of its
original strength and life, there is but one method, and
that is by the culture of it in Wardian Cases. Not only
may many ornamental plants be thus preserved in their full
beauty in the midst of surrounding dust and the fumes of
factories, but the rarest forms of vegetation, which refuse

the tenderest care of skilful gardeners under all ordinary circumstances, readily submit to domestication, and attain their highest development of beauty in these cases, if the requirements of their constitution are severally fulfilled.

It was in the year 1829 that Mr. Ward placed the chrysalis of a sphinx in some mould in a glass bottle covered with a lid, in order to obtain a perfect specimen of the insect. "After a time, a speck or two of vegetation appeared on the surface of the mould, and to his surprise turned out to be a fern and a grass. His interest was awakened: he placed the bottle in a favourable situation, and found that the plants continued to grow, and maintain a healthy appearance. On questioning himself about the matter, the answers readily presented themselves, inasmuch as air, light, moisture, and other requirements of the plants were contained within the bottle."

This was the first Wardian Case. Mr. Ward extended the experiment, and arrived at the conclusion that certain kinds of vegetation readily adapt themselves to an unchanged atmosphere in a *close* structure of glass, and to account for such an apparent departure from the recognised laws of vegetable growth, certain explanations as to the absorption of carbon and the evolution of oxygen were offered, and quite an elaborate theory of vegetable physiology was the consequence. It was admitted, reasonably enough, that it is impossible to make a Wardian Case on such a plan as wholly to exclude the outer air, but at the same time it came to be generally accepted that, for all practical purposes, such a case might be sealed hermetically, change of air, in the ordinary acceptation of the term, being quite at variance with the theory of vegetation as applied to these cases. Mr. Ward himself industriously taught that a plant-case is a self-supporting structure. Once set going, the exhaling moisture trickles down the glass, refreshes the herbage, and rises again to be again condensed; while the air in the case is alternately charged with excess of carbon or

oxygen, the plants being always occupied in restoring it to a normal tone, spite of their tendency to vitiate it; that, in fact, they create an atmosphere of their own, and thrive without external aid, and independent of external agencies. In a former edition of this work I quoted largely from the lecture in which Mr. Stephen Ward re-asserted and explained the original theory propounded by his father; and though I had been haunted by doubts as to the soundness of that theory, I waited long and watched patiently before I would dare to gainsay it. At last I made a series of definite experiments, the result of which confirmed my doubts, and compelled me to regard the Wardian theory as "a delusion and a snare;" and when I insisted that a Wardian Case was nothing more nor less than a *greenhouse on a small scale*, and that all the learned dust about oxygen, and carbon, and the production of local atmospheres, was worthless, I had to bear with much obloquy and perversion of my views, and was even charged with unfair conduct towards Mr. Ward himself. Nevertheless, every line that has been written on the subject since I first broached my views in the pages of a public journal, has added strength to my position; and I once more repeat that Mr. Ward has led the public astray, and that his own theory has been the great impediment to the improvement and the general adoption of plant-cases. Mr. Ward can afford to be told that he is wrong, as can any man who loves knowledge for its own sake. He is a genuine naturalist, a persevering man of science, a successful practitioner of the healing art, and a friend to the poor and needy, in fact, a gentleman and a Christian; *he* therefore will be the last to complain of those who seek to bring his invention to the perfection of which it is susceptible. May his shadow increase!

Now as to the construction and general uses of these cases. In a *close* case some kinds of ferns will maintain their beauty for a length of time, and *then* perish. In a *close* case it is impossible to rear flowering plants of any

kind, and *whatever* may be grown in such a structure will
be more or less drawn, spindling, and sickly; the glass will
usually be in a semi-opaque condition, from the excessive
condensation of moisture, and a succession of disappointments and annoyances will at last determine the cultivator
to abolish it altogether, in the belief that there is some
secret of management to which he cannot attain access,
or that the whole thing is a mistake from beginning to
end. We have only to go to Nature, our best of teachers,
to be assured that the established laws of horticulture apply
to such structures as decisively as they apply to the management of gardens and greenhouses, and that though we do
not usually make the cases air-tight, nevertheless, we must
regard ventilation as a *necessity, not an accident,* of their
management in order to be successful. From that moment
a Wardian Case becomes a miniature greenhouse, in which
we can grow almost anything. Before, we were confined to
ferns, because of all plants they bear a damp imprisonment
with wonderful patience; but now the field is open for the
introduction of flowers of the choicest kinds, and by applying
heat the working department of plant-propagation may be
carried on in-doors with as much success as in the pits
and houses of the experienced nurseryman.

In the design of an oblong rectangular case, graceful
outlines may be attained by the adoption of the following
proportions:—First determine the *general* dimensions of
your case; then whatever is to be its length, let the width
be nearly one-half. If from right to left it is to measure
thirty-two inches, let its breadth from back to front be
fourteen or fifteen. The height of the glass sides should
be the same as the breadth of the case. Then to roof it,
let the summit of the roof be formed of four sloping sides
surmounted by a flat top; and let the flat top be as much
above the edges of the four sides as *half the height* of
those sides; then you will have an angular object possessing
as much grace as can be infused into the simplest rectangular

design; and simplicity and grace have ever been close neighbours. That we may not be misunderstood, let us restate the matter. A square glass box—which the case may be termed before the roof is put on—should be formed on the principle of a double cube; but it should not be strictly a double cube, because the mind has a tendency to resolve it into two portions. Then upon this a glass roof is to be formed of four sloping sides and a flat summit; and this flat summit is to be as much above the upper edge of the box as half the height of the box itself. If the front and back measured each thirty-two inches, then the height, without the roof, would be nearly the same as the width, namely, fifteen inches. The roof itself, formed sarcophagus fashion, would give an additional elevation of eight inches, and the entire height within would be twenty-four inches. One side of the sarcophagus top should be fixed on hinges, to let down as a door to give the necessary ventilation occasionally.

Now, to place this on an ordinary table would be to waste space. Let it have a stand expressly made for it, with four legs, of course, and an elliptical arch of fretted work to break the monotony of the straight lines. If the case is on a large scale—say with a length of four feet, and a height of three—a stand of the kind just mentioned would give it completeness as a noble piece of furniture; and it would only require to be properly planted to realize a genuine conservatory, not of ferns only, but the choicest flowering exotics as well, for which there would be room for a good selection. Ordinary carving or relief ornament has very little effect when set against the light; but open fretwork, by admitting the light through it, produces a beautiful and appropriate tone of ornamentation. Of course the principles of art may be applied to glass structures in many ways, so as to insure grace of outline with the necessary space, which, as has been said above, is only adduced by way of example; at the same time it may here be finally remarked that imi-

tations of temples, villas, and dolls' houses, a multiplicity
of corners and fancy convolutions, or *any intricate* design
that may be adopted for a Wardian Case, is more likely
to produce puerility than grace. Let the form be simple,
and the proportions symmetrical, and you may hereafter
be gratified with your work.

When we have once shaken off the errors that have
cramped the application of the Wardian Case to house
embellishment, the idea expands, and there is positively no
limit to the variety of forms it may assume, and scarcely
a limit to the uses to which it may be put, from the
preservation of ornamental exotics, to the raising of a salad
for the Christmas table; and a few of these forms and uses
here demand distinct description, and first, as to the construction of cases generally.

An ingenious taste will suggest innumerable designs for
the purpose, and of these *built* structures are always
preferable to the mere glass dome or bell, because they
admit of arrangements for ventilation and management
most easily. A few years ago it was the practice to build
a Wardian Case over a deep box for the soil, to allow of
the growth of esculents amongst the ferns, the culture of
radishes and onions being resorted to, to give an air of
utility to the structure, and to help to pay for its cost.
Utility has long ago been abandoned, and the motto "beauty
is the highest use" has prevailed, and henceforth a great
depth of soil may be considered unnecessary.

In constructing a Wardian Case, the bottom must be
double; one case with a perforated bottom, fitting within,
but *not touching*, an outer water-tight one, and from this
the drainage-water must be occasionally removed by means
of a proper exit. The depth of the soil need seldom be
more than four inches, and for small cases a depth of
three inches will generally be sufficient. This soil should
rest on a layer of light porous material, such as broken
flower-pots or clean cinders. By this arrangement, it will

be impossible to drown the plants as they are drowned and rotted on the accepted plan. Air as well as moisture will reach the roots; and instead of confining the selection to such ferns and lycopods as are capable of resisting the destructive influences of excessive moisture and stagnated air, high-class flowering-plants may be brought into the field, and a genuine garden under glass—a conservatory in fact—may be fitted up in the window. Here we come to the design of the thing; and it may now be asked why the everlasting four-sided packing-case pattern should be so perseveringly adhered to by the makers of Wardian Cases. It really seems that if you want to grow a few plants under glass in your room, you must be condemned to accept some piece of angular ugliness, yclept a Wardian Case, whereas such materials as glass, wood, and zinc, are of all others the best adapted for combining into graceful forms; and instead of mean boxes, we might have noble pieces of furniture, or at least a set of graceful outlines.

Other modes of procedure readily suggest themselves; the Crystal Palace gives us one of the best of hints, and amongst others, Mr. Ward's suggestion for the construction of a floral window, merits prominent consideration. In many town localities it is very desirable to extinguish the prospect; the daily view of factory chimneys, grimy walls, and sooty roofs, is by no means cheering or ministrant to the sentiments, and a Wardian Case of a peculiar construction may be adopted to give cheerfulness to a room which otherwise would present but few suggestions of the beauties of nature. Mr. Ward suggested the construction of double window sashes, the space between them to be filled with plants; and if we add that a double trough for soil, and an arrangement above, for ventilation, are to be thought of in the preliminaries, the remainder of the work may be left to the taste of the proprietor, and the judgment of the carpenter, for its completion.

But a better plan still is to construct a proper conser-

vatory, either within or without the window, in the first case serving as a floral blind or screen, as well as a plant case, in the second a place of retreat for the enjoyment of leisure, and in either a source of very pleasurable re-creation. Here is a field for ingenuity; here is the Crystal Palace and Winter-Garden brought to the fireside at once, and the room beautified by a judicious grouping and selection of plants.

To construct a conservatory on this scale would be comparatively inexpensive. An amateur who could use carpenters' tools with a little skill would easily plan and execute such a work at less cost than he could purchase a good-sized Wardian Case; and as the frame-work might be formed wholly of wood, there would be no problem to solve in its construction. The *modus operandi* would include, first, the removal of the lower sash; or that might be left untouched, and the whole of the construction placed before it, the sash being used to form one side of the conservatory. If the sash were removed, one sheet of plate-glass ought to take its place. A depth of from four to six inches would be sufficient for the projection on the side next the room, and that of course would be the breadth from back to front of the conservatory. On each side of the window the necessary wood-work would be fixed; and along the base of the proposed conservatory a suitable trough for the soil would be required. Then the glass-work within, on the side next the room,—the central portion forming a door for access to the plants, and a roof on hinges with a perforated ventilator, to be closed or opened as required,—would complete the structure. There would be ample room for design in the formation of such conservatories. The inner side need not be a mere flat frame-work, but might be made up of simple and symmetrical curves, so as to "*bow*" *into* the room in the same way as a bay-window "bows" towards the street; and a bay-window would be the best of situations in which to form a conservatory of this kind.

One of the prettiest Wardian Cases I have ever had has recently been built up for me by Messrs. Treggon, of Jewin Street. A fine vase, No. 26 in the patterns of Messrs. Ransome, of Ipswich, and formed of their patent artificial stone, is surmounted with a zinc frame-work. The vase stands thirty-four inches high on its pedestal, and its upper edge has a diameter of twenty-five inches. It is fitted with a perforated dish of zinc for soil, and on this, but made separately from it, is a frame-work of zinc, with plate-glass in six divisions, one of them opening on hinges to form a door. From the edge of the vase to the top of the first frame-work is a height of twenty-four inches, where it is bound with perforated zinc for ventilation. Above this is a conical lantern with a domed top, reaching twelve inches higher, the dome resting on another rim of zinc, perforated for ventilation. Besides this I have a duplicate pan for soil, so as to afford facilities for a complete change of plants at any time—a matter on which a few words must be said presently.

The vase is planted with tropical ferns, orchises, and lycopods, arranged with some care as to effect, and the surface of the soil is diversified with a few blocks of granite. Its appearance is chaste and classical; and with a moderate amount of sun, and attention as to moisture and ventilation, it answers admirably.

For halls, staircases, or drawing-rooms, a very classical ornament may be constructed by adapting a glass frame to a large Grecian vase. Professor Allman, of Trinity College, Dublin, thus describes a case of this sort in a communication to the author of the "Hand-book of Town Gardening."—

"It struck me some time since, that a very picturesque Ward Case might be formed out of one of the numerous copies of ancient vases, which are constructed in Roman cement, or some such material, and which may now be easily obtained at any of the principal statuary workshops.

I accordingly procured a large Grecian vase, and fitted upon

it a frame made of patent zinc sash-work, carefully glazed with British plate-glass. The frame is of an octangular shape, curved at the top, and surmounted by a low bell-glass in form of a dome. Its diameter, from angle to angle, is two feet five inches, and its height, to the commencement of the curved roof, two feet six inches. Each of the eight sides is formed of a single plate of glass, and one of them is hung upon hinges, so as to open outwards in the manner of a door. The vase stands upon a quadrangular timber pedestal, and occupies a window facing the south.

From within the vase a metallic tube, open at both ends, passes downwards through the stem into the interior of the timber pedestal, which is hollow. The use of the tube is to prevent any undue accumulation of water, which would act injuriously on the plants, but is by this means carried off, and discharged below into a dish placed in the hollow pedestal, which opens by a small door, and thus admits of the removal and emptying of the dish when necessary. In the manufacture of such vases, the upper part is cast separately from the stem, and generally admits of a free rotation on the latter, a circumstance of importance, for the several sides can with great facility be in this way exposed successively to the light, or turned round to the spectator during examination." Some of Minton's vases present magnificent examples of artistic design, suitable for Wardian Cases, and for those of small size a single bell-glass would be preferable to any metal framing; but beyond sixteen inches in diameter, glass shades are almost unmanageable.

Messrs. Cottam and Hallen, the distinguished manufacturers of horticultural ornaments, have long given their attention to the production of fine examples, selected from ancient and modern designs, and adapted to all the purposes for which vases may be required, either for fountains, gardens, conservatories, or the in-door culture of plants under glass. Among the many examples produced by them the Medici, Warwick, and Lotus vases are perhaps the best of all for elegant Wardian Cases. A pair of such vases fitted with French shades, and mounted on pedestals, would give grace and finish to a room, such as could not be attained by the most tasteful arrangement of any ordinary furniture, or works of art however costly, because art and nature would here be combined; the lines of the artist would contrast against the lines of nature; and while the first remained passive and unchanging, yet ever telling its own story truly, the second would, in the development of its proper life, continually assume new forms, and add the charm of a *living* creation to the *dead* perfection of the human brain.

The effect of a group of vases is illustrated in Mr. Voyez's frontispiece to this article; and another example of a fern vase forms a frontispiece to the paper on the Fernery. In the coloured group of vases the one in the foreground is devoted to ferns, and a smaller case which surmounts it is stocked with cacti. Another is occupied with curious British bog and marsh plants; and from the summit hangs a block ornamented with delicate creepers. Another is devoted to flowering plants—the crocus, snowdrop, and hyacinth, for spring; to be succeeded, as the season advances, with rosy oxalis, pimpernels, and any choice greenhouse or garden favourites which delight in a moist air; though as the ventilation and amount of moisture can be very easily regulated, the selection need not be in any way confined.

The mention of vases naturally introduces some other forms of Wardian Cases, of which the common fern-shade is the chief. This is a cheap and effective contrivance, consisting of a simple glass dish with a rim, into which is fitted a glass dome or bell. It answers well for ferns, but is not applicable for flowering plants, on account of its close character. The pan, too, is in no way porous, and hence drainage must be secured by means of a layer of cinders or broken pots under the soil, and water must be given sparingly until the soil is sufficiently wet; because, should it once get drenched to excess, the only remedy is to get rid of the superfluous water by the slow process of evaporation, during which the stock may perish from positive soddening at the roots. Those ferns which love shade and moisture, and a close air, are the best adapted for these fern-shades; and even then the shade should be removed two or three times a week, and kept off for an hour or two each time, to give a thorough change of air to the plants, and prevent "damping off" at the surface.

When judiciously managed as to air and moisture, and placed within reach of the morning or evening sun, any of the ferns, marsh, bog, and heath plants, which usually flourish under glass, may be kept in common fern-shades.

Another form of fern-shade is that known as Pascall's Patent Propagating Pot, which is manufactured by Mr. Pascall, of the West Kent Potteries. It is an ingenious contrivance, and will be found invaluable for the pot culture of ferns, or for the propagation of hard-wooded plants of all kinds. It is simply a flower-pot with a rim to receive a propagating glass, the glass being pressed down into sand in the groove, thus forming an extemporaneous Wardian Case, in which cuttings of all kinds may be struck close to the pot, and kept moist and dark, or ventilated at pleasure; and in which such ferns as *Trichomanes speciosum* and *Hymenophyllum*, as well as the pretty *Dionæa muscipula*, *Cephalotus*, and fine-foliaged plants and ferns generally may be grown. These pots are made of a beautiful red ware; they are shallower than the ordinary garden pot, and as they are made in sizes from four to twelve inches, they are capable of a thousand different uses, and, with bell-glasses, may be made into Wardian Cases instantly.

I shall mention one other kind of case, and then quit this part of the subject. The common Florence flasks, in which salad oil is imported, make very pretty and useful

vessels for the culture of minute flowering plants and ferns, and for the preservation of the low forms of either terrestrial or aquatic vegetation. I have in my study window a row of these flasks, suspended along a brass rod; each of them contains specimens of plants that would be inconspicuous in a general collection, though full of interest individually. The pretty wall-rue, the true maiden-hair, the adder's tongue, small specimens of *Hymenophyllum unilaterale* and *Tunbridgense*, *Cystopteris Dickieana* and *fragilis*. Some of the spleenworts, with lycopods and mosses, flourish in sandy peat carefully dropped into the flask; while in others half-filled with water, I have specimens of *Riccia*, *Lemna*, *Nitella*, *Conferva*, and other aquatics, making quite a garden of curiosities, worthy at any time of a quiet and studious inspection. Each flask is covered with a piece of oiled silk, kept round the mouth by means of a small India-rubber band, so that it can be removed instantly for the supply of air and water. The only matter of importance in the management of such a collection is to keep the sun off it, or at least to allow only his faintest morning beams to shine upon it, for an exposure for an hour at mid-day, may cause the destruction of the whole. For raising seedling ferns, these flasks are admirable in the absence of other appliances.

A few observations now present themselves as essential to the completion of this chapter on the construction of Wardian Cases.

I have suggested the formation of a double bottom, to ensure efficient drainage—the inner one perforated, the outer one water-tight, to prevent drip or damp in the room.

This plan causes the superfluous water to escape entirely from the soil, and is therefore preferable to a drainage secured merely by a bottom of crocks; because, though the latter may relieve the roots of the plants, it does not readily enable us to remove the water entirely from the case; and unless the case is constructed with very special provisions for the purpose, we may not even know how much moisture may be lurking under the soil, and doing injury to all above it by exhalation and absorption by capillary attraction.

In addition to this provision, it is advisable to make another for a complete change of plants at any time. Two or more soil pans may be used—only one of course being in use at one time. Suppose the vegetation to get shabby from some accident, from neglect, or from the natural decay of the plants when their season has expired, you have only to stock another which fits the same case, and ring the changes. If you have several pans, they may be kept

in the greenhouse or stove, stocked with plants for exhibition in succession, so that every day in the year your Wardian Case may blaze in the brightest colours of the season; the plants being brought into bloom previously, and then the pan containing them dropped into the receptacle, and the frame-work placed over them. In the London season, we see in the houses of the nobility, collections of ferns and flowering plants in cases which a few weeks before were a disgrace to the establishment. Basing our judgments on the idea of the case being *permanently* stocked, we are puzzled to conjecture by what witchery those wretched ferns have been revivified. The neighbouring nurseryman can reveal the secret, for he keeps a number of troughs stocked ready for the purpose, with the choicest ferns, and exotic palms and orchises. It is but necessary to remove the shabby collection, and replace it with one of these carefully-tended pans, and presto! the Wardian Case "blooms in beauty like the smile of love." However skilfully the case may be managed, a change of vegetation may now and then be desirable, and it is easily effected by means of duplicate troughs or pans.

To sustain in health and beauty some of the more tender ferns and flowering plants artificial heat is essential, and to apply this to a Wardian Case is to make it approximate still closer to an ordinary greenhouse. Nothing can be simpler: below the trough for soil let there be a shallow tank of the same dimensions as the bottom of the trough, and made to slide in and out if necessary, or if not, at least, let it be furnished with a tap for drawing off the water, and another for filling it. When filled with hot water it will impart a gentle bottom-heat, and this heat may be either sustained by means of a lamp, or gas jet out of sight, or the water may be changed every morning so as to sustain it at a maximum temperature during the mid-day. This would be combining the Wardian with the Waltonian Case, and as the latter will come to be treated

in detail, in a subsequent paper, this mere hint may here be sufficient.

In regard to the material used in the construction of cases, it should be borne in mind that wood-work is least liable to be affected by sudden changes of temperature. Metal is such a rapid conductor of heat that it rapidly conveys to the atmosphere of the case every change of external temperature; it neither resists heat nor cold, and hence at some seasons of the year greenhouses, conservatories, and Wardian Cases, in which metal is one of the principal materials, are subjected to sudden alternations of temperature that do much mischief. As Wardian Cases are seldom exposed to the weather, the disadvantage of metal is not so readily felt, and it is balanced by the lightness and neatness in which metal is so superior to wood; still it is important that the superiority of wood in this respect should be borne in mind, and in the construction of a window conservatory, or a plant-house of any kind which is to be exposed to the external air, wood will always be found to be the best material. Among metals galvanized iron is decidedly the best.

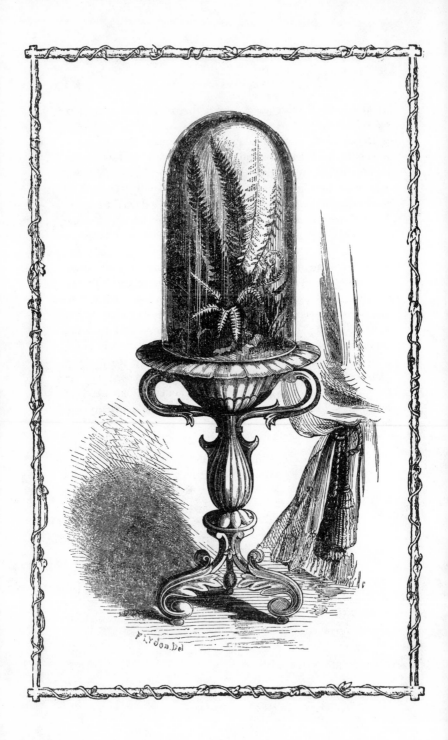

F. Lydon. Del

CHAPTER II.

"MIGHTY Flora, goddesse of fresh flowres, which clothed hath
  the soyle in lusty green,
Made buds to springe, with her sweet showers, by influence
  of the sunne shine;
To doe pleasannce of intent full cleane, unto the states which
  now sit here,
Hath Ver downe sent her own daughter deare."

LYDGATE.

ARDIAN Cases may have innumerable forms and almost innumerable uses, if the principle of their construction is not cramped, and if a sufficient amount of horticultural skill is brought to bear upon management. Now, although I have insisted on the abandonment of the air-tight theory, it must not be supposed that air is to be admitted indiscriminately, or that any excessive dryness of the soil is essential. It depends entirely on what is grown in them, how they shall be managed. The value of such constructions to the townsman arises from the fact that they are partially closed, or, as expressed by Mr. Stephen Ward, "closed to adverse, open to genial influences," that is, sufficiently close to exclude the dust, soot, and noxious gases with which town atmospheres are generally loaded, yet admitting of ventilation when necessary, and at times favourable to the operation. For cases made on the ordinary plan, that is, as close as ordinary workmanship will make them, there can be no better stock than ferns and lycopods, because these naturally love a moist quiet air, and whatever facilities the case may afford for the admission of atmospheric influences, such flowerless plants need less ventilation than most other kinds, and even in the case of flowering plants, those that prefer moisture and partial shade are the most suitable.

Among the many varieties of ferns suitable for culture under glass, there are of course many that require special modes of culture, but the majority do well with one uniform system of treatment, which I will endeavour to epitomise. The soil should be chiefly peat of a friable nature, mixed with soft charcoal, silver sand, and leaf mould. Exact proportions of each are frequently given; but it really is not necessary to weigh and measure the materials of any composts, and we may say roughly that one-third peat, one-third leaf mould, one-sixth silver sand, and one-sixth charcoal, will be found as good a compost for general purposes as can be made. A small proportion of very old and well-rotted dung in a sweet condition may be added to advantage, and when the compost is complete it should have a crumbly character, and bear wetting without suddenly becoming pasty. It should *not be sifted;* in fact sifted soils are generally the very worst for all purposes, but the materials should be well broken and incorporated by the hands. Another good compost may be made with one part loam, one part chopped moss, and one part of silver sand and rotten wood. In this most ferns will thrive admirably, as will also primulas, auriculas, violets, and most British wildings. Mould from heaths or commons, if of a sandy nature and free from clay, will frequently answer without any

addition, except a little old dung to enrich it, but, generally
speaking, the peat compost is the best. An addition of some
finely-broken flower-pots will always improve the soil for ferns.

Those ferns that usually flourish best on limestone soils
or on rocks, may have a compost of a similar kind, but
with a little broken freestone or old mortar added; and
in planting a hole may be formed in the general soil, in
which to insert any such special compost, and then the
plant must be placed in the centre of the soil so introduced.
Among the best known ferns, those that require limestone
or old mortar, are the following:—*Polypodium calcareum,
Allosorus crispus, Cystopteris alpina* and *montana, Asplenium
trichomanes, viride,* and *ruta muraria. Lastreas* and *Brakes*
do not generally do well if their roots come in contact with
calcareous matter, and this should be remembered in the
first arrangements made for planting.

In stocking a case it is necessary to see first that the
drainage is effectual, and besides a definite outlet for superfluous moisture, a layer of crocks should be placed below
the soil, for the roots need a circulation of air about them,
as well as the presence of moisture. The planting of the
ferns will be found a very simple affair, and the pictorial
effect of the whole may be ensured by judiciously grouping
and arranging them. In an oblong case it is generally best
to place the plants in rows according to their heights; in
vases and other circular structures, some one distinct plant
should occupy the centre, rising perhaps from a miniature
rockery, formed of blocks of granite, and with a few low-
growing plants about the base, of which *Lycopodiums* are
the best for general purposes. It tends very much to enhance the beauty of a collection to break the surface in
some pretty way. This is easily accomplished by means of
a miniature rockery, every crevice of which is to be made
use of for plants suitable to such spots.

The Maiden-hair fern, which loves shade, moisture, and
warmth, is one of the very best for such a miniature rockery,

and my lady readers may perhaps like to be informed that two of its fronds, with two spikes of mignionette, at the back of a white camellia, make a splendid bouquet. *Asplenium trichomanes, A. marinum,* and *A. adiantum-nigrum,* (the very common black spleenwort,) are other good plants for the miniature rockery; so are *Cystopteris alpina* and *fragilis,* and any of the species of *Allosorus* and *Woodsia.* Around the rockery the ferns of smaller growth, such as the Hart's Tongue, Polypodies, *Polystichum,* and others of distinct habit may be grouped, but nothing is eventually gained by over-planting, and room must be afforded for the natural increase of the plants.

The plants selected and arranged are then to be firmly planted in their several positions; every decayed frond should be cut off close to the root, and if young fronds are pushing, the plants should be handled tenderly, to avoid breaking them, for on the growth of these depends the beauty of the collection for the next season. When completed, the surface of the soil should be wholly raised above the rim of the case, and the centre should be elevated above the surrounding portions, either by a mound covered with surfacing plants, or by a constructed rockery, or a few handsome pieces of rough stone. Those who like to introduce architectural decorations, such as the imitation of a ruin, may indulge their fancy freely, provided they do not bring into contact with the soil or plants any pernicious material, such as cement, or metal of any kind. I think such decorations very unsuitable, but that is simply a matter of opinion.

Now as to watering, which completes the process of stocking. It is generally thought that as ferns love shade and moisture, they cannot have too much of either; the consequence is that plants in Wardian Cases are usually immured in darkness and drowned in water. I should advise every beginner to give a very slight watering, at first using rain water that has been warmed in the sun, and a

fine-rosed watering-pot. A gentle shower overhead will give the plants a start after their removal, and will settle the soil about their roots. After the watering, the case should be left open a few hours to allow of the escape of exhalations, and for a few days it should be shaded from excessive light. In a day or two give another gentle shower, and leave the case open as before, choosing a time when the air in the apartment is quite free of dust and smoke, and at all times closing the case fast while any household operations are in progress that may occasion dust. Several waterings may be given in this way till the soil is moderately moistened through, and from that time forward water is to be administered only when really required. This plan of wetting the soil through by degrees is a safe one, for watering may easily be carried too far; and if an excess should be given, it is not easily got rid of, and the matured fronds may decay under its influence.

If the soil gets positively dry, water is essential; and if the collection consists chiefly of marsh-growing species, it may be administered liberally, but as a rule, whenever the soil becomes so pasty as to adhere to the fingers, and soil them after watering, too much has been given. It should be moist and friable at all times, never absolutely wet. As to giving air, an hour or so every morning will usually be sufficient; with flowering plants a little more air is necessary, but with very few exceptions ferns and flowering plants in a Wardian Case should have a little sun, as well as abundance of ordinary daylight. The morning sun is preferable, the evening sun next so, but the mid-day sun in summer would be far too fierce for anything that might be grown in such a structure. To keep the collection clean and bright by the removal of every dead or decaying leaf, and to alter or replant as occasion may require, are matters that must be left to the judgment of the cultivator, who must in his attentions keep pace with the changes of seasons and the revolutions of time.

So far the instructions are of a somewhat general character, and apply to such cases as are stocked with miscellaneous ferns; but this chapter would be incomplete were I not to include in it a few hints on the management of a few special favourites of fern cultivators. There are a few delicate and lovely ferns that refuse all our attentions when planted out of doors; however beautiful they may be in their native rocky sites, when transferred to situations carefully prepared to imitate them, they lanquish and die, and we have to thank Mr. Ward for an invention that enables us to coax these shy pets into a very perfect growth. Two of them especially are highly prized, and it may be said in the language of catalogues, "no collection can be considered complete without them." They are the Bristle fern, (*Trichomanes radicans*, syn. *T. speciosum, brevisetium, Hymenophyllum alatum, etc.,*) and *H. Tunbridgense,* (syn. *Trichomanes Tunbridgense,)* the renowned Tunbridge filmy fern. These are the rarest and most delicate of all our British filices, and upon their culture extraordinary patience is lavished, with more or less success, by professional and amateur growers. The Wardian Case is just the place for both, and to secure a free growth they must be kept pretty close under glass; indeed they require so little ventilation, that in their case Mr. Ward may have his way, and point to them as a triumph.

To grow these ferns it is necessary to confine them closely in a warm moist atmosphere, either in a Wardian Case or a pot, and it would even be better to construct a case expressly for them. They should be planted on a mass of porous freestone; if in pots the freestone would be better if fitting the pot exactly, with the exception of a layer of crocks underneath it for drainage. A little silver sand is to be sprinkled over the stone, so as to bring the surface a little above the rim of the pot or case, and the root stock of the plant must be neatly arranged on the surface. A little more sand must be added above the root, and a

surface of sphagnum laid down over all. If the plant does not stand erect when planted, a few neat stakes must be placed to support it; and when the arrangement is complete, a good watering must be given, but with great care, so as not to disturb the thin layer of sand which lies over the root. They must thenceforth be kept constantly damp, moderately shaded, and on no account disturbed, for every disturbance of their roots does them great injury. Mr. Andrews, of Dublin, grows them suspended by the stems across the roof of a fern case, attached to rods covered with bass matting and moss. Mr. Ward brings them to great perfection in the midst of London smoke by means of his close case; and without a case, Pascall's pots, with bell-glasses, may be used for them in greenhouse and conservatory culture. This latter would be a valuable contrivance, if only for the sake of cultivating these delicate ferns, for they come to perfection in them, and form lovely specimens when well established.

Mr. Stephen Ward, in his lecture already quoted, says, "In illustration of the perfection which ferns may attain under this plan, I may notice the success which, in the hands of different amateurs, has attended the growth of one of the most delicate and beautiful, the *Trichomanes speciosum*. Formerly, in consequence of the occasional dryness of the atmosphere, and the presence of adventitious matters even in the best constructed conservatories, it was almost impossible to cultivate this plant. Now, in one of these cases, where it has a perfectly pure and highly humid atmosphere, it will grow as well in the dirtiest parts of the metropolis as in its native locality; and in the first experiment made with it under this plan it produced fronds one-fourth larger than native specimens either from Killarney or elsewhere. As small triumphs in the culture of this plant, I may notice a fine specimen reared by my brother in the heart of the city, and another by Mr. Callwell, of Dublin, which, remarkably slow as the plant is of growth, has produced in a few years, two hundred and thirty fronds, varying in length from fourteen to twenty inches and a half." It is here that art beats nature; in such positions seasonal changes make no havoc with their delicate fronds; they revel in their glass prison, and far excel in beauty their sisters that still linger in the wilds.

We now come to the adaptations of the case for flowering plants; and it must be candidly stated that as a rule flowering plants should rather be exhibited than grown in them; and I will suggest a plan by which a good-sized case may be kept unusually gay. In the illustration which adorns the head of the first chapter, it will be seen that the artist has introduced a very refulgent rose and other gay bloomers in a group. Where there is room for a rockery, greenhouse plants may be freely used by the following plan: —Let a large flower-pot be placed as a basis for the rockery. Build the stones and soil up around it, so as to hide the pot, but yet to keep the pot itself open for access. Plant the mound as you will with lycopods, sun-dew, cyclamen, pennywort, common and rosy oxalis, etc. The other parts of the case may be planted with lilies of the valley, auriculas, primulas, violets, myrtle, anemone, mignionette, musk, nemophilus, dwarf ipomeas, and common ivy, which is one of the most classical ornaments that can be introduced into a case. Such neat-growing climbers as *Tropæolum Jarattii*, *Convolvulus*, and *Pentanthus* may also be used. Some ferns that do well in a moderate amount of sunshine may be added according to space; and when the general planting is completed, throw a little moss into the empty pot, and drop into it a well-blown plant to occupy the centre, and conceal the edges of the pot by bringing the stems of the *Lycopodiums* over it, or with a little fresh-gathered moss neatly arranged for the purpose. Occasional sunshine, air, and water are all that are needed to carry the plants through their bloom. When that is over the centre one can be changed in five minutes; those that are planted in the soil can be removed, and their place supplied with others of suitable character; and with very little trouble the drawing-room may be kept gay, and the Wardian Case brought into repute as a very tasteful ornament; or if there are several trays made to fit the case, they may be brought on in succession, and removed from the greenhouse as wanted, to take the place of the tray that is removed. A few suspended plants, one or two small vases with specimen ferns, or an aquarium may be placed underneath it, and a very charming collection of living objects will be there to greet all comers.

A large number of flowering plants may have permanent occupancy, and especially if such be selected as have variegated or cheerful foliage, and which will give an agreeable air to the scene when not in flower. A few orchids suspended from the roof in the outer shells of cocoa-nuts, or in pieces of rough bark, with a vase containing creepers above the case, will give a complete and fairy-like aspect to the whole; and with a judicious selection of ferns for the general stock would ensure a pretty scene at all times. Gesnerias, gloxinias, achimenes, hydrangeas, roses, calceolarias, fuchsias, auriculas, and pansies are all suitable for the more striking features, and thrive well in a moist atmosphere if planted for permanent occupancy. Pelargoniums, verbenas, and others of dryer texture, would require a drier air, and a little knowledge of greenhouse economy will be essential to a successful issue of the enterprise; with a little such knowledge, and means provided for drainage and ventilation, there is scarcely any limit to the selection that may be made; but it will generally be found the best plan to shift the plants as they go out of bloom, and thus keep up a permanent exhibition of choice things in full floral perfection.

In the selection of plants it is a grand point to bring together in the same case only such as are of similar con-

M

stitution, especially when they are to remain together permanently. Cacti are very much admired by those who use Wardian Cases, but they seldom do well unless grown by themselves, and treated in a distinct manner. They love extremes of heat and moisture, but desire plenty of light at all times. The *Mammillarias, Echinocactus,* and *Opuntias* are found on dry levels and volcanic slopes; the creeping *Cereus* and the brilliant *Epiphyllum* flourish on the borders of woods and rocky places abounding in moisture; and the *Peraskias* are inhabitants of the hot, damp jungles of Guiana and Brazil. In the culture of these in Wardian Cases, there must be ample means for ventilation when necessary, very efficient drainage, and if heat can be supplied, as suggested in the previous chapter, their culture can be more successfully prosecuted. The last-named genera are the best for this mode of culture; the soil should be a compost of yellow loam, silver-sand, and potsherds; during the season of growth the plants should have frequent waterings of liquid manure, weak at first, and the strength gradually increased till they flower, when it should be gradually discontinued, and the plants suffered to rest.

Unless properly rested by the entire withdrawal of moisture after growth, the best stock in the world will soon be ruined; but if their strange tempers are humoured by the opposite excesses, which they love so much, the varieties of cactus are among the most curious and beautiful plants that can be introduced in Wardian Cases. These and many other plants may be grown in pots in Wardian Cases: ferns so grown look extremely well, especially when their foliage conceals the pots themselves, and such a system of culture affords many facilities for successful management and occasional change of scene.

But the selection is not yet exhausted. If you have any love for your native land—any warmness of heart for its grey woods and green slopes—its rustic beauty and its Saxon freedom—just set apart the finest case you have

for a collection of British wildings. You will create a
picture that will make your friends stare again, when they
learn that every gem within is next of kin to the little
things they have trodden under-foot all their lives in
wood-side and meadow rambles. Some will doubt your
word, and *internally* ejaculate "fudge!" but should any
man once openly drop a hint that you are imposing on
him, rebuke him severely for his ignorance of the productions of his country, and finish off with Scott's lines—

> "Breathes there a man with soul so dead
> Who never to himself has said"—

You know the rest; and now for this National Floral Exhibition. Prepare the case in the usual way; if deep, with
a bottom of broken flower-pots; if shallow without them,
fill up with the compost already recommended for ferns,
and then plant in it a small sprig of the *smallest-leaved*
ivy you can find on a tree stump in the woods, or on an
old bridge above a sylvan stream, then tufts of marsh pennywort, common pimpernel, germander speedwell, toadflax,
wood oxalis, bird's-foot trefoil, lythrum, anemone, potentilla,
tormentilla, cranesbill, wild vetch, primula, violet, squill,
forget-me-not, orchises, lily of the valley, and indeed any
neat wildings of small growth found in damp woodlands
and marshy grounds. Plants of dry texture, such as heaths,
wild thyme, and others found on sandy banks and road-
sides, will not do so well; but all of those above-named will
associate together in the same soil and a damp atmosphere,
and they are all of a similar succulent texture, and exquisitely
beautiful.

For a drier atmosphere, and a soil composed chiefly of
sandy peat, very old mortar, and a good sprinkling of
potsherds and fragments of limestone, the most suitable
would be the pretty heaths, especially *Erica tetralix*, the
common ling or "heather," the lovely harebell, wild thyme,

tormentilla, toadflax, ivy, rest-harrow, bladder campion, cranesbills, hawkweeds, and that most elegant of spring flowers the stitchwort. Neatness of habit and gaiety of colour are the necessary qualifications, and any wild flowers met with in rambles may be carried home for planting under glass, but it will always be preferable to have them planted before they are in bloom; and it will be best to remove them tenderly with a little of their native soil attached to their roots. No one who may devote a little time and care to the stocking of a case with such gems will ever regret it; and the exercise of but ordinary judgment will ensure success. Then you will have a scene that will repay you for your attentions, and that will every day suggest something green and sunny to the mind, and give to many a page of poetry a new and higher meaning than it ever before presented to your mind. You will certainly read "The Daisy" of Burns, the "Wild Flowers" of Campbell, the "Wood-side Sketches" of Bryant and Brainard, the glorious primeval pictures of our old English poets, and the hearty rustic songs of our dear Shakspere, with a new pleasure; you will mark many a page in Spenser, and Thomson, and Clare, and Carrington, and revel in the fine apostrophe of Pollok, with which I shall here quit the subject.—

> "Ye flowers of beauty, pencilled by the hand
> Of God, who annually renews your birth,
> To gem the virgin robes of nature chaste,
> Ye smiling-featured daughters of the sun!
> Fairer than queenly bride by Jordan's stream,
> Leading your gentle lives retired, unseen,
> Or on the sainted cliffs of Zion's hill
> Wandering, and holding with the heavenly dews,
> In holy revelry, your nightly loves,
> Watched by the stars, and offering every morn
> Your incense grateful both to God and man."

LISTS OF PLANTS,

SUITABLE FOR WARDIAN CASES.

In the vase described by Dr. Allman, are the following:
—"In the centre a *Chamærops humilis*, the dwarf palm of
the south of Europe; covering the base of the ground at
its stem, are the delicate and beautiful little ferns, *Hymen-
ophylium Tunbridgense* and *H. Wilsoni*, while *Adiantum
capillus-veneris*, *A. formosum*, *Asplenium marinum*, *Pteris
longifolia*, *Scolopendrium vulgare*, *Aneimia fraxinifolia*, *Cassebeera hastata*, and the beautiful *Trichomanes speciosa*,
are other forms of ferns whose variously shaped fronds contrast well with one another. Under the shadow of the ferns,
several *Jungermanniæ* grow luxuriantly, and the *Oxalis acet-
osella* thrives wonderfully in the company of its cryptogamic
neighbours, while *Lycopodium denticulata* and *L. Stoloniferum* surround the whole with a perennial hedge of verdure.
Beside these, *Maxillaria rufescens*, an epiphytical Orchid
has attached itself to the rough bark of a piece of suspended
elder branch, and in order that no space may remain un-
employed, the husk of a cocoa-nut has been filled with
earth, and hung in the dome at the top, and from this
may be seen descending the graceful fronds of various pendulous ferns and lycopodiums."

In a case fashioned in imitation of the Crystal Palace,
and measuring in extreme width five feet, and in the central transept a height of five feet, each wing being two
feet high, the following were planted:—In the centre
Chamærops humilis. At its base some dwarf ferns and
lycopods, such as Wilson's filmy fern, the true maiden-
hair, *Adiantum capillus-veneris*, *Asplenium marinum;* the
lovely little bladder ferns, *Cystopteris fragilis*, and *C.*

alpina; with *Lycopodium stolonifera, formosa, denticulata,* and *apotheciæ.*

In the left wing specimens of *Lastrea cristata, L. filix-mas,* the lovely hart's tongue, *Scolopendrium vulgare,* of which there are at least twenty-five distinct varieties; *S. vulgare proliferum* being very desirable as a diminutive curiosity: it bears little plants on its fronds. On the right of the hart's tongue, *Osmunda regalis,* the most renowned of British ferns.

In the right wing the graceful Lady fern, *Athyrium filix-fœmina,* with plumes of verdant feathers. At her feet the common polypody, *Polypodium vulgare;* the commonest and most easily cultivated, and, with two or three exceptions, the most beautiful and distinct of all the British ferns. Another polypody, *P. dryopteris,* rises from the hollow below it: it has one clear stem, with three branching divisions of the frond; the colour a most refreshing green, and the whole aspect of the plant distinct and elegant. The common brake, *Pteris aquilina,* and *Lastrea spinulosa,* complete the planting on this side.

For covering the diversified surface, and filling the hollows of the rock-work, the following were used:—Spleenworts, the adder's tongue, *Asplenium lanceolatum, A. trichomanes,* and *Trichomanes radicans,* are low-growing ferns that delight in the moist air of a Wardian Case; and among flowering plants, the pretty *Drosera rotundifolia,* marsh pennywort, ground ivy, hound's tongue, wood oxalis, rosy oxalis, (a border-flower,) germander speedwell, and common small-leaved ivy.

A SELECTION OF FLOWERING PLANTS,

Sufficient for a Wardian Case six feet long, three feet six inches wide, and three feet high.

Gesneria Suttonii,	scarlet,	2ft.	0in.
Gesneria splendens,	scarlet,	2	6
Gesneria tubiflora,	white,	3	0
Gesneria faucialis,	scarlet,	2	6
Gloxinia speciosa,	blue,	0	8
Gloxinia rubra,	rosy crimson,	0	8
Gloxinia Cartonii,	pink,	0	8
Gloxinia candida,	white,	0	6
Gloxinia violacea,	violet,	0	8
Gloxinia speciosa alba,	blue and white,	0	6
Achimenes longiflora,	blue,	1	6
Achimenes grandiflora,	rosy purple,	2	0
Achimenes picta,	scarlet spotted,	2	0
Achimenes rosea,	rose colour,	1	0
Sinningia guttata,	cream spotted,	1	0
Drymonia punctata,	white-spotted creeper.		

PLANTS FOR SUSPENSION.

Æschynanthus pulchra major, Hoya bella, Torenia Asiatica, Cereus frageliformis, C. Mallisonii, Mesembryanthemum barbatum, M. Floribundum, M. inclaudens, M. rubrocinctum; Achimenes and Orchises may be added.

A SELECTION OF THE MOST SUITABLE FERNS.

Tall—Pteris aquilina, vespertilionis, Lastrea decomposita, Davallia canariensis, Goniophlebium sepultum, Gymnogramma calomelanos, Asplenium bulbiferum, Nephrodium molle, Adiantum formosum Onychium lucidum, Polystichum falcinellum, Polypodium dryopteris. *Dwarf*—Adiantum cuneatum, concinnum, hispidulum, affine, assimile,

Asplenium odontites, obtusætum, ebeneum, Cassebeera hastata, Cheilanthes profusa, Doodia aspera, caudata, Davallia pulchella, Polypodium reptans, Lomaria nuda.

PENDANT AND CLIMBING FERNS.

Lygodium scandens, palmatum, hastatum, Goniophlebium latipes, loriceum, Cheilanthes spectabilis, Nothochlæna tomentosa, (tender,) Davallia pentaphylla, Asplenium flabellifolium.

FOR SURFACING.

Lycopodium cuspidata, densa, denticulata, Martensii, stolonifera, and Willdenowii.

THE WALTONIAN CASE.

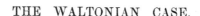

"No works indeed
That ask robust, tough sinews, bred to toil,
Servile employ; but such as may amuse,
Not tire, demanding rather skill than force."

COWPER.

EFERENCE has been made in a preceding page to the possibility of applying heat to a Wardian Case, with a view to extend its uses; I will now very briefly describe a special form of plant case, the invention of Mr. Walton, of Surbiton, known as the Waltonian Case, in which the principle of a heated plant-house is brought to perfection. Strictly speaking, it is not a Wardian Case at all, but a propagating pit—in fact a hot-house suited to the drawing-room; and it is of such practical value, and withal so simple in structure and management, that it may be accepted as an adjunct to the very best cultural contrivances, as it will also be found the most efficient scheme the inexperienced lover of flowers can adopt.

Mr. Walton himself never struck a cutting before he invented the case for himself; but after setting his first case to work, he learned to perform operations that in the ordinary way require years of tuition and experience. Now that the best form, the best measurements, and the exact

details of construction have been determined by experiment, no one, however previously ignorant of ordinary gardening operations, need find it difficult to produce an abundance of stock for the garden, the greenhouse, or the window; for it may be a hothouse, an intermediate house, or a cool pit, just as you please, by a very simple regulation.

The Waltonian Case is fashioned in the style of a garden-frame, the framework being of wood, with side and top lights, a boiler and lamp for supplying heat, and a tray

of sand on which the pots are placed. The annexed figures are drawn from one which I have in use, supplied me by Mr. West, of Surbiton, who is the original maker of the cases, to whom, indeed, we are indebted for many improvements based on Mr. Walton's first idea, and the suggestions of that eminent horticulturist, Mr. Donald Beaton.

As this description must be brief, I will at once refer the reader to the perspective view of the structure, closely stocked with seeds and cuttings, as it adorns my study window at the moment of writing this. The framework is of wood, and may be either plain deal, as mine is, or any ornamental wood with elegant mouldings. The front and the two ends are fitted with glass; the back is wholly of wood; and on the top are two lights laid on loosely. There is room inside for thirty-two four-inch pots, in four rows of four each, under each light, and these pots stand on a thin layer of silver-sand kept constantly damp, and heated by the boiler immediately beneath it. The lamp in front is a common tin one, burning colza oil, and the cost of working is barely a shilling a week. The lamp is understood to burn eight hours, but I find that I can, if

No. 1.

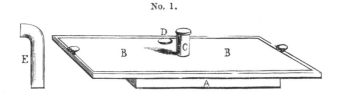

necessary, so trim it that it will burn twelve, or even fourteen; so that five minutes twice a day is all the attention the case ordinarily requires.

Having glanced at it so far, let us now take the case to pieces. The top lights lift off without troubling with hinges, hooks, or attachments of any kind. They are simple squares of glass let into a zinc binding, and with a ring by which to lift them. This plan allows them to be shifted to give air to any extent that may be necessary. Having removed these, we find the pots standing on clean damp sand. When the pots are removed, it is an easy matter to lift out the whole of the heating apparatus by means of the two handles attached to the zinc tray, and its appearance is that in figure 1. The upper tray B B, is an inch deep, and in this the sand, an inch deep, is evenly

spread all over. Attached to it is the boiler A, which is
in reality double, one portion enabling the hot air and
smoke of the lamp to circulate around the tank, and
escape by means of the flue D, to which the funnel E is
attached when in operation, the tank itself being filled by
means of the vapour-tube C, on which a cap fits to prevent
any excessive escape of steam. The boiler holds about two
quarts of water. If we turn the tray upside-down, we
have the appearance presented in figure 2, where F is the
boiler, and G the entrance to the hot-air chamber, into
which the flame of the lamp enters when the case is at
work.

Replacing the tray, it will be seen that the hole in the
boiler fits over the box which contains the lamp. The

No. 2.

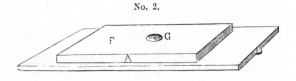

flame of the lamp plays upon the inside tank, and the
smoke escapes by means of the flue G, which conducts it
out through the back of the case, quite away from the
plants. Practically speaking, there is very little smoke,
and whatever soot forms inside the hot-air chamber flakes
off and falls on the lamp, so that in these respects the
case is self-acting, and cleanses itself. The exact measurements of these several parts are, in the case I am describing,
as follows:—Length of the tray B B, thirty-four inches and
a half; breadth, seventeen inches. As the pots stand inside
the tray and the latter fits the frame, there is therefore
a working space for plants of five hundred and sixty square
superficial inches. Depth of the boiler A, two inches. The
entire case measures outside along the front, thirty-six inches
and a half; from back to front, eighteen inches and a half.

The price of this size and make is forty-eight shillings.

When placed in a window or greenhouse, light is admitted only at the top, but the case might be made with lights at the back, to suit a low window, and additional light would be obtained. But as the chief use of the Waltonian Case is to raise seeds and strike cuttings, a partial admission of light is usually sufficient.

In managing a Waltonian Case, it is important that the sand should be kept constantly moist, or the heat will not rise freely, but any excessive moisture may lead to damping off. It is a good plan to sprinkle a little silver-sand over the surface of the soil in pots containing cuttings, as this is a great safeguard against damping; it is also important to strike cuttings, and indeed to sow seeds in *small* pots for such a pit—the smaller the pots the greater the safety. Those which require the greatest amount of heat must be placed towards the centre, immediately over the lamp, to be succeeded by others as soon as they are sufficiently started to be moved towards the sides. I find it a good plan for lessening trouble to keep one side partially open, and the other quite close, and to keep a regular shift from the close to the open side, as the plants make root, and demand more air. The work of re-potting and hardening off is as simple as in any other form of tank-bed—the great point being to shift them before they get drawn through close confinement with bottom-heat. Watering must be regularly attended to, and the water must be of the same temperature as the air of the case. The pots may be removed for watering, and drained well before being returned to the case; though I use a fine rose, and water them as they stand, so as to irrigate the sand as well as the plants; and if the sand gets a little too moist, I get rid of it by a little extra ventilation.

When set to work, it is really astonishing how much may be done with a Waltonian Case. It is a little plant factory, in which seeds and cuttings of all kinds may be started, and carried so far with the aid of bottom-heat,

that they may be safely hardened off for the greenhouse or the window, or, during spring, for planting out in the garden. It has many advantages over a common hotbed. In the first place, we are certain of heat, and can regulate temperature from any degree up to nearly 90°; the ordinary temperature, with a partial admission of air and the lamp freshly trimmed, being 75° to 80°. It requires an experienced hand to make up a hotbed with dung that shall give a steady heat for any length of time, and with the most experienced accidents are not at all uncommon, such as damping off, burning up, failure of heat, and necessity for linings; but here we have simply to fill the boiler, and light the lamp, and then keep the case as close and damp as we please, or give air and light according to circumstances. Besides this, there is no soiling of the hands, no wetting of the feet, no anxiety about frosts and mats, and the most serious part of gardening economy is brought within reach of a lady's delicate fingers, and the merest beginner's unripe judgment. The limited size of the case may seem to militate against it somewhat; but though it is not intended for the commercial florist, who must strike cuttings by the thousand, it nevertheless will perform such an amount of work when well managed as to meet the wants of most amateurs who delight in a garden of limited dimensions, or who require the aid of close bottom-heat in connection with a greenhouse or conservatory. Geraniums, fuchsias, calceolarias, everything which comes from cuttings with bottom-heat, may be struck safely, and in quantities sufficient for all ordinary wants; the work of propagation being kept up during winter, and till the close of May, after which time most half-hardy plants may be propagated out of doors, without any artificial heat whatever. In other respects there is no difference in the management of seeds and cuttings in a Waltonian Case and in a common hotbed.

FLORAL ORNAMENTS

FOR THE

TABLE AND WINDOW.

"BRING flowers, young flowers, for the festal board,
To wreathe the cup ere the wine be poured.
Bring flowers! they are springing in wood and vale,
Their breath floats out on the southern gale,
And the touch of the sunbeam hath waked the rose,
To deck the hall where the bright wine flows."
MRS. HEMANS.

NUFF-TAKERS usually find a welcome everywhere; they never get snubbed, and are always familiar in the first three minutes of conversation. The "pinch" is a talisman, it introduces folks to each other, smooths away any discordant feeling, and perhaps the sneeze that follows explodes any angry word that would otherwise have carried bitterness; but the gift of a few flowers will make any one your friend. The most granite-hearted misanthrope cannot withstand those fragrant pouting lips of coral, those eyes of azure, those nodding leaflets, that never shrink or blink at the hardest, sternest, most stony, grey-eyed hater of everything and everybody.

It would be rather a difficult matter to sum up all the social qualities of flowers. Do we not always feel welcome when, on entering a room, we find a display of flowers on the table? Where there are flowers about, does not the hostess appear glad, the children pleased, the very parrot

garrulous, at our arrival; the whole scene and all the personages more hearty, homely, and beautiful, because of those bewitching roses, and brugmansias, and pavonias, and mignionette? Assuredly, of all simple domestic ornaments flowers must have the first place.

"Better hang a wild rose over the toilette than nothing," says Leigh Hunt; "the eye that looks in the glass will see there something besides itself, and acquire something of a religious right to respect itself, in thinking by how many objects in the creation the bloom of beauty is shared."

Speaking of breakfast in summer, the same prince of essayists says "Set flowers on your table, a whole nosegay, if you can get it, or but two or three, or a single flower; —a rose, a pink, nay, a daisy. Bring a few daisies and buttercups from your last field walk, and keep them alive in water; and preserve but a bunch of clover, or a handful of flowering grass—one of the most elegant as well as cheap of nature's productions—and you have something on your table that reminds you of the beauty of God's creation, and gives you a link with the poets and sages that have done it most honour. Put but a rose, or a lily, or a violet on your table, and *you and Lord Bacon* have a custom in common; for that great and wise man was in the habit of having the flowers in season set upon his table—morning and, we believe, noon, and night; that is to say, at all his meals; for dinner, in his time, was taken at noon; and why should he not have flowers at all his meals, seeing that they were growing all day? Now, here is a fashion that shall last you for ever, if you please; never changing with silks and velvets, nor dependent upon the caprice of some fine gentleman or lady. The fashion of the garments of heaven and earth endures for ever, and you may adorn your table with specimens of their drapery—with flowers out of the fields, and golden beams out of the blue ether."

Now it would be sheer conceit on my part, were I to assume that my readers need any persuasions to adopt the practice of adorning the inside of the house with flowers; for who is there that does not rejoice in a bright boquet, or a vase of newly-gathered roses, or a window screened with fresh foliage and pyramids of bloom? Children are always busy in making posies for mamma; little Emily gets clever in arranging them; flower-stands come home in the carrier's cart, and all are impatient to see them filled with their glorious burden, and the good old soul who gets ready that same carrier's breakfast, ere he sallies out into the

hot dusty road, has her box of mignionette and her jug
filled with wallflowers, and the smoked mantel in her little
kitchen is smothered with dry grasses, with a sprig of
asparagus berries in the midst, while the window of her
parlour, where every Saturday she exhausts her strength
in polishing the old mahogany table and the spinnet that
her grandmother excelled in playing, opens on a garden
that brims over with verdure, and spangles, and odours
that keep her heart alive in the practice of homely virtues.

You who have gardens may multiply your enjoyments
of them a hundred-fold, by keeping in mind the genial
suggestion of Leigh Hunt. Make the most of every ray
of light that falls out of heaven to bless you at the window,
there you may woo beauty, and have it nod to you in a
hundred forms; with a pair of scissors you may, every
morning, cull a posy for the breakfast table; you may make
the tables, and the mantel-pieces, and the quiet recesses of
your rooms gay at all times, and the whole atmosphere of
the house as odorous of flowers, as it is already morally
sweet with the interchange of love's language, and the
expressions of high emotions of the heart.

There are many ways in which cut flowers may be preserved, both with and without suitable appliances. In spring
time you may delight yourself by culling a few violets—
which I will never be without, as long as I can keep
a rod or two of garden ground—and placing them in a
glass dish, in which there is a little wet silver-sand. The
short stems stuck into the sand get sufficient moisture, and
a glass over the whole confines the fragrance, so that whenever you are inclined to inhale a full breath of unadulterated
violet perfume, you have but to lift off the glass, and enjoy
it to your heart's content. In the same simple way any
short-jointed flowers may be preserved for a considerable
time; the partial shade, and the confinement of moisture
secured to them by the glass, preserves their beauty and
fragrance, sometimes even for a fortnight, but the most

fragile will, in this way, continue fresh and beautiful for at least a week.

An extension of this idea is carried out in an invention called the Elizabethan Vase, but which is, of course, not necessarily made in Elizabethan designs, but may take Grecian, Etruscan, or other forms, according to the fancy of the maker and the purchaser. The vase is covered with wire-work and a glass shade, and thus becomes a sort of Wardian Case, not for the *culture,* but for the *preservation* of flowers.

The principle of a vase for cut flowers requires that it should

have a groove or gutter all round the upper edge, to receive the glass shade, and wholly exclude the atmosphere. Within the vase may be constructed in any way most suitable for supporting the flowers, and if there is any convenient way of introducing a little silver-sand, into which to insert their stems, the better. When the flowers have been arranged, and the glass shade put on, a little water should be poured into the groove, around the glass, to render it air-tight. The advantages are evident, a moist air surrounds the flowers, and they continue beautiful and fragrant for weeks; and

whenever it is desired to inhale their fragrance, the glass
may be lifted off, and *kept off* for a considerable time without
injury, the damp sand sustaining them against the exhaustive
influence of the atmosphere. Another advantage of this kind
of vase is that, as the flowers do not stand in water at all,
they may be safely moved about, whereas in the ordinary
way of sticking them in vessels of water, they fade quickly,

their stems putrefy, and instead of enjoying their fragrance,
we are nauseated with their putrescent exhalations.

A still more efficient invention for cut flowers, is that now
coming into use at the flower shows, and which is known
as the "Pyramidal Boquet Stand;" the invention of Mr.
Daniel Stead, of Huddersfield; supplied in London by Messrs.
Henderson, of St. John's Wood. This is a most ingenious
contrivance for effecting the double object of *preserving* and
displaying the flowers to the highest advantage; it is very

philosophical too in its construction, for though it holds water, there is no need for the water to be frequently changed, and there is none of that rapid decay below, and exhaustion above, which always takes place when flowers are plunged into ordinary vessels.

The Boquet Stand consists of a pyramidal cylinder of metal, pierced with holes at uniform distances, and within it is another cylinder fitting so as *nearly to touch* the outer one, and with just enough space between to receive the stalks of the flowers which are inserted in the holes. At the top of the outer cylinder is a tubular orifice, stopped with a small tube, reaching to the bottom of the cylinder. The small tube is lifted out, and a little water poured into the central bore or tube, and then the small tube is again inserted, and a little water poured into that also. The flowers are then inserted according to the fancy of the decorator; and as each flower should have no more than an *inch of stem*, they sit close to the outer cylinder, and make a continuous pyramid of colours. The stems touch the inner cylinder, and by the process of capillary attraction, get from it just enough moisture, without being actually wet, as serves to sustain their freshness of colour and odour. Nothing can be more simple in use, though so thoroughly philosophical in construction, as this Boquet Stand. Flowers may be cut singly from trusses, and every *single bloom* will show to advantage, to greater advantage indeed than *trusses* on any other plan, because being set out flat on the green metal surface, the whole of the petals are fully displayed. I find that most of the flowers last a fortnight in it; a pyramid of scarlet geraniums only, or asters, pansies, and verbenas, all of which may be cut so as not to be missed from the borders, make a glorious show on the table, and one that may be kept up by replenishing only once a week such as show any signs of shabbiness. Chrysanthemums in regular rows of the same colour, with a fine bunch at top, is another good display, so is a mass of pansies with a row of white asters around the bottom; in fact you may turn to artistic account whatever you have, and by cutting *single blooms* out of trusses, the poorest bed or border, or even a few pots, will make a show without detriment to the source of supply; but where there is a well-kept garden, as there is to every Home of Taste, every table in every room may have its bright boquet. You may dress with flowers at your side, eat, read, talk, romp, lounge, meditate—wherever you are, and however occupied, flowers are wholesome companions, and Stead's Boquet Stand just the thing in which to preserve and display them. I must, however, not quit the subject without a protest. They are not made as elegantly as they might be. Mine is mounted on a turned mahogany stand, which is destitute of design, and *pimping* in dimensions, and I shall not be happy till I have it mounted on a more elegant and substantial basis—that, however, is a matter of taste, easily rectified, and does not affect the *principle* of the invention.

When you have secured a boquet for the drawing-room, you may turn your attention to the windows, and flowers will help you to screen off intrusive eyes, or an ugly outlook, or to improve a fine view; and there is no end of devices by which to make a lover's bower of a window, and at the same time create a recreative employment, replete with successional delights.

A well-filled flower-stand is a noble window ornament, and one on which we need say but few words. Lightness and elegance of outline are to be studied in choosing them, and no little care must be exercised to keep them gay at all seasons. It is a folly to suffer plants to pass all their days in such receptacles; their proper use is to exhibit fine specimens of blooming plants; and of these, greenhouse exotics are most suitable. Where a greenhouse is well managed, there will be no difficulty in furnishing the stand with a succession of fairy roses, geraniums, fuchsias, heaths,

genistas, azaleas, camellias, calceolarias, etc.; and it should be the aim of the possessor to preserve the brightness of the scene all through the year. The moment a plant goes out of bloom, it should be removed and its place supplied with another; for as to rearing plants in such situations as many do, it is wasting one of the best opportunities which art affords us for a display of successional pictures. As

well might the actors dress and rehearse before the audience, as a collection of plants be allowed to present themselves in all their preparatory stages to the eye of either visitor or host.

A flower-stand should always be bright, clean, and gay; and since it is a purely artificial arrangement, it should *in itself* be ornamental, with not a trace of *the rustic*, what-

ever there may be of *the rural* about it. Designs and
patterns might here be multiplied without end were they
needed, but they are not. A visit to any of the established
makers of iron and wire ornaments will enable any one to
choose better than a whole sheet of engravings. Such a
house as that of Cottam and Hallen, already referred to,
would afford the largest choice at the most reasonable prices
of flower-stands of all kinds; and all I need do here is just
to hint that strict *appropriateness* is all that need be thought
of (except price) by any purchaser of such a floral necessity.
The size, the form, and the general arrangement must be

such as to adapt it to the place it is to occupy; and if any
special form deserves special notice, it is that which admits
of the grouping of other ornaments, such as vases and fern
shades with it; and this is easily accomplished—with a stand
of an arched form, which admits of additional objects being
placed beneath it.

The mention of Messrs. Cottam and Hallen reminds me
that Crystal Palace Baskets are now in high favour everywhere, and that this house takes the lead in the manufacture
of them in a multitude of choice designs and sizes. The
splendid display of these ornaments at Sydenham has given
a popularity to suspended baskets, and we are all taxing

our inventive powers to find suitable places for them. The rafters in greenhouses and conservatories, the ceilings of corridors and passages, the windows of the house, and the trees that branch over the garden path, are all made available for these suspensionary elegances. Still it is quite possible to *over do* anything, and this aerial gardening needs a bit of a check to prevent it running to an excess that would be ridiculous. In suitable places they are certainly charming; they have a grace of their own; and though nothing suitable can be too good for them, they look well if planted with the commonest bit of ivy, saxifrage, or any ordinary flowering plants that trail about and form flowering festoons. It should be borne in mind, however, that when galvanized wire is used for this purpose, the basket should be made before they are put in the galvanizing trough; if merely made with galvanized wire, every cut end will rust and disfigure the whole; if made of common wire they should have two good coats of dark green or dark brown paint.

Added to their elegance, other advantages of these baskets are that they show off suitable plants to the greatest advantage, and admit of fancy pots, or balls of moss, or masses of bark, in which the plants may be inserted. The most ill-shaped fancy-pot—and fancy-pots seem to me to be always ill-shaped and ugly—looks well when plunged into the surrounding wire; in fact, common pots are out of keeping, and should not be used for them.

As to the planting, that will depend very much on individual taste, and the resources of the garden and the greenhouse. Verbenas, petunias, fuchsias, the Persian cyclamen, most choice annuals of slender growth, common ivy, creeping saxifrage, and common toad-flax may be named as among the plants most readily attainable, all of which tell well in these aerial nests. For a small basket to adorn a staircase or boudoir window, what can be better than the ivy-leaved toad-flax, *(Linaria cymbalaria,)* which is such a favourite of mine, that I begin to fear the public will soon be tired of my repeated recommendations of it. It is abundant everywhere on old walls and ruins; here at Tottenham any number could be procured from the old walls in Lordship Lane, and along the meadows before Bruce Grove. On Blackheath I have seen it in abundance; on Rochester Castle it forms magnificent masses, so it does in many of the stone walls which divide the fields in the north of England; in fact it is to be met wherever there is a scrap of very old mortar to afford it a nidus. Those who are not acquainted with it may recognise it as a delicate trailing plant, with purple twine-like stems, and small dark green ivy-shaped leaves. The blossoms are pale lilac, and of true snap-dragon shape, for it is a snap-dragon, and the prettiest of its family. Planted in October in a small pot in a compost composed of three-fourths silver-sand and old mortar, and one-fourth of any kind of garden mould, it becomes a permanent ornament for the window in a wire basket for the top of a Wardian Case, or for any position where a delicate creeper may be required.

Then we have our established greenhouse trailers, *Maurandia Barclayana*, a gem in its way; the noble *Cobea scandens;* four species of passion flower, the *Rhodochiton volubile*, the tuberous *Tropæolums*, especially the new cross between *Canariensis* and one of the darker kinds lately produced by Mr. Melville, of Dalmeny Park; not forgetting either *Tropæolum Schuermanniana, Brachyceras, Brickwoodii, Jarattii, Pentaphyllum,* and *Tricolorum,* and the old *Peregrinum* itself, which has lately been so finely metamorphosed. For small baskets the trailing cystuses, the variegated mint, and the variegated ground ivy might be used, with the beautiful ivy-leaved geranium and the creeping sedums, the noble *Sedum Seboldii,* not last or least of its family. All of these require roomy baskets and careful training, but not one of them would occasion more difficulty than the most ordinary half-hardy plant intended for the

borders. *Hibbertia grossulariæfolia* is another of the very best of trailers for a suspended basket.

The pretty *Lotus luteus*, a thoroughly hardy perennial, ought not to be forgotten; nor the fine *Æschynanthus*, which would dangle freely all the summer, if grown through the winter in a pot in the greenhouse, in the compost used for ferns, with a mixture of a little dry cow-dung. It would also look well in a wicker-basket filled in with sphagnum, the plant of course turned out of the pot, and daily watered by dipping the whole.

A wire basket is just the thing to show off abronias; they creep gracefully over it, and are so nearly hardy, that a cool frame does as well for them all winter as a greenhouse; and if started in a little leaf mould, any common soil does for their after-growth. In habit these are much like verbenas, and more easily manageable where gardening is not pursued with vigilance; hence abronias commend themselves to amateurs generally.

If a more rustic kind of ornament is required for suspension, baskets of wicker and bark are suitable, but when these are used, it will be found better to fill them with suitable soil, surrounded with a lining of moss. A few rough unbarked logs put together with wooden pegs, or galvanized wire, may soon be converted into a very charming window ornament, and a fine display of ferns may be so obtained with very little trouble. The common polypody looks very beautiful when grown in this way, and indeed is just in its element; for we find it in dark woods crowding the summits of old pollard alders, and finding in the bark and accumulating leaves a soil congenial to it.

To keep such ornaments gay requires not profound skill, but *regular* attention. If pots containing suitable plants are inserted in baskets, they must have a suitable aspect and daily watering, for the evaporation is in such positions very rapid. As the tendrils and trailing stems crowd about the outside of the receptacle, they must be regularly disposed

for effect; and as a rule it will be found better to grow one showy plant in each basket, than to crowd together several of different habit. Masses of one colour generally tell better than mixtures, though when annuals are grown, mixtures are scarcely avoidable. With wicker-baskets and logs containing ferns, ivy, and toad-flax, the best mode of watering is by dipping, and leaving them to drain off before replacing them; and if the roots are well surrounded with moss, these will not require water so frequently as the plants in pots.

Another branch of this department of in-door gardening, is the culture of suitable plants in the form of canopies and parasols. A stout plant of common ivy makes an admirable canopy of this sort, if carried up a central stem, and then trained over a spreading wire frame of a parasol shape. For a juvenile gathering, or the adornment of a ball-room, half a dozen of such canopies would add much to the charm of the scene, and might be placed behind rout seats, and in alcoves, where beauties, fatigued with dancing, take refuge from the light. A row of green canopies formed of alternating plants of ivy, *Calystegia pubescens, Bignonia, Hexacentra Mysoriensis, Abutillon striatum, Rhodochiton volubile,* or any other free-growing trailers brought into fine condition by previous good management in the greenhouse, would convert any lighted drawing-room into a palace of Alladin, and realise more of enchantment than the profoundest spells of a magician, or the fertile invention of an Arabian story-teller, and with very simple materials too. When done with the plants would go to their places on the terrace, the gravel walk, or to occupy glass passages and corridors, which they would help to

"Immantle in ambrosial dark."

Now let us consider the windows, not to shut out the light, but to soften its glare in summer, and in winter shut out the view of leafless stems and leaden skies.

"Hail! holy light, offspring of heaven,
First born."

Without it no flowers, no colours, no life, so "open the

shutters and let in more light," that it may come in through
chequered leafiness, and tinged with rainbow colours.

Where a mansion stands amidst its own grounds, and the

garden and park offer their slopes and wooded knolls, and water scenery, and geometric beds of flowers, there may not be much need of a floral display at the windows; but in suburban villas the views are not always of the finest, and besides the opportunity the window offers for flower culture, it is sometimes advisable to shut out the glances of too curious eyes, and screen ourselves from the glare of the sun, the driving dust, the keen wind in spring, when the blue sky and inviting greenness tempt us to throw up the sash in spite of the lingering north-east; in fact, a bowery window is often desirable for strict utility, as well as for ornament; and nothing is easier than to break the angular outlines with plants, and create a choice garden within and without, such at least as may give a lady full employment, and add vastly to the grace and pleasure of the home.

The shape, dimensions, and aspect of a window will, of course, pretty much determine what is to be done with it. To begin inside, you may, if there is sufficient space, and particularly where a large window is built in a recess, place at each side a neat box lined with lead, and of a depth proportionate to the height of the window-sill. Twenty inches may be considered a good depth; and each box should occupy not more than a third of the window, so as to leave the central space open for the view and the transmission of unbroken light. Then from each box let an elegant trellis of wood or wire—and wire is *always best* —ascend nearly to the top of the glass, and then arch over and meet in the centre. Indeed the centre-piece should be made separately, so as to admit of removal in winter, if desirable, and it may be attached to the two side portions by a little simple carpentering. Most of the climbers require to be shortened in autumn, and the few rods left must be well ripened by the plentiful admission of light and air; and when this is accomplished the upper portion forming the arch of the trellis may be removed, to give full access

to the winter light, which is, heaven knows, scanty enough
in our climate. These boxes, if fully exposed to the daylight,
may be stocked with choice half-hardy plants, which, having
the shelter of the room in cold weather, will do as well
there as in a greenhouse. Against the trellis may be planted
a few tender climbers, such as you cannot well grow outside,
and the best for the purpose will be *Passiflora racemosa*
and *Colvillii*, the one pinkish blue, the other a true blue;
Mandevillea suaveolens, white; *Cobea scandens*, purple;
Bignoica chirere and *jasminoides*, the first deep orange,
the second purple and white; *Jasminum nudiflorum*, yellow,
and very early; *Tacsonia pinnastipula*, rose; and *Maurandya Barclayana*, blue. All of these will, of course,
not be wanted; they are named here, as elsewhere, to give
room for selection, according to the taste of the cultivator
and the space at command. In the absence of any of the
foregoing, or to take their places while they come forward,
major convolvulus, or even sweet peas and Dutch runners,
may be used; but it should be observed that whenever fast-
growing plants are used to cover a space for which something
else is in preparation, they must not be allowed to choke
the slow-growing plants which are to have permanent occupancy. In planting, a bed of crocks must first be laid
down, then rich sandy loam, or well-rotted turves, that
have been frequently stirred over and washed with lime-
water to remove vermin of all kinds. *Tropæolums* may
be used here, so may those quick growers *Eccremocarpus
scaber* and *Lophospermum scandens*, and indeed a grape-vine.
I have eaten many a fine bunch of grapes grown in this
way, but the root was usually outside, and the rods brought
in and trellised over the window greenhouse fashion; and
a lovely spectacle it makes as we catch the daylight through
the emerald of its noble leaves. Indeed, plants seen thus
against the light have the most charming appearance possible; every vein and pore is visible as the light streams
through them, and on the room the light falls beautifully

tinted with a soft green, and chequered with a thousand interlacing shadows.

Outside we must adopt similar tactics. Let us suppose a window facing the south-west, which is the best of all aspects for window gardening. It is a French window, opening in the form of glass doors, and has a handsome balcony, in which there is sufficient room to do something more than swing a cat, though a cat, of course, is never to be swung there. Along the wall, close under the iron balustrade, there is room for a stone trough, which is to be so moulded as to match the mouldings of the balcony; or, if stone should be considered too expensive, a trough of sufficient depth may be formed by means of a few of Hogg's edging tiles, mounted on brick-work. These tiles are obtainable of Mr. Blackett, of Witham, Essex, at a cost of only fourpence halfpenny a yard; they bear the closest resemblance to a stone moulding, and are equally durable. In place of either stone or tile, a wooden trough with a moulded edge may be formed. At each end of the trough may be placed a box, formed terrace or step fashion, that is, rising one foot from the trough, and at the distance of a foot rising again, each step being a distinct compartment for mould and flowers. The walls on either side of the window are to be covered with trellis-work. In filling the trough and side boxes, the first care requisite will be to secure good drainage, and a layer of broken crockery or potsherds will be the best for this purpose. The mould should be light and rich, and, if taken from the garden, it should have been previously well turned over, with an admixture of well-rotted dung and silver-sand. When filled, the trough may be stocked with choice annuals and herbaceous plants, and the side boxes with plants of larger growth, or with very neat evergreens. Supposing such a work to be commenced in spring, seeds might be sown of *Collinsia bicolor*, *Nemophilas*, *Silenes*, Virginia stock, ten-week stock, sweet alyssum, mignionette, Clarkia of sorts, gilias, annual lupines,

and candytufts; and as any of these grew shabby, their places might be supplied with flourishing plants in bloom or annuals of a second sowing picked out from pots or the garden borders. The side boxes would look well if some

hearty anarbas and rhododendrons were plunged into them, or shrubby plants of holly, box, or Portugal laurel. The lattice-work may be speedily covered with such cheap but

o

truly elegant climbing annuals as the dark major tropæolum, the major convolvulus, and sweet pea; and while these hide the temporary nakedness of the land, white jasmine, *Clematis cerulea*, common white clematis, and *Passiflora cerulea* may be coming on to take permanent occupancy. *Calystegia pubescens* would also do well, but would have to be planted in a pot and plunged, or it would ramify through the whole of the soil, and monopolise trellis, window, and balcony, in spite of knife and shears, for it is an inveterate underground worker.

For additional embellishment to the borders, or to take the place of the first lot of annuals, the greenhouse would supply verbenas, geraniums, lobelias, nolanas, Brompton stocks, calceolarias, balsams, cupheas, petunias, schizanthus, and senecios. Since it would be better not to dim a scene so close to the house by the spectacle of plants in slow progress towards perfection, it would be better to grow on all the plants required in pots, till just about to bloom, and then plunge the pots where the flowers are required; on this plan you need never be without a gay show, from the first of January to the thirty-first of December, for no sooner would the greenhouse plants come out in autumn, than you would plunge in a few potted dwarf hardy shrubs, some wallflowers to add their cheerful winter green, patches of stonecrop, alyssum, and chrysanthemums, and between the plants on the edge of the border you would plant clumps of crocus, snowdrop, and early tulip; or, if the border was well filled with plants for the winter, these also could be brought on in pots, and plunged out in spring, just in time to add their lustre to your window garden.

It will be obvious that any aspect, and any kind of window may be ornamented on this plan, with such modifications as the case may require. An east aspect will be too cold for the majority of choice plants; a north aspect too dark, and frequently a due south aspect too likely to scorch all before it, considering how walls reflect the heat, and generally

how shallow would be the soil about the plants; yet the worst aspect, and the worst position, need not prove fatal to the enterprise. Ivy and Virginian creeper grow in any aspect, and under the most careless treatment, and the shears will always keep them within bounds. The evils of a south look out may be obviated by liberal watering, and a blind fitted outside to give shadow when necessary; and as to the east and north, there are plenty of hardy things that will brave the keenest winter winds; in fact most evergreens do best when fully exposed, and late-blowing flowers do as well in such a position as anywhere. The chief objection to north and east aspects for this kind of gardening, is that some of the choicest climbers would be likely to fail, such as the blue clematis, the passion flower, jasmines, and most roses. Yet even here we need not be utterly beaten, the *Félicité Perpétuelle* is a rose that does well in any aspect; *Jean Desprez* will also face the north without blenching; and for plunging out during summer only, those quickest of climbers *Lophospermum scandens*, *Eccremocarpus scaber*, and *Maurandya Barclayana*, would do, except in very bleak and exposed situations.

As to the fittings of a window where there is no balcony, a stone or wood shelf is easily fitted, and with the gnarled branches of an old apple tree, stripped of the bark by means of steam, a very elegant rustic balcony might be made, and this plan might be extended so as to be still more ornamental, if three brick walls, enclosing a space in front of the window, were first erected to the level of the window-sill, and then a bank of earth, sloping down to the garden, built up against it. The walls would form a pit in front of the window, and the top of this pit would form the soil of the balcony garden, to be enclosed by rustic wood-work, and flanked on each side with a trellis of wood, or galvanized wire stretched on frames; and the front of it, towards the garden, would form a slope, either for a smooth turf or for shrubs and flowers. The effect of such an arrangement would be very pleasing if well done, and it would connect the garden with the house, without any violation of the rules of taste. The openings in the rustic wood-work might be planted with verbenas, abronias, or masses of ivy-leaf geraniums, and the creeping habit of these plants would cause them to stream, and, as it were, flow down the sloping bank in rich masses, so that either from the window or the garden, the scene would have a completeness about it, and an elegance quite unique in its way.

Where neither balcony, nor slope, nor trellis, would be deemed advisable, the old refuge of potted plants would be left, and a common flower-pot being scarcely as gay a thing as it should be for such a position, the pots containing the plants should be plunged into ornamental pots, with a lining of wet moss between the two, to prevent the scorching of the roots in hot weather. Pots are now made, in a variety of good designs, by Blackmore, of Praed Street, Paddington; Mortlock, of Oxford Street; Copeland, of Stoke-upon-Trent; Messrs. Hunt, of Pimlico; and, I think, Mr. Willmot, of Lewisham; and other makers scattered up and down the country. Some small pots which I have in use for creepers, inserted in wire baskets, are made of a dark ware, coloured to imitate bark, the whole of the pot being formed in open work, covered with green vine leaves and tendrils. Where they came from I know not; they are *really* ornamental, and that is more than I can say of, at least, half the fancy pots offered for sale at Covent Garden, and elsewhere. Fancy pots should only on exceptional cases be filled with mould; it is always better to drop into them the common pots in which the plants have been grown; and if the fancy pots are not made in an open pattern, to fill round the inner pot with moss. In fact plants on window-sills, in a south aspect, should always be so treated, either plunged into fancy pots, or into common pots of a size larger than those containing the plants, and the space between filled with moss, or, if that is not handy, silver-sand will do. If not so treated, do not express surprise if they go out of bloom before their time; if they shrink and wither by quick degrees, and at last become mere scare-crows, fit only for the rubbish-heap.

There are not twelve greenhouse plants to be found out of the hundreds we may have to choose from, that can long withstand the summer sun beating on the exposed pot which contains their roots, assisted by the heat reflected and conducted from a white window-sill, a burning-hot wall,

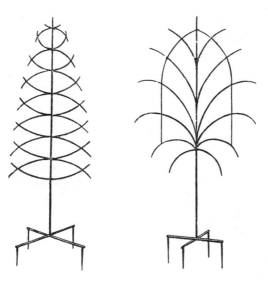

a mass of glass, and adjacent wall and buildings; in fact we must neither boil nor bake our window pets, but plunge them into moss, keep them cool and moist, trim off shabby blooms as fast as they appear, administer water liberally in hot weather, and allow *none* to stagnate about their roots, and they are sure to prosper, and preserve their beauty to the last. The baking and soddening process may be seen in operation everywhere in the suburbs of London during summer, and the folks who practice it are always crying

out about the expense of flowers, the *impossibility* of keeping
them, unless you also keep a nursery; whereas it is only
their own ignorance and stupidity that makes the thing
either impossible or expensive.

This department of window gardening may be extended
considerably by the culture of climbers on trellises in pots.
Trellises and wire-work designs of light character suit for
such climbers as *Passiflora*, *Rhodochiton*, *Cobea scandens*,
the tuberous *Tropæolums*, *Maurandyas*, and fuchsias of pendant habit.

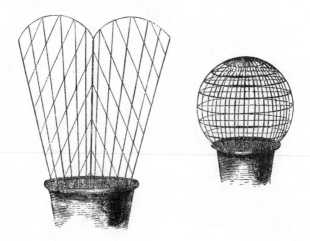

Fitted to fancy pots, and covered with climbers, such
trellises make noble window and terrace ornaments. The
choice kinds of *Tropæolum* are among the best of plants for
the purpose. To carry them over the entire surface it is
necessary to watch the young shoots as they make progress,
and lead them regularly. Fine lead wire will be found useful
in all cases where creepers have to be led over trellises.
The thread-like fingers of the *Tropæolum* make the best
effect if trained over the interior of a sphere, but for plants
of stouter growth, such as the pyramidal bell-flower, a flat

and somewhat fan-shaped design will be most suitable.

I ought not to quit this subject of window gardening, without suggesting that sweet-smelling plants ought not to be forgotten in selecting plants for such a purpose. It is delightful to have the odour of mignionette, wallflowers, stocks, and roses wafted to us from the open window, and mingled with the fresh air, such perfumes are as wholesome for the mind as for the body. These, and indeed all other plants mentioned for window culture, may be obtained of the nurserymen, in much better condition, and to flower earlier than if raised by the amateur, except where gardening is carried on in high style, and then the amateur may occasionally beat the nurseryman. But every amateur should include among his window operations the winter culture of mignionette, and he can have no better instruction in this choice work, than is given in the "Journal of the Horticultural Society," which I shall here transcribe, and then quit the subject.

"To flower the mignionette at, or soon after Christmas, the seed should be sown in the beginning of August, in pots of any convenient size. The soil should be good loam, moderately enriched with rotten dung, and kept open by a pretty liberal intermixture with old mortar or lime rubbish. It is essential that the pots be thoroughly drained, and upon the drainage a handful (more or less, according to the size of the pots) of one year old pigeons' dung should be placed. After sowing the seed, set the pots in a frame or pit, where they may be covered by the lights in rainy weather. As the plants increase in size they should be gradually thinned, ultimately leaving three or five in each pot The principal point to be attended to now, is judicious watering; by this is meant giving water only when the plants really require water, and then in sufficient quantity to moisten the whole of the soil. Pinch off any premature flowers that may appear, keep the pots free from weeds, and far enough asunder to prevent the plants from being crowded; and when they are removed to winter quarters, set them near a glass in an airy situation.

I have recommended, continues Mr. Whiting, who proposes this plan of cultivation, the seeds to be sown in the pots, which is the method I prefer; but if more convenient, a sufficient number of self-sown plants might be taken up and potted, only a few extra should be put in to allow for casualties, as the mignionette transplants badly. The best mignionette I ever saw grow was treated in this way; but as it is not every gardener who can procure pigeons' dung, I may add that guano will be found an excellent substitute. This admirable fertilizer must, however, be applied in a liquid state, and not before the pots have become well filled with roots, when a small quantity of guano, given at intervals of a week or so, will increase the vigour of the plants in an extraordinary degree. A second crop might be sown in the beginning of September, and managed in the same manner. Single plants will attain a large size in six or eight-inch pots, if the main branches are pegged down as they grow, and the flowers are kept pinched off for a time."

On this plan you may enjoy the odour of summer along with the winter scent of roast beef and horseradish. If the last ministers to the social feeling, and confirms us in the love of Christmas, when old hatreds are forgotten, and we join hands to part in friendship with another old year; the first will suggest the dawn of spring,

> When rosy plumelets tuft the larch,
> And rarely pipes the mounted thrush;

A time which is to find us on the look-out for crocuses, and under the inspiration of the blackbird's song, full of fresh schemes for improving and beautifying the garden, in the midst of which we shall meet again in a future chapter.

> We shall tread amongst the blue-bells,
> We shall rest where violets grow.

THE AVIARY.

BIRDS, the free tenants of land, air, and ocean,
Their forms all symmetry, their motions grace;
In plumage delicate and beautiful,
Thick without burden, close as fishes' scales,
Or loose as full-blown poppies to the breeze;
With wings that might have had a soul within them.
                                        JAMES MONTGOMERY.

CHAPTER I.

ALAS! they are "free tenants of the air" only while they elude the clutches of the bird-catcher. Man lays tribute on creation: the poor worm that hides in the sand at the sea-bottom, and the "bonny lark,"

That beats against the sky,
With a canticle that stirs a heart to leap aloft and sing,

are equally brought prisoners, to minister to his bodily appetite or his desire for amusement. Of all the creatures reduced to subjection by man, for pleasure or profit, birds seem to plead the hardest against the transition from a free life in their native haunts, to confinement in wretched cages. And sometimes we are ashamed of our acts, not sufficiently so to turn the poor birds loose again, but enough to set our wits to work to compensate them, if we can, by placing them in circumstances as nearly approaching to freedom as incarceration admits of. We build our Aviaries, and keep the conscience quiet by deluding ourselves into the belief that now they are happy. But they have no free woods wherein to roam at large, no pebbly pools to bathe and drink in, no store of red and white berries to choose from as they will, no insect food of their own choice; and if they half forget the precious freedom they have lost, and once more sing as is their wont, we conclude that we have satisfied the instincts of their nature.

> "Inhuman caught, and in the narrow cage
> From liberty confined and boundless air,
> Dull are the pretty slaves, their plumage dull,
> Ragged, and all its brightening lustre lost."

Still, something may be said in defence of imprisonment, even in this case. It would be worthy of consideration how much of the cultivation of the moral sensibilities we owe to the keeping of household pets; how many refined domestic virtues, how much of the love of things gentle and beautiful springs out of the imprisonment of wild creatures, and the consequent endeavours to soften their lot, in administering to their instinctive necessities. Their gratitude in acknowledgment of kindness, their various and winning ways, their progress under tuition and capabilities for being taught, not to speak of their beauty and companionship, beget a love for them, which cannot but soften the heart, and win the passions from less worthy pursuits. If Jasmin was fired with poetic ardour when he saw the buxom Kitty —type of innocence—feeding doves at the top of a ladder, how much more elevated must Kitty herself have been in ministering to the typical favourites? Who could hope to bring up children so as to insure the development of the gentlest sentiments of our common nature, without the help of a pet bird, or dog, a tame squirrel, or a motherly cat with a brood of helpless kittens? What would Margaret Fuller, in her childish days, have given out of her full heart for the possession of a pair of doves, or something living to lavish her affections upon, in that house which had no toys, no garden, nothing for a child to build its hopes upon?

Who will aver that kindness grows without exercise, pity without objects of compassion, the love and thirst of knowledge without some pleasing causes of excitement, the domestic sentiment without domesticating toys and playthings, and scenes which endear home, and give it interest in the memory when it is home no more; when the grey parrot is remembered as well as the grey cap; or the warm heart, ready in the mission of goodness, traces the first budding of its benevolence to the demands of some poor helpless bird, which the child has saved, and reared, and made its own.

There may be, and there is, cruelty in the indiscriminate imprisonment of helpless creatures, but out of evil springs some amount of good; and if we can reduce the evil, so that at least the good shall overbalance it, we shall be gainers, not utterly to the injury of humbler creatures. The well-disposed may enjoy the possession of tame birds if, by the exercise of a kindly discrimination, they inflict the least injury on those they keep, and leave untouched, uncaged, those that are least able to bear the loss of freedom.

If we are to derive pleasure and instruction from the daily watching and attention which our birds require, we must exercise some skill in providing for their necessities;

not merely as to food and drink, but as to the shapes and sizes of their cages, the influence of seasons and changes of weather on their health, and the adoption of means which may conserve their health and vigour, and give them as large a measure of happiness as imprisonment admits of.

Herein, indeed, lies the truth of the charge of injustice, brought too sweepingly against all who indulge the passion of bird-love. But too many of the gay songsters of the woods are yearly brought from their own mossy haunts to perish miserably through excessive heat in carpeted rooms, or through unseasonable exposure in porches or balconies. Ill-fed, neglected, exposed to colds and heats, buried in dark corners, or flung into an intolerable blaze of sunlight, thousands of these helpless creatures are sacrificed; yet not often without a pang, and, we would fain believe, never wilfully.

> "More offend from want of thought,
> Than offend from want of feeling;"

and while we deplore the ignorance which leads to such results, we must avoid making a general protest against the taming of birds altogether.

The amiable William Kidd, the first of advisers as well as the most delightful of gossipers on bird-keeping, says, "People *do* and *will* keep them, and I write to shew how birds already confined may be comparatively reconciled to their solitude. If they are doomed never again to rise on wing, I would win their hearts by kindness, to take some little pleasure in things nearer the earth. I would procure them what they most delight in, administer a bath, give them a flight in a spare room, play with them; in a word, I would study as much as possible to efface the recollection of scenes passed in their early youth in the fields of ether." The nature to which such feelings are common has not been dwarfed or brutalized by bird-keeping; austerity never had a home in the heart of a naturalist.

How many an invalid or lonely sorrower has lost her one

pet, or rather her one faithful companion, through the heedless freak of a servant, or the teasing propensity of some wanton visitor, who, while gratifying an idle whim, knew not he was destroying an innocent life, a life dear at least to one who could appreciate its simplicity. Yet we would fain believe that kindness is very universal, and that if it need development, nothing will so certainly insure its growth as the introduction to our homes of creatures demanding its exercise, and repaying us for it in a thousand winning ways—in beauty of form and plumage, in gentleness of disposition, and in glorious song.

> "Each day I listen'd to thy varied song,
> Pleased with the labours of thy little tongue;
> Sweet was thy song when morning shed its ray,
> Sweet was thy song when evening closed the day;
> When care oppress'd me, thou couldst bid it flee,
> When friends were far, I found a friend in thee."
>
> *Fawcett.*

It must be confessed that an Aviary is an expensive luxury, whether on a large or small scale; but the lover of birds may do much to gratify his taste without the necessity of a heavy outlay. An Aviary that a lady would delight in, must be fitted up in a conservatory; or a separate structure of elegant design, accessible from the house at all times without exposure to the weather. A spare room may easily be converted into one, if its situation be to the south or south-east, or if visited for a few hours daily by the sun. Ventilation and a good share of daylight at all seasons are essential. Where these requisites are not attainable, it is better not to attempt bird-keeping.

Excellent Aviaries are sometimes fitted up by ladies in small rooms, looking over gardens, or adjoining the breakfast parlour or study, by means of a glass door, and a second inner door of wire netting; and on this plan of procedure the expense is very much reduced; wire netting for the windows, with perches and feeding-boxes being all that is

required, except the birds themselves. A room of this kind, fitted with perches at various heights, or, better still, with one or two dead trees, and some living shrubs in boxes, may be made to render a very tasteful exhibition, not certainly of still life, but of active bustle, cheerfulness, and drollery. A good addition to such an Aviary would be a large box planted with grass, moss, and such weeds as groundsel, plantain, and chickweed, of which the garden will usually supply more than is required, for bird-food makes a conspicuous figure among the garden weeds. A fountain may be introduced with good effect, and the masonry so fitted as to afford convenience for the birds to drink, thus obviating the necessity of water-troughs or glasses.

My kind friend Lady B—— has converted a large conservatory on the east side of her house into an Aviary; the opening glass door being fitted with wire gauze, and the whole of the glass with blinds outside, to screen off, when necessary, excessive sunlight. Within, it is furnished in a truly tasteful manner, worthy of the fair hands whereon the little favourites delight to perch, and ask for dainties, and submit to be fondled. On one side is placed a sloping bank or miniature garden. Here is a piece of sward well-filled with clover, and a group of evergreens in the midst. Round this runs a narrow border stocked with wallflowers, plantain, ornamental thistles, poppies, groundsel, chickweed, and some varieties of salads. The other portions are covered with clean gravel, except the centre, where stands a fine stone fountain, so designed as to afford convenience for the birds to drink and bathe without encountering the splash of the jet; though some prefer to cling to the scrolls of the jet itself, revelling in the gentle shower-bath. The shelves and feeding-boxes are all rendered ornamental; the flowers get mangled and despoiled, but they are regularly replaced by sinking pots containing new plants; and the brilliancy of the scene is thus kept up, so as to present its gifted owner with a perennial festival of odour, colour, and song.

An Aviary should certainly be an ornamental object, and in its construction there is every opportunity offered for a display of good taste. In the adjoining engraving a design is given for a highly ornamental garden structure, which may be used both as a bird-house and conservatory; one wing being appropriated to the display of choice exotic shrubs, and the other to a collection of British and Foreign birds. The whole may indeed be used as an Aviary, and with the adornment of shrubs and fountains, will present as pleasing a scene within, as the building is attractive without. By its entire appropriation to birds, room is afforded for keeping separate, in ornamental cages, such birds as cannot be allowed the full liberty of the enclosure. To give full effect to this design, it should be worked out on a somewhat large scale. If the elevation is adopted, with all the details given in the figure, the façade will make it worthy of a conspicuous position. The entrances will be at either end, unless considerable depth be given; in which case the entrance may be from the front, with a corridor on each side, screened off from the central aisle by fine wire netting. The dome surmounting the centre may be used as a vinery, or for any choice flowering climbers, and when covered with verdure will add greatly to the beauty of the scene. Stained glass, wood carving, statuary, bronze and filigree work, may all be used abundantly in the embellishment of an elaborate work of this kind, wherein the gayest songsters and chatterers of the tropics may rejoice in a home well adapted to their wants, and the advantageous study of their habits and rare beauties.

The coloured design of Mr. Voyez, is intended only as a summer Aviary, for the embellishment of a lawn. The interlacing branches form the framework, to which is attached within a fine wire netting, the latter painted a gay ochreous yellow, or pale brown. The nests and reeds around the base are happily disposed, and appropriate in character; while the falcon poised above suggests the security of the sheltered inmates of the cage. At the close of the season the birds should of course be removed to winter quarters.

The design might be worked out in metal or wood. If cast in iron, it would require to be appropriately painted or bronzed; if in wood, the general framework might be formed of well-selected tree-loppings, with carved nests at the base, on a firm timber or iron foundation. In any case, it would be well to attach near the summit either a wire with rings, or any other simple contrivance, for the reception of a light blind or screen to shade off excessive sunlight, or give shelter during spring or autumn frosts.

At Knowsley, in Lancashire, an Aviary on an extensive scale has been formed, by an immense extent of wire netting thrown over the tops of trees, and supported by posts or hollow rods, so as to enclose a portion of natural scenery, which is still further adapted to the uses of the birds by the planting of reeds and aquatics, long grass for partridges and larks, spruce firs for pheasants, furze bushes for linnets, and various weeds for the uses of other birds. Catharine of Russia formed an Aviary on a similar plan in that memorable burlesque of taste and despotism, the Hermitage Palace. The Aviary at Kew is perhaps one of the finest generally accessible, and affords admirable opportunities for observing the habits of birds to persons visiting those wonderful gardens. Such extensive operations, however, are not generally within the compass of our suburban friends; and a small building of wire-work, or a conservatory fitted with perches and boxes will, with most of our readers, be the scene of their ornithological studies. Wire netting for Aviary purposes, and Aviaries fitted with every requisite, are manufactured by Messrs. Cottam and Hallen, of Winsley Street, Oxford Street; Messrs. Morton, 9, Basinghall Buildings, Leeds; and Barnard and Bishop, of Norwich.

It must be borne in mind that in stocking an Aviary, granivorous and insectivorous birds can only be associated together during the summer. The seed birds may remain

all winter in the Aviary, but the soft-billed birds must, during that inclement season, enjoy some amount of artificial warmth. Hence it is better either to form a double bird-house, one portion of which admits of being warmed; or, in the absence of such arrangement, the tender birds must be removed to the dwelling-rooms, for if left to winter in any ordinary Aviary, they will infallibly perish. In any case soft-billed birds are difficult to preserve through the winter, and any sudden change of temperature either of heat or cold, is certain death to them. These matters must be thought of in time, and the Aviary constructed so as to afford every facility for the successful management of the collection at all seasons. I cannot do better here than quote the instructions given by Mr. William Kidd, in his new and delightful work on "The Aviary and its Inmates," wherein every detail of the subject is treated in that poetical, though highly practical manner, which distinguishes Mr. Kidd's writings from *all others* on this subject. He says,—

"The proper length of a detached Aviary is eighteen feet; width, twelve feet; height, sixteen feet. Of course, should two Aviaries united in one be required, the proportions will be just, or nearly, double, as regards the length; with a glass door, and a latticed-wire partition across the centre.

In the winter, the latticed-wire should be covered over with green baize, and all draught excluded, as far as is practicable. The ceiling should, of course, be flat; and the external roof shelving from the front backwards. Cover the latter with zinc, and let a gutter of the same material be made, to convey the water from one corner of the roof, at the back, downwards into the ground.

Our building was entirely of wood, with three windows in the centre of the front; equally divided, and boarded above and below. Also, there were two windows at one end of the Aviary, equally divided, and boarded above and below. At the opposite end was a glass door of entrance; immediately over which there was a double window, opening

outwards on hinges.   To protect it, and to prevent the
escape of the birds, a moderately close net-work of galvanized
wire was nailed on, from the inside.   The birds were thus
able to get plenty of fresh air, and to introduce themselves
to their brethren in a state of freedom, who assembled in
numbers on the adjoining trees and branches to join them
in their song.   Our present garden has ever been the resort
of multitudes of these song-birds; and the harmony during
the seasons of spring and summer—not excepting the piping
of the thrushes and blackbirds in the winter months, has
been delightful.

One of the panes at the opposite end of the Aviary should
also be made to open outwards, with hinges.   Let the interior
be lined with wire-work, whereby free ventilation will be
secured.   This is important.   The back of the Aviary should
be entirely of wood, by which means it will more readily
be kept warm and snug.   Let the front be painted white,
with at least three coats; and afterwards ornamented with
double cross-barred lattice-work, painted green; not too close,
but arranged with a due regard to relief or effect.

Between each window, and at the extreme ends of the
windows, let there be upright fluted pillars of wood; which,
though really hollow, appear, when viewed from a distance,
perfectly solid, and important withal.   These pillars should
be strongly painted in green; excepting the plinths (top and
bottom,) which should be white; the facia of stone-colour;
and the ornaments running round the top of the building
of a vandyke pattern—painted green.

With respect to the 'look out' of the little musicians;
this requires some judgment.   There can be no doubt that
they are most in their element (during confinement) when
in the immediate neighbourhood of trees, shrubs, flowers,
and plants.   It will be desirable, therefore, to render the
Aviary as umbrageous as possible; and to have it overarched,
at all events in the summer season, with drooping foliage.
An ivy plant would greatly assist in this matter, and a

honeysuckle; also some fine aucubas, which would soon grow bushy, and look very handsome on either side. A palm and a sycamore tree would also be of rapid growth. The more secluded—except at the front, which must be kept more open—the better on every account. It attracts the wild birds, and tempts them to take up their quarters with you; thus strengthening your own orchestra, and improving the taste of the respective performers. We must ever concede, after all, that nature is the best teacher.

Round all the windows, on the outside, let a miniature balcony be affixed, in which may be placed pots of geraniums, calceolarias, sweet williams, pinks, sweet peas, and other varieties. These, when properly bestowed (not too crowded,) show off your birds to great advantage; for while they sit singing on their perches at the window, their plumage and action will be distinctly visible between the flowers, from one extremity of the garden to the other.

We should recommend that the flooring of the Aviary be of thick tiles, about twelve inches square each, and made of brick earth. This would effectually prevent the entrance of vermin. Let the walls all round the room be cased with floor-cloth, of a white marble vein, with a black pattern on it, in the form of a large diamond. This looks remarkably well, both in summer and in winter, and it can be readily cleaned with a sponge and warm water.

In each of the four corners of the room, about twelve inches from the windows, a square upright pole, fourteen feet long and one inch and a quarter thick, should be let into the floor, and carefully secured by nailing the feet to the ground. To steady these at their summit, square perches of sufficient lengths, and of a quarter of an inch in thickness, should be nailed one upon the top of each. This will form a kind of rail all round the room, leaving the centre open, so as not to interfere with the grand fountain, which will be in the middle. On these lofty perches the birds will, for the most part, roost. Indeed, in the winter, they will always use them for roosting on. The cause is evident. Being immediately below the ceiling, and not exposed to draught, they will sit warmly, cosily, and snugly—defying the most severe frosts.

Through the four square upright poles, round perches, five inches long, and a quarter of an inch thick, should be inserted, at a distance of five inches apart, every alternate perch being let in transversely. This arrangement will prevent the plumage of the birds being unnecessarily dirtied by those which are sitting the one immediately over the other—as they will do in the day-time, when they are singing. Another rail of round perches, a quarter of an inch thick, should run all round the windows; let them be about five inches from, and immediately level with, the bottom of the lower panes.* The birds, by this plan, will be readily and constantly seen from the dwelling-house, and the variety of their colours will be shewn to a great advantage. The beauty of the latter will be materially enhanced by reflection and refraction in the looking-glasses, of which we shall presently speak.

At the back of the Aviary, five inches distant from the wall, a long round perch, a quarter of an inch thick, must run from end to end. Let all the perches be painted over four times at least, in the best green colour, that they may be thoroughly dry before they are taken into use. Round the ceiling there should be a neat moulded cornice, and a narrow skirting-board, painted stone-colour, all round the bottom of the room.

The door of entrance, which should be of glass, must be at one end of the Aviary, and must open outwards; over it the double window before spoken of, also opening outwards. Just within this glass door, let there be constructed a three-sided mahogany framework or partition, fourteen inches deep, having a painted shelving top of wood. The front should form a door, opening *inwards*.

* Support these perches on about half-a-dozen slight iron brackets.

The sides of this partition should be faced with closely-meshed galvanized iron wire, and the door of it never opened until after the outer door has been closed, and *vice versâ.* By adopting this precaution, none of the inmates can escape.

The next thing to be considered is the fountain. This should be of zinc, strongly painted, and its circumference about eighteen inches, with a turnover lip, and .sides gradually shelving downwards to the depth of about four inches. The position of the fountain should be immediately in the centre of the room. To carry off the superfluous water, a waste-pipe should pass through the wooden support of the fountain and under the floor. A second pipe, similarly introduced, would carry off the foul water every morning, by the withdrawal of the plug attached to the bottom of the basin·

The same aperture that conveys away the waste-pipe, will also admit the pipe which is to supply the water, which last must be forced up by high pressure, and regulated in its ascent by a moveable jet. To accomplish this, let a large zinc cistern be fixed immediately over the Aviary, on the outside, and let it be kept constantly filled with spring-water.*

To prevent the possibility of any of the birds being accidentally drowned, and to afford them no facilities for acts of 'self-destruction,' pieces of coral, stone, or crystal rock should be introduced into the water. On these they will stand in security, and, placing themselves immediately under the descending shower, they will lave themselves in the limpid stream at least twice every day, retiring from 'the bath' in a perfect ecstacy of delight.

The birds having performed their ablutions, which they do in the most perfect order, will now necessarily require to make their toilet. And here let us tell our reader, if he has never yet witnessed this sight, he has a rare treat

* Any practical plumber would understand this matter, and would fix the whole at a small cost.

to come. The 'ceremony' observed on such occasions is worthy of royalty itself.

In furnishing them with 'Aids for Reflection,' we should recommend three looking-glasses, each three feet long by eight inches wide. These should be mounted in narrow frames of flat oak, and nailed to the back of the Aviary, just above or nearly level with the long perches. Let them be twelve inches apart. The introduction of these glasses will afford a never-ending source of amusement to all parties concerned, and they will ensure 'respectability of appearance,' at least, among all the inhabitants.

The 'hoppers' or food troughs for the seed birds are made of mahogany, on the principle of a rack, having a moveable slide of transparent glass in front, and a cover or lid with hinges, lifting up at the top to receive the seed. All along the front of these 'hoppers' is a projecting rail, on which the birds sit while eating, and, underneath, three or four round holes, through which they put their heads to get their seed. As the latter is being cracked and eaten, the hull falls to the ground, and a fresh supply descends from above, the apparatus itself being self-supplying.

Four of these 'hoppers' should be suspended on the wall, between and on each side of the looking-glasses. They should be regularly emptied and cleaned out twice every week, as a quantity of dust, etc., is apt to collect in them, thereby spoiling the food. If kept half-filled only, this will prevent waste.

Let the pans for the food of the soft-billed birds be kept always on the ground. We should advise their being made of glass or china, and of a square form.

Let the floor of the room be cleansed *daily*, and always kept well supplied with small and pebbly gravel, well dried, and old mortar well bruised."*

* "The Book of British Song Birds and Aviary Companion." By WILLIAM KIDD, of Hammersmith. London: Groombridge and Sons, 5, Paternoster Row.

Respecting the winter management of the Warblers, Mr. Kidd advises the removal of them about the middle of August to one large separate cage. His own cage for this purpose measured nine feet in length, six feet in height, and three feet six in breadth. It was lined throughout with green baize strained and nailed; the front of the cage only was of wire, the other portions were made of stout deal. A fountain, covered with wire-net to prevent the birds bathing, completed the arrangement. One or two other smaller cages similarly made will be necessary for any birds that prove sulky or quarrelsome; and each cage, whether large or small, must be provided with a green baize curtain to draw down at night, and secure them sufficient warmth. An open fire-place will afford the necessary warmth to the room in which the birds are kept, and will be preferable to any kind of close stove. On this point Mr. Kidd is minute in his instructions, but as space does not allow me to quote further from his pages, even if I were inclined to pirate him by wholesale, I strongly recommend his work on the "Aviary and its Inmates" to every one who may contemplate setting up an Aviary, indeed to every one who loves a bird in a cage or on a tree, for it is a work full of delightful gossip and anecdote, and brimful of most practical instruction. Indeed a lover of birds should consider Mr. Kidd's books as essential portions of the furniture of bird-keeping. His "Treatise on the Canary," and his delightful works on "British Song Birds and Warblers," are portions of our British literature, already rich in works on natural history, but now crowned with these last chaplets on bird lore and the love of country. Mr. Kidd is a true bird-master; he knows the magic method of winning a bird's heart, and keeping possession of it; and he writes with an accuracy worthy of Wilson, and a fervour and graphic simplicity which remind us of the finest passages of Audubon. A mere linnet in a cage has a story to tell, and no one

ever translated it into human language so truly and felici-
tously as Mr. William Kidd, who brings to his task an
experience of thirty years in Aviary management. One
who keeps four hundred songsters of all kinds ought to
know something of their ways—he should have some rare
things to tell; and this ornithological enthusiast does know
and tell rare things in a rare way.

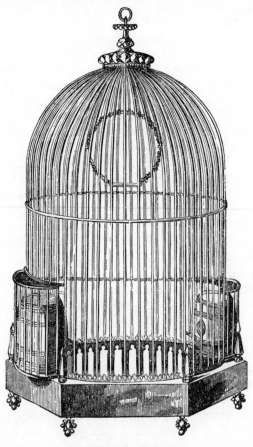

Kidd's Fairy Bird-Cage.

CHAPTER II.

THOU wast not born for death, immortal bird,
  No hungry generations tread thee down;
The voice I hear this passing night was heard
  In ancient days by emperor and clown;
Perhaps the self-same song that found a path
    Through the sad heart of Ruth, when sick for home
      She stood in tears amid the alien corn;
        The same that oft-times hath
    Charmed magic casements, opening on the foam
    Of perilous seas, in fairy lands forlorn.

KEATS.

MONG the feathered favourites most suited to the cage or Aviary, the canary stands the first. He is a favourite everywhere, and holds the first place among our little *Lares*. To those of tender feeling on the subject of animals, it is some consolation to know that the canary is no longer to be considered a captive. His cage is his home, he is a domesticated citizen, and has long ago forgotten all the circumstances of his aboriginal wildness. He pines no more for the sloping vineyards of the fortunate purple isle, where erst he wandered an untamed savage; he is proud of the fetters that bind him, and from his little throat he warbles no plaint for perished freedom.

Except the nightingale's, there is no song so fine as his,
for besides the power he has all the skill of a musician.
There is something so joyous, so bold, in his articulations,
that if colours were accepted representatives of sounds, we
would describe his song to be as golden as his plumage.

It is often said that the canary in a wild state is a poor
songster; that it is the child of culture, dependent on the
teaching of other birds for the perfection of its song. It is
true canaries require teaching, but not more so than young
birds of other species. Dr. Heineken* describes the habits
of the wild canaries of the Madeira Islands. He says "they
build in high shrubs and trees, and construct their nest
of roots, moss, and feathers. They pair in February, and
rear five, sometimes six, broods in a season. It is a familiar
bird, frequenting gardens in the outskirts of the city of
Funchal. It is a delightful songster, with much of the
nightingale's and skylark's, but none of the woodlark's
song. Yet, where are the nightingales and skylarks to
teach the young birds as they issue from the nest. There
is no wild nightingale or skylark in Madeira; there may be
a few in confinement in the city, but they are not the
tutors of the young broods which issue full of song from
the woods. It is therefore absurd to suppose the song of
the canary a mere imitative performance. It is in full song
nine months in the year, and sings on the wing, passing from
one tree to another." Each flock has its own song, and
individuals differ in their respective musical capabilities.

The colour of the wild canary is grey brown, with a
dash of olive green, clearer on the under parts; the caged
birds which present these colours are stronger than those
of a pale yellow; but those of a rich deep gold colour
usually sing well, and are unquestionably the handsomest.
These birds sport into a variety of tints, as most animals
and plants do under culture; and not only do canaries vary
in their tints, but in stature, symmetry, and proportion.

* "Zoological Journal," vol. v.

The London amateurs have very much improved the
English breed of canaries; and to their persevering efforts
we are indebted for many excellent qualities. At one time
the long-bodied Belgians were the fashion; at another the
Norfolk, which is a neat and excellent bird; and now
German canaries carry all before them, and certainly merit
the esteem in which they are held. Bird-fanciers seem to
want fixed rules of properties, such as have long been

laid down for the culture of various kinds of flowers, and
which florists are now bound to observe. Judicious rules,
framed in accordance with the natural excellences and
properties of the object of competition, are as useful to
the public in purchasing, as to the professional producer
seeking fame and fortune by his success in bringing his
pets within the subjugation of generally received dicta. It
is, however, very much a matter of taste what kind of

birds are chosen; they are *all* good in their way. Some like the mealy and others the jonquil kinds, and for song the German birds are prized on account of the softness and fulness of their notes. They are not so loud and *squally* as the birds from Yorkshire and Norfolk.

The best time for pairing canaries is April, and the male should be not less than two years old. Good attentive males are not easily obtained, and attentive and assiduous dams are not so plentiful as might be wished. Some will lay without sitting, some will pick their own babes to pieces, and some are so bad as not to be worth keeping at all. The cages ordinarily sold for breeding canaries are much too small. You cannot rear healthy children in courts and hovels, and even birds want breathing-room. There should be sufficient space for flying as well as hopping about, and hence better birds are bred in rooms or in an Aviary properly fitted for the purpose. Another objectionable practice is the removal of the eggs as fast as they are laid; the custom is opposed to the course of nature, and it is a positive cruelty to give the poor hen a series of ivory eggs to brood over till she has ceased laying. The eggs are injured by removal, and when given to the hen all together, exhaust her by too sudden an abstraction of vital heat; and again, instead of the chicks coming into the world one at a time successively, they are all hatched at once, and the anxious parents have half-a-dozen helpless babes to provide for suddenly, instead of their parental cares increasing as ours do—or as we hope them to do— by one at a time. There should be more nest-boxes than couples where they are bred in an Aviary, so that the hens may have a choice, otherwise they are apt to quarrel for shady corners. A fir growing in a tub affords a good *nidus* for canaries to build in, and if one is supplied them they seldom use the nest-boxes.

Caged canaries should not be kept in heated rooms; it causes them to moult before their time, and to moult badly.

They should have fresh air summer and winter, whenever the weather permits the opening of the windows; but sudden chills and undue exposure are to be avoided. Our little favourite has warm southern blood in his veins, and in his island home enjoys a happy ignorance of March frosts and November fogs. Provision for bathing is another great necessity. To keep a good canary in perfect song, let him be at a safe distance from any common chirping bird, for he is a great imitator, and will soon incorporate some of his neighbour's barbaric chirpings with his own classical voluntaries.

A song canary should be fed on summer rape-seed, (not black, but *brown*,) with canary-seed, bruised hemp, and poppy-seed occasionally—the hemp and poppy should be but seldom given. It is usual to give a bird a little green meat now and then, as a treat; but this is one of the common fallacies of bird-keeping; the relish is so tempting to the bird's appetite that he eats too much, and his health is injured; but let him have it regularly, not as a luxury, but as daily food, and he gets used to it, eats sparingly, is always in health, and needs no other medicine.

The practice of giving pet birds pieces of loaf sugar, morsels of cake, or sweet dainties of any kind, is highly reprehensible. It injures a bird as much as it does a child. A pretty belle would never indulge in sweetmeats before sitting to the piano to sing; and just as such things injure the voice, appetite, and health in human warblers, do they ruin speedily the excellence of a bird.

Canaries are but little subject to disease, and when they are attacked, it is usually a consequence of neglect or improper management. If at any time a canary shews signs of ill health, if it takes an after-dinner nap, appears languid, or sits huddled as if its feathers had been brushed the wrong way, let it be examined an hour or two after dark. If any red insects appear about the bird or cage,

remove the bird at once, bathe him in warm milk and
water, and place him in a clean dry cage. The cage from
which the bird has been removed must then be plunged
into boiling water, and well scrubbed, and not used again
till it has been exposed to the air, and several times cleansed.
If the case is very bad, it is better to burn the cage at

once; but such a proceeding needs courage, and is sometimes expensive. This pestilence is very common where
birds are pampered with sweets, or neglected as to cleanliness; but as the parasites do not show themselves by
daylight, it is necessary to look for them after dark.

Sore feet is another affliction to which canaries are incident.

Fresh air and cleanliness are the only remedies. Surfeit may be cured by the administration of a little oatmeal, mixed with bruised maw and hemp-seed, and at the same time steeping a little groundsel in the water. To obviate the evil consequences of uncleanliness, accustom the bird to an occasional bath, not in the cage, but by means of a porcelain bath fitted for the purpose in a smaller cage, and which is attached for the purpose when required. I teach every young canary of my own to fly about the room, and take his bath at such times. Little attentions of this kind do very much to increase the enjoyment of both parties, and quickly bring about that close acquaintance between ourselves and animals, which is the chief delight of keeping them.

THE SISKIN.

THE siskin, or aberdevine, is a great favourite for the Aviary. It is bold in character, most easily tamed, and takes to its cage almost as soon as caught. The song is a poor one, but it may be taught a better: its treatment must be the same as directed for the canary. In a cage it should be supplied with food for only one day at a time, for it is a voracious bird, and will eat to-morrow's dinner as well as to-day's, on the plan of "a feast and a fast," and if kept from the latter enjoyment, will soon grow so fat as to be worthless. Siskins, as well as bullfinches, linnets, and other birds, frequently

"Die of plethora, through excess of health;"

and one of the main points of bird-management is to check unruly appetite for enjoying health without exercise; most birds eat more than they require, if they can get it. The siskin pairs with the canary, and the produce is generally very pretty.

Q

FINCHES.

ALL the finches are, generally speaking, easily tamed, either in an Aviary or in single cages. Linnets thrive best on summer rape-seed, or, if in a room, the universal paste (hereafter described) is best. The finches are all hardy, and devour greedily all kinds of small seeds, and almost every kind of edible vegetable. Their beauty, docility, gay plumage, elegant attitudes, and lively movements, render them the most entertaining of any of the inhabitants of an Aviary. The attitudes and movements of a goldfinch when picking the seeds from a thistle top, are very engaging and funny, and only equalled by the tomtit when tapping at the door of a bee-hive, to eat up the porter who opens the door. Square cages are best for single birds; and as to food, poppy, hemp, rape, and canary-seed may be given indiscriminately, with common paste, chickweed in blossom, lettuce, chopped watercress, and any salads of the season.

In Germany the chaffinch is a great favourite, though with us it is held in no esteem. Bechstein describes the varieties of its song with a minuteness worthy of Mr. Oxenford, when introducing to the world, through the medium of the "Times," a new Prima Donna of the opera. Not a single tone of the chaffinch's song has escaped the experienced ears of the German fanciers. A workman will give a *Louis d'or*, or sixteen shillings, for a bird he admires, and willingly live on bread and water to obtain the money. In Germany a good chaffinch is proverbially said to be "worth a cow," and all the enthusiasts of a town in Thuringia will turn out to hear one that performs the Reiterzong or the Bräutigam perfectly. The bird is certainly capable of much instruction, and is a playful inmate of a room; but in this country we accord it no fame as a songster.

The greenfinch is a beautiful member of the family of

finches, and, though no musician, should not be neglected in forming a collection, on account of its beauty, playfulness, and familiarity. It may be taught, but not rapidly. The bullfinch is another pretty finch, too well known to need description here. It is dangerous in a general collection, but an excellent cage-bird. It is necessary to guard against allowing these birds to grow fat; otherwise, they are hardy, and easily managed.

LARKS.

AMONG the larks the skylark must have the first place as a cage-bird. The woodlark is a fine songster, but impatient of confinement; both sing better if closely confined. But a skylark in a cage is a painful spectacle, its habits are so wild and free; the space between heaven and earth seems scarce enough for its bold flight, and imprisonment of so happy a creature seems a sin. He no longer soars in graceful curves,

"To bathe his plumage in a fount of light,"

but stands panting on the dry floor of his cage, looking upward beseechingly, as if he would in one mad bound dash through the white roof that shuts him down from his own heaven, if only once to breathe the free air and die uncaged. The skylark, the robin, and the nightingale, are the strongest in their appeals against slavery; their most prominent instincts are those which claim liberty for their exercise; and these are never extinguished while they have life left them to weep for the franchise they have lost. Most other birds suffer but little; confinement is to them but a temporary trouble, for which food, and shelter, and fondling compensate; they grow fat in prison, familiar and contented. But these three never lose the recollection of their native wilds, and when they do submit to sing, it is so unlike their "native wood-notes wild," that every trill seems a reproach to us for the despotic exercise of our power over helpless innocence. The free wild life of the skylark,

> ————"A spirit of the sun,
> A soul with all the dews of pathos shining,"

his exuberance of song, his homely-dappled rustic plumage, his bold flights toward the morning sun, or into the grey dawn before the sun has risen, singing as he soars from the cool turf, and the brilliant array of images, epithets, and allegories, which the poets have entwined around his name and history, from the great Greek epics, down to the Ettric Shepherd, calling him

> "Bird of the wilderness,
> Blithesome and cumberless,"

all plead against the captivity of so true a type of joyous freedom.

> Spare the soft tribes; this barbarous [act forbear;
> If on your bosom innocence can win,
> Music engage, or piety persuade.

Still larks are kept, and will be kept in cages, and therefore it is better to make the evil less. by proper treatment, than to wage a war vainly against a passion which has many gentle traits to redeem it. Few birds are so easy to preserve as the skylark. All he wants is fresh turf and paste, or yolk of egg boiled hard and grated, whole hemp-seed, and now and then a little bread crumb soaked in water, and pressed dry.

The best cage for a skylark is that described by Bechstein. The cages in general use are much too small, in character approaching very closely to a condemned cell, from the bars of which we expect to hear groans and curses, rather than the merry trill or the melodious canticle. Bechstein

says, "Whatever form may be given to these cages, they must be at least eighteen inches long, nine wide, and fifteen high; the bottom should have a drawer, in which enough of river-sand should be kept for this scratching bird to be able to roll and dust itself conveniently. It is also a good plan to have in a corner a little square of fresh turf, which is as beneficial as it is agreeable. The top of the cage must be of linen, since, from its tendency to rise for flight, it would run the risk of wounding its head against a covering of wood or iron wire, especially before it is well tamed. The vessels for food and drink must be outside, or, which I prefer, a drawer for the food may be introduced in the side of the cage: sticks are not necessary, as the lark does not perch." They should never be kept in an Aviary.

The rock, meadow, and tree pipits are sometimes kept in Aviaries, but require the care of an experienced bird-keeper. The rock pipit is most easily preserved, but is very local in its distribution; it is seldom seen in the south of England, and is most frequently met with on the northern rocky shores of our island. I have frequently seen them among the limestone crags at Sunderland harbour, and along the coast between Shields and Hartlepool, where they are taken by the bird-catchers. The song is very pleasing, and is performed during flight. The bird rises by a tremulous motion of the wings over the furze and brake above the cliffs, and when at a great altitude breaks into a fine fife-like trill. It then gradually descends in an oblique direction to the earth. Its food consists of marine insects and worms, and in confinement it thrives upon the universal paste.

The woodlark differs in many points of its character from the skylark, and is not to be preserved without considerable care. He is a bird of fine spirit and fluent song, and is a useful member of an Aviary, singing generally from a retired corner, where he stands as still as a stone, but

warbling most melodiously: in the house he sings from February to August. The birds taken at Michaelmas hold their song longer than those taken at other seasons. The female sings, as is the case with all kinds of larks, but her song is less sustained than that of the male.

The purchaser of a woodlark must depend entirely on the dealer, for it is most difficult to distinguish between the sexes; though, as the female sings respectably, the consequence of a mistake is not so serious. Woodlarks require plenty of clean sand, frequent change of food, and water at all times in abundance. The best food is rape, millet, and poppy-seed, with fresh vegetables and insects.

THE NIGHTINGALE.

"So sweet the tawny nightingale,
  When spring's approaching steps prevail,
  Deep in leafy shades complains,
  Trilling her thick-warbled strains."

THE prince of British song-birds is the nightingale, the hero of many a wild lay and legend, the subject of innumerable metaphors, myths, and moral eclogues; the joy of spring-time, the enchanter of the woods. The literary history of the nightingale would furnish materials for many a huge but not ponderous tome, of classic and legendary lore. The epithets applied to this

"Light-winged Dryad of the trees,"

as compiled by Cuthbert Bede, in the pages of "Notes and Queries," number some three hundred; while the odes, sonnets, idyls, and pastorals to which it has furnished inspiration, are numberless. There is the great question still unsettled, whether its song be sad or merry—

"Oh nightingale, what doth she ail,
  And is she sad, or jolly?"

and there are many points in its history still undetermined, affording as broad a subject for inquiry in the future, as the stored-up ideal wealth of symbol and metaphor provides an immense treasure of nightingale lore from the past. Alas! that we dare not here tread even on the green borders of such holy ground, but must fain prose about Aviary details, and matters of practical management.

The nightingale is a bird of passage, and visits our island at the close of April or the beginning of May, rears its young in our gardens and coppices, charming our woods meanwhile with its heavenly melodies, and returns to its southern home in August. Its favourite haunts are close coppices and humid valleys, shrubby coverts, old-timbered lawns, and highly-cultivated garden districts. It is quite a mistake to suppose that the nightingale sings at night only; its strains are to be heard at all hours, and after the beginning of June the nightingale

—————All day long
Cheers the village with his song.

Around London nightingales are much more numerous than is usually supposed. In the shrubberies at the New River water-works, in Lordship Road, Stoke Newington, the nightingale has been a regular visitor for years; and from the privacy of the spot is likely to continue so, for the benefit of Londoners. Dulwich and Peckham are favourite spots on the south; eastward, in the Essex marshes, and even on the borders of the Wanstead and Epping Woods, it appears to be rare; but to the west, from Westbournia to the Thames at Hammersmith, there are many spots haunted yearly by birds of excellent song. The nearest point to London where the nightingale is to be found in plenty, (speaking from my own experience,) is Cheshunt, Herts., where this bird and the blackcap seem to abound, much to the delight of cockney sojourners, who, like myself, make trips at the proper season, to enjoy that finest of country pleasures—the spontaneous song of happy uncaged birds. Here, at Tottenham, he has of late become a *Rara avis.*

"The strength of his vocal organs," says Bechstein, "is indeed wonderful, and it has been found that the muscles of his larynx are proportionally much more powerful than those of any other bird. But it is less the strength than the compass, flexibility, prodigious variety, and harmony of his voice, which make it so admired by all lovers of the beautiful. Sometimes dwelling for minutes on a strain composed of only two or three melancholy tones, he begins in an under voice, and swelling it gradually by the most superb *crescendo* to the highest point of strength, he ends in a dying cadence; or it consists of a rapid succession of more brilliant sounds, terminated like many other strains of his song, by some detached ascending notes. Twenty-four different strains or couplets may be reckoned in the song of a fine nightingale, without including its delicate variations; for among these, as among other musicians, there are some great performances and many middling ones. His song is so articulate that it may be very well written." The song is certainly less attractive when written; it almost amounts to a burlesque on the art of syllable-making. Here it is from Bechstein— "zozozozozozozozozozozozoz zirrhading, hezezezezezezezezeze- zezezezeze cowar ho dze hoi, higaigaigaigaigaigaigaigaigaigai, guaigai coricor dzio dzio pi."

Bechstein considers that there are two classes of nightingales—day-singers and night-singers. The "night-singers prefer mountainous countries, and even mountains themselves; whilst the others prefer plains, valleys, and the neighbourhood of water." British naturalists do not agree in this view, and as far as my own experience goes, I agree with Mr. Kidd, that the same individuals sing both by night and day, as we all know *caged* nightingales do, no matter *where* they have been caught; there is no such distinction

as that laid down by Bechstein, between daylight and
nocturnal songsters.

Nightingales reared from the nest seldom prove good songsters, they need tuition from their parents. Young birds
caught in August, and which have learned their parents'
music, invariably prove good, especially if in the following
spring they are placed beside a fine singer. The bird-catchers
prize these young birds when they are heard "recording,"
that is warbling over in a low tone the songs which they
have recently learned. The birds caught at their first
arrival, when the males precede the females some days,
generally prove fine songsters, but if taken after they have
paired, are sure to pine for their mates. At five or six
years old, the nightingale in captivity loses its voice—its
strains get broken, the mellifluous flow of song is checked;
and after this happens he has not long to live, unless freed
from the shackles that crush the soul out of him. Two or
three years are sometimes sufficient to bring about this
calamity; and the humane owner of such a bird will not
fail to open the door of the cage when April comes, and
give the pining captive his long-prayed-for liberty. Birds
so restored to freedom, often regain their song in all its
original vigour and fulness. Doubtless they seek that companionship with the gentler sex, without which both men
and nightingales are very forlorn creatures.

The best treatment for a nightingale is to give him two
or three meal worms a day, now and then a spider, though
two spiders a day are *quantum suf*. A regular supply of
ants' eggs, or earth from an ant's nest, is most essential,
and but poorly compensated for by roasted ox heart and
grated carrot. A good staple food for nightingales may be
made of raw sheep's heart and the yolk of hard-boiled
eggs, chopped together exceedingly fine. It should be
prepared fresh every day; and every particle of fibre
removed from the heart. The fine threads should be carefully removed, for if one gets round the tongue of a bird,

it is pretty sure to cause its death. The only remedy that can be resorted to in such an extremity is to take hold of the bird gently, and remove the fibre from the tongue by means of a needle.

Fresh-water for bathing is very essential, and the utmost attention should be paid to cleanliness, for our princely songster has a royal delicacy of constitution, and cannot bear the least neglect or careless usage. Numbers die soon after they are caged; and in every sense nightingale keeping is a precarious undertaking. Unfortunately, like skylarks, they are most easily caught, and their unsuspecting nature proves their moral ruin. Perhaps no one sooner than the owner of an Aviary would desire to place the bird-catcher beneath a ban, none, surely, know better how heartlessly these men pursue their inhuman craft than those who are intimate with bird history, and who truly regret the thinning and destruction of the British Fauna, which these men hasten by their indiscriminate trapping of birds, and their settled plan of never letting one escape, even if the quarry, as an article of commerce, be worthless.

BLACKBIRDS AND THRUSHES.

BLACKBIRDS, thrushes, and starlings, readily adapt them-selves to a civilized life, and ask only a few berries and worms in addition to the universal paste. Blackbirds are rather quarrelsome in an Aviary, and had better be kept in separate cages. They are easily taught to whistle airs, though the wild woodland song of the blackbird is to us far preferable to all the acquired performances that ever blackbird received from a human master.

The real song thrush, *(Turdus musicus,)* is a very superior bird to the missel thrush, *(T. viscivorus.)* The latter is not worth much attention as a song bird; but the bold throstle, the mavis of the old poets, has a melody unsurpassed for

wildness. The nightingale reminds us of a first-class opera singer, skilled in the most refined details of classic melody, but the throstle gives us the ancient mountain music which thrilled the glens, and peopled every crag with armed men, hurrying to their chieftain's standard. The throstle and blackbird must ever stand to represent old-world rusticity, such as buds perennially in the Saxon verses of Dan Chaucer.

A blackbird may have a bone (not a salt one) to pick occasionally, or a little chopped meat. Starlings and thrushes should be kept on rather low diet; oatmeal, or bran moistened with water, is a good staple food for a thrush, with now and then a worm, a few hips from a wild rose, or some blackberries. The starling and blackbird are neither of them so cleanly as the thrush, and all require abundance of water for bathing and drinking.

BLACKCAP, WHITETHROAT, AND WREN.

An Aviary stocked with such birds as we have already described, would present a respectable appearance, and afford a pretty good morning chorus, and some amount of vocal confusion; but there are several other British birds that are easily domesticated, and well suited to the companionship of the more notable inmates of an Aviary.

The blackcap must take the first place amongst the miscellaneous tenants of an Aviary; the collection is indeed worth little without him, for he rivals the nightingale; and like Essper George, can perform almost any feat with the smallest possible amount of teaching.

The blackcap is of shy recluse habit, partial to caterpillars and insects, but omnivorous, nevertheless; feasting with equal pleasure on ants' eggs, meal worms, cherries, currants, and the universal paste. It is excelled in song only by the nightingale, and in captivity it sings at every season of the year, by night as well as by day. It is a great imitator, and inexperienced persons often mistake its song for that of the nightingale, when it warbles from a coppice by moonlight, like a true British mocking-bird. They require great care as to diet, and a regular supply of water for bathing. The male may be known by the blackness of

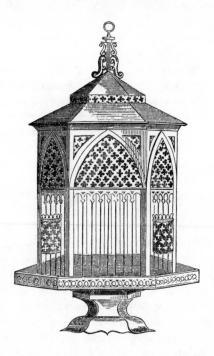

the poll; the female has the top of the head of a reddish brown. They become very tame when once domesticated, and even impudently familiar.

The garden warbler, or pettychaps, is a useful member of a feathered community. Its motions are so lively, and its warble so soft and sweet, that it is sure to repay any trouble it may occasion, for it is a delicate bird, and needs the same care as the blackcap. Another bird of passage sometimes kept in the Aviary is the whitethroat, or *fauvette* of Buffon, which arrives in our islands in the spring in considerable numbers, frequenting copses and hedge-rows, where it moves from bush to bush in a sort of spasmodic shake, warbling the while its pleasing but gossipy song.

The chiff-chaff, the wood wren, and the lovely gold-crested wren are all useful birds of the soft-billed kind for an Aviary. Dr. Bechstein recommends for a gold-crest a paste of crumbs of white bread, "dried in an oven, and powdered; a tea-spoonful of this put into a cup, and three tea-spoonfuls of milk, as hot as it can be made without boiling, poured over it." Flies and ants' eggs are also necessary.

THE ROBIN.

How many attempts have been made to tame the robin redbreast! and how many of these familiar haunters of the cottage threshold are sacrificed to man's passion for subjecting everything that is endowed with life! But who would cage a robin? who would infringe the laws of hospitality, and make a captive of the poor wanderer who comes confidently to beg at the door? He thinks you have a crumb to spare for him

"When the hips and the haws are all gone,"

for he saw the barns stacked at harvest-time, and boldly asks to share the refuse of a table which Providence has bountifully covered for you, repaying you for it with his cheerful minstrelsy, for he belongs to the rustic "waits" who fill the tingling Christmas air with songs that make the heart throb, and the eye moist with feelings of hearty benevolence. He puts his trust in you, and should go unscathed to make his little foot-prints in the snow, and exhibit his pretty warm-tinted breast upon the garden railings, full of song, and sprightly cheer, and unsuspicious courage.

It may not be so bad to confine him in a roomy Aviary, where he can quarrel with other birds if he will, and as he is sure to do, to such an extent as to make him a dangerous inmate of an Aviary, but in a cage he becomes a downcast exile, and dies of grief for perished freedom. Yet we would rather persuade our readers not to burden their consciences with the sin of keeping a captured robin anywhere; let him associate with the dryads and wood-nymphs for the sake of old story and song—for the sake of the "children in the wood," for whom he performed the rites of decent Christian burial, warbling over their graves (so the story says) a melancholy requiem for inno-cence blighted, even in the opening bud, by avarice, and craft, and cruelty. If you do keep him, let him have insects, German paste, a bit of soft cheese now and then, and water to bathe in. He is naturally tame, and will take to a room quickly, and make himself *very* familiar with his fond proprietor. *This* is the way to keep a robin; let him fly about as he pleases, and teach him to take a meal worm from your hand.

WHINCHAT AND WAGTAIL.

The whinchat is a very pleasing but noisy bird in con-finement. It sings the whole year through, suffers little or nothing from imprisonment, and will learn the songs of any birds that it may hear. It is rather tender, but feeds freely in the house on any of the pastes, and needs only protection against cold to ensure it long life and con-stant cheerfulness. The wheatear is another of the useful and easily-managed Aviary tenants. It is a handsome bird, and very abundant on the downs of the south coast, where

thousands are captured annually for market. It arrives here in March, and leaves in October. Mr. Sweet says "it is an interesting bird in confinement, and is almost continually singing; it will also sing by night as well as by day if there be a light in the room where it is kept. It has a very pleasant, variable, and agreeable song." When a pair of them are kept together in a large cage or Aviary, it is very amusing to see them at play with each other, flying up and down, and spreading their long wings in a curious manner, dancing and singing at the same time.

The grey wagtail is another bird but seldom caged, which may be turned to good account in furnishing an Aviary. The distinctness of this *(Motacilla Yarrellii)* from the continental species, *(M. alba,)* has but recently been determined by Mr. Gould, and the specific appellation *Yarrellii* applied to it. It is a permanent resident in the south of England, but in the north it is migratory. The colouring of the bird is pretty, and its habits are very pleasing. Mr. Yarrell quotes a letter by Mr. Rayner, in which the writer states that he had several wagtails, both pied and yellow, *(M. flava,)* in his Aviary, in 1837, "both of which were very expert in catching and feeding on minnows, which were in a fountain in the centre of the Aviary. These birds hover over the water, and catch the minnow as it approaches the top, in the most dexterous manner. I was also much surprised at the wariness and cunning of some blackbirds and thrushes, in watching the wagtails catch the minnows, and immediately seizing the prize for their own dinner."

The song of the pied wagtail is sweet but not powerful. Indeed capability for fine song is not essential in every inmate of an Aviary. As in a converzationé we want some quiet folks, so in the bird-house we do not want a fierce competition of rival voices, but an assembly of pleasing and interesting personages, each amusing us by its individual ways; the songsters falling into their places, as they do in a dramatic performance, to give tone and purpose to the scene, yet not to absorb the undivided attention of the auditor.

PARROTS, MACAWS, ETC.

PARROTS, paroquets, macaws, and cockatoos are handsome and amusing birds. There is something pleasing in the harsh wild scream of a parrot, when placed among trees in a garden; it is a fragment of wild nature that we contrive to carry into the town with us, and is sometimes more congenial to the feelings from its unsophisticated barbarism, than the most melodious song. Who can help envying ladies the leisure they enjoy in teaching a noble bird to talk, even if it talk nonsense? for there is something so apparently human in the queer ways of an old family parrot, who struts out of his cage to steal a fragment from the sugar-bowl, or a cherry or gooseberry from the side-table. It is amusing to see the sly criminal mount to the top of his cage with the purloined treasure, to handle it with his scaly fingers, while he eats and mumbles in a low chuckling tone, for all the world as cleverly as if he had read Leigh Hunt—

> "Stolen sweets are always sweeter,
> Stolen kisses much completer,
> Stolen looks are nice in chapels,
> Stolen, stolen, be your apples."

This class of birds looks best on poles and stands, and if kept in cages should be allowed to roam occasionally about a room. When well tamed, they go in and out of their cages in a very orderly manner. I have always fed parrots on bread, scalded and then moistened with milk, with hemp-seed and any of the ordinary viands of the table. When well tamed, they are admirable companions at break-fast, and omnivorously rejoice in bones to pick, scraps of meat, fruit, cooked vegetables, and indeed anything that happens to be on the table. The familiarity which this sort of feeding engenders benefits both parties.

One old favourite green parrot lived with me for years in the full enjoyment of liberty. True, one of his pinions had been mutilated before he came into my possession, still he could fly tolerably, yet never committed trespass on property beyond his own; and I believe they never need be chained or caged at all if made companions of. The great joy of this fellow was to perch all day in a lilac tree, where, by croaking and threatening, he drove away cats and sparrows, as fast as they came in sight. When hungry, he descended and straddled to his open cage to feed, returning to his favourite locus, or perhaps taking a stroll over the garden, where he refrained from nibbling even the tendril of a weed.

Tame magpies and jackdaws, that I have kept in this way, have punished me sadly by their destructiveness; their great delight in a garden is to pull up every small plant by the roots, and lay it out in the sun to perish, a process that makes a wonderful change in the aspect of a gay border in the course of an hour or two.

Parrots and cockatoos require to be kept scrupulously clean. As a general food for parrots, there is nothing better than the crumbs of stale white bread, scalded, and then slightly squeezed in the hand, and moistened with milk. They prefer it slightly warm. To this add hemp-seed, crushed biscuit, nuts, and fruit of all kinds.

Some young macaws are fed on hemp-seed, which must always be of the year before, as the new would be too warm and dangerous. Yet they must not be fed entirely on this food, but there must be added white bread soaked in milk or water, as has already been mentioned, some fruit and nuts, but never bitter almonds, though sweet almonds never injure them. In all cases the excrements of the birds will indicate the state of their health, and whether the food ought to be changed or not. Although macaws rarely want to drink, as their food is very moist, yet they must not be left without water, which is generally placed in one of the divisions of their tin drawer. It is also a good thing to entice them to bathe; nothing is more favourable to their health, or better facilitates the painful operation of moulting, or keeps their feathers in better order. For the smaller kinds of the parrot tribe, hemp-seed is a good staple food.

A parrot-house might very well be combined with a vinery, where, under the shadow of purple grapes a large number of choice birds would find sufficient room to be happy. Our design for a structure of this kind is in the Moorish style, and is well adapted for use as an open bird and vine-house during summer. Sashes or trellis-work, made to fit accurately, would render it secure in winter; and many rare animals and plants might be displayed at all seasons by judicious economy of the space within. A collection of parrots and paroquets would have a splendid effect in such a building, and give it a truly oriental appearance.

CHAPTER III.

"COME banish thy grief, nor past folly bewail,
My love is a storehouse that never shall fail;
At evening, at morning, at noon, and at night,
To feed my sweet bird shall give me delight."

IN selecting birds for purposes of amusement, it must be borne in mind that birds of passage are always most difficult to preserve. Those which are permanent residents take to confinement kindly; but the former, when their season of migration returns, are much agitated, sometimes for several days together, and not unfrequently die under the mysterious influence of the passion, which, if they were free, would lead them over oceans and continents, to the sites of their winter resorts. This is one of the chief reasons that it is so difficult to preserve nightingales. If the first shock of imprisonment be passed through safely by the help of skilful treatment, there is still the season of migration to be got over, during which the birds are more or less possessed of an intense desire to escape imprisonment, for the purpose of joining the flocks which are then leaving the country. At the time they would naturally migrate, they become so agitated, especially during the night by moonlight, (the hour at which they commence their journey,) that they often fall ill and die. This impulse to migrate effects all birds of passage; they flutter their wings, beat wildly against the bars of their prison, forsake their food, and gasp for breath; and when the frenzy has subsided, they are for some days dull and dispirited, only gradually recovering their wonted health and cheerfulness. Little can be done beyond keeping the birds as undisturbed as possible, to mitigate the agitation which, at particular days and hours, affects them in confinement; the separate cage already recommended tends very much to obviate losses from this cause.

Birds are frequently purchased when newly caught, the purchaser having to perform the operation of reducing the savage to a civilized life. If a newly-caught bird exhibits impatience of the cage, he should be put aside without food and water in a quiet place, and the cage covered with a dark cloth. After three or four hours, half fill the food-box with some tempting food suited to the particular bird, according to instructions already given, or to be given, and at the same time give a supply of water. Then take out the bird, and plunge it in a pan of cold water, so as to drench it thoroughly; replace it in the cage, and hang it up in the sunshine or in a warm room. The shock of the cold water will so exhaust the bird, that he will for a time forget his imprisonment, and will at once set about preening his feathers. As he recovers from his bath, his appetite will press him hard, and he will be unable to resist any longer the choice morsels offered him, however sulky he may be at his position. Having once eaten, proper care will complete his subjugation. For a few days new birds should be kept in a quiet place, even if well reconciled to the cage; the bustling about of strange persons, and other disturbing causes, act prejudicially, and more especially with

birds recently caught. As a rule however it is better at all times to purchase birds that have undergone the necessary treatment in the hands of experienced dealers, who obtain them at the *proper time*, as well as at the *proper age* for the purpose.

With regard to feeding, birds may be classed in three divisions:—First, those that live on seeds only, as canaries, siskins, and most finches; secondly, those that eat seeds and insects, as quails, chaffinches, and all kinds of larks; thirdly, those which subsist on berries and insects, as the thrush, blackbird, and nightingale.

There are two leading kinds of paste, suitable for birds of every variety of appetite, and which may be considered staple foods for the Aviary, as well as occasionally useful for any parlour pets. They are made as follow:—To make the first paste, take a white loaf which is well-baked and stale, put it into fresh water, and leave it there until quite soaked through, then squeeze out the water, and pour boiled milk over the loaf, adding about two-thirds of barley-meal with the bran well sifted out, or what is still better, wheat-meal.

For the second paste, grate a carrot very nicely, (this root may be kept a whole year if buried in sand,) then soak a small white loaf in fresh water, press the water out, and put it and the grated carrot into an earthen pan, add two handfuls of barley or wheat meal, and mix the whole well together with a pestle.

Bechstein describes the first paste as agreeing so well with all his birds, "which are not more than thirty or forty, at liberty in the room, that they are always healthy, and preserve their feathers, so that they have no appearance of being prisoners. Those which live on seeds, or only on insects, eat this food with equal avidity; and chaffinches, linnets, goldfinches, siskins, canaries, fauvettes, redbreasts, all species of larks, quails, yellow-hammers, buntings, blue-breasts, and redstarts, may be seen eating out of the same dish. Sometimes, as a delicacy, they may be given a little hemp, poppy, or rape-seed, crumbs of bread, and ants' eggs.

Every morning fresh water must be given to the birds, both for drinking and bathing. When a great many are left at liberty, one dish will do for them all, about eight inches long and two in depth and width, divided into several partitions, by which means they are prevented from plunging entirely into the water, and in consequence making the place always dirty and damp. A vessel of the same size and shape will do for holding the universal pastes, but then it must have no partitions. Quails and larks require sand, which does for them instead of water for bathing.

Some birds swallow directly whatever is thrown to them: great care must be taken to avoid giving them anything with pepper on it, or bad meat. This must be a general rule. I shall also remark, that food sufficient for one day only must be given to birds kept in cages, for they are accustomed to scatter it about, picking out the best, and leaving only the worst for the next morning; this makes them pine, and puts them out of humour."

The second paste will seldom be wanted; the first, with proper care in other respects, will be found to serve every necessary purpose, and there is no kind of food so easily prepared. For nightingales the food used by the bird-fanciers is preferable; it is made of raw sheep's heart and the yolk of eggs boiled hard, and both chopped together as finé as possible. This keeps the bird in full song better than the paste: it is nourishing and stimulating. Mr. Kidd recommends the "nut" of boiled bullock's liver grated fine, with occasionally a little stale bun. The liver must be quite fresh, and prepared *daily*, and the birds must be accustomed to it by degrees, by gradually mixing more and more of it in their food.

Recurring to Mr. Kidd's work on the "Aviary and its

Occupants," he says, "The seed boxes should be half-filled with a mixture of the best canary, flax, and rape seeds. Of these, the proportions should be—canary, one-half; the other half consisting of flax and rape. A small quantity of the latter will suffice, it being eaten principally and sparingly by the linnets. Flax is good for all the seed birds, keeping their stomachs in a healthy state. The "hoppers," as we have before noted, should be carefully examined, at least twice a week; and the seed remaining in them should be sifted, to cleanse it from dust and refuse matter, before re-filling.

For the soft-billed or insectivorous birds, the general or 'universal' food must be made as follows:—German paste, one pound; the yolk of six eggs, boiled hard; one ounce of blanched sweet almonds (pounded;) half a pint of hemp-seed, well bruised; six plain stale buns; two table-spoonfuls of best moist sugar. These ingredients, after being placed in an earthen pan, (glazed,) should be well incorporated with the naked hand, till they amalgamate. Throw in a small quantity of maw-seed before putting it into the birds' saucers, and place the latter on the floor of the room. Above all, bear in active remembrance that *the food must be fresh every day*.* Scald the hemp-seed.

In addition to the above, one or two of the saucers should contain grated bullocks' liver, (from the part called 'the nut,') boiled hard, and some grated Cheshire cheese; both rubbed fine, and mixed with stale sweet buns, of which all birds are excessively fond. The buns should be purchased of a first-rate confectioner, otherwise they stand every chance of being manufactured from 'kitchen-stuff.' Many a school-boy's stomach, ('digestive' though it naturally be,) will give satisfactory evidence of the truth of this remark.

All your birds, from a canary upwards, will freely share in this soft food; and they will thrive nobly on it. By

* You must be guided in *the quantity* of food made, by the number of the inmates. We give the proper proportions.

leaving it to their own option what to select, you will find
they seldom, if ever, will have any ailments.

The room must be kept well supplied with ripe chickweed
and groundsel; lettuces (in season;) cherries; strawberries;
ripe, mellow, juicy pears; and now and then a boiled mealy
potato, bruised. The 'Warblers' eat greedily of the two
last; also of soft-boiled, tender cabbage. Nightingales and
blackcaps are dearly fond of the latter; also of elderberries
when ripe; and they greatly luxuriate in a little raw, scraped,
tender rump-steak, free from fibre. This, when scraped,
should be moistened with cold water, but not made too
'pappy;' and it must always be sweet. If tainted in the
slightest degree, do not attempt to introduce it.

In the way of live food, throw in occasionally ants' eggs,
small red worms, spiders, earwigs, mealworms, liver-gentles,
et hoc genus omne. The windows being kept constantly open,
hundreds of flies, gnats, and other minute ephemera, will
find their way in; and no small amusement is it to watch
the gyrations of the birds, as they topple over to catch their
prey. The wagtails, whitethroats, and titlarks,* in particular,
are most elegant in their motions while thus occupied.

There have been many opinions on the subject of giving
your birds hemp-seed. It certainly does tend, homœ-
pathically, to shorten the duration of their lives; but still
—strange though true—they cannot live without it! It
warms their stomach, and possesses, moreover, an oleaginous
peculiarity of flavour, which, mixing with the other food,
forms a good general diet. It must be given sparingly.
Many people feed goldfinches in cages with hemp-seed;
this is quite a mistake. Canary and flax is all they should
be allowed. They thrive well on it, and escape getting
over fat—the ruin of half the race. Their plumage, too,
is always in beautiful order.

---

* The titlark is a delicate bird, not at all adapted for a cage, although he
thrives nicely in an Aviary. *Here* he is at home, and sings very sweetly—very
joyously.

To prevent the necessity for "medicine," properly so called, let some crumb of bread be scalded with boiling milk; into this put some grocers' currants, after previously soaking them two hours in cold water. All soft-billed birds—nightingales, blackcaps, garden warblers, and white-throats in particular, eat voraciously of this dish; and as boiled milk acts medicinally on all birds, its curative properties will speedily become apparent.

If these instructions be fully carried out, and plenty of *old mortar*, well bruised, be kept constantly on the floor, no sanitary commission needs ever be appointed. It is with birds as with ourselves—air, exercise, temperance, and a proper diet, will pull us through to a good old age."

With respect to the assortment of the birds so as to realize a truly "happy family," certain important matters must be borne in mind. Birds of a pugnacious temper, such as the robin, must be excluded, or you will not be safe from one day to another. *Pairs* of birds are also objectionable, for though many, and especially finches, do breed in the Aviaries, their domestic habits too frequently lead to a row; they are attacked by the bachelors, the eggs rolled out and smashed, the hens worried, and the whole place put into confusion. Hence, though one or two pairs of *canaries* may be admitted to build and domesticate, it must never be a matter of surprise if very few young birds ever arrive at maturity. Beside the canaries, *one pair* of wagtails may be admitted, for these are too handsome and lively to be omitted, and too pugnacious to be introduced *singly;* they certainly agree better with their neighbours when they have domestic affections to occupy them; like ourselves, they must be occupied to keep them out of mischief.

Now as to the selection, let it consist, among the soft-billed kinds, of thrushes, blackcaps, tomtits, garden warblers, hedge sparrows, nightingales, redstarts, wheatears, willow

wrens, reed sparrows, stonechats, whinchats, titlarks, woodlarks, whitethroats, babillards, and wagtails.   Among the
hard-billed birds most suitable, are goldfinches, canaries,
siskins, chaffinches, greenfinches, linnets, redpoles, twites,
yellow-hammers, and Java sparrows.

Though this, like other pursuits, admits of experiment
and extension, the amateur is strongly advised not to place
in an Aviary a single blackbird, robin, skylark, bullfinch,
jenny wren, oxeye, hawfinch, or starling.   These are all
spiteful and quarrelsome, with the exception of the neat
little wren, and that is too tenderly constituted to bear
up against the bustle and row of an Aviary.   It is indeed
difficult to keep this little pet in any way, so let him be
left to hurry through the hedge-rows, and brave the winter
out of doors.   Mr. Kidd says the bullfinch may be kept
with other birds without danger, and though I must bow
to him in all matters pertaining to birds, his experience
in them outweighing mine at least the eighth of a century in time, and a round *hundred or two* in number, I
will not here bear the responsibility of recommending that
which of my own experience I do not feel to be perfectly
safe.

As to numbers, finches of all kinds may be kept in
plenty, so as to form the general bulk of the population,
but one nightingale only should be kept, and one thrush,
and he must be young; when he gets into his second, or
early in his third year, he must either have his liberty or
be consigned to a cage.   If more than one nightingale be
kept, the rivalry of these proud songsters will create either
a feud or a deadly sullenness.   One will sing and rejoice
in his power of outdoing every other inmate, but none of
the minor vocalists will take umbrage at his superiority.
Lastly, take care that no single bird obtains a mastery in
the house.   This frequently happens, and a thrush or
wagtail is as likely as any to accomplish the usurpation.
Should it happen, remove the bird at once, and supply

his place with another young one already prepared by a proper course of previous treatment in a cage.

Where there is no regular-constructed Aviary, much may be done towards securing a greater share of enjoyment for birds than cages afford them, as I have already suggested. Most suburban villas are now built with conservatories attached at the back, and these make excellent bird-rooms. The fancy German cages, gaily coloured and elegantly designed, are great aids in the ornamentation of such retreats, as well as for ordinary rooms. A few choice shrubs, some bright flowering plants, and a row of cages stocked with choice British and Foreign birds, among the latter love-birds, paroquets, Java sparrows, and the lovely waxwings, may make such a place infinitely more attractive as a resort when "the cares of day are done," than one half of them are at present, being left to the cats and spiders, or *embellished* with a few withered geraniums fit only for the muck-heap. The large Aviary cages made of mahogany and wire, and mounted on mahogany stands, are also useful as well as elegant, and do well for small collections of finches. There is no occasion for keeping such interesting, lively, and beautiful creatures as birds in the ugly cages that have so long been used; let their homes be beautiful, to match themselves, and their happiness will be increased the more we lavish attention upon them, and humour their pride by consigning them to respectable dwellings.

Since bird-cages form important items in the furnishing of "Homes of Taste," a few words may be added here to what has been already said respecting them. The fancy German or Zollverien cages, of which several examples are figured in these pages, were originally invented by Mr. William Kidd, and are now in very general request. They are made entirely of metal, stamped and perforated in many beautiful designs, the one here represented being a good example of the taste displayed in their construction. But

the most striking feature of these cages is the colouring, which is gay in the extreme, the patterns being picked out in the brightest tints of orange, scarlet, crimson, green, and blue, so that as window and conservatory ornaments they are very showy and effective. Whatever objections may be urged against them will arise out of their being made wholly of metal, which sometimes proves too cold for tender birds, and hence the inmates of such should not be too rashly exposed to currents of air or adverse weather. But another recent invention of Mr. Kidd's may be described as the perfection of a bird-cage; it is an invention which fulfils every requirement of conserving the health and plumage of the feathered pets, and is at the same time so beautiful in itself as to merit the appellation "Fairy cage," applied to it by the inventor. This cage is figured as a foot-piece to the first chapter, but no engraving can convey an idea of its brilliancy, lightness, and prismatic hues. Mr. Kidd thus describes it:—

"It is a showy bird-cage of pure crystal glass, (a material now used for the first time,) altogether dispensing with wire and other disfigurements, and allowing a bird's plumage to be viewed to the best advantage. In praise of the workman, it must be observed that those only who know the nature of glass, will be able to comprehend the obstacles that have had to be surmounted in rendering it thus obedient to the human will.

The 'fairy bird-cage'—so named because of its lightness, elegance, and extreme brilliance—is of very simple construction. All the bars are of solid transparent glass, compacted together so as to unite in a strong body. The form of the cage is an oval. It is mounted on a sexagon base, and supported by six lapidary-cut crystal knobs, beautifully prismatic. The six panels in front are of fine-grained satin-wood. On each of the six corners rises a brilliant pyramid, of the purest (cut) crystal glass.

Immediately above the panels, and between each bar of

glass, is introduced a *moveable* length of polished ornamental glass, richly cut. Of these lengths, or pieces, there are no fewer than thirty-six. To secure them at their bases, (they are made to fit close between the bars,) there runs all round the cage an ornamental gilt metallic band. When adjusted, no joins are observable. We see only a polished surface of radiating gems.

These fringes, (as they may be termed,) when fixed, serve a two-fold purpose. They prevent the seed being scattered over the table or carpet; and when exposed to the rays of the sun, or the reflection of a fire or candle, they shine with a lustre worthy of fairy-land. Their prismatic colours are really beautiful. The fringes are easily removable and readily cleansed; but, as before hinted, it requires the light gentle hand of a fair maiden to prevent accidents. After two or three experiments, she will enter *con spirito* upon her pleasing daily duties, and never care to relinquish them to a stranger. The interior of the cage is so constructed as effectually to exclude all vermin; it also affords unusual opportunities for extreme cleanliness. The seed and water, too, are quite removed from contact with any impurities. Both are supplied in miniature cut-glass barrels, which are fixed in glass galleries, projecting, one on either side of the cage, externally. Each of these galleries revolves on a pivot, so that fresh seed and water can be readily given to the bird. They are so contrived as to admit of a bath being supplied, in summer, at the same opening. They also form an invisible cage-door.

The perches (square) are made of Bohemian ruby-glass. There is also a swing-perch of crystal and malachite. These colours add greatly to the beauty of the inhabitant. The top of the dome is of richly-cut crystal glass, powerfully refractive; and above it is a strong metal ring, by which the cage is suspended. It hardly needs be added, that when raised above the head it is seen to the greatest advantage, though it is ornamental anywhere. To prevent

the bird being subjected to draughts when standing on a
table, a moveable screen, made of strong tinted cardboard
and mounted on hinges, may be placed round one side of
his cage. The screen, if painted, would be a neat ornament.

With a view to secure the uniformity and elegance of
the exterior of the cage, the tray, or drawer, is *not* introduced in the usual manner. *The bottom of the cage itself
forms the drawer.* This is removed by turning a screw
fastened (externally) in its centre. On its removal, a tripod
is in readiness to take its place. On this flat surface, adapted
to the size of the opening, the cage is quickly placed while
the drawer is being cleansed and sanded. Once more lifting
the cage with the left hand, the drawer is adroitly supplied with the right, and the screw turned from below. All
is then complete. Two minutes, or less, suffice for the
change.

The happiness and whimsical conceit of birds living in
these 'fairy bird-cages'—particularly love-birds, Australian
paroquets, canaries, bullfinches, and goldfinches—can be but
faintly conceived. They *feel* their importance, and they
know they are objects of admiration. It is, perhaps, difficult
to say which is the happier—the bird or his mistress."

I may here add that Mr. Hawkins, of 6, Bear Street,
Leicester Square, is an extensive importer of the original
Zollverien cages, and a most conscientious dealer in birds
of all kinds. He has supplied me for some time past with
both English and Foreign birds, and I am so well satisfied
that I feel a pleasure in here recommending him. Mr.
Hawkins is a naturalist and a gentleman, and no lady
need fear to enter his establishment and pick and choose
from his extensive stock, and that, unfortunately, cannot
be said of many of the London bird shops; the majority
of them are *dens* that reek with effluvia, and pain the heart
by the abject condition of their leprous captives. Mr.
Hawkins' plan of keeping song-birds in a room by them-

selves, apart from parrots, is an additional advantage of preserving their melody uncorrupted.

It must be remembered that cats and rats are deadly foes, and no bird is safe within their reach. Mr. Kidd's loss of nearly four hundred birds by rats is a harrowing history, told by him in energetic terms. The grand purifier is *carbonate of baryta*, mixed up with fish, and laid about where these vermin will be sure to find it. I have been compelled to depopulate my own neighbourhood lately, but not till my losses were too terrible to be any longer borne. I used the baryta rubbed into portions of Yarmouth bloater, spread it about the garden, and since then the only cats to be found here are those figured in Mavor's Spelling Book. As Mr. Kidd says, they soon become "matters of history." It is painful to take life of any kind, but in this case it must be cat or bird, not both together. Your neighbours will not tie up their cats, *ergo* you must kill them.

> "A light broke in upon my brain,—
>   It was the carol of a bird;
> It ceased, and then it came again,
>   The sweetest song I ever heard,
> And mine was thankful till my eyes
> Ran over with the glad surprise,
> And they that moment could not see
> I was the mate of misery."
>   *Prisoner of Chillon.*

THE APIARY.

In belted gold, the bees with "merry march,"
 Through flowery towns go sounding on their way,
They pass the streak'd woodbine's sun-stain'd arch,
 And onward glide through streets of sheeted May,
 Nor till they reach the summer-roses stay,
Where maiden-buds are wrapt in dewy dreams,
 Drowsy through breathing back the new-mown hay,
That rolls its fragrance o'er the fringed streams,—
Mirrors in which the sun now decks his quivering beams.
                              MILLER'S "SUMMER MORNING."

CHAPTER I.

MANY of our readers will be surprised to find bee-keeping entered in our catalogue of recreations for town-folk. Many may perhaps imagine at first sight, that we intend

the bee-house as a useless ornament, an empty sham, devised
to deceive the visitor, after the fashion of the Empress
Catherine's painted villages, or the shrines and altars which
Watelet set up in his utilitarian grounds, wherein theatrical
sacrifices and pagan rites were enacted in the finest style
of child's play; or like any set of modern ruins, woods of
canvass, or fairy palaces, temples, and fountains, of painted
timber.   Such things are abhorrent; they are like those
deceptive Arabian fruits which attract the eye, but fill the
mouth with ashes.   Our suburban Apiary is a reality not
to be thrust upon the unwary as a plausible experiment,
but a *fait accompli;* and so favourably, that we look forward with hope to the day when the townsman shall regard
the bee as his intimate neighbour and bosom friend, his
moral preceptor, his purveyor of sweets, his companion, adviser, and by his yearly gift of virgin honey, the sanitary
guardian of his household.

But supposing it to be possible to keep bees in healthy
suburban districts, or even in the closer parts of towns,
what inducements are there to enter upon a pursuit which,
time out of mind, has been the hobby of village school-
masters, farmers' wives, overworked curates,

"Passing rich with forty pounds a year,"

and naturalists addicted to the narration of what a great
portion of the world regard as fictions, and not moderate
fictions either, but wrought to the fullest with extravagances
which beat the "Arabian Nights," out of all hope of competition.   Why should the townsman turn Apiarian?   He
can afford to buy sugar, and honey too, if he wants it—
though but few British citizens have ever tasted the pure
commodity; he can read about bees much more than he
cares to know; he has grown familiar with the shape of
a hive from the gilt signs hung out at taverns and linen-
drapers, and over the gateways of suburban tea-gardens;

and he classes the bee with vipers, scorpions, hornets, and toads; creatures that sting, bite, or spit fire—the evil genii of creation—to be avoided by all except country bumpkins who can't be hurt, and mad naturalists who have lost all regard for the smoothness of their hands, or the safety of their persons.

There are many, of course, on whom our warmest persuasions will fall as dead as drone music. We may urge and urge, but they will not be led into bee-keeping, from a fear of the bees themselves, or strong doubts as to its possibility. We leave such to the pursuits they have chosen, and wish them as much happiness as can be obtained without the help of home-grown "trickling honeycombs;" who have no desire to see their own

> "Bees
> Hum about globes of clover and sweet peas."

There are two classes of persons on whom we may hope to make an impression. The first are those whose minds are stored with the rich honey of classic lore, who dream about Aristæus and Aristomachus, who can quote the great old Stagyrite, Columella, Celsus, and Pliny, who know the fourth Georgic by heart in the original, and love the happy old Corycian as a grey-beard father. To these the buzzing of a swarm will recall the green youth of the world, when Hymettus flushed with wild thyme, and Hybla's flowery slopes were odoriferous gardens of sweets.

> "Ille terrarum mihi præter omnes
> Angulus ridet; ubi non Hymetto
> Mella decedunt."
> *Horace.*

For that happy unchanged roamer, the bee, the "free-born wanderer of the mountain air," blows his bugle to the same tune over our "fallow leas," as on the sixth day of creation, when he made his first sally among the new-born wood-cups, or rifled the sweets from Eve's Eden garlands, which she

"Bred up with tender hand,"

not feloniously seizing on the hidden treasure, but helping the flowers to perfect their seeds for the benefit of all future generations, and freely sharing with man his store of golden honey-combs when the curse was passed, and the barren ground was watered with the sweat of human toil. And the bee shared the fall; brambles and briars sprang where amaranths had bloomed before, and he had to wing his flight far over dry slopes and tangled wastes, to collect the scanty honey-drops that erst had dowered his very threshold, trickling from blush roses, in cool grottoes where angels "watched silently."

The scholar will adorn his home with hives of "singing bees," that he may hear the hum of Pan's great festival, and study the mysterious workings of an instinct that perplexed antiquity, and has furnished modern science with the most brilliant evidences of the minute workings of that great Designing Will, which maintains the balance of a million worlds, and equips a creature scarce bigger than a rain-drop with implements, armour, and a system of mathematics that strike the philosopher dumb with wonder and admiration.

There is another class to whom we may make a more homely appeal, asking them to remember—as perhaps they do, but not too fondly—the scenes of early youth, the rustic home, the flower-garden with its row of dark brown hives, tended by hands, doted on by hearts that now

"Rest beneath the clover sod."

Hearts that doted upon them too, hands that pushed back from the forehead the truant curls, and in the hour of childish suffering moistened the fevered lips with the cool nectar of those well-remembered hives. Our towns are crowded with children of the manor-house, the farm, the cottage, and the way-side smithy; feet that hurriedly pace the dry pavement still retain the elastic step with which they brushed the cool dew from heather bells, or threaded the maze of mossy woodland, under the pattering of beech-nuts or the flutter of cooing doves.

Who, then, can wonder that our smoky towns are belted round with flowery gardens, and ornamental slopes and shrubberies? Who can wonder that amid the deadening influences of city life the natural instinct of man rises superior to circumstances, and that he will have beauty with him wheresoever he may be; that he will conquer difficulties, and though he himself fall before the city plague, his favourite flowers shall escape unhurt, if not to brighten his pathway while living, at least to soften the sunshine that falls upon his grave.

These lovers of

"Silvery oak-apples and fir-cones brown,"

these cherishers of early memories, and rustic images of peace and contentment nestling under tall elms and grey hawthorns, will not sneer at the idea of suburban bee-keeping, but will welcome whosoever shall shew them that the joy is possible—that they may have the companionship of their old friend the confectioner, whistling over his work, wherever there is a few square feet of garden-ground for his stall, a daily blink of sunshine, and access to the sugar-market of gardens and meadows a few miles beyond. For the bee is a free roamer, he does not care for the raw material on the spot, but travels far for the treasure, and, like man himself, sets a high value on that which comes from a distance.

The pleasures of bee-keeping are not trivial, nor are the advantages few. If only for the flowery life he leads, it must be wholesome to have him about us, humming all day of

—"Tendrils green, of every bloom and hue,
Together intertwined, and trammelled fresh:
The vine of glossy sprout; the ivy mesh,
Shading its Ethiop berries; and woodbine
Of velvet leaves and bugle blooms divine;
Convolvulus in streaked vases flush;
The creeper, mellowing for an autumn blush;
And virgin's bower, trailing airily."

But the highest pleasures are those the observant mind will derive from a study of the economy of the hive, wherein we see displayed a social scheme of an intensely practical character, working out its results by means of order, industry, and skill; a scheme designed by the Almighty himself, subject to none of the flaws which beset the plans of human theorists, but perfect in its minutest details, and as instructive to the student of political economy as to the lover of nature and the searcher after wondrous truths. Here is a perfect queendom with its three estates of sovereign, aristocracy, and workers. Here is the division of labour in practical operation; here chemistry and mathematics are made subservient to the wants of life; while respect for persons, obedience to authority, industrial activity, patience, and concord, give a moral completeness to the miniature world within, which renders it so striking a picture of what the human world without *should be;* that to have such a scene at our command through the windows of an improved hive, must ever rank one of the finest pleasures of the observer of nature.

The educational uses of such rustic ornaments as are here introduced, to those who love homely pleasures and communion with nature, are of the highest value in opening the minds of the young, and giving renewed zest to the recreative hours of the mature; and none so fascinating, so replete with food for curiosity, so suggestive, so likely to improve the head and refine the heart, as the colony of bees conspicuously placed, ingeniously plying their tasks under our every-day gaze; the emblems, in all time, of

industry and thrift, and the most entertaining beguilers of a spare half-hour.

The increased attention paid to bees of late years indicates an increased appreciation of their moral as well as physical attributes. To the growing fondness for these highly-endowed but modest rustics, we are to attribute the many improvements for the humane treatment of them, which promise ere long to banish all the black associations of wanton and unnecessary slaughter which has so long impeded the culture of the bee, and kept aloof so many who could not purchase pleasure by the infliction of injustice and cruelty. It is now so well known that no bee-keeper can kill even a single bee except to his own cost, that the pleasures of the Apiarian are unalloyed, while his profit increases with every act of kindness which his skill and benevolence enable him to perform. There is nothing more domesticating than the love a good bee-keeper bears his bees, except, indeed, it be the love of his wife, his children, and his God: may such love increase and be its own reward.

Next to these, and of a different sort, but still improving to the nature, is the tender regard we have for these helpers of our lot, who cheerfully give us of their store, making more than they need in their active, persevering, and serious endeavours; while every bee-keeper knows that the bees love him in return, get used to him, and allow him to come amongst them at times when none other dare approach, and cheerfully submit to a very hard fate if he imposes it, having faith in him that he will do no wrong. If I could here unravel, as fully as the subject deserves, the history of the bee, and detail the structure and operations of the hive, who would read and live another day without setting about having the means at hand of verifying for themselves all that Schirach, and Reaumur, and Huber, and Lord Brougham have said and written on the subject? And that is the great pleasure of bee-keeping—to be able to verify facts already known, but too wonderful to be believed till we have seen them, and to hope some day to discover new facts ourselves. For such a pleasure the student of Almighty Wisdom will ever cherish the bee, though it cost him much; but if he can be gratified at no cost, but greatly to his profit, (speaking in the worldly sense of commercial gain,) who would not wish to share the pleasure, and find in the Apiary the best-drawn pictures and the best-written books?

As to the advantages of bee-keeping, but little need be said, because the products of the bee have been famous articles of commerce ever since the first caravan set out on its first mission of barter. But there is one service, not everywhere recognised, which the bee performs for the horticulturist, deserving of mention here. The bee is the great fertilizer of flowers. Without his help, but few of our plants would produce seed, and therefore he is somewhat a purveyor of fruits, as well as honey, helping to insure the husbandman's harvest, and to perfect the seeds of the choice flowers, on which the florist lavishes his love and enthusiasm. Did not the bee bustle in and out of the blue-bells at the proper time, sprinkling and brushing the fertilizing pollen-dust over the half-hidden stigmas of flowers, it is questionable if many tribes of plants would not pass out of existence, while others would be but scantily spread, which now prosper in abundance.

> "The bee transports the fertilizing meal
> From flower to flower, and even the breathing air
> Wafts the rich perfume to its appointed use."

Now, as to the honey, Mr. Taylor, one of our highest authorities, says, "I have known as much as eighty or ninety pounds obtained from a stock by deprivation." Such results, however, are rare, and Mr. Payne estimates the average harvest at from twenty to thirty pounds annually from every good stock. Let us take the medium of this moderate estimate, and four stocks, no great number, will furnish a hundred pounds of honey yearly, at no cost beyond the first outlay for hives, which last for years; the honey, too, of the finest quality, untainted by brimstone, unmixed with pollen or brood, and free from adulteration.

In the town Apiary, the produce will be less, but not contemptible; the worst situations ought to produce annually ten pounds per hive, leaving the bees twenty-five or thirty pounds for their own winter consumption, whilst in good suburban districts, opening on the country, with clover-fields within reach, and lime-trees and garden-flowers in abundance, the produce will nearly equal, with good management, the best country Apiaries, and exceed the ill-managed, swarming, and suffocating hives which help small farmers to pay their rent, and country wives to clothe and educate their children.

This may be taking a sordid view of so noble a pleasure as bee-keeping; but a practical basis gives stability to an ideal superstructure; and most of us love gain, however small, as an apology for pursuits which lie out of the beaten track of our every-day duties. There is not a lady from Belgravia to Bow, from Park Village to Peckham, but takes an interest in sweets, cordials, perfumes, and confections, and there are few families but might use honey more extensively than they do, for economy, for enjoyment, and for health. We find a finer flavour in fruits of our own growing; our children prize the one peach which the one neglected tree produces, and when we grow honey for our own consumption, it is really sweeter than any we can purchase. In every corner of our land, the well-wishers of our race cry to their neighbours, "keep bees! keep bees!" and, wherever bees are kept, the ground seems sanctified to the genii of homely comfort, hospitality, virtue, elegance, and thrift.

Will our blue-eyed, our auburn-tressed, dark-ringleted, cherry-lipped, noble-minded "Women of England" steal

one hour a day from Potichomanie, Diaphanie, and the
knitting of superfluous anti-macassars, and give it to the
bees?—for the hive is a feminine empire, where the only
worthy part of the population are of the gentler sex,
where a queen holds perpetual sovereignty, and where the
triumph of female unity and perseverance is marked by a
periodical annihilation of the strongest stubborn gender.
Nor do we fear the lessons you may learn herein; we
have too much faith in your tenderness of heart to fear
that the fate of the wretched drones may befal us. You
would not extirpate *us* as the female bees do our droning
representatives; we judge so from your angel ministrations
when we need them most, your winning tenderness and
devotion, your confiding love.

There remains the question, which should be disposed
of here—*Can* bees be kept in towns in any other state
than that of wretched exiles from their proper home? Is
it absolutely necessary to dwell in the country to enjoy
the pleasures of bee-keeping? or are bees constitutionally
adaptable to circumstances, capable of the transition from
rustic to urban scenes, without curtailment of life, or
deterioration of faculties. We answer that wherever sunshine and air have free access, bees may be kept, even in
the most crowded parts of a great city, though better, of
course, in its suburbs, and best of all in the open country,
within reach of hedge-rows and commons. All they want,
as to position, is a free circulation of air, morning and
midday sun, a free causeway—which their wings will ensure
them anywhere—to the country, and immunity from the
vibration of machinery, and the effluvia of factories. A
garden is not even necessary, a window affords an excellent
locus, and professed Apiarians frequently fit up their observatory hives in such a position.

The ordinary rate at which bees travel is estimated at
thirty miles an hour, and it is well known that however
rich a garden may be in flowers, bees prefer to roam

away in search of honey; for the bee is eclectic, and will pass a hundred blooms before alighting on one, and when he alights, he often does no more than just poke his nose in, as much as to say "good morning," and goes on again, making a long journey before fairly settling to work.

The author of the "Essay on the Honey Bee" says, "We believe that two miles may be considered as the radius of the circle of their ordinary range, though circumstances will occasionally drive them at least a mile more." The adventurous person who kept bees for many years *in the garret of a house in Holborn*, performed an experiment to ascertain how far, and to what pasturage, his bees travelled. As they came out of the hive in the morning, he sprinkled them all with a red powder, and immediately set off to Hampstead, thinking it most likely he should meet them there. What was his delight at beholding among the multitudes of humming workers, some of "his own little fellows which he had 'incarnadined' in the morning." From Holborn to Hampstead Heath, is about four miles, and, if this is more than the ordinary range, it at least shews how far bees will travel, rather than come home "empty handed." Mr. Huish states that he observed bees on the Isle of May, at the entrance to the Frith of Forth, which is distant four miles from the mainland, though there was no hive on the island, and the journey was made across water, on which they could not rest in their progress. There can be no fear, therefore, but the bee will find pasture, though he have but a mural home.

Dr. Bevan says, "Those who reside in towns may consider it indispensible to the success of an Apiary, that it should be in the immediate vicinity of good pasturage, and be thereby deterred from benefiting and amusing themselves by bee-keeping. It may be satisfactory to learn that the Apiary of the celebrated Bonner was situated in a garret in the centre of Glasgow, where it flourished for

several years, and furnished him with the means of making
many interesting and valuable discoveries; which he gave
to the world about thirty years ago." Mr. Payne, the author of an excellent work called the "Bee-keeper's Guide,"
kept an Apiary, for many years, in the middle of a large
town, where it afforded him both profit and amusement,
and flourished in a manner worthy of a heath tract.

Who cannot remember the working bees exhibited by
Mr. Milton, of Great Marylebone Street, and the Messrs.
Neighbour, of Holborn, that attracted thousands to the
gallery of the transept of the Great Exhibition, in 1851.
What delight, surprise, curiosity, wonder, was excited there,
as the little labourers, visible to all eyes, plied their tasks
—emblems of the great industrial energies which had crowded
the Crystal Palace with the most glorious fruits of ingenious
handicraft—yet in that assemblage of the choicest products
of all climes, there was nothing so wonderful as that product
of Almighty Power—the bee, building comb, kneading pollen,
elaborating honey, rearing young before the daily gaze of
thousands of astonished spectators.

That admirable exhibition may be now referred to as a
bold, because practical, defence of bee-keeping in towns; it
established the fact that bees may be kept successfully in
the midst of bustle and noise, at a great elevation above
the ground, and in a district where, of necessity, the bees
must have travelled far for their supplies; a combination
of circumstances less propitious than most town and all
suburban localities would afford.

But a still more striking instance may be cited. Mr.
Marriott, who for some years carried on business as an
Apiarian, and who exhibited bees by gas-light at several
places of popular resort, had, in October, 1855, a stock at
work in one of the windows of his place of business in
Gracechurch Street, in the very centre of the city of London.
When I saw these bees the hive and depriving glass con-
tained nearly sixty pounds of honey, and *the store was still*

increasing, though the season had passed, and the bees were located in the very centre of the city. On inquiry, Mr. Marriott said his bees "visited the fruiterers and apple-stalls," perhaps went as far as Covent Garden to collect the exudation of filberts, grapes, and peaches. The proof of this was before our eyes—the bees were active, and honey was being stored in recently-formed cells.

There are few amusements so well suited to the tastes and inclinations of ladies as bee-keeping, and the suburban residence can have no more fitting ornament than a tastefully designed and well-furnished bee-house, or, at least, one or two cottage hives, on the lawn, within view of the windows, or an observatory hive in a conservatory, or greenhouse, or even in the window of an ordinary room.

Every ordinary residence affords some convenience for an Apiary, either on a limited or extensive scale; and in any suburban district, where proper means are used, bees may be kept so successfully as to be profitable as well as amusing; though we would rather say nothing on the score of profit, while so many higher inducements exist. Neither is a great outlay essential, for a common straw hive, made for deprivation, and costing from half-a-crown to half-a-guinea, will furnish as good honey as the most expensive appliances of the bee-keeper's art, and much of the entertainment to be derived from more costly hives, though, as a matter of course, these latter have high claims on those who can afford them. The trouble of attending bees is less than most other pets occasion; they seldom require feeding, they manage their own household in their own way, and indeed the less disturbed, except at some particular seasons, the better.

Lastly, the amusement they afford is ever-varying; with proper appliances, free from danger and every cause of alarm, and accompanied with economical advantages, such as the wealthiest and most refined may take delight in. A lady may well prefer to grow flowers rather than kitchen

vegetables, to bestow her care upon pet beauties in pre-
ferment to pigs or poultry; but no lady will shrink from
the utilitarian suggestions of virgin honey, which is everywhere regarded as one of the most welcome additions to
the stores of a household. In fact, every phase of bee-history,
bee-management, and the harvesting of bee-produce, is fraught
with elegance; and where elegance is accompanied with
instruction and usefulness, there do we ever hope to meet
the attentive eye and approving smile of female beauty.

> They whom truth and wisdom lead
> Can gather honey from a weed.

CHAPTER II.

Thou cheerful Bee! come, freely come,
  And travel round my woodbine bower!
Delight me with thy wandering hum,
  And rouse me from my musing hour!
Oh! try no more those tedious fields,
Come, taste the sweets my garden yields;
The treasures of each blooming mine,
The bud, the blossom, all are thine.

Professor Smythe.

INCE it is impossible, in a work of this kind, to attempt anything like a full history of the honey bee, I shall briefly state a few particulars only, as introductory to a code of bee management; the culture of the insect being, of course, based on its constitution and habits.

An ordinary well-stocked hive contains from fifteen to twenty thousand bees. Dr. Bevan estimates that hives managed on the depriving system, have their numbers sometimes swelled to fifty or sixty thousand. In their wild state there is no doubt they frequently exceed this number, owing to the vast extent of space which a colony usually has at its command. Two thousand bees will fill a pint measure, and five thousand weigh a pound. A swarm ought never to weigh less than four pounds; sometimes they reach to six, which will give a total of thirty thousand bees.

A community is made up of three kinds of bees. The
first in importance is the queen, or, as she is called by
the Germans, the mother bee; for she is the mother of
the whole community, and maintains a sovereign command
over the affairs of the hive. The next in importance is
the worker, or neuter bee, which is really of the female
sex, of similar constitution to the queen, but undeveloped,
and hence differing from the queen both in size and
appearance, and in the capacity of reproduction. The
third kind is the drone, or male bee, which exists merely
for the propagation of the species, and is doomed to perish
as soon as a continuance of the race has been insured.

The queen is the largest of the three, and has a tapering

Queen.　　　　　　Worker.　　　　　　Drone.

body one and a half times the length of the worker. Her
sole province is to lay eggs, and thus supply a continually
increasing population. The queen is seldom seen, yet, as
it is sometimes necessary to capture her, the bee-keeper
should be familiar with her form, as represented in our
engraving. The queen usually begins to lay on the fifth
day after her arrival at maturity, and continues fertile for
four or five years, producing during the season of her
greatest productiveness, from one to two hundred eggs a
day, indeed as many as one hundred and thirty-five eggs
have been counted as the produce of a single night. They
are united at the bottom of the cells, and are of a long
oval shape. Though queens differ as to fertility, the

average production of eggs is estimated at from sixty to eighty thousand a year.

The queen is the soul of the hive; where she goes the bees follow, paying homage to her and studying her wants. Remove her, and the operations are immediately suspended; the peaceful orderly industry is changed to confusion. Honey is no longer stored up for future use; the bees are content to live from day to day; it is not for themselves they labour. The queen, separated from her subjects, becomes dejected, pines, refuses food, and dies. Yet when an emergency removes the queen at a time that the hive is full of unborn brood, the bees, once convinced that their queen is lost, select a few of the grubs of common workers, and, by a peculiar course of treatment, secure the development of the sexual organs, and thus, as it were, create a queen. This process has been witnessed, and repeatedly confirmed, and is one of the many wonders in the general economy of the hive.

The workers are the smallest and most soberly-coloured members of the community: the form and appearance are well known. They constitute the bulk of the inhabitants of a hive, the drones seldom numbering more than fifteen hundred, while the workers reach as many thousands. A brood of common workers is almost always to be found in a hive; they are the first eggs laid by a young queen, who continues to lay worker eggs only for the space of eleven months during the season. These eggs are hatched in four or five days, and remain in the grub form for about six days longer; they then pass into the chrysalis or nymph state, and spin themselves a cocoon. In about twenty-one days from the first laying of the egg, the young bee issues from its cell, and in another day or two makes its first roaming expedition to gather honey in the fields.

Worker bees are short-lived, and the abettors of the destructive system of bee-keeping adduce this fact in defence of their cruel theory, alleging that, if not destroyed by art,

T

they only suffer a lingering death, worse than the more
merciful one of sulphur. But the fact of their short existence is no defence of suffocation—rather the contrary;
the six or eight months allotted to a bee affording the
best argument for making the most of it while it lives.
As early as February there is an increase in the number
of workers. During the summer the breeding goes on
rapidly, and there is an enormous increase, and, if common
straw hives are used, swarms go off.

The bees bred in the early part of the year are dead
before winter, and "every bee existing at Christmas was
bred during the latter part of the spring or summer." By
preserving the lives of these we have a sufficient number
of nurses to tend the brood-combs in spring, and these
having performed their kindly office, die in their turn, and
leave the hive stocked with a large and vigorous population
of young bees. In depriving hives, the workers die as soon
as they become useless, and to exterminate them before
their natural period is complete, is to lose their services
at a time when they are of the greatest value—namely,
in fostering a strong population for the ensuing summer's
work. Paley says, "A bee among the flowers in spring,
is one of the cheerfulest objects that can be looked upon.
Its life appears to be all enjoyment; so busy and so
pleased."

The drone is the butt of all who have written on bees.
He is only tolerated, not cared for, by the worker bees.
He lives in idleness and gluttony; gathers no sweets, performs no labour; is a mere voluptuary, and dies at last a
miserable death, the consequence of the disgust with which
his laziness has inspired the whole of the industrial population. In a good stock-hive there will be from one to
two thousand drones at the beginning of May; these are
the produce of the first-laid eggs; two months afterwards
there is commonly a second laying of drone eggs, which
appear in public twenty-five or twenty-six days afterwards.

These two generations of drones meet with two separate but determined massacres, the first slaughter of the voluptuaries taking place in June or July, the second in August.

Various duties have been assigned to drones. One author fancied them "hewers of wood and drawers of water" to the establishment; and others have thought that they brooded over and hatched the eggs like hens, "in which case the hair on their tails would seem to serve the same purpose as the feather-breeches which Catharine of Russia had made for her ministers, when she caused them, as a punishment, to hatch eggs in a large nest, in the ante-chamber."

Huber hit on the correct explanation, that fecundation of the queen takes place during flight, and that hence a large number of drones are necessary, that she may be sure to meet with some in the upper regions of the air, the queen having been observed to leave the hive soon after the drones. Her embrace is said to be fatal.

Let us now briefly consider the internal history of a hive of bees, as upon the details of this history we must base our method of arrangement. In February the breeding of young bees commences, and the thin population of the hive is soon augmented by fresh bodies of young workers. Towards midsummer the crowd becomes so great that the old queen and a number of the workers prepare to depart, and found a new colony. Supposing them to swarm, and the swarm to be hived safely, the first thing the bees do is to clean out the new hive, block up all its chinks, fix it by means of a resinous substance to the hive-board, and to varnish it all over thoroughly within.

The first material they seek is the resin of willows, poplars, alders, and birch trees; this they prepare till it becomes a greyish brown tenacious kind of cement, being firm in texture, and aromatic. With this they cover all protuberances, and sometimes contract the entrance to the hive with it, the latter use having given rise to its name *propolis*, meaning "before the city."

While one body of workers is engaged in the work of plastering and varnishing the hive with propolis, another set are laying the foundations of combs. The cells of the combs are made of wax, but the combs are attached to the roof by means of propolis. A large number of cells is usually made the first day that the hive is taken possession of. They have been known to construct a comb twenty-seven inches long, by seven or eight inches wide, in the space of twenty-four hours; and in the course of five or six days they will half-fill the hive; hence it appears that

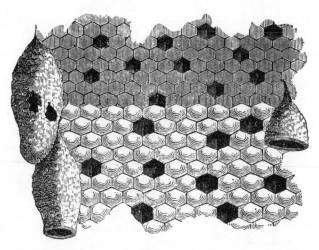

in the first fifteen days after they take possession of a new habitation, there is as much wax made as they elaborate during the remainder of the year. The wax is secreted by workers, who first feed on rich saccharine food, and then repose in clusters till the wax scales are formed under the rings of the abdomen.

There are three sorts of cells; the first are for the larvæ of workers, the second for those of the males or drones, the third are the royal cells. Worker brood cells are usually in the centre of the hive, drone cells around these in patches, and queen cells are invariably on the outer edges of the combs. In the adjoining cut the purse-shaped combs are those containing royal eggs. An inattentive observer might perhaps be led to infer that the various cells composing a cake are little habitations in which the workers might repose themselves after the labours of the day, each in his own house. This, however, is not the fact, for some of these are filled with honey, and others closed up, though when starved out the helpless creatures creep into them, and perish. On a more careful inspection, it will be seen that most of the cells contain a little worm—the young of the bee—an object evidently of the most anxious care and attention to those appointed to watch and feed them,

The results of these varied operations are even more wonderful than the orderly industry with which they are conducted. The combs are usually suspended from the top of the hive, each comb being formed of two layers of six-sided cells, united by their bases. The combs do not touch, but are separated by intervals sufficiently wide to permit the bees to work at the surface of each contiguous comb, and approach any cell without touching each other. Besides these highways, there are narrower causeways for ready communication between one portion of a comb and another.

The cells are usually placed in a horizontal position, so that their mouths open towards the sides of the hive. The bottom of the cells, instead of forming one flat square, is composed of three lozenge-shaped pieces, so united as to make the cell end in a point; consequently the whole is a hexagonal tube, terminating in a pyramidal cavity.

Their combs, or clusters of cells, are arranged in vertical and parallel plates, with a space of about half-an-inch betwixt contiguous pairs; and each comb is nearly an inch in thickness. At the outset, when one wax-making bee leaves the suspended cluster alluded to, and lays the foundation of a cell, others follow in rapid succession, not only

adding their wax to that of the first, but soon commencing
new combs, one on each side; and so the work goes on, in
most cases, until the whole roof is covered with foundations.
The architects proper, also, are meanwhile at their finishing
work.   They have, says Reaumur, to solve this difficult
geometrical problem:—'A quantity of wax being given, to
form of it similar and equal cells of a determinate capacity,
but of the largest size in proportion to the matter employed, and disposed in such a manner as to occupy the
least possible space in the hive.'

Wonderful to reflect upon, this problem is solved by
bees in all its conditions, in their construction of hexagonal,
or *six-sided* cells. The square and the equilateral triangle
are the only other two figures of cells which could make
them all equal and similar without interstices. But cells
of these figures would have either consumed more material,
or have been weaker; and they would also have consumed
more space, being less adapted to the form of the bee. In
short, the hexagonal form combines all the requisites of
economy and capacity. Another wonderful arrangement is
seen in the construction of the bottoms of the cells. Each
of these is composed of three rhombs, or plates of wax in
the shape of card-diamonds, disposed in such a manner as
to form a hollow pyramid, the apex of which forms the
angles of the bases of three cells on the opposite side,
giving to each of them one of the three diamond-shaped
plates which is required to form their bases. Now, the
three rhombs, composing each cell-bottom, have the two
obtuse angles each of 110 degrees, and, consequently, each
of the two acute angles of 70 degrees.

The cells of the bee are extremely delicate, two or three
plates or sides being of the consistence only of a common
leaf of paper. They are made strong, however, by mutual
support and other means. Besides a sort of froth which
the insect mixes with the wax, the cells, at first of a dull
white, soon appear yellow on the interior, the change arising

from the plastering over them of a compound varnish of wax and propolis. Each cell is soldered, too, at its mouth, by a similar compound of a reddish colour, having in it more propolis; and threads of the same substance are laid around the walls, to bind and strengthen them. It is now to be observed that all cells are not alike. They have four different uses in the economy of the hive, and are constructed variously to suit these. One set of cells is for holding the eggs or embryos of worker-bees; a second for those of males or drones; a third for those of young queens, hence called royal cells; and a fourth set are for the reception of honey and pollen. The first are generally about five lines in depth, (or less than half-an-inch,) and two lines and two-fifths in diameter. The cells of the young males are much less numerous, and measure from six to seven lines in depth, by three and a half in diameter. It is worthy of note, that in passing from the construction of worker-cells to those of drones, in the same comb, the architects do not alter the size at once, but gradually; thus disordering in the slightest possible degree the delicate arrangement of the bases of the cells. In shifting from larger to smaller, the same rule is observed. After the chief breeding season is over, (to some extent young bees are produced at every season of the year,) the cells, both of worker and male bees, are used for holding honey. Those made purposely for that end are chiefly marked by a greater divergence from the horizontal plane, that the honey may be better secured; and it is curious to observe that, in a very warm season, these wise insects give the floor a still greater dip from the mouth inwards. As the store enlarges, they seal up the mouth with a ring of wax, to which they gradually add concentric layers till the cell is filled, when they close it altogether—reserving its treasure for use during winter and spring. Pollen, as brood food, is kept in cells of considerable size.

The maturation of the eggs is not left to chance. Huber

observes that there is a distinct class of workers, whom he denominates, in his poetical technology, *nurses*. These watch over the larva or worm with tender care, administering supplies of pollen, honey, and water, and performing other offices essential to the development of the helpless nursling. So assiduously is this nursing duty performed, that where stocks are thin, and there is much brood-comb in the hive, honey gathering is almost entirely suspended, and the bees suffer from want, even during a season of plenty, owing to their unremitting care in tending the brood. Hence large stocks thrive better than small ones, as, if labourers be scarce, the whole are occupied in the internal duties of the hive. When this happens, feeding may be necessary. As the brood leave the combs, the bees cleanse the cells, and prepare them again for eggs or honey, but always neglecting to remove the silk cocoon which was spun by the worm. Hence in course of time the combs get contracted in size, and the bees hatched in them become smaller; so that to keep up the breed undegenerated, it is necessary to remove the old combs occasionally, and thus compel the bees to construct new ones. The use of the bar hive enables the operator to remove combs periodically, and thus prevent any degeneracy of the brood.

The massacre of the drones is an important event, and takes place differently according as the hives are managed on the swarming or depriving principle. The manner in which this massacre is performed was ascertained by the exhaustless ingenuity of Huber. Six swarms were put on glass tables, and watchers underneath waited to see the result.

"This contrivance succeeded to admiration. On the 4th. of July we saw the workers actually massacre the males, in the whole six swarms, at the same hour, and with the same peculiarities. The glass table was covered with bees full of animation, which flew upon the drones as they came from the bottom of the hive; seized them by the antennæ, the limbs, and the wings, and after dragging them about, or, so to speak, after quartering them, they killed them by repeated stings directed between the rings of the belly. The moment that this formidable weapon reached them was the last of their existence; they stretched their wings and expired. At the same time, as if the workers did not consider them as dead, as they appeared to us, they still struck the sting so deep that it could hardly be withdrawn; and these bees were obliged to turn round upon themselves, with a screw-like motion, before the stings could be disengaged.

Next day, having resumed our former position, we witnessed new scenes of carnage. During three hours, the bees furiously destroyed the males. They had massacred all their own on the preceding evening, but now attacked those which, driven from the neighbouring hives, had taken refuge amongst them. We saw them also tear some remaining nymphs from the combs; they greedily sucked all the fluid from the abdomen, and then carried them away. The following days no drones remained in the hives.

These two observations seem to me decisive. It is incontestable that nature has charged the workers with the destruction of the males at certain seasons of the year. But what means does she use to excite their fury against them? This is a question that I cannot pretend to answer. However an observation that I have made may one day lead to a solution of the problem. The males are never destroyed in hives deprived of queens; on the contrary, while a savage massacre prevails in other places, they there find an asylum. They are tolerated and fed, and many are seen even in the middle of January. They are also preserved in hives which, without a queen properly so called, have some individuals of that species that lay the eggs of males, and in those whose half-fecundated queens, if I may use the expression, propagate only drones. Therefore the massacre takes place in none but hives where the queens are completely fertile, and it never begins until the season of swarming is past."

This last observation is somewhat confirmed by what takes place in improved hives, where no swarming being intended, and hence no new queens needing fecundation being allowed by the bees, the massacre of the drones takes place much earlier than it would do if the bees were allowed to swarm; as in the latter case the new queen would require to be fertilized. The bees in this, as in all other cases, adapting their operations to circumstances, not as a blind instinct would teach them, but by a faculty for which we can find no more appropriate term than reason.

We are indebted to Mr. Taylor, the author of the "Bee-keeper's Manual," unquestionably the best practical work on bees extant, for a correct explanation of the causes of the difference in the period of the expulsion of the drones, observed in swarming and depriving hives respectively.

Respecting the advisability of rendering the bees assistance in expelling the drones, Mr. Taylor says, "If it can be done at once, without annoyance to the workers, I think much fighting and valuable time may be saved by it; but no advice can be worse than that of attempting to accomplish the work piecemeal. When attacked, the drones, to avoid persecution, will congregate together in a remote part of the hive. Observation led me to think they would be glad to retreat for still greater safety into a separate box, so placed as to be accessible to them. Accordingly on the 14th. of June, in one of my collateral stock-hives, where the drones for a day or two had been hard pushed by the others, I opened a communication on the ground floor into an empty side-box. My theory was completely realized, for the poor drones gladly made their way into this, where they remained clustered at the top like a swarm, not a single common bee accompanying them, and would proba-bly have been starved. The following morning I took away and destroyed them, counting rather more than two thousand two hundred, besides some few that escaped. I did not find among them a solitary working bee; nor could I dis-

cover in the parent stock-hive one remaining drone. The bees peaceably at once re-commenced work and did well, as if glad in this wholesale way to be rid of their late unprofitable inmates. What was the cost of their daily maintenance? and what proportion to the entire population of the hive did the drones bear?" One great advantage of the depriving system is here manifested; the drones are expelled much earlier than in swarming hives, and hence the amount of their keep for the intervening period is added to the honey harvest.

Before closing this brief notice of the natural history of the bee, a few words should be said on the subject of swarming; for though I do not anticipate that a single suburban Apiary will, in these enlightened times, be established on the destructive system, yet swarming will sometimes happen spite of our precautions, especially during the earlier periods of Apiarian experience.

When the old queen and a number of her subjects determine to expatiate themselves, and trust to chance for a future home, there is usually a dozen or more royal infants in embryo; and as but one queen is ever tolerated in a hive, these must either be slaughtered, (as they are in depriving hives) by the old queen, or she must leave to make room for one of them. The increased heat of the hive is another, though not the chief cause, as many writers have asserted; Mr. Nutt, especially, having been led into many errors through adopting such a view.

"The issue of a swarm," says Mr. Taylor, "is to be expected when the bees have remained for some time previously in a state of seeming inertness, followed by an unusual commotion among the drones; and more especially if these make their appearance in the morning. But mere clustering at the mouth of the hive is not invariably the precursor of a swarm, and the bees not unfrequently continue to congregate in apparently unmeaning idleness on the outside, even though honey may be abundant."

The thermometer affords but little help in this matter, and those who depend entirely on Mr. Nutt's otherwise admirable instructions, will be led astray. The thermometer rarely reaches 95° in a stock-hive, and swarms will depart at a temperature of 90°; indeed Mr. Taylor records one instance at 80°, and adds a note in which he says that a *very* high temperature does not accompany swarming, "for I have proved that the combs collapse and fall at a temperature a little above 100°." This experiment cost Mr. Taylor the destruction of a fine stock-hive. A swarm always consists of the *old* queen, a large number of workers, old and young mixed together, and some hundreds of drones.

Swarming is not so formidable an affair as the amateur usually regards it. The tremor with which every Apiarian hives his first swarm, forms a ludicrous contrast with the confidence with which he deals with the event, when he has had some experience. Indeed so far from the bees being irascible at this time, as they are when bent on the slaughter of drones, they are more than usually submissive, seeming conscious of the aid that man may render them in their extremity, so that, with moderate skill, they may be handled without risk, or the least necessity for hurry or confusion. In my own experience I never remember to have been stung while hiving swarms, and now that I am used to such work, I doff my coat as soon as the alarm is raised, and hive them in my shirt sleeves. The excitement is magnificent, and many a time I have had from twenty to thirty neighbours assembled to witness the scene.

The swarm seldom proceeds far before it alights, and usually takes up its position on the nearest tree or shrub. When this happens in an old-fashioned village, where depriving hives are regarded only as toys for the curious or insane, it is the scene of one of the most pleasing events in the round of rural memorabilia. Away go the dames and the damsels, beating frying-pans, saucepan lids, ringing bells, and making such a clatter as rouses the village from

its noontide lethargy, and sets the whole population, including, sometimes, the parson, the schoolmaster, the beadle, and the gouty squire, to a game of hop, skip, and jump, till the bees having clustered, and the bee-master, "big with importance," having brought an empty hive, and mounted a table under the tree, where they hang like a shower of tea-leaves, sweeps them into it, and, with his swarm safe, leaves the hubbub to subside by gradual evaporation.

He who does not love this ancient custom, which Mr. Taylor is pleased to call "absurd," is unworthy to keep bees, and can be no lover of Lucretius or Aristotle, or Varro, or Virgil, all of whom dwell upon the clashing of cymbals, which was the ancient method of *tanging*, with a fervour worthy of classic poetry and bee music. Still such a scene would not be very appropriate in a populous locality, where itinerant dealers, servant-maids, tax-gatherers, penny postmen, and perambulating boarding-schools, would make a strange melange to dodge a swarm over the walls of a suburban seminary, or into the green retreat of a deaf invalid. There must be no swarming in towns for many reasons; but if it should accidentally occur, the swarm may be hived without danger if the operation is performed with confidence, and *at once*.

On this point Mr. Taylor says, "A clean dry hive is the best; and, if of straw, cutting off the loose ends. They usually alight very shortly after quitting the family domicile, and cluster on a bush, or branch of a tree, when they are easily shaken into a hive put close under them. Turn the hive in its proper position, a little raised on its board, and shade it from the sun. If the queen bee is in it, the others will soon join her." If a hive is not at hand use a hive cover, a depriving cap, or an old basket. *Secure* the swarm first, and dispose of them afterwards.

The new swarm should be at once placed where it is to remain. It is the custom in the country to let it remain till night, before assigning it its proper place, but all ex-

perienced Apiarians agree in condemning the practice. The
lives of many bees are sacrificed every time a hive is
shifted, and at the critical period of swarming, they should
be disturbed as little as possible. In fact, the swarm once
hived should be conveyed to its proper place if possible,
without leaving the hand of the operator at all, and many
valuable lives will be saved in consequence. Where unusual
difficulty attends the capture of a swarm, it is advisable
to look for the queen, who may generally be found by the
extraordinary clustering of the bees around her. If she is
taken in the hand with a few bees, and placed in the hive,
the remainder of the swarm will join her in a few minutes.

To comfort the timid Apiarian, we will conclude this
chapter with an anecdote, which the author of the "Honey
Bee" quotes from a Scotch newspaper, "of an elderly
gentleman, on *whose face* a swarm of bees alighted. With
great presence of mind he lifted up his hat, hive-like,
over his head, when the bees, by their natural instinct,
at once recognising so convenient a home, betook themselves to his head-gear, which he then quietly conveyed
into his garden. Had he fidgetted and flustered, as most
old gentlemen—and young ones too—would have done in
his situation, he would doubtless have presented the same
pitiable object that our readers must remember in Hood's
ludicrous sketch of an unfortunate *Bee-ing*."

A young swarm will frequently throw off a swarm, while
the parent stock will also throw off swarms in addition to
the first, so as at last to get broken up into swarms and
casts. The object of the bee-keeper should be to hold
these together, and by consolidating one strong community,
to insure activity and regularity in the operations of the
hive, which it is impossible to have where swarming absorbs the attention of the bees, and distracts them from
work at the very best season of honey-gathering. There
are various modes of preventing such accidents, and these
will be dealt with in a chapter on management.

CHAPTER III.

WHETHER thou build the palace of the bees
With twisted osiers or with barks of trees,
Make but a narrow mouth: for as the cold
Congeals into a lump the liquid gold;
So 't is again dissolv'd by summer's heat,
And the sweet labours both extremes defeat.

VIRGIL, FOURTH GEORGIC.

 IN describing the Apiary and its furniture, I shall contrive to meet the wants of those who may take to bee-keeping, either as a source of amusement or a means of profit; for both may be admirably combined in this pursuit, which is fruitful in rustic amenities, and at the same time characterized by utilities of the sternest cast. I write for the behoof of those who love rural scenes and rural occupations, but whose avocations compel them to dwell in the vicinity of towns, but who, nevertheless, would surround their homes with as many of the cherished rusticities as the "local habitation "admits of. Therefore, in treating of the aspect of the Apiary, and the structure of the hives, I may have regard to picturesqueness of appearance and facilities for study, rather than smallness of outlay and largeness of profit, though I am at the same time sure that if the bees pay their

own expenses, and something "to boot," it will be an additional and not unworthy inducement for many suburban readers to make the experiment of keeping them.

The author of the charming "Essay on the Honey Bee," whom I have already quoted, says, "It would be an excellent plan to attach a stall* of bees to the south wall of a gardener's cottage or lodge, with a glass side towards the interior, so that the operations of the bees might be watched from within. The custom of placing them within an arched recess in the wall of the house was one of old Rome, and is still observed in some countries. We look upon this as a very pretty suggestion for a fancy cottage in any style of architecture."

Unfortunately our suburban cottages seldom have the arched recess, although the tenant might construct it if he thought proper, and it would really add very much to the rural tone, indeed to the classic completeness of a country box, if a fourteen or sixteen-inch wall, filled in with rubble, were run up sufficiently high for architectural purposes, for the sake of leaving an arched recess for a bee-stall on the east or south side. If attached to a summer-house or conservatory, the "glass side" might be adapted to increase the enjoyment of a garden retreat.

The requisites for an Apiary are dryness, a free circulation of air, exposure to the south-east during summer, and to the north-east during winter. It should be sufficiently near the house, that the bees may get used to the inmates, and the inmates familiar with the bees; if too far removed the bees get shy and wild.

The bee is a delicate creature, and cannot abide cold or damp. The bee is an early riser, too, and unless the first beams of the sun gild his doorstep, he loses courage in his work. Where there is plenty of garden room, it is easy to choose a suitable spot; and in most suburban localities little difficulty will be experienced in fulfilling

* See engraving at the head of Chapter I.

the requisite conditions in the establishment of an Apiary. A terrace under a parlour window, a conservatory or greenhouse, a small open yard, where the air is sweet, or even a parlour or garret window, are all suitable sites for an Apiary in town. It is no unusual thing to find persons regretting they have no suitable place for a bee-stand, when half-a-dozen good positions, unappropriated, and requiring little or no alteration, stare them in the face. There is no better situation for bee-stands than a grass-plot, the drier and quieter the better, with shelter towards the north, and some amount of shade from the midday sun in summer.

Mr. Taylor says, "The hives ought never to be put near a wall, but must have a good approach at the back, where all operations should be performed. Nothing high should be allowed in front; but a few shrubs of no greater height than the alighting boards of the hives are rather an advantage as a resting-place to the bees on their return from work, for, from apparent fatigue, they frequently fall to the ground just on reaching home. All should be kept clean and well-mowed around, and nothing offensive be permitted in the vicinity."

Except where bees are kept on an extensive scale, a bee-house is scarcely necessary, except for purposes of ornament. Hives last longer, and bees thrive better under cover, and if the suburban Apiarian determines to erect a bee-house, the style of the erection must, of course, be made to agree with the general style of the garden. An arbour, pavilion, or summer-house, may be turned to account for bee-purposes, in which case the hives should be ranged so as to be visible from some good point where a seat will afford an opportunity to watch them. One of Nutt's Collateral Hives would make a very appropriate ornament to a Chinese or Italian summer-house, or any of the wooden bee-boxes, from their angular outlines, would suit a trimly-kept and formal scene; though for a rustic aspect, nothing would be more appropriate than straw hives. The bee-houses represented on pages 255 and 268 are adapted for ornamental garden scenes, the second being truly rustic in design; the south side fitted with a continuous shelf for the hives, and the north left open as a summer-house, though in a dry and sheltered spot the hives might be arranged *all round*, and an entrance made in the centre of the north side. The hives might be enclosed with moveable glass sashes within, for the purposes of observation. If the plan of conducting the bees out by means of tunnelled floor-boards were adopted, glass sashes would not be necessary inside. Milton's Cork Hive, hereafter described, is specially adapted for the adornment of a lawn.

Every form of bee-hive is graceful, from the humble dome of straw perched among hollyhocks, with which we became familiar when we learned Dr. Watts' lines—

"How doth the little busy bee
Improve each shining hour,"

to the dignified pavilion which Mr. Nutt calls the Temple of Nature. There is no such thing as an ugly bee-hive.

Mr. Taylor says, "I should recommend a covered shed or verandah, in a well-screened spot, partially open in front only, with ample space inside for a passage behind the hives. Our more scientific and experimental Apiarians, however, often like the complete seclusion of a closed but well-lighted building, within which the hives are ranged, with suitable covered passages opposite to each, leading through the wall, for the ingress and egress of the bees, the latter having otherwise no admission into the room itself. There is no reason why any design that may be adopted should not be made conducive to the ornament of a pleasure-ground." My own bee-house is a simple shed with a thatched roof, with three rails along the centre for the hives, which are open to view in all directions. In the

winter a screen is attached to the north side to protect the
hives from cutting winds.

When exposed fully to the south, provision must be
made to afford shade in hot summer weather, for exposure to intense heat irritates the bees, and interrupts the
labours of the hive. A mat or screen of some kind must
be used during the hotter months, to shade them from the
midday sun, though the same end may be attained by having
the roof of the house projecting sufficiently forward to give
the necessary shadow. In my own bee-house the straw-roof
projects twelve inches to the south, so that the hives are
sheltered effectually from driving rains and the fierce rays
of a vertical sun.

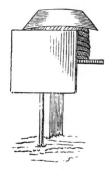

Beside the convenience a garden affords, one or ·two
hives may be placed in the window of a room. For this
purpose Collateral Boxes are very suitable; they should
be furnished with glass windows at the back and front, to
admit the light freely for purposes of inspection. The
doubling-board is represented in the cut projecting outwards
through the window, which is shut down upon it to prevent
the entrance of bees to the room. All the manipulations
would be performed in the room, and as not a single bee
need ever gain admission, their management would be
attended with the most perfect safety. Mr. Milton, of
Marylebone Street, has invented a very elegant hive for

window-management; it is called the Royal Alfred Hive, and is highly suitable for the conservatory, library, or boudoir. It is very portable, and is so constructed that every part of the interior may be viewed at any time without the possibility of the operator being stung or alarmed. Neighbour's *Unicomb* Hive is also well adapted for similar purposes.

It is pretty well known that there are two methods of keeping, or rather two methods of *treating* the honey bee; by one it is killed, and the whole of the honey taken; by the other it is preserved, and man profits by a part. The

theory of the latter mode is, that bees swarm on account of the increased heat of the hive; and though the theory may be open to debate, the practice based upon it is unquestionably sound. It consists in *enlarging* the hive at the proper season; the enlargement prevents swarming, and the chamber added is afterwards taken away with what it contains, and the two objects of improved hives are accomplished, namely, prevention of swarming, and partial deprivation of the honey store. Thirty pounds, hive and all, is considered sufficient for the bees, the remainder man appropriates as his share for the expense and trouble of tending the bees. There can be but three ways of adding to a hive; first by enlargement at top, called by bee-masters *supering*, or *storyfying*, because additional *stories* or *supers* are added above the stock-hive. Another process is that of adding extra room at the bottom, called *nadiring*, which is seldom practised. The last method is by enlargement at the sides, by adding boxes, called the *collateral system*. Each of these methods has its peculiar advantages, according to the kind of stock to be operated on, and also according to the desire of the Apiarian, who may want an increase of bee-stocks, rapid formation of honey, or improved facilities for studying particular operations of the hive.

To enter into all the advantages and disadvantages of these plans would occupy a volume, but as the destructive process does not come within the province of this work and as many of the improved hives will not need to be described, it remains for me to treat of a few select hives only. When the construction and mode of working these is understood, it is an easy matter to appreciate the peculiarities of any other hives at a first view, so that anything like a catalogue would be as unnecessary as distasteful.

One of the best and cheapest forms of straw depriving-hives is that recommended by Mr. Payne, and improved somewhat by the ingenuity of Mr. Taylor. This consists of a stock-hive, thirteen inches wide and eight inches deep, withinside. The stock-hive is open at both ends alike, and is stopped at top by means of a moveable wooden crown-board, made of two circular boards glued together, the grain of the wood crossing to prevent warping. The boards are of different diameters, one being cut so as to fall within the inner diameter of the hive, the other large enough to project beyond the edge of the hive. In the centre of the crown-board is a four-inch hole, which is stopped with a piece of mat or zinc. At the proper time the straw mat must be removed, and a straw cap or glass placed over

the hole. This must be covered by the *super* or upper hive, which fits on the stock-hive, and has a crown-board uniform in appearance to that of the stock-hive. The bees pressed for room will ascend to the cap or bell-glass, through the hole in the crown-board or adapter, and commence filling the cap with new comb. When filled the cap is removed, and its place supplied by another, to be removed in its turn, and so on as long as it is considered judicious to deprive the bees of the very finest of their

produce. If the straw of the stock-hive is worked on a hoop, so as to lift the straw above the floor-board, it preserves the straw from the action of damp, at the same time securing the bees against the intrusion of enemies. The entrance should also be cut in the floor-board instead of the base of the hive, which affords additional security; and windows for observation, as well as a thermometer, may be added if required.

Another simple and easily-managed hive is Messrs. Neighbour's "Ladies' Observatory Hive," which certainly does merit the attention of ladies, from the ease and safety with which the operations of the bees may be observed in it.

In this the stock-hive is formed wholly of glass, and exhibits at any time a complete view of the entire structure. Deprivation is effected by means of a bell-glass placed over the centre of the stock-glass, which the bees quickly fill during the season of abundance. Over the glass is placed a straw cover to insure darkness.

This is one of the best hives for an in-door Apiary; it is easily fitted to a window by means of a tunnelled floor-board running across the ledge inside, and opening outwards by means of a hole three inches wide and three-eighths deep, cut in the window-sash. The hive then occupies the centre of the window inside the room; not a bee can gain admission to the room, and the straw cover may be removed, and the whole of the miniature city exposed to view at any time, without the slightest risk. This is well named the Ladies' Hive. Surely there can be no more pleasing amusement than a lady may derive from one of these fitted to a window looking on a garden, where the bees may be seen going and returning, while comb-making, nursing, and all the other wonderful processes of the hive are proceeding undisturbed under the gaze of the fair proprietor.

The Humane Cottage Hive, which might very well be called a Ladies' Hive also, is a more elegant affair than the last, and certainly more productive in honey, while in cost it is a trifle cheaper. This one does not afford so complete a view as the glass box, but the windows and storyfying glasses above make some amends for the loss of complete transparency; while there can be no question that the bees will give it a preference, for, to speak the truth, they have but little vanity, and do not care to be stared at, much less hived in glass, and made transparent morally as well as physically. This is perhaps the prettiest

of all the straw depriving-hives—it is the perfection of a
fancy hive; for while the bees take to it kindly, and work
as well in it as in any, whether new or old, it serves
well for study, and may be managed with ease by the
most timid. The adapter is pierced with three or four
small holes, or with one large one, according to the fancy
of the purchaser, and over these are worked correspondingly-
sized bell-glasses; the communications being cut off when
necessary by means of zinc slides. These ingenious inventions are represented in the adjoining engraving.

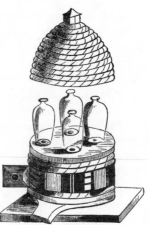

Ladies' Observatory Hive.   Humane Cottage Hive.

Many other kinds of straw hives might be enumerated,
but as the principle of action is but little varied in them,
lengthy descriptions are unnecessary, as any of the experienced dealers in hives will give information and advice
on any special points. Messrs. Neighbour, of 127, High
Holborn, and 149, Regent Street, London, will give every
information that purchasers may require.

We cannot leave the subject of straw hives without
referring to the Grecian Bar Hive, invented by Mr. Golding,

of Hunton, the author of the Shilling Bee Book. This hive is intended to carry out an experiment first suggested by Huber, namely, that if a piece of comb be attached to the roof of the hive, the bees continue it, and range all their subsequent combs parallel with it. In this hive there are seven wooden bars resting loosely on the upper rim of the stock-hive; by attaching a small piece of comb to each of these bars, the bees "follow my leader" and construct a separate comb on each bar, so that by lifting the bar any comb may be taken out at pleasure—an admirable help to the study of the bee. Bar Hives are unquestionably among the best contrivances for experimental bee-keeping, and have been brought to great perfection by Mr. Taylor, as we shall see presently.

We now come to the more elaborate constructions in wood, to which straw hives must yield the palm of superiority; if not for picturesqueness, at least for grace and artistic perfection of outline, as well as for admirable adaptability to the wants of the bee.

The plan of the Grecian Bar Hive, as first adopted by the ingenious Mr. Golding, has, by Mr. Taylor, been brought to a perfection which leaves nothing to be desired; and to him we are indebted for many other improvements both of hives and modes of management. The Amateur's Bar Hive, as constructed by Mr. Taylor, in extension of Mr. Golding's plan, is unquestionably the best bee-box extant, and just the thing which the suburban student requires to secure good honey, abundant and novel opportunities for study, with the greatest possible safety and ease of manipulation.

The Amateur's Single-bar Hive is made of wood, of an inch and a quarter thickness throughout, and consists of a stock-hive, and one or two supers for storyfying. The engraving A represents the floor-board, which is an inch and a half wider on all sides than the box, and from the line which marks its projection beyond the box, it is

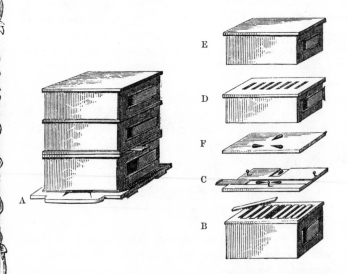

chamfered down every way to three-eighths of an inch at the edge. From the outer edge the entrance is cut quite level till it enters the inside of the hive, when it gradually slopes upward. Should it be necessary to contract the opening at any time, small blocks of wood, cut for the purpose, can be fitted as may be required.

B is the stock-hive, which measures eleven inches and three-quarters square, withinside, and has a height, including the bars, of eight inches and a half. The windows and shutters are the same as those just described in the plain box. The stock-hive B and the super D are each furnished with seven or eight moveable bars, one inch and an eighth wide, and three-quarters of an inch thick, fitted rather loosely into shallow recesses cut from the upper inner edge of the box. Between the bars are spaces of half-an-inch.

The crown-board C is peculiarly constructed, and evinces a happy ingenuity. It is fastened down by means of long screws, and serves the double purpose of a crown-board to the stock-hive, and an adapter for supering—a great advantage to the amateur, who, even when enveloped in clouds of tobacco-smoke, is not always "possessed of the nerve requisite to perform periodically the operation of changing the cover immediately over an over-flowing stock." Mr. Taylor's plan renders so alarming a process unnecessary. Grooves three-eighths of an inch deep are recessed out of the under side of the crown-board near its front; these grooves run across the bars, and allow a passage for the bees beneath the crown-board from one part of the hive to another. As there are eight spaces between the bars and the sides of the box, these two grooves running across the bars will afford the bees sixteen three-quarter inch wide openings for communication.

On the lines of these grooves holes or slits are cut through the crown-board for the admission of the bees to the super boxes, and in the arrangement of these one of the great advantages of this hive consists. The upper surface of the crown-board is recessed or grooved, so as to admit two slides of zinc over the slits through which the bees pass to the super. These slides or dividers are four inches in width; they traverse the groove and meet in the centre, and when a little drawn out the holes with which they are pierced serve to ventilate the hive through the slits in the crown-board beneath them. To obviate danger to the bees in passing the dividers, the openings in the crown-board are cut to a point at the inner extremity. The top-box, E, is cut at the edges under the cornice to admit air for ventilation. The arrangement of the three holes through which the bees pass to the super is seen in cut F.

In this hive three boxes are frequently used. The centre one is either made exactly like the lower one, with a crown-board of the same kind, or it is a mere case corresponding in outward form to the stock and super above it, with a square frame between it and the super, to preserve exteriorly the same appearance as if it were fitted with a crown-board. This latter form is generally far preferable, because if we give the bees a third set of bars, they must lose time in laying new foundations, whereas by introducing a mere case between the super and the stock-box, they are enabled to continue the combs down into it, and in depriving, the whole of the store above the stock-box may be lifted away in the two boxes; the combs hanging from the bars in the super. The triplet or centre-box should not be so deep as the stock by at least two inches. This hive on its stand, with three boxes in their places, and the entrance hole fitted with a porch of bent zinc, is represented in the engraving on the next page.

In respect to the working of bar hives, Mr. Taylor gives the following instructions:—"In the swarming season, the lower box must be stocked by hiving a family of bees into it in the usual manner. On this occasion the dividers on its cover should be temporarily made fast in their places, previously, however, it will be necessary to attach what are called *guide combs* to two or three of the bars. The object in view is to furnish foundations, on which the bees will continue their works, without placing the combs across the bars, as they might otherwise choose to do. In other words, they must be constrained to build in straight lines, one comb not being attached to another, which would render their subsequent extraction difficult or impossible."

Pieces of clean *worker* comb should be chosen, *drone combs,* and those with *elongated* cells, are to be avoided. To attach them, let a common flat-iron be heated, and then warm the bars with it, and then melt a little bees' wax upon each. "The comb is now drawn quickly across the heated iron, and held down upon the bar, to which it firmly

adheres if properly managed." These pieces of guide comb need not be more than two or three inches in diameter, and should' be attached on each of the side-bars nearest the centre one.

The proper time for giving additional room to the bees must be a matter of judgment, depending, in part, on the

weather and season. The super must be prepared with
guide combs, in the way already described; and the dividers
being withdrawn, the bees will ascend into it; and perhaps
the more readily if a little honey is smeared on the guide
combs. The dividers will now be out of use, and the
recess they had occupied hitherto can be turned to a beneficial
account, as a means for supplying ventilation to the super
standing across it. For this end the space should be kept
clear.

When it is desired to obtain possession of the combs
from the super hive, in the middle of the day the dividers
must be pushed under it into their places. Do this gently
to avoid injury to the bees, and without noise or jarring.
The communication being thus cut off from below, the super
may be wedged up a little on one side where it stands.
The bees will probably soon shew signs of a desire to
escape, unless, indeed, it should turn out that the queen
bee is therein—not often the case. In such an event, the
tumult would most likely be perceptible in the stock-box.
An emergency of this kind is to be met by restoring matters
to their previous state, and again withdrawing the slides
for another trial a few days later. If, however, all is right,
the bees will rapidly quit the box, when the top may be
unscrewed, and the stragglers brushed out between the
bars with a feather or twig.

Possession can now be had of as many of the loaded
bars as you may choose to remove, taking care that your
partners in the concern are well provided with family store
for the winter. In case of need, or doubt, a comb or two
had better be left for an emergency in the spring, which
might perhaps then save the trouble of feeding. The bars
may be replaced, or spare ones inserted in the super, into
which the bees can again be admitted, time and season
permitting, and fresh work commenced. On removing the
combs from the bars, the latter should not be scraped
clean, but a row or two of cells may with utility be left

attached. This is always agreeable to the bees, and saves future trouble in the fixing of guide combs. In no other description of hive can there be witnessed a more beautiful sight than combs thus regularly worked to the bars; and one may be taken whenever required. Nor is it possible in any other way to have them so perfect and unbroken when detached.

When it is required to operate upon a *stock-box*, a different mode of proceeding becomes necessary. In such an event it is desirable to have ready a piece of board of the same width and thickness as the top. In the middle of the day unscrew the latter, sliding it sideways, the extra board filling up the vacancy as you proceed. In this way only as much space as is wanted to extract any given bar need be uncovered.

A few puffs of smoke will intimidate the bees, and drive them down. When once intimidated by smoke, almost anything may be done with them. Such is the mode of working the best bee-box ever constructed, for neither Nutt's Pavilion, nor Huber's Leaf Hive, can be compared with Taylor's for ease of manipulation, convenience for study, and availability of the harvest; and, we think we may safely say, beauty of appearance, though Nutt's would compete fiercely here.

From the foregoing description the reader will readily understand the construction and mode of working the celebrated Stewarton Bee-boxes, which, for the *profitable* culture of the bee, deserve to be regarded as the most ingenious contrivances extant, as they are also cheap almost to absurdity. I have just (May, 1857) set up a series of these boxes, supplied by Mr. Eaglesham, of Stewarton, North Britain, and the annexed cut represents the boxes as they stand on the bench of my Apiary. They consist of a set of four boxes, three of them formed exactly alike, with the exception that the fourth, which forms the summit, is a little shallower than the others. They are octagonal;

the *inside* measure of each is thirteen inches and three-quarters from side to side, or from back to front; the height of each of the three lower boxes is five inches and three-quarters, the bottom open in all. With the exception

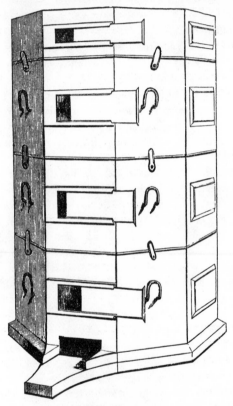

Stewarton Bee-boxes.

of the top or shallow honey-box, the construction of each is the same; the roof is flat, and consists of seven fixed bars, each one inch and a half wide, and between each of the bars are grooves three-eighths of an inch wide, which are capable of being closed by strips of wood. When the boxes are severally placed above the stock, these slips are withdrawn, to allow the bees to ascend, and they are prevented from escaping at the openings outwards of the grooves by little blocks of wood fitted in at the back of the hive. The two lower boxes have an additional *cross-bar*, to give strength to the combs. Each box has a window back and front, closed by a moveable shutter, and every one of the three larger boxes may be used as a stock-box by the withdrawal of a slip of wood from the front, which immediately forms an entrance for the bees to come and

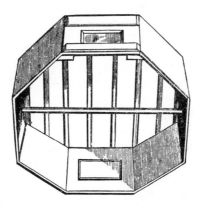

go. Of course they are worked on the storyfying system, or rather a combination of storyfying and nadiring. The swarm is hived into the two boxes joined and communicating with each other. When these are filled, the super or honey-box is added, the bars of the super being first furnished with guide combs. As more room is required, another of the large boxes is added *below* the stock, the original entrance is closed by a slide, and a new one opened by a similar slide in the nadir. In the winter this lower box is removed, and the combs left in it undisturbed for the future use of the bees. The boxes are readily adjusted

by means of buttons, and each has a set of hooks attached
to give facilities for lifting and weighing.

In a communication received from Mr. Eaglesham, he
says, "In a good season I have known a skilful hand take
honey to the value of six or seven pounds from a single
hive, besides leaving an ample store for winter." I said
they were absurdly cheap—let the fact justify my remark;
the boxes are sold at *five shillings each*, or twenty shillings
for the set of four, the carriage of the set to London being
but two shillings and sixpence additional. If I add that
the carpentering is admirable for strength and neatness,
the reader will wonder, as I do, whether the project of
making them is based on commercial or philanthropic
grounds.

Among the fanciful bee-hives Nutt's must take first place.
Nutt's Collateral Hive is an imposing structure, consisting
of a central stock-box, A, called the Pavilion, which is
stocked with a swarm in the usual way. As the stock-box
gets filled with comb, a bell-glass is worked above it, over
which is placed the octagonal cover B. As indications of
crowding are exhibited, swarming is prevented by withdrawing the slides which close the communication between
the stock-box and the side-boxes C C, into one or both of
which the bees enter, and commence the deposit of honey,
which is afterwards removed without injury to the inmates,
and the bees driven back to the stock-box for the winter.
The winter management is facilitated by means of the
feeding-drawer F, to correspond with which, for the sake of
uniformity of appearance, mouldings E E, are attached to
the fronts of the side-boxes.

One of the chief features of Nutt's plan was the improved
system of ventilation, by means of perforated ventilators
D D, which contribute also to the ornament of the boxes.
The ventilation is regulated according to the temperature,
and to facilitate the accuracy of the working a thermometer
inside the glass window of the central stock-box A.

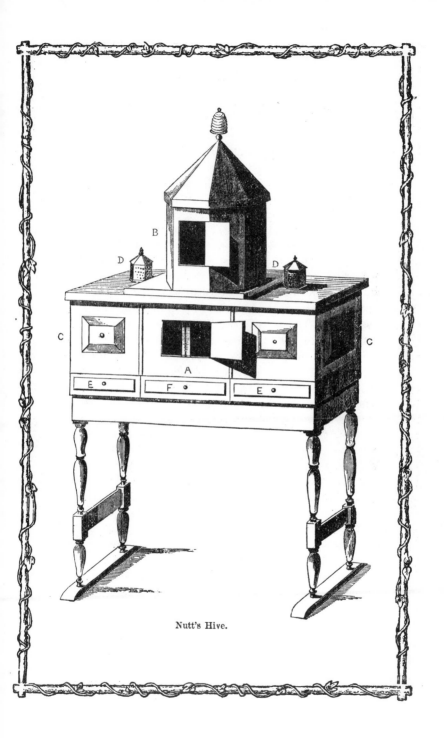

Nutt's Hive.

Still, though this hive looks pretty, there are many objections to it in practice, which are aggravated by the promise of wonderful success held out by the inventor. Mr. Nutt certainly drew attention to the ventilation of hives—a matter of great practical importance, but has not achieved a perfect triumph in his very fanciful "Temple of Nature." This hive, as improved by Mr. Taylor, is described by the latter in his highly-practical and indeed essential work to Apiarians, "The Bee-keeper's Manual." Mr. Taylor also describes a very simple and practical mode of managing collateral bee-boxes of a different structure to those of Nutt's, and which would serve well for the window culture of bees. As a matter of experience, collateral hives are the most difficult to manage, and the beginner should be cautious in his adoption of any collateral system.

The last of the out-door hives to be described here is one of the many high-class inventions of Mr. Milton, of 10, Great Marylebone Street, London, who is a real successor of Wildman, a lover of the bee, and a master of bee management. The hive here figured is almost wholly constructed of *cork*, a material not much used for such purposes hitherto, but one, nevertheless, well adapted to conserve that constancy of temperature on which the prosperity of the bee so much depends. It is adapted to stand on a lawn, or to ornament any open position where a colony of bees would afford an agreeable object of contemplation from the windows of a sitting-room.

The hive is double, the working portion being enclosed in an outer case, by which means a circulation of air is maintained around the inner hive, which obviates the need of ventilation in summer; and as air is as effectual a' non-conductor as cork, the warmth of the hive is preserved during winter.

In the engraving, A represents the apex of the outer cover; B the summit of the cover or lid. Opening the door F we see the hive within, where C represents the

supering glasses worked on a cork hive, of which D is the window, and E the top of the hive. Another window is seen at G. The entrance H slopes downwards to guard

Milton's Cork Hive.

against the entrance of wet; and at I is another entrance for occasional use, and for the removal of dead bees and other refuse. Altogether this is a picturesque, substantial, and practical hive, far preferable to the fanciful pavilion of

Nutt, and as an ornament to a lawn, graceful in exterior and fitted to stand all weathers.

It has been long a matter of dispute among naturalists, whether bees can be made to prosper in glass hives fully exposed to the daylight. That question is at last settled in the affirmative, and a new and splendid field of study opened for the cultivation of the bee. Mr. Marriott's glass hives were exhibited under a full glare of gaslight without in the least disturbing the operations within; and they were

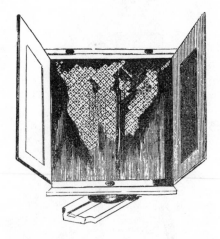

also fully exposed to daylight at all hours. Messrs. Neighbour have also experimented at the Regents Park Gardens and elsewhere, and the fact is now established that bees "do not manifest the least dislike to a continual flood of light." The amateur may therefore safely venture on the use of hives wholly formed of glass, bearing in mind that the bees should not as a rule be wintered in them, and that during the whole of the season bees in such hives require careful ventilation.

There are several admirably-constructed glass hives now in use. For ordinary purposes Neighbour's Ladies' Observatory, (already described,) and Taylor's Bar Hive, constructed with glass sides, will be found suitable. But for window study, the Unicomb Hive, made by Messrs. Neighbour and Sons, will bear away the palm before every other. It is elegant, easily managed, and adapted exclusively for study.

In the annexed engraving the Unicomb Glass Hive is seen to be composed of two sheets of plate-glass, placed so far apart as to allow of the formation of *one comb only*. Shutters to promote uniformity of temperature are attached, but may be entirely dispensed with, if a perpetual view be desired. The floor-board and entrance exhibit an improvement on that adopted by the Messrs. Neighbour, for, as the hive works upon a pivot in the centre of the floor-board, the comb can be inspected on both sides, and the queen bee discovered in an instant.

Messrs. Neighbour's Unicomb Hive is on a similar plan, but the hive is not placed on a pivot, and hence the comb is not so readily inspected on both sides. A window is perhaps the best position for a hive of this kind; and it may be remarked, that since it has been demonstrated that bees *will* succeed exposed to daylight, it would be possible to dispense with the shutters entirely.

I shall conclude this chapter with a recapitulation of the leading arguments which may be adduced in favour of the depriving, as opposed to the suffocating system of Apiarian practice. These may be summed up in brief in the following

TWELVE REASONS FOR PRESERVING THE LIFE OF THE HONEY-BEE:—

I.—Humanity prompts us to preserve the lives of the creatures that associate with us, and more especially of those which render us special service.

II.—The honey harvest commences earlier in depriving hives, and is less interrupted by excessive heat or sudden changes of weather.

III.—In depriving hives the drones are sooner expelled, and the labour of workers is not suspended to prepare for swarming.

IV.—The stocks may be much more rapidly increased on the depriving system, and more hives kept in operation.

V.—Deprived honey is of higher quality than that obtained by suffocation; it may always be had *new*, and free from the taint of sulphur. The same may be said of the bees-wax.

VI.—The honey can be taken at the best period, and as it is wanted.

VII.—As swarming seldom takes place at the height of the honey harvest, there is no fear of the loss of swarms, no cause of alarm to the bee-keeper, and the work of the hive is free from interruption.

VIII. In the old straw-hives the same comb is used again and again for worker-brood, and the bees rapidly degenerate in consequence. In improved hives the comb may be periodically removed, and the population maintained in its natural vigour.

IX.—As the autumn bees live through the winter, their preservation conduces to the success of the spring campaign and honey commissariat.

X.—The humane treatment affords the best opportunities for the study of bee history and economy.

XI.—For purposes of ornament depriving hives excel all others; the latter are restricted in design as in use.

XII.—The world holds the name of Herod in abhorrence; therefore let no lover of rustic life and scenery stain his hands by a slaughter of the Innocents.

CHAPTER IV.

FIRST for thy bees a quiet station find,
And lodge them under covert of the wind;
But near a living stream their mansion place,
Edged round with moss and tufts of matted grass;
And plant (the wind's impetuous rage to stop)
Wild olive trees, or palms, before the busy shop.
VIRGIL.

 HE best way to stock a hive is by a swarm of the season; old hives are seldom worth having to an amateur Apiarian. When a swarm is purchased in the country, it should be carried home the same day as it is hived; a coarse clean cloth securely tied around the bottom of the hive, and over the top by the four corners, so as to prevent the escape of the bees, will afford the means of carrying it easily, even for miles.

The pleasure of bee-keeping is much enhanced if a record of all occurrences be kept in a journal. If it is intended to make entries in a journal, the weight of the empty hive and its floor-board should be accurately ascertained beforehand, and when the swarm is hived it should be weighed again with the bees in it. A tripod and steelyard for weighing hives is manufactured by Messrs. Neighbour and Sons. The cost, weight, and character of the stock should form the first entries in the bee-journal.

The new swarm should be placed where it is to stand

at once, and should there remain undisturbed. When placed
on its stand, which should be accomplished before night,
the bees will sally out and reconnoitre. The next day they
will begin work in earnest, and comb will be formed
rapidly. The hive must not be fixed, the bees accomplish
that in their own way; clay and plaster are sometimes
used, but most injudiciously.

There are two requisites to the success of bees—pasturage
and water. The latter must be near the bee-stand or house;
it should be fresh and clean, and on its surface should be
floated a piece of thin perforated wood, "or a trough may
be filled with moss or pebbles, pouring in water to the top,
and placing it near the Apiary."

For pasturage the bees will travel far and wide, but
there is some utility in supplying as far as we can a suitable pasturage for young or weak bees. Mr. Payne says,
"I have always found the advantage of planting in the
vicinity of my hives a large quantity of the common kinds
of crocus, single blue hepatica, *helleborus niger*, and *tussi-
lago petasites*, all of which flower early, and are rich in
honey and farina."

"Large heaths, sheltered with woods," says the Naturalists'
Library, "are extremely productive of honey, as the wild
thyme and other flowering plants with which they abound
are not cut down by the scythe; and the heath itself remains in bloom till late in the season. The plane tree, the
whole willow tribe, the furze or whin, the broom, especially
the Spanish kind, furnish a rich store both of honey and
farina. When a variety of bee-flowers flourish in the same
field, it is said they will first collect from those which
furnish the best honey; if, for example, several kinds of
thyme grow together, they prefer the lemon variety, which
is of a sweeter and richer fragrance.

But while mainly depending, as they must always do, on
the natural products of the country, the bee-master will do
well to supply his favourites with such flowers, etc., as are

not growing spontaneously in his neighbourhood. In addition to the gooseberry, currant, and raspberry bushes, and the several orchard trees, the flower-borders in his garden should be well stocked with snowdrops, crocuses, wallflower, and above all, the mignionette, which affords honey of the richest flavour, and which continues flowering till the near approach of winter. The rich melliferous blossoms of the *Buddlea globosa*, too, the bees are very fond of; and some of the *Cacalia* tribe afford an ample store. 'The *Cacalia suaveolens*,' says Darwin, 'produces so much honey, that on some days it may be smelt at a great distance from the plant. I remember once counting on one of these plants above two hundred painted butterflies, which gave it the appearance of being covered with additional flowers.' Besides these, the plants of borage and viper's bugloss yield a very considerable quantity of the rich liquid. The former is eagerly resorted to by the bees; it is an annual, and blossoms during the whole season, till destroyed by the frost. In cold and showery weather, the bees feed on it in preference to every other plant, owing to its flowers being pendulous. The bugloss appears as a troublesome weed among corn, and grows on dry soil in great profusion: it is a biennial plant. Turnips, particularly the early garden kind, should be sown, and allowed to remain in their beds during the winter; and they will in consequence, by their early flowering, afford a seasonable supply of farina, and also a small portion of honey early in the spring. The whole cabbage tribe also may be made to contribute their share; and mustard, when sown in successive crops, will continue to blossom for many weeks together." In my own garden I usually sow a few rows of mustard and borage, to flower on in succession till the end of the season, and I find the bees resort to them most gladly. But the best of all bee-flowers is a species of clover called *Melilotus leucantha*.

In selecting sites for your hives, give a preference to a south or south-east aspect, and place them where they will

be partially shaded in summer, and quite dry in winter. Well-painted hives may be exposed, but before the late autumn rains set in, a roof of sloping timber or thatch should be placed over them. The hives will become very populous as breeding goes on successfully, and unless prevented, your young stocks will probably determine on swarming. It is not usual for swarms of the same year to throw off swarms, but it will happen occasionally. Three weeks after the first founding of the colony, make an inspection of the hive. Here will be found the advantage of an improved hive, with good arrangements for storyfying. If the combs are worked nearly down to the floor, and the cells in a good measure filled, no time should be lost in placing a super over the stock; more especially if symptoms of crowding and increased heat are apparent, for by this time young bees are coming forth.

If straw hives with bell-glasses are in use, set one or two to work, not all at once, introducing the others in the course of a few days. If one large bell or cap be used, it must of course be brought into requisition; at mid-day this should be done. Place the cap in its place over the hole in the crown-board, then draw away the zinc divider, most easily effected in improved cottage hives, and then replace the cover-hive, and leave the rest to the bees. The mode of working supers to Payne's straw hives, has been already described. Instructions for manipulating hives, not described here, will be given by the makers when purchased. If Taylor's or Stewarton's bar-hives are used, the operator must attach guide-combs to the bars of the super. Glasses for supering are recommended by Mr. Taylor to be broad and shallow,

rather than of the usual tall bell-shape. They are now made according to Mr. Taylor's directions, and are to be obtained at any Apiarian depôt; they are entered in catalogues as "Taylor's new shape." If made with a hole in the top, and fitted with a ventilator, it is

all the better, and the bees take to a glass more readily if
the ventilator has a small piece of decoy-comb attached to
it; or if you would have the bees work out any particular
pattern for you, such as a series of combs radiating from
the centre, attach a few pieces to give them the direction,
and they will work to it, as in the Bar System. The
pieces of comb must be attached by warming the glass over
a lighted taper.

When first placed the supers should be closely covered
up to exclude light and confine the heat, for they chill the
bees at first. As they get warmed a little air must be
admitted, especially in sultry weather, by slightly wedging
up the edge of the top hive. If ventilators are adapted
to the hive, they should be opened gradually as the heat of
the weather increases, so that the thermometer should never
go higher than from 68° to 80° of Fahrenheit.

Triplets or additional supers should be placed between
the first super and the stock-hive, so that the bees may
continue the combs down into them. First cut off the
communication, and then wedge up the super, to allow
the bees to escape from beneath its edge. The super may
then be lifted off, the triplet fixed, and the super placed
above it, and the bees re-admitted without so much as a
sting upon the fingers, provided it be performed at mid-day
and without jar.

Towards the end of July you may think of contracting
the space the bees occupy. At this time the bees get
ill-tempered, and must be handled with caution and confidence; the fact is, they have now accumulated their
store, though old-fashioned country-folks give them till
Michaelmas to complete it, and having something to defend,
they are very jealous of interference. However, you feel
entitled to take some of the harvest, and as long as you
are satisfied that there is a sufficient winter supply in the
stock-hive, you are entitled to it.

Whatever be the kind of hive on which the operation is

performed, the process is much the same. At *midday* and during *bright weather*, quietly cut off the communication between the stock and the super or collateral box. Then, after waiting about two minutes, so that the bees in the super are sufficiently alarmed at the passing of the slides, gently lift up the super on one side, and insert a wedge to keep it tilted. If the queen is not there, the alarmed bees will escape without attempting an attack. Should the super contain the queen or brood comb, the operation must be deferred to a future day. "All attempts at ejection of the bees by tapping, smoking, or driving, do much more harm than good."

For the removal of the comb from the boxes, proper knives must be used, which may be obtained at any Apiarian depôt. The honey should be at once strained off, and put away in jars tied down with bladder, for exposure to the air soon spoils it.

Various kinds of drainers have been used for separating the honey, and keeping it as much as possible from the external air. The honey which runs off naturally without breaking down the combs, and passes through muslin, is held to be the finest. A second kind is procured by cutting the combs in pieces, and letting the honey pass through a drainer, under exposure to a gentle heat. A third quality is procured by subsequently putting the combs in a vessel placed on a fire; the product, strained through canvass, is used in feeding bees. The separated wax of the combs is introduced into a woollen bag, firmly tied at the mouth, and put into boiling water. The pure wax oozes through and is skimmed off the surface, where it floats. It is then to be allowed to cool slowly. The best honey is supposed to be that formed from heath. The famous bees of Hymettus were nourished by that plant.

> "And still his honey'd store Hymettus yields,
> There the blithe bee his fragrant fortress builds,
> The free-born wanderer of the mountain air."

Before the stocks are made up for the winter, it is necessary to be sure that they have sufficient food. Twenty pounds of honey will be required, and comb, hive, and honey ought to weigh at least thirty pounds, or the bees will suffer from want of food before they begin honey-collecting in the spring. They had better have too much than too little, for they waste nothing, and repay you in the spring for the liberality you shew them in the autumn.

It is at this season of the year that calamitous accidents befall bees, not so much through their natural enemies, or alterations of weather, but through the mismanagement of bee-keepers; the great mistake, so disastrous, yet so universal, being that of removing the honey harvest late in the season. Not a particle should be removed after the last week in July; for after this period there is little or no increase of the stock, though country wives have a strong faith that this is just the hey-day of the rich honey season. Nor is there any need to push the bees hard, even where they are regarded as a sort of agricultural stock; for with good management they will pay an abundant profit to the bee-master long before July closes.

The inexperienced amateur, to whom the loss of a stock, or perhaps the whole of the Apiary in the spring, will be a sad calamity, had better take the wiser course of giving the bees too much, and after having gathered the honey harvest, supply them liberally with food, the more especially in the neighbourhood of towns, where late-blooming honey pasture is not always within reach. In an improved hive, feeding is easily accomplished, and feeders should be purchased at the time of stocking the Apiary. These are made to suit particular hives, though there are feeders which suit almost any hive or box. Mr. Taylor, with his accustomed fertility of invention, gives instructions as to the formation of several kinds of feeders suited to different hives. The principle of all feeders is, however, the same —the bees are admitted to a perforated float, underneath which the food flows to them from an adjoining reservoir. If supplied with food in a bee-feeder towards the end of autumn, they store away a large quantity in their combs, and even enlarge their combs to receive it.

Mr. Taylor says the supply of food should not be delayed later than the beginning of October. "Food must never be given in the open air, or in the day-time, but about sunset, otherwise a great commotion would take place, and the smell would attract wasps, or what is worse, strange bees; in the latter case a battle generally follows. To prevent the scent escaping from the pan, let it be covered."

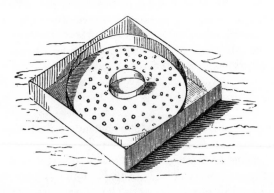

The best food for bees is honey, and in harvesting, all broken combs should be saved for feeding. If honey in sufficient quantity is not at hand, take one pound of loaf sugar, a quarter of a pound of honey, and half-a-pint of spring water; boil up half-a-minute, and allow it to cool; give it to them before it is quite cool. Another good food is barley-sugar. Mr. Taylor says, "The sooner the feeding is ended, the better; the bees, if in health, being on these occasions much excited, and extremely irascible. Let enough be given while you are about it."

Union of Swarms.—When two or three swarms can be united in one hive for the winter, the anxieties of winter

management will be much reduced, the bees will pass through the winter more safely, and the Apiarian will have an increased honey harvest. This is one of the great points in improved bee-keeping, and is not only valuable in making up stocks for the winter, but in the height of honey-gathering, when united swarms prosper amazingly.

The method of uniting swarms now adopted is that of fumigation, which is easily performed, and is certain in its operation, requiring only a little every-day judgment and careful handling for the most inexperienced person to succeed.

The fumigator consists of two pieces of tin tube, of three-quarters of an inch diameter. One piece is about nine or ten inches long, and is attached at one end to a round tin box, the other end being expanded so as to adapt it for insertion in

the mouth of the hive. The other tube is much shorter, and is attached to that portion of the tin box which serves as a lid or cover, and which fits into it after the fashion of a sliding telescope.

The material used for fuming is a fungus, called puck-fist, fuzz-ball, Devil's snuff-box, and half-a-dozen other picturesque names. It is common in meadows and plantations, and is the *Lycoperdon giganteum* of botanists. Mr. Taylor says that the difficulty of obtaining this led him to use another kind, called *Racodium cellare*, which may be found growing in large wine or beer vaults, in immense dark-coloured bunches or festoons, suspended from the roof.

These fungi, ready prepared, may be obtained, along with the apparatus for fuming, at most Apiarian depôts. Mild tobacco will serve the purpose if proper caution be used; we

Y

have seen gold-leaf Turkey tobacco used successfully, but should not recommend the amateur to adopt any but the established plan.

Having determined which hives are to be smoked, proceed (at dusk) to close up the entrances of *all* your other hives by means of the slide for that purpose, or with some cotton-wool, to prevent confusion and robbery; then proceed as follows:—Have the tin box three-parts full of fungus; then lighting the fungus, fume without moving, the hive from which the bees *are to be taken.* The first puff will cause a roaring sound within the hive that will alarm an operator who performs it for the first time. No bee-keeper ever forgets his first essay in fumigation; the sound is like that of the sea surging on a rocky beach; for a few seconds it is awful, but quickly subsides as the fungus takes effect. As soon as you hear the bees falling freely on the floor-board, cease blowing the smoke in, and give the hive a gentle tap, to make them fall faster. Then turn the hive upside down, and you will find the bees heaped as though dead on the floor-board. If you can pick out the queen, do, and place her under a glass at some little distance; if you cannot find her, she must be left to her fate. Brush out with a feather any bees that stick about the combs, and sweep the whole in a little heap, giving them one more puff to keep them quiet. Then smoke the hive into which you intend to transfer these bees. As soon as they fall freely, turn it up, floor-board and all, and set it in a pail, or if flat-roofed, on a bench upside down. Remove the floor-board, and the bees will be found as stupified as the first lot, clustered in the combs.

Now sprinkle both of the intoxicated parties pretty freely with sugared ale, and before they revive, sweep the whole of the first lot into the turned-up hive with a feather. Clean the floor-board of the last smoked hive, and replace it, putting the hive in its proper position, see that the doorway is clear for air, and leave it. As the bees revive,

they will set to work to lick each other clean of the syrup; had they been united without previous stupefaction, they would have fought till scarce a bee would have been left to tell the tale. In the course of a few days another stock may be added in the same way.

Stocks made up in this way get through the winter more safely, and consume scarcely any more food than each separate single stock would have done, so that the bees are benefitted, and the bee-master rewarded with a larger harvest, by the adoption of the excellent plan of uniting swarms. These strong stocks perform wonderful labours in spring; one well-stocked hive producing more than half-a-dozen thin ones. Swarms that come off late in the season may be returned to the parent hive by the same process, and two or more weak stocks may be so united at any time, so as to produce one powerful colony; weak stocks seldom succeed, either for their own good or that of the Apiarian.

We now come to the critical period of winter. The safest rules that can be given for winter management are to exclude from the hives the rays of the sun, and to keep them at an equable low temperature. Damp at this season is most destructive, and so is a confined air. For the first it is advisable occasionally to place a piece of perforated zinc over one of the holes in the crown-board; and over this one of the feeding pans, from which the perforated bottom and glass cover are removed. Over this place a bell-glass, which will attract and condense within it the moisture as it arises from the bees below. In this way the exhalations of the hive may be conveyed away, and dryness assured. The hives should never be closed up in winter, nor shifted from their original quarters. They should not at any season be disturbed, but in winter, quiet is more than ever necessary. Should it be necessary at any time to shift a hive from one part of the garden to another, move it a foot at a time only, and let this be done after dark, and in the most quiet manner possible.

February is the beginning of the bees' year. But they begin the year with no flourish of trumpets, or tidings of gladness, for at this season they are usually weak, and young bees are coming forward in the combs, so that their labours are heavy while food is scarce. If feeding appears to be necessary, defer it as long as it seems safe to do so; and then give food sparingly inside the top of the hive. "It usually suffices to give it three times a week, in one of the pans; but the latter must be completely covered up to exclude cold air, or the bees will not at first ascend into it. At this season it is well to give the food on a fine day, and sometimes slightly warmed." A still better way of feeding in spring is to insert small sticks of barley-sugar in the mouth of the hive. This method is admirable for beginners, who might be awkward in feeding from the top of the hive. If the barley-sugar is without flavouring of any kind, the bees will prefer it.

When once the bees shew signs of real activity in spring, remove any screens that may have been used to keep the winter sun from reaching them, and encourage the warmth of the hive by the admission to it of sunshine. Now will be found the benefit of strong stocks, which bring their brood forward long before there are any signs of life in scantily-populated hives, in consequence of the greater warmth of numbers. Spring flowers in the immediate neighbourhood of the hives are very serviceable, for the bees are now weak, and incapable of long flights; the weather, too, is trying, and if pasture is close at hand, it is a great benefit to them. They soon get strong, however, and disdain the scattered honey-bells of the garden.

As spring advances the temperature of the hive increases, the population becomes more dense, and the work of making

"Boot upon the summer's velvet buds"

begins in earnest. Supers come into use; swarms, if wanted for stocking other hives, are to be obtained; and once more the amateur may look out for well-filled caps and bell-glasses, and an abundance of that choice nectar they never fail to give us when

"--Summer has o'erbrimm'd their clammy cells."

We have as yet said nothing on the subject of bee-stings; we have treated the subject much as if the bee were a patient, inoffensive creature, who would put up with any usage quietly, and with no desire for resentment of injury. Such certainly is not the popular opinion as to bees, yet the fear of being stung is the last thought which enters into the

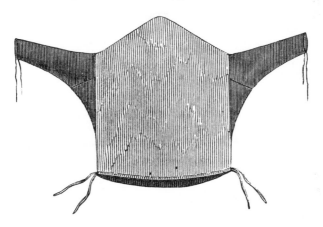

mind of the experienced Apiarian, except in autumn, when it does sometimes happen when *strangers* make too free with the neighbourhood of the bee-house. The fact is, confidence is the best protection; if bees are handled skilfully, there is nothing to fear; and no one will ever succeed who does not love bees; and whoso loves the bees, will be loved by them in return. There is no romance in this; bees do get accustomed to persons, while there are some to whom they are always spiteful. Like ourselves, they have their "likes and dislikes." I can, at any season of the year, inspect my hives, operate in any way that occasion may require, without the need of any kind of protection. To beget this natural confidence, the bee-keeper should take daily interest in them, not in vain meddling, but in quiet observation, and the bees will soon shew that they respect a benefactor. But as every one must have a beginning, and many may begin timidly, the Apiarian armour will be found useful. It is made of a light net, called leno, and passes over the head and face, and fastens round the waist. The cost of the complete garment is only five shillings. The hands should be protected with thick woollen gloves, from

which the bees may easily withdraw their stings. If leather gloves are used the bees cannot withdraw, and are lost in consequence. The loss of the sting is certain death to a bee. Great care should be exercised not to kill a single bee in any operation, for not only do you lose a good servant and friend thereby, but the smell of a dead companion exasperates the whole hive, and an attack is never to be desired.

The sting is rather painful, and as we hope that our lady readers will soon become practical bee-keepers, we advise the immediate use of an alkali, pure ammonia being perhaps the best. My *cara sposa* keeps the blue-bag in readiness when she knows that I have Apiarian duties to perform. It does not often come into use, but when it does it is certainly valuable. A thoroughly effective sting is no joke at all. Bees are much annoyed at being breathed upon, and this should be carefully avoided in all operations with them.

In this account of the honey-bee, and its management, many matters of interest and importance have not been touched upon. My object is to induce residents in town and suburban districts to adopt bee-keeping into their circle of home recreations, and the bee-hive and bee-house into their collection of home adornments. These instructions are more than sufficient to set afloat any beginner who may bring to the task sufficient perseverance and love; without these, and as a mere idle curiosity, the best advice that can be given is, *leave the bees alone*, for, to use a country term, "they want a deal of shepherding."

Those who enter fairly upon the delightful recreation of bee-keeping will find much valuable instruction, as well as many matters of high scientific interest, in that best of books on the subject—"The Bee-Keeper's Manual," by Mr. Henry Taylor. The works by Golding, Nutt, Bevan, and Payne are also of high merit. Mr. Milton's "Practical Bee-Keeper" is another work of the highest merit.

It would be slighting the bees were I to omit from this letter of introduction of them to the family circle at least a couple of recipes for the making of mead, a renowned drink of old times, the favourite beverage of Queen Elizabeth; these, therefore, shall form the postscript.

The first is from the "Encyclopædia Britannica."—"Into twelve gallons of water put the albumen (or white) of six eggs, mixing these well together, and to the mixture adding twenty pounds of honey. Let the liquor boil an hour, and when boiled, add cinnamon, ginger, cloves, mace, and rose-mary. As soon as it is cold, put a spoonful of yeast to it, and barrel it, keeping the vessel filled as it works; when it has done working, stop it up close; and when fine, bottle it off for use."

The next is for the brewing of the veritable drink whereof the immortal Queen Bess—of happy memory—was much enamoured. "First, gather a bushel of sweet-briar leaves and a bushel of tyme, half a bushel of rosemarie, and a pek of bay leaves. Seethe all these (being well washed) in a furnace of fair water; let them boil for the space of an hour or better, and then pour out all the water and herbs into a vat, and let it stand till it be but milk-warm, then strain the water from the herbs, and take to every six gallons of water one gallon of the finest honey, and put it into the boorne, and labour it together half-an-hour; then let it stand two days, stirring it well twice or thrice each day. Then take the liquor and boil it anew, and when it doth seethe skim it as long as there remaineth any dross. When it is clear put it into the vat as before, and there let it be cooled. You must then have in red-diness a kive of new ale or beer, which as soon as you have emptied, suddenly whelm it upside down and set it up again, and presently put in the methæglen, and let it stand three days a-working, and then tun it up in barrels, tying at every tap-hoal (by a pack-thread) a little bag of beaten cloves and mace, to the value of an ounce. It must stand half a year before it be drunk."

> "If thou hast found a honey-comb,
>   Eat thou not all, but taste on some;
> For if thou eatest to excess,
>   That sweetness turns to loathsomeness;
> Taste it to temper, then 'twill be
> Marrow and manna unto thee."
>   *Herrick.*

THE PLEASURE GARDEN

To deck the shapely knoll,
That softly swelled and gaily dressed appears
A flowery island, from the dark green lawn
Emerging, must be deemed a labour due
To no mean hand, and asks the touch of Taste.

COWPER.

TASTE IN GARDENING.

T is difficult to conceive of either an elegant or happy home, which has not, at least, some amount of garden attached. It would doubtless be a libel on the characters and capabilities of the inhabitants of our towns, to say that, without the help of a garden, it is impossible to cultivate chaste ideas and refining feelings; but it is certain that the more we are called into the midst of greenery, and incited to the observation and culture of things that grow and change with the seasons, the more do our minds expand in the appreciation of what is true, and good, and beautiful; and the better traits of our humanity expand, and by degrees obliterate whatever harshnesses and asperities may lurk within us. In fact, none but the most sordid and abandoned are utterly without either a garden, or the best substitute that can be had for one. Where the necessities of life compel men to immure themselves in the midst of

"The dust, and din, and steam of town,"

we find a hundred devices resorted to, to keep the soul freshened in its thirst for something living to lavish its love upon. Flowers in pots, boxes of mignionette, Wardian Cases, Aquariums, pet birds, and affectionate spaniels, are severally adopted as aids to the mind in its constant endeavour to ignore the eternal stone, and brick, and smoke, and noise, that are so foreign to its innate love of life and beauty; and these are cherished because they continually remind their fond possessors of the larger life that lies beyond them in the region of tangled woods and trim gardens.

Now, though it would not be fair to say that a Home of Taste cannot be created except in the vicinity of a garden, it is certain that a garden is a very essential portion of such a home. It has always been so, for at the birthday of the world "the Lord God planted a garden eastward in Eden; and there he put the man whom he had formed," "and the Lord God took the man, and put him into the garden of Eden, *to dress it and to keep it*," for until this first of men and first of gardeners received "into his nostrils the breath of life," "there was not a man to till the ground." So far then from the tilling of the ground being a special part of the curse of the fall, it was from the first an occupation sanctioned by divine command, and though man's highest duty was to love and worship the Father of all things, he was, nevertheless, made to till the ground, created *ab initio* a gardener. Nor did the Almighty spare his mercy, when the fall brought on "the man" a merited punishment. The joy of gardening was still vouchsafed to him, and the eternal penance of himself and his race was to be tempered by a consideration of the lilies *"how they grow;"* for when he went "forth from the garden of Eden," his first sweet task was renewed to him, "to till the ground from whence he was taken."

Through every succeeding period of human history, the culture of plants has taken prominence among the sober occupations, as well as among the amusements of mankind, and this "iron age" finds a strong contrast to its harsh commercial tendencies, in the increasing love of flowers, and the expansion of taste in their arrangement and cultivation. Gardening is now one of the completest of the arts, for it is an art, as well as a pursuit, subject to rules as definite as those which control its sister arts of painting, sculpture, and poetry; and to which indeed it furnishes innumerable materials, and acts at once as nurse, teacher, and standard of comparison.

I cannot hope, in one short chapter, to convey anything like a full expression of my views on the display of taste in gardening, for the subject ranges, wide and far, over a variety of associated topics; but I will here condense into as brief a space as possible, such suggestions as seem to me most likely to be useful to the reader, who, I shall assume, possesses a garden, and wishes to make the best of it according to its extent and capabilities. And the first thing that occurs to me is the fact, that as very few of us, especially in suburban districts, build our own houses, and plan our own grounds, so it is often impossible to realize fully our own ideas of gardening taste; we cannot have any great varieties of surface when we take up our residence on a flat plain, nor can we command a slope to the south where the house is already built on a slope to the north. But where the choice can be made, it is undoubtedly of the first importance that a garden should slope to the south, that its surface should be diversified, that it should admit of some kinds of water scenery, and be surrounded either with fine open country or picturesque woods, or with some objects natural or artificial, on which the eye may rest with pleasure when the walks themselves are exhausted, and we have arrived at the boundary of the domain.

Then as to the laying out, every person who really loves a garden has some idea of the plan and style that will be most pleasing to himself, and a predetermined opinion as to the extent of space to be devoted to the several departments of wood and water, gravel path and lawn, flower-borders, shrubs, and the culture of edibles. The nature of the ground itself must always be first considered in relation to such matters, but whatever the arrangement, every thing must conform to certain principles of taste, or the most sincere efforts will be wasted.

By principles of taste I do not imply any cut and dried formula of ovals, squares, curves, and oblongs, but the sub-ordinating of every detail to the production of a *complete effect,* in which every contrast helps to conserve the harmony of the whole, and in which the details are so disposed as mutually to assist each other in creating a succession of pleasing cares, anxieties, and occupations, and a varied scene of ever-changing delight. It should be borne in mind by every cultivator of taste in gardening, that a garden is an *artificial* contrivance, it is not a piece scooped out of a wood, but in some sense a continuation of the house. Since it is a creation of art, not a patch of wild nature; a part of the house or the town, not a slip from the moor-land—

"God made the country, and man made the town;"—

so it should everywhere show the evidence of artistic taste, in every one of its gradations from the vase on the terrace, to the "lovers" walk in the distant shrubbery. True nature is not to be shut out of the scene, but nature is to be robed, dressed, and beautified, and made to conform to our own ideas of form and colour; and while we delight in some amount of picturesqueness, we are to consider art rather than nature as the basis of every arrangement.

There can be no doubt that, climate and circumstances considered, the Romans hit upon the true theory of gardening. Their pleasances combined all the graces of the modern terrace, the display of architectural and sculptural beauty, the freshness of well-kept lawns divided by clean paths; with the old geometric evergreens and the fanciful arbours that delight us in pictures and descriptions of old English gardens. To the formal scene they added the umbrageous coolness of quaint grottoes and retired nooks, each in its place; the rustic scene removed from the immediate vicinity of the house, and approached through the groves of myrtles, lotus, and pine, all reduced to order by the skill of the gardener. The interior of the house itself formed the first portion of the garden. Here was an open space surrounded by walks, and enclosing a grassy plot with a fountain in the centre. This was the *viridarium*, sometimes ornamented with the myrtle and the plane, and always with the ancestral laurel, a tree sacred to many an old divinity, and which is still a household god with us degenerate Britons. The inner court, or *cavæ dium*, was indeed a sheltered garden, and formed a distinct portion of the house; and even the *Atrium*, which was next the entrance, had its rows of pillars, its fountain, its plots of grass, and vases of flowers, all placed within the daily gaze of the inmates, as essential portions of the domestic furniture. Then the *Tablinum* and other choice rooms opened upon the *Peristyle*, or colonnade, and this was the true Pleasure Garden of the affluent Roman citizen. Sometimes the *Peristyliæ* were of vast extent, with superb fountains, vases, and statuary, and gloomy groves of evergreens; and frequently a forest of umbrageous leafiness, in which singing birds found happy homes amid the shadows which gave coolness to the retreat. Nor were flowers wanting to perfect the artistic arrangement, spite of the sneers that modern writers have heaped upon the old patricians for their love of fruits and other eatables, as elements of a well-planned ground. Aristophanes frequently alludes to the floral glories of Attica; and every classic poet, not forgetting even Juvenal, has in some way or other celebrated the *elegance* of the gardens in and about the imperial city. Virgil describes the old Corycian as rejoicing in his "white lilies," his "roses in spring," as well as his "apples in the fall;" and did he "not so near his labours end," he says he would sing, not only of the cucumber and parsley, but of "*flowery gardens*," and of the roses of Pœstum, as well as of the narciss, green myrtles, and the trailing ivy.

> "Quôque modo potis gauderent intyba rivis,
> Et vrides apio ripæ, *tortusque per herbam
> Cresceret in ventrem, cucumis: nec sera comantem
> Narcissum, aut flexi tacuissem vimen acanthi,
> Pallentesque hederas, et amantos litora myrtos."
>
> *Fourth Georgic, v.* 120.

So far indeed from the gardens of the ancients being composed only of "potherbs and sepulchral cypress," the legends that remain of Semiramis and Adonis, Alcinous and Laertes; and the historical instances of the gardens of the academies, the villas, and gardens of Cicero, Pliny, Sallust, and Mæcenas; and the splendid grounds of Lucullus on the Pincian Hill, overlooking the field of Mars and the Flaminian Way, sufficiently attest that a taste for horticultural embellishments is by no means of modern origin—nay, did not the Romans, cooped up two millions strong, in a space of less than fourteen thousand yards circumference, revenge themselves on the *city*, by placing the *country* above it; that is, did they not build indestructible roofs of larch, and beech, and pumice stones, in order to lay down mould for the growth of fruit-trees, myrtles, laurels, arbutuses, oleanders, and roses? So they not only had their gardens on the house tops, but frequently miniature forests there also, in which wild birds found nesting quarters, and tame birds in cages were hung about to increase the melody of the scene.

Indeed Horace makes it a special subject of complaint, that in his time the ornamental gardens were fast usurping the place of the old olive and apple grounds, and that the demands of luxuriance were fast destroying the profitable groves and orchards; proof enough that a cabbage or bulb of garlic was not the *ne plus ultra* of a Roman garden.

> "Jam pauca aratro jugera regiæ
> Moles relinquent; undique latiùs
> Extenta visentur Lucrino
> Stagna lacu; platanusque cœlebs
> Evincet ulmos: tum violaria, et
> Myrtus, et omnis copia narium,
> Spargent olivetis odorem,
> Fertilibus donimo priori."
>
> *Lib.* II., *Ode* 15.

Though these roof gardens might be worthy of revival at the present day, in London and other great towns, it concerns us most here to get back quickly to the garden proper, and review the thread thus broken, in an attempt to set forth something like a code of taste in gardening.

This discursion demands pardon, because, after all the styles and schools of gardening have been considered, that which prevails at last is based upon the Roman plan. Our modern terraces, vases, sculptures, fountains, glowing parterres, refreshing lawns, and bright gravel paths, formal and artistic, near the house and verging by degrees towards the scenery of the surrounding country; all so nobly worked out at Sydenham, are the several features of a Roman garden, which was always regarded as a work of art, and now as a work of art retains its place, after the schemes of many Browns, and Langleys, and Kents, and Le Nôtres, and Watelets have been long exploded to the winds, as pervertive of good taste, and obnoxious to the mind that has come to regard a garden as a choice appendage to a house, rather than as a toy-shop, a gingerbread stall, or a receptacle for mole-hills and wayside rubbish.   If the *old* Italian, and French, and Dutch, and English gardens had their several good features, the *modern* English garden admits of the combination of them all, without it being necessary to jumble them together, or to crowd into a small space a number of incongruous elements.

How then should a garden be planned? It should first of all be laid out so that every diversity of surface may be turned to good account to increase its beauty; the hollows should be made deeper, the elevations higher. Near the house the artificial tone should be highly cultivated, for here at least the garden is but an amplification of the house itself—here, if you can, have a terrace to overlook the brightest scenes you have. Along the southern and west sides of the building, if the garden be on that side, construct a terrace half as wide as the house is high.   Let this terrace be truly Italian, with balustrades, vases, and statuary; with climbing plants of the richest character to scale its most salient angles. From this terrace let a flight of stone steps lead to another terrace, of double the width of the first, and let this lower terrace be laid out as an elaborate flower garden, on a ground of turf, with stone fountains, statues, vases, and one or two highly-wrought tables and seats of iron or bronze. Here, in the summer, your gaudy parrots will chuckle on their poles, your fountains will splash and sparkle in the sun, above glowing parterres of flowers laid out in Italian patterns, and a few of the choicest shrubs, with perhaps a monster vase or two, loaded with gorgeous flowers, will set off the angles, and serve as a framing to the whole.

From this lower terrace let your paths lead off over lawns sprinkled with evergreens, flower-beds, avenues of deciduous trees, for which hornbeam, lime, or horse chesnut, would be best. Converge the paths so that every slope forms a

separate scene complete in itself, when so contemplated, and
yet forming but a part of the whole. From the drawing and
dining-rooms you have glass passages, leading to your conservatory, greenhouses, bird and bee-houses; and from one
side of the grounds the whole of these houses are visible,
and form a noble addition to your home of taste.

At every opening point in the shrubberies you will place
some object to arrest the eye—a statue, a pile of rock, a
fine acacia, an orange or azalea in a tub, a trained pyrus or
weeping ash, to form a distinct object on the sward or on a
border beyond the path; in some places where you would
have a shady passage leading to a view of the open country,
you will plant an avenue, perhaps a quincunx, and the path
here will be of mossy sward *closely shaven*, instead of gravel.
Where this moss-walk opens again on the outer path you
will place your rosary, arching the path with the richest
of the perpetual bloomers, breaking the sward into elaborate
patterns of dwarf roses, on their own roots in masses of
separate colours, and bounding the whole with a space of
turf, dotted with the finest standards in clumps of threes,
each triad being bound into one head of odorous beauty
by the copper wire which passes like a cord through their
several stems. Beyond the rosary across the lawn is an
immense sweeping background of holly or rhododendron, or
at least of two sorts of shrubs only, and these are broken
here and there to open views of other portions of the garden.
From this point the ground rises, with lawn on the left
hand, and on the right a continuous bank, studded with
wild thyme, strawberries, masses of roses, honeysuckle, and
here and there grand pyramidal avenues of hollyhocks. As
the path ascends we come into view of a dense shrubbery,
before or amidst which here and there arise the tall outlines
of some majestic firs, or the red cedar, the cyprus, the
arbor vitæ, the white poplar, or the hemlock spruce. When
the summit has been gained, the scene that opens is
entirely new.

Below on the left lies the sloping sward, dotted with roses, tree peonies, and hollyhocks, and backed by the rich and dark borders of shrubs; above on the right is the bank covered with roses and trailing cystuses, and broken here and there by immense clumps or knolls of ivy; and this bank extends round in front of us, so as to cross the path and lead the way to a rustic summer-house perched on a hillock, the front of which towards the lawn is faced with rockwork, and planted with ferns and alpines, and the base of it dips into a mimic lake, not fashioned so as to deceive us as to its size, but neatly margined with aquatic plants, and its bosom dotted with a few majestic swans, and some curious water-fowl.

If you found places on your terraces and near the windows of the house for flowers, in elaborate patterns of mosaic, for noble vases, statuary, fountains, sculptures, and gay climbers to festoon the balustrades, here is the proper place for such rustic work as you may care to indulge in. You may embellish the lawns with bark baskets of flowers, tree-stumps filled with flowers and ferns, masses of rock covered with ivy and wild creepers, with, in suitable spots, a rustic seat, a table, a summer-house, or a thatched bee-shed, each object being so placed as to form the key to a separate scene, and to have a visible use to sanction its adoption. Wherever your walks wind they should lead to something or somewhere; they should not wind merely to form ovals and parabolas, but to disclose a scene, a view, an object, or a group of objects; where something which you cannot remove requires to be hidden, throw over the path an archway, build a knoll and cover it with ivy, construct a bower, plant a group of shrubs or trees, but let every detail form only a part of the whole, however each may be to a certain extent complete in itself. Here is a resting-place umbrageous with branches on one side, open on the other to your own grounds, and if you have a view of a neighbouring church, a distant hill, a coppice, a wood, or a sheep-walk, let some good point be selected for observing it, so that you can either revel in the glory of the sunrise with a grand natural panorama before you, or retire to your summer-house to read

> Many an old philosophy
> On Argive heights divinely sung.

From this nook of coolness and verdure four walks may lead back in another direction to your American garden, blushing in its pride of purple blooms, through other lawns covered with fruit, where every visitor may pluck as he pleases, nor barred out by a tantalizing gate, or prevented from approach by a five-feet fence of thorn. Then your kitchen-garden, which you enter through a screen of filberts and raspberries, brings you once more towards the house, and you have only to cross the few borders of shrubs that intervene between the lawns and vegetable ground, to reach again the Italian garden, where the fountains once more delight you with their musical splashing, the flower-plots load the air with fragrance, and the sinking sun gilding the soft edges of the masonry; and the rounded outlines of the groups of sculpture warns you that the dews are increasing, and the lights are ready in the drawing-room, you take a farewell glance at a scene of which you cannot tire, and join the family circle in the best of tempers for coffee gossip, books, or kisses and romps with the children.

But it may not be in the power of every reader of this work to plan a garden on such a scale. Nevertheless, the *idea* of such an arrangement may be carried out in a small plot of a hundred square feet, and no matter what the size, shape, or position of a garden, the leading principles of taste in gardening must be kept in view at every step to insure success in the end. I have just seen a notable instance in what may be done in a narrow space to realize a lovely scene, and how that scene may be marred by one simple oversight. The instance is that of a handsome villa, with

a small fore-court and very limited space of garden ground behind. The villa has a handsome portico entrance and a passage through the house, the rooms are arranged on either side of this passage, and of course there are two front windows, one on each side of the portico. The house itself is a pattern of chastity; the windows bright, the blinds elegant, the window-sills filled with flowers, the fore-court planted with grass and shrubs. Looking through, the eye catches a beautifully-stained glass fan-light, which surmounts a door of enamelled glass, opening into a conservatory. The conservatory is well stocked, and as well arranged; it is a garden in itself. Another glass door, opening at the side of the conservatory door, opens into a small garden, fenced with a well-trimmed hedge of yew, and laid out in parterres of shrubs and flowers, with a small patch of turf in the centre, embellished with a pair of vases. Everything is so bright and cheerful, and complete within, that on emerging at the gate we take one last look at the scene through the open door in the portico, and then we find the whole spoilt by a pair of rustic baskets, placed opposite the windows in the fore-court, one on each side of the central path, leading from the highroad to the house. Contrasted against the stone facings, the trim windows, the stained glass at the further end of the passage, and with the highly-polished *tout ensemble* of this neat country box, those abominable rustic baskets seem fit only to be burnt. A pair of vases would have made the scene complete, but these rustic things betray the wooden-headedness of the proprietor, and prove that he has yet something to learn ere he can realize a home of taste.

I would have every garden symmetrically arranged; the paths should never diverge at sharp angles, a large proportion should be devoted to lawn and shrubs, and the chief display of flowers should be not only near the house, but immediately within view of the windows of the chief dwelling-rooms. Macintosh, in his "Practical Gardener," says,

"In all cases, unless in small villas or cottage residences, the flower garden should be entirely concealed from the windows of the house, and be placed, if circumstances will admit of it, in the shrubbery." He would, in fact, light his candle to place it under a bushel; create a beautiful object and hide it, or at least place it where it could be seen only on high days and holidays, instead of placing it where it should hourly gratify the senses, and suggest to the mind the perfection of the pencil, which, in the fingers of the Almighty, has painted creation in tints of gorgeous and contrasted colouring. Even where the garden slopes away to a splendid prospect of open country, I would still have flowers in the foreground, and around them works of high art should cluster, not to draw the eye from natural scenes, but to combine happily the efforts of art and nature in the production of a living picture.

I would have no puerile conceits anywhere; no attempts at *the picturesque* should be made; as far as the eye could reach, from terrace or window, all should be artistic, and every separate feature subordinate to the whole. Bruccian's casts and copies of the antique should mingle with the Etruscan and Grecian vases of Ransome or Cottam and Hallen. No rock-work should deface the slopes except *artificial* piles, constructed to receive groups of plants, such as verbenas, lobelias, gentianella, specimen ferns, and rock roses. I would have no meaningless curves winding upon themselves, like eels in misery; wherever the paths turned aside it should be to show me something. Water should be seen in plenty in the midst of flowers, and grass, and sculptures, not in green stagnant pools, but in basins of stone, splashing from the mouths of dolphins, or fluted tazzas of classic design. There should be no wilderness of a shrubbery to entangle the eye from a distance, or the head when near, but my belts of holly, arbutus, and rhododendron, my groups of ornamental pines, with the araucaria, the deodora, and the larch should be sprinkled about in

rounded masses, opening at intervals to other walks and
scenes, so increasing the apparent extent of the ground, not
by a trick, such as Evelyn would have delighted in, of
painted canvass and imitative perspective, but by the judicious
mingling of open grassy spaces, parterres, Dutch gardens,
and full masses of green shrub, beyond which should tower
some lofty elms, chesnuts, poplars, and limes, so as to give
richness as well as variety to the scene. Every advance
from this point should prepare the eye for a gradual change
from the highly-artificial to the semi-natural. Here oval
should balance oval, and colour balance colour. If in my
geometric garden I planted from half-a-dozen to twenty
tints, they should be so arranged that no particular one
should snatch the eye aside from the whole, which might
easily be the case if just *one* plot only were filled with
shrubby calceolarias.

The great point to be observed is to fit things together
properly, and to preserve such an arrangement of outlines
and colours as shall present at every point a pleasing view,
and from the windows of the dwelling a picture *complete
in itself*. And not only are the truly rustic features of a
garden inappropriate if brought too near the house, but in
such a position they lose all charm.

"'Tis distance lends enchantment to the view."

The vivid colours of well-kept borders, and smooth plots
of turf, the refined tone of plastic embellishments, and the
idea of order which prevails in the foreground of such a
scene, appear to greater advantage against the darker back-
ground of massive evergreens, deciduous shrubs, and trees
which increase and thicken in the distant prospect, whereas,
if submerged in such a prospect, the classic household gods
would either be lost or appear ridiculous.

But all legitimate contrivances for increasing the apparent
extent of the ground, by breaking the view here and ex-

tending there, are approvable. Where space is limited, or where a cheerful scene involving but little trouble to preserve its beauty is required, an extensive lawn, broken by clumps of trees in variously rounded compartments, the paths winding through it in a series of gentle curves, the whole enclosed by a continuous thicket of shrubs and trees, would, when established, afford a noble scene, varying its aspect at every step, and by its very diversity of outlines, help out the idea of extensive surface.

The subjoined engraving is intended rather as a suggestion than a plan, because a *plan on paper* is always a different affair when worked out on the ground, and can never be of great value unless prepared specially for the ground to which it is intended to apply; hence no work on gardening in general can provide all for the various circumstances of position, extent, and varieties of surface that may require consideration in laying out a garden. It consists of a continuous walk, which, if possible, should have a breadth of seven feet, but should certainly be not less than five. It enters the garden through a border of mixed shrubs, mostly evergreens, and then breaks upon a lawn, which in truth consists of two distinct lawns, one within and one without the path. At various intervals, there are on either side of the walk compartments for flowers, shrubs, and trees, though, unless well managed, shrubs and flowers do not mingle well in the same compartments. The shrubs and trees may be mixed, deciduous and evergreens in about equal proportions. The deciduous kinds may consist of lime, outario, poplar, weeping ash, common ash, chesnut, American thorns, American oak and beech, birch, laburnum, lilac, almond, and *Ribes sanguineum*, one or two of each only in each compartment, those of largest growth occupying the principal positions, so as to aid, not hide, the shrubs around them. For evergreen sorts, hollies in large masses, say hollies alone in at least two compartments balancing each other; and in the mixed masses, tree box, Portugal laurel,

rhododendron, in belts and masses unmixed, lauristinas, Aucuba japonica, snow berry, arbutus, myrtle, (which stands the winter in sheltered positions,) magnolia, privet, common

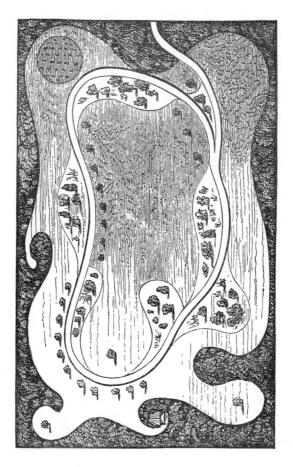

laurel, arbor vitæ, and evergreen cypress. These, of course, are named for selection; some might not suit the soil or climate, some might be preferred in quantities, to the entire

exclusion of others, but a practical gardener in working out
the plan would plant well and make judicious selection,
though for special points of tasteful arrangement he might,
perhaps, want occasional suggestions from the proprietor.

Around the right hand side of the inner lawn a row of
handsome shrubs or deciduous trees might be planted,
and they should be all of one sort; limes might be chosen
for their brightness in spring and their fragrance in summer; the weeping lime would make a delightful sweep of
branchy verdure throughout the season. If there were
not many hollies elsewhere, and especially no clumps of
hollies anywhere, a row of tall specimen plants would
contrast nobly with the bright turf and the various foliage
and borders around. A belt of rhododendrons or American
thorns would also look well, but cypresses or firs of any
kind would be too gloomy for such a position. At the
lower or the outer lawn a similar belt of trees might be
advantageously placed, the whole formed of *one* sort; if mixed,
the glory would be gone. In gardening, repetition in its
place is as useful as variety. In suitable spots a weeping
ash or willow might be planted as a distinct object; a
fine arbor vitæ is useful for such a purpose, so is a pair
of aspen poplars, or a well-spread specimen of American
beech. The willow is certainly appropriate to form "a
key to a position," but it so invariably suggests the idea
of water, that, spite of its own intrinsic beauty, its presence
sometimes mars the effect where water is not to be found.
In planting the clumps, spaces will be left for such landscape
flowers as befit the scene. Roses, (on their own roots,)
the tree peony, the hollyhock, the tall varieties of evening
primrose, aconites, pyramidal bell-flowers, and any tall massive flowering plants or shrubs may occupy the foremost
places, where their beauty will be heightened by the verdurous background against which they are set. In such
a ground some pleasing effects may be produced by very
simple means. A knoll formed of brick rubbish filled in

with soil, and planted thickly with ivy, will in a couple of years form a splendid object to bound the curve of a path, or arrest the eye where an object for the purpose may be required. At the summit of such a knoll a handsome shrub may have a suitable place, and at its base room may be found for a few bedding plants; even half-a-dozen Tom Thumb geraniums, or a patch of *Lobelia ramosoides*, would give it a magical aspect. I have in such positions obtained a cheap ornament to occupy a centre of a knoll for a season, by sowing a dozen seeds of the common hemp, and the graceful group of plants, six feet high and of a rich dark green, has served me as well for the time as if it were composed of costly exotics. In fact, it is not the amount expended on a thing that insures excellence and fitness; it is the judicious use of whatever we may have or whatever we can most easily obtain.

The outer border of shrubs and trees would afford space for a goodly variety, and with occasional patches of colour next the path, and a few objects to give interest to the walk, such as a circular bed of American shrubs in one corner, a weeping ash or birch in two others, a pavilion or summer-house at the remote end, deliciously embowered with fruit trees, and surrounded by patches of sweet-scented plants, and backed by flowering shrubs and deciduous trees, would make up a garden that Lord Bacon would not have sneered at, and one, too, that would in a great measure be self-preservative, the lawn and flowers requiring the only constant attention, the shrubs pretty well taking care of themselves. It should be borne in mind in planting a garden of this character that, however densely the outer borders of shrubs may be planted, the clumps on the lawns must be planted thinly rather than otherwise, and as time goes on, the evergreens should be allowed to extend themselves, so as to break the regular outlines of the compartments with their own rich masses.

This combination of park and pleasure-ground has been treated as if the whole were a level surface. Now I have no hesitation in saying that to lay out a *flat surface* with diversified curves and clumps demands a very small amount of skill, and, moreover, a flat surface, if ever so intricately laid out, is a tame affair after all. It is like a wall paper or a carpet, an everlasting doubling over and over; it is repetition after repetition, ovals giving place to fig-leaves and circles ringing changes with curves that have no name. To make a noble garden you must have a diversified surface; your water must be *below* the general level, and your rockery above it; the green carpet must have furniture in the shape of tree stumps, knolls of ivy, piles of stones to catch the eye as you traverse a path; the eye wearies on a plain, but is ever delighted with a surface judiciously broken into hills and hollows, every rise or fall presenting some feature of interest. The effect intended may not always be realized, but it is the duty of one who plans out a garden to calculate judiciously what its effect will be, not next season, but in years to come. As Cowper says—

> "He who would see his flowers disposed
> Sightly and in just order, ere he gives
> The beds the trusted treasure of their seeds,
> *Forecasts the future whole;* that when the scene
> Shall break into its preconceived display,
> Each for itself, and all as with one voice
> Conspiring, may attest his bright design."

Like all other things that pertain to earth, this chapter must come to a close, so here let us part for awhile, to take up in the succeeding chapters a few of the special features of the garden in their practical bearings one upon the other, and as distinct things in themselves.

THE FLOWER GARDEN

ALONG these blushing borders, bright with dew,
And in yon mingled wilderness of flowers,
Fair-handed spring unbosoms every grace.
  *   *   *   *   *
Infinite numbers, delicacies, smells,
With hues on hues expression cannot paint,
The breath of nature and her endless bloom.
                                        THOMSON.

THIS chapter is to be sternly practical; and I shall endeavour to compress into it a complete series of suggestions for the formation of a Flower Garden, not so much with a view to thrust upon the reader my own notions of what a Flower Garden should be, as to help those who may have special views, to carry them out successfully. For this reason I shall endeavour to shape my suggestions so that they may severally apply to gardens of large or small dimensions; to the Flower Garden as a feature of an extensive pleasure-ground, or as confined in narrow limits within the walls of a suburban property.

First, then, as to its plan. When a lawn or terrace is

to be enriched with a display of flowers, the geometric garden is most appropriate. This must have a symmetrical

arrangement, and whatever the shapes of the several beds, the *whole*, when viewed collectively, must present a distinct and decided pattern of some kind, and that kind must be one that will please the eye. There is no need of harsh outlines, indeed curves of some kind should predominate, and the whole should in some measure correspond with whatever borders or detached beds are in the vicinity. Since a geometric garden always looks best when accompanied with architectural accessories, such as vases and fountains, and is usually to be viewed from a higher level, as a terrace, for instance, the design must be studiously adapted so that the eye may take in the whole from more than one point of view. If possible, a geometric garden should be on a flat surface of closely-shaven lawn. Between the beds the spaces should be only large enough for the gardener to work conveniently, and the beds themselves must not be wider

than can be conveniently managed without the necessity
of treading on them. The more simple the general design
and the parts of which it is composed, the more effective
will it be when furnished.

To these rules a few exceptions may sometimes be necessary. I have frequently laid out a geometric garden,
or a pair of such gardens, one on either side of a main
path, on a sloping lawn, and when the slope is towards

the house the appearance is admirable. Between the beds
narrow paths of gravel or silver-sand may intervene, or
the grass of the lawn may be broken only by the beds
themselves, and gravel divisions entirely dispensed with. I
should usually prefer the latter plan, for the appearance
of a net-work of sand is seldom good, indeed the fewer
small paths in any garden the better.

When detached beds are used for flowers, as they frequently are, on the sides of lawns adjoining walks, simplicity

of design will generally be found most effective, though we do frequently see examples of the most grotesque patterns, which tell well when there is a complete set of such beds, say at four sides of a small lawn, forming a whole when viewed collectively. Detached beds of this kind may be made pleasing, but, as a rule, should be planted with mixed colours, the plants chosen as much for the interest they excite in us as for their beauty. Close-growing flowers, such as the minute campanulas, squills, primulas, pansies, some varieties of sedum, verbenas of quiet colours, ageratums, heliotropes, and petunias, look well in such detached beds if set before or mingled with taller-growing kinds, such as agapanthus, iris, peonies, dwarf roses, wallflowers, aconites, gaillardias, sweet-williams, and other hardy or half-hardy plants that are of quieter character than those used in Dutch gardens. Here annuals of all the choice kinds tell well, and may be grown freely.

Another mode of embellishing a lawn is that of pincushion beds. These are most appropriate where a long walk is bordered on one or both sides by grass. In fact, there must be a continued series of them to produce a good effect and sufficient variety, but they are not only most effective, but economical and easily managed; every little thing stuck into them tells to advantage. Mr. Beaton, the distinguished experimentalist in floriculture, thus describes, in the pages of the "Cottage Gardener," the pincushion beds in his experimental garden at Surbiton:—

"Every one of the pincushion beds must be exactly of the same form and size. If one of them was bigger or less than the rest, the whole effect and the character would be entirely lost; and the same if the least variation is made in the shape. They are all circles; and after trying and studying the different sizes, that which I think is nearest to the truth, and which is adopted, is just one yard in diameter, and, strange to say, there is not a bit of garden ground lost by the use of them, and this of

itself will bring them into use in all places under five acres in extent.

The fact is this: there is a good selection of standard roses planted on the grass along the walks in the experimental garden, just one yard from the sides of the walks; and we began at one end, and made a pincushion bed round each rose-tree, a yard in diameter, and four inches above the level of the grass. Generally, when standard roses are thus planted, there is from a foot to eighteen inches free from grass, and *below* the level of it, so as to take the watering. Now, and all my lifetime, I have been thoroughly convinced in my own mind that this was only a rude and unartistic expedient, forced on us because roses are so thirsty, that to raise them on circular mounds, as they do the fancy trees at the Crystal Palace, and, I hope, in all other places, would be little short of madness, for then all the watering in the world would only prove what the Horticultural Society, in their daft experiments, proved in the first rose-house at Chiswick; that is, proved the death and destruction of every rose so 'operated' upon. Then, to get rid of the ugly hole for ever, and to be able to cultivate the rose-tree on grass, as the rose-tree requires to be cultivated, wherever it is, the scheme of pincushion beds is exactly the 'balance of power' between good and bad cultivation; between the rude attempts of the middle ages, and the present knowledge of 'common things;' and you have the flowers as the second bird down by the hit.

The philosophy of the thing stands thus:—All the cultivated roses like a *cool, moist bottom*, but no standing wet; and all the standard roses *on grass* ought to get a good spadeful of right rotten dung every winter of their lives, and as much water in summer as will keep the space occupied by the roots constantly moist. The present hole in the grass system can only allow a make-believe in all those essentials, and no more.

The manner of doing the thing is this:—The rose-trees,

perhaps, are planted on the grass already; but you may know, from the rusty-brown leaves, that they are three-parts starved. Open the grass in a circle of a yard across round each rose, then scrape off the soil carefully till you find the roots. When you find the roots, pour two large watering-pots full over those of each tree, supposing that you are doing the work as soon as this is printed; (July) then put two or three inches of very rotten dung all over the roots; water again with the rose put on the spout of the watering-pot, and pat down the dung with the back of the spade. Now, the dung is just level with the grass, or nearly so, more or less, and you must keep it out of sight. Any good light garden-mould will do to cover the dung; let it be full three inches deep, or rather more; and, to keep up the sides from the grass, you must use an artistic edging to give dignity to the whole. What we use is the best and cheapest; burnt brickbats, and whole bricks of a dark grey colour, such as are too much burnt in the making; but stones would be as cheap, or cheaper in many places, and stumps of larch poles or of any other poles would do if cut into six-inch lengths and sharpened at one end, to be driven down two or three inches close to one another all round. The soil is as high as the top of the edging—ours is four inches high, and quite level on the top, or rather with a hollow towards the stem of the roses. Three nice *Tom Thumbs*, and three equally good calceolarias out of about forty-eight-sized pots, will fill one of these beds except the edging. As we do not go quite close to the rose stem, *Œnothera prostrata*, all the little blue lobelias, *Campanula fragilis, Garganica*, and two or three more of them, and many more such 'tit bits' will do for edgings.

Again, (among geraniums) *Flower of the Day*, all by itself, or Lee's *Attraction*, or Gain's *Attraction*, or *Mountain of Light*, or Kinghorn's *Countess of Warwick*, or *Annie*, both exquisites for pincushions; or, again, for a plainer collection, take *Glow-worm*, or *Harkaway*, or *Baron Hugel*, or *Tom Thumb*, and make one bed of any of them, and the opposite bed with the other, and see the difference without an edging; or to come to the *dandyfication*, use only a selection of the best bedding *Quercifoliums*, *Diadematums*, and such like.

If your garden is too dry, or too wet, or too heavy for this class, make the pincushion bed accordingly. It need not be more than three inches deep if your soil is very stiff and damp, and the compost may be poor or rich: it is just like making a bed inside a sieve or a tar barrel. No dwarf plant that is at all suitable for beds will come amiss here; but they should all be very choice; and ought to be considered the cream of the place. Next winter, and every winter, when it is dry, empty out every one of these beds, and mulch the roses afresh; after that, let them always have it in winter. Mix what remains of the old dung with the top soil, and that will do for some years, as you only put it on, as it were, to hide the dung, merely planting to hide the mulching. Very shallow flower-beds want much water in dry weather—the more the better for the roses, as every watering gives them a fresh feast from the dung. *Crocuses* in spring, choice annuals in May, and *late* propagated choice plants for summer."

As to borders, there is no doing without them; they fringe walls, fences, and grass-plots, and beautify the walks everywhere. In suburban gardens, and in the gardens attached to town villas, the borders often present the most attractive features, owing to the limited capacity of the garden precluding geometric arrangements and pincushion beds. Borders should never be wider than can be conveniently reached across; in fact, a very broad border under a wall or fence does not look well. Borders on grass and in open grounds frequently take the form and arrangement of detached beds, and when they are planted with shrubs, care should be taken to break them here and

there into sweeping outlines, so as to open an occasional space for the eye to escape, as well also to increase the means of transit from one part of the garden to another.

For regular borders, especially where they have considerable length, the style of planting known as *ribbon gardening*, so finely carried out at Trentham, is usually most appropriate. Many will prefer the old-fashioned mixture of shrubby flowers, evergreens, and annuals; and if the borders are well cared for, this old-fashioned style gives us variety and symmetry at the same time. But the line of the path being somewhat formal, the line of the border being ditto, and the garden perhaps rendered very formal in the whole by its enclosures, *ibbonism* may have encouragement without fear of a Hibernian skirmish.

What is meant by ribbon gardening? It is the arrangement of plants in lines, each line being of one colour or one set of blended tints, and the plants forming the several lines of the border are so selected as to contrast against each other, and produce a harmony in the whole, one essential part of the arrangement being that every successive row from the path is a trifle taller than the last, the wall, fence, or boundary of the border being either covered with climbers, trailers, hidden by the tallest-growing flowers, or formed of a line of mixed luxurious shrubs. On the planting of borders and beds of all kinds, I shall occupy a few pages presently.

Having determined on the general plan of your ground, and having in that plan made the most of every old tree, or existing ornament of any kind, you will proceed to the work of laying out, and the paths will form the skeleton of the garden. I have already laid sufficient stress on the necessity for broad walks, in an extensive garden they should be seven feet in width at least; in a small suburban spot nothing will be gained in the end by any stinting of gravel, and it will be better generally to make them five feet at least, than to cut off a foot for the sake of increasing the

width of borders and lawns. At the same time the walks
may be as few as possible, consistent with the space
they are to cover, and they should be decided in character,
no two walks running parallel near each other, indeed if
one walk is kept out of view from another so much the better,
though it is seldom advisable to conceal walks by a stratagem;
above all things avoid meaningless curves and tortuous
twistings anywhere.

A labyrinth of little walks that look like ropes of sand
is always contemptible. In the practical part of the work
nothing is of more importance than to make every walk
as sound and complete as possible. The soil should be taken
out to a good depth, and where mounds and elevations are
required, soil for them will be easily attainable from the
excavations made for this purpose. I invariably take out
the bottom of a gravel-walk to a depth of eighteen inches
or two feet, and, if possible, work as I go on, throwing
up the knolls and mounds so as to save the labour of carriage.
The trench is to be filled up to within two inches of the
top surface with building rubbish, clinkers, or any dry, loose,
hard material that may be attainable; the neighbouring
dust-yard, a builder, or a brickmaker can usually supply
as many loads as may be required. Upon the top of the
rubbish lay a stratum of large gravel, and upon this the
finer sort which is to form the rolled path. The walk
will perhaps sink a little here and there, though if the
workmen are up to the mark there will be but little
sinking, and at the end of the first season the walk will
take another layer of gravel without rising too high in
consequence. Here I must make a note that I consider
very important. A well-made walk ought to be dry enough
for walking on five minutes after the termination of a twelve
hours' rain; in fact, it ought never to be really wet. Where
a good foundation is wanting, it will be rather difficult to
insure such rapid drainage, and to obviate this, some folks
have their walks made so convex that it is only possible

to walk with safety exactly in the centre; in fact, to enjoy such walks one ought to have had some few lessons on the tight-rope, so neat a balance of body does it require to preserve one's equilibrium on these convex ridges of gravel. Even then, if two or three walk together, they must travel in a line, not abreast; it must be a game of follow my leader, or the person in the centre must allow one on each side of him to take tight hold of his arm, and the three must move along cautiously, and as if the outsiders were the worse for liquor. Now there is no need of this ridiculous convexity; a well-made path may be nearly as flat as a deal plank, a rise of an inch at most being sufficient from the margin to the centre.

As to edgings for borders and beds, there is no end as to variety, but really very few that are not open to some kind of objection. In small gardens, strips of wood are frequently used, but they rot quickly, and from the day they are put down harbour all kinds of vermin, slugs and snails especially. Box edging is admirable anywhere; it is fresh in appearance, always neat if properly attended to, but, like wood, it affords a very safe retreat for slugs and woodlice. Then we have gentianella, mixed hepatica, crimson thrift, double daisy, cowslip, pansy, and ivy. The first two and the last are admirable live edgings, and, with dwarf box, may be considered the best of all for really ornamental grounds. The others are pretty but troublesome, and rather belong to the cottage garden than to grounds laid out with any pretensions to excellence. An ivy edging of from four to six inches in breadth makes a splendid line of green for a border of mixed flowers, or for a narrow border in which scarlet geraniums, single white petunias, shrubby calceolarias, and patches of nemophila and blue lobelia are placed in one line at intervals under a wall or trellis also covered with ivy, Stauntoniæ, or Virginia creeper. When ivy is so used to run along the edge of a border, and then spreads out bravely over a knoll, it then becomes a choice thing, and will not be parted with very readily.

Then we have the "burrs" or spoilt bricks from the kilns, which look well in front gardens that abut on high-roads in the suburbs. Placed in regular order along the borders and around large central beds in which there are masses of evergreen, nothing can be more appropriate; every year increases their fitness, as they get greened over by the confervoid growths that take possession of all dead edgings in winter. After all, I have not mentioned among this large number one single edging suited to the divisions of a garden kept in high taste. Here an architectural edging is the thing wanted to carry the eye along the lines from balustrades, and stone steps, and fountains, and vases, into the midst of grass and flowers. For this purpose stone mouldings are the most suitable, but the cost of a few thousand feet of them would be tremendous. Let those who can afford it give the mason work, and those who cannot may take refuge in the best garden edging ever invented, at less cost than is usually paid for dwarf box.

The author of that delightful essay on the "Flower Garden" which Mr. Murray reprinted from the "Quarterly" in his Railway series says, "In a symmetrical garden, and where they harmonize with the house, strips of stone-work might be introduced; and we think a tile might be designed of better shape and colour than any we have yet seen." This suggestion proves to have been prophetic, for the new tile invented by Mr. Hogg, is just the thing that our trim gardens have been crying out for for years, and now they are all but presented to us for nothing. Hogg's Edging Tile is constructed so as to bear the closest possible resemblance to a neat stone moulding. When put down, the appearance is that of a continuous line of chaste edging of stone, the summit standing just two and a half inches above the gravel on one side and the border on the other. They are constructed, as shewn on the next page, so as to sink into a trench, which should be three inches deep, the tiles being five and a half inches high. The spreading sole is placed on the side next the walk, and when filled over with gravel they bite the ground so firmly that no clumsy foot or erratic wheelbarrow can shift them out of their place. They are made of a very hard but porous ware, and each tile is tunnelled through above and below, so that they drain the border and the path, and preserve constant dryness for the feet. They are of a warm stone-colour, very durable, and resist sunshine, frost, and ill-guided garden rollers, so that they fulfil all the requirements of usefulness as well as ornament. The price of these tiles is fourpence halfpenny per running yard, which is just twenty-five per cent. cheaper than box edging, and, as I suppose they will last for ever, the first expense is also

the last. I am now getting rid of a thousand yards of box edging, to replace it with these tiles; the edging will produce me more than the cost of the tiles, and I shall make the exchange with possibly a trifle profit, certainly, after paying for labour and carriage, without loss. Where slugs abound, I should advise others to follow my example, for where those gentry once make a footing in an edging, it is not easy to get them out, and it is hard to have one's pansies open as big as penny pieces to-day, and to-morrow fade into invisibility. In fact, stone is the thing, and this invention of Mr. Hogg's is equal to stone in every respect, and superior to it considering the ease with which it can be put down either in straight lines or curves of any kind. There is one final matter to be dealt with before we get

back to the flowers again, and tnat is the fence, or boundary
of a garden. It was the crotchet of Betty Langley, the
noted timber grower and "planter of gardens after a rural
and more grand manner," that "the true end and design
of laying out gardens of pleasure is, that we may never
know when we have seen the whole." Bridgman and Kent
worked in a similar manner, to mix the garden with the
woodland, and confound the two; but modern taste requires
that a garden should be a garden, not a wilderness, nor a
prairie, nor a "boundless contiguity of shade." It is an
artificial affair, or wild weeds would be allowed to riot in
it; it is trim and bright, and in some sense a picture, and
hence a framing or boundary of some kind is essential. If
a boundary is essential why should it not be visible, and
in its way ornamental. Town gardens do not open the
question—the bricks determine the matter—and it becomes
a matter of taste how and with what the walls shall be
covered.

Into that question I shall enter anon, but here I must
impress upon every "lord of a noble domain," in fact every
possessor of a garden surrounded by open country, the
necessity of setting up a visible boundary line of a substantial
and definite character, and to all sunk fences, ditches, and
invisible frontiers, let the reply be a derisive "ha! ha!" To
the immortal Kent we owe this "ha! ha!" idea, and to
separate paddocks, so as not to break up a view, it is a
very good thing, but for a boundary to a garden it is the
last scheme that a man of taste will resort to. Why?
well, just imagine a couple of ladies to be rambling in a
lovely garden, and suddenly, as they emerge from "an alley
of limes," or a flowery lawn, they see half-a-dozen oxen
staring them in the face, from what appears to be one of
the lawns of the garden. They would scream and fly, and
when assured there was a "ha! ha!" or, in other words, a
ditch between the paddock and the garden, they would
still "refuse to be comforted," and would not make another

tour of the grounds unless each had her lover's arm to support and protect her.

If we are made secure against real or imagined dangers, it does not follow that a frantic horse, or a bellowing bull should form part of the apparent stock of a garden, and hence, if they must be shut out let the fence be visible, and *in appearance*, as well as in reality, substantial enough to effect its object *à la Ruskin*. Thorn, privet, hornbeam, yew, dwarf oaks, clipped hedge maple, holly, Asiatic barberry, and many other close-growing plants will suit. For dividing portions of the ground what can be better than wire fence covered with roses? Of course *Sempervirens* would be most useful for such a purpose, and if the fence was wanted in a portion of the ground much frequented, a rose border might be added in front. To carry up the fence the best would be *Perpetuelle*, *Mirianthes*, *Princess Maria*, and *Princess Louisa*. Between the climbers a row of *Gloire de Rosamène* might be planted, and in front of these a row of *Souvenir de Malmaison* and *Geant des Batailles*, alternating with each other; the edging of the whole to be formed of either *Grand Capitane* or the close-growing *Burgundy*. All except the climbers should be on their own roots; the *Malmaison* would want pruning close in every second year, and the *Rosamène* every third year, and the edging would have to be kept in order by a gentle use of the shears every year.

Lastly, there is a large variety of fences in cast and wrought iron, in tasteful patterns suited for forming boundaries where views are to be preserved. There are many makers of such scattered up and down the country, but for those who find any difficulty in obtaining these fences in good character, and at reasonable prices, I here refer to Messrs. Cottam and Hallen, of 76, Oxford Street, London, who keep the largest stock of every kind of horticultural ornaments and implements anywhere to be seen. Messrs. Dray, of Swan Lane, also deal largely in such things.

Now let us return to the domains of Flora, and for a brief season revel amongst the flowers.

> Bring orchis, bring the foxglove spire,
> The little speedwell's darling blue,
> Deep tulips, dasht with fiery dew,
> Laburnums dropping wells of fire.

The leading elements of a Flower Garden are its flowers, lawns, shrubs, and walks, minor ornaments fall into their places, and give the final touch of grace to the whole. There are but two of these prime features to be treated of now, namely, the flowers and the shrubs, and as the latter are permanent occupants, and form striking portions of the scenery at all seasons, it will be well to discuss their merits and uses first. As to the plans of the shrubberies, that has already been pretty freely dealt with, but here in the practical department I will add a final suggestion. Let every clump, border, or bed of shrubs, give form and character to the lawns and the walks. The flat surfaces are those which most display their own outlines, and the shrubs and trees must be so planted as to break up the lawns, not into higgledy piggledy patches, but into symmetrical forms, the one opening to the other, giving range here and confinement there, but nowhere compressing the grass into pimping spaces. In my last chapter I gave a pretty good list of the most useful trees and shrubs for gardening and landscape uses, but will here touch on the subject again in a different way.

The front of the house seldom has such a range of garden as the back, and as a south or south-west aspect for a garden is preferred, the front usually faces the north or north-east. Here is just the place for some bold masses of evergreens, with a few deciduous trees on the border next the footway. A breadth of lawn, with a bold walk or drive to the house, may be graceful in themselves, but in front of portico, steps, and windows, there is a thin look about it unless shrubs be added. A central compartment of the lawn is usually allotted to hollies, lauristinus, aucuba japonica, tree box, rhododendron, common and Portugal laurel, snow-berry, and such like shrubby-growing evergreens, and these look rich when they get to their full size, and well massed together. The borders, if there are any, may be edged with brickmakers' "burrs," or, still better, Hogg's tiles, or if a live edging be preferred, common ivy is just the thing. The borders may also be of shrubs, for this front court should present a *fullness* of character, to give the house a substantial aspect, but all must be as trim as the Corporal's boots; no ugly branches straggling out of the line, no rampant growth to shut out light and suggest that you can't afford to keep a gardener. You need not lavish much upon the forecourt, but what you have must be in first-rate order. Then for the border next the public path what can be better than limes, or a pair of the rose-coloured horse-chesnut, with a mixture of almond, lilac, laburnum, lady birch, and acacia, or even apple and pear, all planted out in order, and with a facing of hardy rhododendrons on the side next the house to cheer the eye from the windows with their lovely purple blushes in June and July. The Irish yew and evergreen cypress look well in single plants or pairs on a trim lawn, but all these are better suited for planting apart from clumps and borders, either on grass or gravel, and as they are somewhat gloomy, though very substantial and respectable, must not be chosen without at least some consideration.

In a north or east aspect such a mode of planting a forecourt would afford shelter for flowers, which, of course, should be grown on those borders which were quite within view of the windows. The flowers most suitable for this purpose are the old-fashioned perennials, with a few bedded greenhouse plants, such as geraniums, fuchsias, calceolarias, and myrtles, but high-class flowers or glowing masses of

contrasted colours are, in my opinion, quite out of place
here, as much so as wire arches and rustic baskets would
be. Architectural embellishments are admissible, but they
should be sparingly used, for what gives perfect grace and
luxuriance to the private grounds has an air of ostentation
when exposed to the daily gaze of an "admiring public."
Spring flowers are unquestionably as much for the joy of
the wayfarer as for the proprietor of the house. The invalid
who creeps out in spring on the first day that the weathercock
indicates a change to a warm quarter, the artizan plodding
to work at daybreak or returning fatigued at dusk, nay
even the overworked postman and news-boy hurrying to
your gate with glad or sad tidings, are entitled to a little
of the cheerfulness which you can give them by displaying
some of those precious snowdrops, crocuses, hyacinths, and
tulips that are never out of place anywhere.

Near the house it is advisable not to plant thickly,
though some substantial mansions *do* look all the better
for the green boughs that hug them with fond arms; and
if strict attention be paid to symmetry of arrangement,
some tall laurels or hollies, or, better still, Portugal laurels,
to break the angles of the house, and screen the descending
pathway where the butcher and baker enjoy a right of way.
A gaudy display is most unmeet in a forecourt; so is the
gloomy darkness of overgrown and overplanted firs and
yews; so is a tangle of forest trees that might have looked
very well when young, but which have grown into dimensions that suit them for the park; so is an elaborate
pattern of any kind, especially if laid out for flowers with
labyrinths of gravel between; so, indeed, is any decided
flower garden, even if the place be large; and I would
not tolerate, except far away in the country, a display of
standard roses or a bed of tulips. Mix the flowers and
plant them sparingly, support and vary them with graceful
masses of azalea in bloom, iris, agapanthus, delphinium,
lily, hydrangea, peony, and chrysantheum, but keep away

for use elsewhere every dahlia, hollyhock, rose, verbena, *fancy* calceolaria, pelargonium, and fuchsia that you have, unless you are determined to make a Flower Garden of it, and even *then* dahlias, hollyhocks, and roses, unless on their own roots, will generally be inappropriate. Lastly, balance your work against the outline of the house, for *that* is not to be hidden or treated as if it did not exist. I have just seen an instance that I will note here to explain my meaning. A very showy villa has a very showy portico and flight of steps in the centre, with an elliptic window on each side. The portico is surmounted by a sort of spire, or steeple, or miniature minaret, of a nameless order—or *dis*order—of architecture, and on *one* side of this portico towers a tall holly cut to a tapering form, so as to match the pyramidal entrance; but not only does the dark holly look ridiculous against the white facing of the house, which otherwise is in no way screened at all, but it towers so high above the steeple beside it, and is not balanced by a corresponding tree on the opposite side; the whole affair, house, steeple, holly, and doorway, look as if they would fall over together. Things of this kind should balance well, and be strictly appropriate. I would not possess that portico and tree *as they are* for a trifle. A perpendicular line may be balanced by a horizontal one, but the two cannot balance each other, unless they form a decided *pair* of objects. If you kept your dahlias, and standard roses, and hollyhocks away from your forecourt, you will now find the use of them, for—presto!—we leave the van for the rear, and can more safely indulge our whims in gardening.

What will you put in your borders? If they are not to be in ribbons, but in the old style of mixed plants, there will be very little difficulty in making them gay, but the cold pit, the forcing pit, and the greenhouse, must be carefully managed to keep up a succession; and now, we may say, not a week in the whole year need pass without

offering to the ladies something from the borders for a
bright boquet. But in the absence of such aid as pits
and houses afford, any extent of borders may be kept
beautiful, owing to the immense variety of high-class
hardy plants we have suitable for beds and borders. In
spring the bulbs will commence the floral year, single
snowdrops, crocuses, tulips, and hyacinths, lead off the way.
Plant them in clumps in the borders, each clump of a
distinct colour, and the same in the beds if you cannot
use them by thousands. Otherwise, a grand display may
be made of all the spring bulbs by planting them in
masses so as to fill the beds each with a sort, or with
two or three colours in a geometric pattern. Take a circular bed, mark out in it a diamond in the centre, and
fill that diamond with white crocuses, almost touching each
other, and then cover the remainder of the space with
yellow or blue, and you will have a blaze of colour in
spring that will glorify the centre of a lawn opposite a
window in magnificent style. An ivy edging would add to
its lustre; or, if there are several beds, say three or five,
and odd numbers are always best, clump out several distinct colours in masses, each mass large and distinct in
itself, and with white always intervening between other
colours. Mixed bulbs also tell well, as one lot goes off
another breaks out; the snowdrops hold on till the
crocuses begin to sparkle; then the tulips and hyacinths
follow; and then the spring bursts upon us with the
first show of autumn-sown annuals, to lead the way till
the time for most of the hardy perennials, and the greenhouse bedders.

Plant your bulbs early, say the end of September or
beginning of October, and plant them deep, in rich compost, well worked with a mixture of sand. All small bulbs
should have at least four inches of soil above them,
and larger sorts five or six inches, and in spring a top-
dressing of short old dung will bring their colours to

perfection. Hyacinths, tulips, crocuses, and snowdrops require to be taken up every year as soon as their foliage decays, and not before, but iris, gladiolus, jonquils, narcissus, lily, fritillaria, crown imperial, and squills, should be but seldom disturbed; an occasional forking round and a top-dressing being all that they ordinarily require.

Spite of all that has been said against annuals, it is not possible to do without them where successional variety and cheap effects are desired, as they are of course wherever the love of a garden warms the breast that is not "incrusted with worldliness." There are plenty of exquisite sorts, hardy, half-hardy, and tender, that may be sprinkled about on beds and borders, and the great point in using them is to choose good sorts, and to arrange them tastefully as to colour. What should we do without *Nemophila insignis* and *Lobelia ramosa* and *ramosoides*, and the long catalogue of varieties of calliopsis, Clarkia, Collinsia, leptosiphon, gaillardia, œnothera, commelina, dianthus, eschscholtzia, godetia, Jacobea, schizanthus, xeranthemum, zinnia, aster, and those old, old favourites, stocks and mignionette? Take them from us, and our hearts would pine for the pets that won our earliest love for floral dainties; for flowers of sweet scent are prized by the young before those of grandest colour and most elegant form.*

Not only are good annuals useful for the show they make, and the variety they add to a floral display, but the judicious gardener, "forecasting the whole" of his work prepares them as "stop-gaps" to fill up beds and borders while other and more dignified plants are completing their growth, and as the spring bulbs go off, the autumn-sown annuals come on to keep up the glow of colour, till the greenhouse perennials are ready for bedding, and the established hardy

* For descriptive lists and modes of cultivation of a thousand varieties of Autumnal and Perennial Bedding Plants, see "The Town Garden; a Manual for the Management of City and Suburban Gardens." By SHIRLEY HIBBERD. London: Groombridge and Sons. 2s.

plants break their trusses and spikes of bloom. This mode of using annuals is philosophical, for but few of them are of long duration; and as their glory fades they are removed and their places supplied with stock that will eke out the remainder of the season. At the end of September sow the best varieties of the following plants, let the soil be poor but light, and the position of the seed-bed freely exposed to the south:—Calliopsis, candytuft, Clarkia elegans, Clarkia pulchella, collinsia, convolvulus minor, godetia, German larkspur, new hyacinth larkspur, new branching larkspur, leptosiphon, lupinus, mignionette, nemophila, double poppy, scabious, dwarf schizanthus, Venus' looking-glass.

The half-hardy sorts are equally valuable, but must have the protection of the greenhouse all winter, and the earlier they are sown after the first week in August the better. The most useful sorts for autumn sowing are Ipomopsis, Drummond's and other phloxes, salpiglossis, large schizanthus, a selection of dwarf and intermediate stocks, and zinnias. In February a hot-bed must be set to work for a succession of the same, to which may be added asters, especially the French double-quilled, which, if well grown, come nearly as large as dahlias; balsams, amaranthus, browallias, calandrinias, Cleome grandiflora, pentaphylla, clintonia, pulchella, and elegans. A succession of the whole and any others that seem desirable must be planted in spring.

Then for perennials of course we must have a goodly show of carnations, picotees, wallflowers, some of the new sorts being deliciously odorous, as well as gaily painted; antirrhinums, campanulas, rockets, Delphinium, especially the splendid D. Barlowii; digitalis—superb ornaments for wilderness walks; the pretty gentians, lychnis, œnotheras—taraxacifolia being one of the best; hollyhocks, potentillas, sweet williams, dahlias, and chrysanthemums. To these hardy sorts the greenhouse will add seedlings and rooted cuttings of mimulus, ranunculus, imperial Queen and Brompton stocks, pansies, zauschneria Californicæ, hibiscus, anagallis, cineraria,

gloxinia, gesneria, loasa, and that new and fine hardy plant
Dielytra spectabilis, which, when once brought to a moderate
size, will stand the winter without protection, and in February may be divided for increase of stock.

To arrange borders so as to have them at all times gay,
and symmetrically arranged as to colours, demands not only
vigilance in preparing a regular succession of varieties, but
a nice taste in disposing them, so that each plant or patch
of plants shall fully exhibit its beauties, and enhance those
of its neighbours. Colours, heights, and habits must be
carefully attended to, and though a formal disposition is
essential, there are certain ways of breaking a rigid formality,
which, to a tasteful eye, gives much pleasure. It is not a
great profusion or a vast variety that will suffice to produce
a good effect; indeed a spareness of plants and *a repetition
of the same plant* at intervals will generally prove more
successful than the most lavish enamelling of confused colours.
Then along the lines of various heights how gladly the eye
rests upon large masses of shrubs, or grand groups of plants
of large growth, or specimen plants from the greenhouse,
such as huge geraniums, Dielytra spectabilis, myrtle, andro-
meda, calceolaria, fuchsia, and others that form objects in
themselves, placed far apart, and breaking the linear formality by their shrubby masses and their brave powdering
of colour. The geometric garden does not well admit of
this, except as centres for beds; but mixed borders, when
extensive, are greatly improved by an occasional breaking
of the whole arrangement, by means of groups and specimens of larger growth, not set back in the row appropriated
to the taller kinds, but rising from the midway line from
a broad patch of some close-growing gems that clear a
space for them, and make a carpet round their feet. If
the borders are broken by mounds, the effect is still finer,
and the same kind of planting is suitable for their summits.

In the ribbon arrangement of borders we have a still
more formal, but highly artistic, arrangement. The lines of

colour must be sharp and distinct, or delicately blended together by a judicious selection of harmonizing tints. In spring a ribbon display may be admirably accomplished with bulbs, the sorts and colours having been judiciously selected in autumn, and planted in lines. A border of tulips alone would look magnificent so managed, so would hyacinths, and indeed crocuses, or the whole might be blended into one design, though generally spring bulbs do not mix well in such cases, owing to their not coming into bloom simultaneously.

With regard to the summer flowers, which indeed are most suitable for this style, it is important to choose only such as are of very bright tints, and which continue in flower a long time. Plants that have variegated foliage are very suitable, and as these seldom produce showy blooms, the foliage only must be depended on for effect, and in most cases it will be well to nip every truss off such plants as fast as they appear. If plants are mixed in the rows, as they may often be to advantage, those which grow the same height should be chosen for mixing, though if each line is formed of one sort only, there will be greater ease in securing a good result, except in very experienced hands.

As to the culture of the plants, it is important to have them brought on early, so that when planted out they shall be stocky and in bloom. Spring-struck cuttings will seldom do well, because it will be September before they "come out" well; whereas those sown or struck the preceding autumn, and grown at as low a temperature as possible through the winter, and kept near the glass to prevent spindling, and re-potted in March, will, by the beginning of June, be in a vigorous state, only requiring a little careful hardening off in cold pits to go safely to their quarters, and continue gay till the middle of October. The soil of the border needs only to be light and dry; if it requires a dressing, leaf mould and sharp sand will be the best, and in a heavy wet soil, good drainage must be secured by a

bottom of rubble. The majority of bedding plants do best
in a dry soil, excess of moisture gives them a rankness of
growth that developes foliage and long joints at the expense
of the trusses of bloom. The planting should be performed
in dry weather, and the operation will be facilitated if the
pots containing the plants are arranged on the border first,
then with the aid of the line set the back row, clear away
the pots, and proceed till the row next the walk completes
the work. The border will then want forking over to erase
foot-marks. Cloudy weather which forebodes rain, is always
the best time for bedding out.

The following admirable arrangement of plants for borders
of various widths is given in the sixteenth volume of the "Cottage Gardener," on the high authority of Mr. T. Appleby:—

Ribbon No. 1. Front Row next the walk or turf.—Lobelia ramosoides, dwarf blue. Golden Chain geranium.
Flower of the Day geranium. Calceolaria aurantia multiflora. Dahlia Zelinda. Fuchsia corallina. Salvia patens.
Dahlias, three to four feet, various. Hollyhocks, various.
This ribbon should be at least fourteen feet wide, and a
considerable length, to look well.

Ribbon No. 2. Front Row.—Lobelia ramosoides. Golden
Chain geranium. Verbena purple king. Flower of the Day
geranium. Tom Thumb geranium. Calceolaria amplexi-
caulus. Antirrhinum cretia, or any dark crimson. Phlox
antagonist, white. Delphinium Barlowii. This ribbon will
require a border eight feet wide.

Ribbon No. 3. Front Row.—Lady Plymouth geranium.
Calceolaria Kayii. Geranium trentham rose. Dahlia Zelinda.
Fuchsia Riccartonii. For this a border five feet wide will
be sufficient.

Ribbon No. 4. Front Row.—Lobelia ramosoides. Alyssum variegatum. Tom Thumb geranium. Calceolaria am-
plexicaulis or angustifolia. Dahlia Zelinda. The last may
be omitted if the border is only three feet wide; four feet
will hold the whole.

Now for the geometric garden, and the beds on terraces and lawns. Here the colours are to blaze like the variegated lamps at Vauxhall,* or the fireworks of the Peace celebration.

> And what a wilderness of flowers!
> It seemed as though from all the bowers,
> And fairest fields of all the year,
> The mingled spoils were scattered here.

The art of bedding is not to be learnt in a day, nor is it to be taught by books; yet a book may at all events help a beginner in the right direction, and haply give a useful hint to an experienced hand. What constitutes a bedding plant? Strange to say this question cannot be answered in any impromptu manner, for many a neat thing that promised to be the best of bedders has been found quite unfit when put to the test. As a rule, we require plants of a decisive character; they must either bloom profusely and gaily, or must give us a showy foliage to compensate for poverty of blossoms. A close dwarf habit is another essential, and where this is combined with a free habit of flowering, some of the desiderata are supplied. Fancy flowers are invariably unfit for the purpose; when grouped in masses and blended with others, their high points of excellence are not to be seen; hence pansies, auriculas, fancy pelargoniums, and all tall shrubby spreading plants are the worst of bedders for geometric gardens.

Our selection must be made from the dwarf geraniums, such as Tom Thumb and King David, and the many varieties of variegated ivy-leaved kinds; from verbenas, abronias, heliotropes, calceolarias, petunias, cupheas, and others that produce *short joints and long flower-stalks*, and shew little tendency to seed, and then we must mix and blend them so as to produce the effects desired; rings, bands,

* There was once a garden of public resort bearing this name; it is not now to be found on the maps.

and blotches of separate colours, or "shot-silk" blendings of rich harmonizing tints.

On lawns that extend on either side of a walk, beds of one colour, every bed on the right having its match on the left, gives a very bold tone to a garden; but wherever such a plan is adopted it will need a careful arrangement of the several colours to prevent any pair from becoming a special point of attraction. The same may be said of beds disposed in any way so that the whole or a definite part of the whole may be seen at once. A bold dash of orange at a distance will draw the eye away from the most taste-fully planted beds in the foreground, and if one bed of a set be planted with orange, yellow, or white, the balance of the whole will most likely be spoiled from the powerful attractions such tints have for the eye; yet such colours produce glorious effects when rightly used.

The beds may be mixed or in separate colours according to the demands of the case, or the fancy of the gardener; and in filling them, the various habits of the plants must be thought of. Geraniums spread about into bushy tufts, and room must be allowed for them to meet as their laterals extend. Calceolarias do not extend so rapidly in lateral growth, but make wood upwards; and verbenas and helio-tropes must have bare spaces over which to spread as they are pegged down, or must be so placed that their runners will mix with the adjoining plants, and produce good effects when the several colours come into juxtaposition. Lastly, no plant, however beautiful in colour or close in habit, is fit for bedding that does not, uninjured, bear the vicissi-tudes of hot sun, drenching rain, occasional cold nights, and which does not either support its blooms without props or trail on the ground, to enamel the general surface.

Among showy plants the scarlet geraniums may take the first place as bedders, for their foliage is as fresh and hearty as their blooms are brilliant and continuous. Among the scarlets *Tom Thumb* and *King David* are just the

thing that we require for striking masses of foliage and colour; then there is the noble *Rosea compactum* of Mr. Salter, which may be grown to almost any size, and bedded alone, or with an edging of a variegated kind, would glorify a terrace garden, or show bravely in single plants in vases. Among the newer kinds, having the dwarf habit and fullness of bloom, we have *Lady Caroline Courtney*, *Sir Colin Campbell*, *Sir William Middleton*, the lovely *Bishopstow scarlet*, and *Harkaway*. Of the *Nosegay* section, Henderson's new *Duchess of Kent*, which is a rich scarlet, with a white eye—a fashionable marking of late, has proved itself equal to all that was expected of it. *Mrs. Ricketts* may be commended as a neat bedding or pot geranium, with a horse-shoe leaf, and dark scarlet blossom.

For single beds of one kind we should use *Tom Thumb*, which is very dwarf, or *Rosea compactum*, or Mr. Kinghorn's new and magnificent scarlet geranium *Prim*, which bears its splendid trusses on stalks of eighteen inches, and if either of them were edged with the variegated *Flower of the Day*, something would be done towards the furnishing of a high-class garden. Most of the sorts named mix well plant and plant with others; but *Compactum* does not mix, though for a line of colour it is perhaps the best that can be had.

In suburban districts, where the folks are not quite up to the sorts they ought to use, we frequently see what would be very respectable beds ruined by the use of old horse-shoe geraniums, that have been in the family for a century, regularly propagated from year to year, and very much beloved for the size some of the pot specimens have attained to. The kind of geranium I refer to has a faintly-marked horse-shoe leaf, a robust habit, so robust indeed that it towers above every other plant in a bed before the season is half out, and its trusses are large and stand up well, but the blooms are of a dull brick colour, and of a loose windmill shape. *Tom Thumb* compared with it is

"Hyperion to a Satyr." This old scarlet horse-shoe completes its inefficiency by seeding most inveterately, so that every truss soon becomes a perfect nest of stork's bills, and its fertility a perfect nuisance. Avoid all such, whether new or old, and if you are burdened with them, get rid of them at the first opportunity, and supply their place with *Commander-in-Chief*, which is a neat horse-shoe bedder, or *Mrs. Ricketts*, or *Baron Hugel*, also horse-shoed, admirable sorts for edgings to other kinds. *Sir Colin Campbell*, *Fire Queen*, and *Shrubland Scarlet* are other good new ones of somewhat similar character.

Then for beds and edgings we have the variegated geraniums, scarcely one of which is worth much for its blooms, though for the beauty of the foliage, *Flower of the Day*, which everybody knows, is a splendid thing when bedded, especially if edged with a showy colour. There is no scarcity of geraniums in this section, and the best for bedding, besides *Flower of the Day*, are Mangle's *Variegated*, *Attraction*, *Silver Queen*, *Mountain of Light*, Lee's *Attraction*, which has a dash of purple in the leaves, and *Countess of Warwick*, which is also stained with purple. *Richmond Gem*—a gem of first water—mixes the horse-shoe with the purple and white Lee's Attraction, and is a splendid thing for edges and ribbons. The *Blushing Bride* would be used in thousands if its price did not all but preclude its use as a variegated bedder, except by the wealthy of the land.

The *Quercifoliums* have not many of the points requisite for bedders, and will never be much used, except where there is space sufficient for an immense variety. The Messrs. Veitch lately brought out a new geranium of this strain called *Quercifolium floribundum*, which has taken a high place, and is likely to keep it; *Delicatum* is also good, but must be used judiciously to bring out its high qualities.

Then what can be more chaste, especially for edgings to showy beds of scarlet geraniums, than some of the ivy-leaved kinds? Not the fast-growing and ancient *Peltatum*, which looks so fine in a basket, or about rustic work where it has space to climb, and where it will climb superbly; but the neater-habited *Etiole de Vaise*, lately ushered into the world by the Messrs. Henderson, of St. John's Wood; or the white-flowered *Lateripes roseum*, which grows so neatly and looks so bright as to combine the strength of the ivy with the grace of a florists' flower. There are some other kinds of ivy-leaved that are good in their way, but when selecting stock for the geometric garden or the borders, beware of *Peltatum purpureum*, which is a fast grower, and too anxious to "multiply and replenish the earth," ever to be admitted to a gay parterre.

After the geraniums the calceolarias follow for their intense colours; here at least is a California suitable for a poet, though of sorts suitable for bedding are not many, the herbaceous section refusing to adapt themselves to the necessities of the case. Among the shrubby and continuous bloomers the best are *Goldfinder* and *King of the Yellows; Ajax*, an old dwarf variety; *Crimson King*, a rich dark crimson; *Purity*, a lovely white sort, which beds well in poor sandy soil; *Eclipse*, one of Mr. Cole's raising, a brilliant crimson with dwarf habit; *Harlequin*, a quaintly-coloured orange and brown flower; *Orange Boven, Wellington Hero, Golden Chain*, and *Sulphurea splendens*, all splendid yellow bedders; *Aurea floribunda* is a very showy dwarf yellow calceolaria. Half-a-dozen others might be named, and then the sorts suitable for bedding would be exhausted, though for greenhouse and show-flowers the choice is wide indeed. What we want is a good cross, uniting the shrubby habit and continuous blooming of the bedding kinds, with the rich colourings of the herbaceous calceolarias; such a cross has been attained, but it would be premature to introduce it here as a good subject for the geometric garden.

In the way of high colours, verbenas, especially the scarlet and crimson sorts, are admirable, and where beds are

wholly planted with them, so that the tints blend into a perfect rainbow or harlequinade, the effect is fine. Verbenas mix well with heliotropes, ageratums, abronias, and petunias, but with plants of shrubby and robust growth they tell best as edgings, and may be mixed so as to produce bands of luxuriously-blended tints, softening one into the other with the perfection of the rainbow. Of the bedding verbenas the best are *Rose Ricant*, a splendid scarlet with light eye; *King of the Scarlets; Brilliant de Vaise*, a rich crimson with purple eye; *Duchess of Northumberland*, delicate peach; *King of the Purples*, rich purple; *Purpurea magnifica*, a crimson self; *Wonderful*, lovely purple; *Crimson Perfection, Imperialis*, mulberry; *King of Sardinia* crimson; *Loveliness*, rosy pink; *Moonlight*, pure white; *Helen*, rich plum; *André*, purple; and that exquisite purple and crimson verbena, *Madame Adolphe Weick*.

For other effects we have for a splendid orange the *Cheiranthus Marshallii*, the neatest wallflower ever grown; for golden yellow the double buttercup, (*Ranunculus repens flore pleno*,) if you can get it true; the new *Salvia porphyrata*, a lovely scarlet flowering sage of dwarf habit and profuse bloom. Abronias, too, for raised beds, over which they can trail and meet, are splendid, so are whole beds of *Sanvitalia procumbens* and *Saponaria calabrica*, or for a position where other colours would not spoil its beauty by contrast, a bed or pair of beds of mixed Columbines.

Mr. Beaton gives the following as the arrangement of four beds, forming half of a series of eight on the lower Terrace Garden at Shrubland Park:—No. 1 is banded outside by a double row of *Harkaway*, the best of all the green-leaved geraniums for an edge, the colour being more like Chinese than European—a peculiarly rich tint of orange scarlet; then about eighteen inches of Mangle's *Variegated;* then a great breadth of *Punch;* and the centre of *Shrubland Scarlet*, with the plants so sized as to appear no higher than in the exact proportion of a gentle slope from the

outside to the very centre of the bed. No. 2.—*Tom Thumbs,*
(young plants,) *Mountain of Light,* with *Punch* and *Shrubland Scarlet,* as in No. 1. No. 3.—*Baron Hugel* first;
Golden Chain, three rows, next; *Blue Cape Aster, Cineraria annelloides,* backed with *Ageratum;* and the centre
of *Salvia patens,* intermixed with *Larkspur.* No. 4.—*Baron
Hugel, Golden Chain, Purple Petunia, Love lies bleeding*
round *Prince's Feathers,* the side of the *Purple Petunia*
next the *Golden Chain* being trained down to meet it, and
the back left to rise sufficiently to meet the drooping tassels
of the *Love lies bleeding,* and no more is seen of the
Feathers than the purple spikes of bloom. The other side
is a double of the same. The secret of success in such
arrangements is the keeping everything in the several beds
exactly to the style of growth required of it, so that throughout the whole of the season "shoot, leaf, and flower look
as if the whole was just turned out of a band-box." This
is an arrangement that many an amateur with but a limited
space of lawn might adopt with ease, for it involves no
elaborate experiments, and but a few *sorts* of very easily-
managed plants. Indeed the best effects are invariably produced by means of *many plants* of *few sorts,* the more
the variety is extended the more likely is it that the result
will be confusion and emptiness.

For ground outlines to plants of intensely bright colour,
there are few things better than germander speedwell, or
variegated ground ivy, or Neapolitan violets. A bed of
Lobelia fulgens on a ground of Neapolitan violets, with a
broad edging of *Flower of the Day* geraniums, would be one
of the neatest things that could be produced; it would
even tell in the grounds at Sydenham, where geometric
gardening has been brought nearer to perfection than it ever
attained before. Another arrangement for a detached bed
might be first a broad zone of ivy—basket fashion, or a
ring of ivy-leaf geranium; then a mass of scarlet geraniums,
and in the centre a fine plant of *Humea elegans,* which is

one of the finest of plants for centres of clumps, and for baskets and vases in the immediate vicinity of an architectural garden. It should never be planted out till June, and should be potted and sent to a cold pit at the end of September, and after a month transferred to the house, and kept at a temperature never below 40°. At the end of February, or early in March, another shift will be wanted, and then they must be grown on as slowly as possible till the middle of June, and be carefully hardened before being put out. Rich sandy loam is the best soil, but a large plant may have liberal top-dressings, and manure-water occasionally.

Many of the plants already named will furnish masses of white to relieve and heighten other tints, but white flowers deserve to be used much more freely than they are in beds and borders. We have not many good white flowers, but what few we have are very splendid in their appearance when massed out, especially when seen at dusk or nightfall, when they give a garden an altogether new character, that surprises the first time it is so viewed the very eyes that have watched the growth of the whole from seeds and cuttings to full bloom in the beds.

Among the high-class bedders there are not many *pure* whites. Verbenas, geraniums, calceolarias, penstemons, and petunias have all furnished white varieties, but these are none of them to be compared with the double white rockets, white stocks, white phloxes, that make a light in the midst of darkness. The double white petunia promised to open quite a new field for the ingenuity of those fond of contrasts in beds, but though a superb flower for pot-culture, it is utterly unfit for bedding. The *double white saxifrage* is a pretty thing for an edging, so is the *Arabis alba;* and I should think *Silene pendula alba* might be grown so as to produce a most perfect edging of white; an occasional clipping would perhaps be necessary to check seeding, and preserve a permanency of bloom.

As to edgings generally, most of the bedders may be used for the purpose, if adopted on good principles as to colour and habit, but the low-growing sorts would always be preferable. A broad margin of mixed colours, formed of heliotrope, lobelia, verbena, and ageratum, arranged so that their tints should soften one into the other, would look superb if centred with a mass of one colour—scarlet, purple, or white. For such an edging, verbenas alone might be used, the colours selected to produce a "shot-silk" effect; or if distinct contrasts were preferred, it might be had by using *Koniga maritima, Lobelia erinus oculata, Verbena melindres, Œnothera vivipara, Calceolaria rugosa,* (pegged down,) and *Verbena melindres alba.* Fifteen inches should be the breadth of the edging, and the centre should be selected from any of the showy bedders already named—geraniums, calceolarias, or *Montreal Purple,* or *Crimson Perfection* petunia. A more simple arrangement of a similar kind would be a centre of *Calceolaria rugosa,* margined with *Lobelia ramosoides, Verbena melindres alba,* and *Koniga maritima.* Many would prefer the annular arrangement for a single large bed, and for one of twelve feet diameter a beautiful effect would be produced by planting first as the outside ring, *Anagallis azurea grandiflorœ,* mixed with *Calceolaria rugosa;* for the next ring, Mangle's *Variegated,* or *Flower of the Day* geranium, mixed with verbena *Brilliant de Vaise;* and in the centre a fine Irish yew, cut to a symmetrical outline, or a standard rose of sterling quality, such as *Geants des Bataille, Queen Victoria, Crimson Perpetual,* or *General Jacqueminot.*

Many annuals and plants of humble growth may be worked into mixed beds, either to relieve the colours, cover the ground between shrubby plants, or to serve as edgings. For this latter purpose the variegated mint, (*Mentha rotundifolia variegata,*) is an admirable adjunct. There is no beauty in this except the leaves, and its chief use is to cover the ground with a close-growing variegated foliage, to

set off the high tintings of true bedders, or form a sort
of fairy turf around the roots of standard roses. It must
never be put into rock-work, or it will usurp the whole in
a year or two, and resist all attempts at ejectment, and in
beds it must be transplanted every second year at least;
mixed with *Tom Thumb* geranium, its effect is beautiful;
and it is of great value to cover the ground between shrubby
plants of any kind that are not intended to meet, such as
dwarf and standard roses or borders of flowering shrubs.
For nosegays it is an old favourite. Blue *Nemophilas* and
Lobelias have already been referred to as choice edgings
to showy beds; the *Nemophilas*, sown at the beginning of
March, will bloom till near the beginning of July, and may
then be followed by *Lobelia ramosoides*, or a succession of
Nemophila may be had by sowing again from the 20th.
to the 30th. of May; the second sowing will continue gay
till the end of the season.

After all, the success of any plan of arranging masses or
mixtures of colour must depend very much on the exercise
of individual taste, in adapting tints and blendings that
assort with the surrounding scenery. Mere geometric patterns
look bald and bare, however splendid in themselves, if not
well supported with architectural and arboreal embellishments.
The walks require the adorning graces of groups of shrubs
and weeping plants, the terraces the chaste touches of art
in vases and noble specimen plants, and the ground beyond
the beds and borders ought to give the darker shades of
rounded outlines, rich in the greenery of shrubs and trees
artistically arranged, and forming frameworks on that side
to the blushing glories that irradiate the lines of the terrace
and the patterns on the lawn.

A constant watchfulness will be necessary to eradicate
weeds. The hoe must be plied to keep the earth fresh in
its appearance, and the lawns must be kept closely shaven
and clipped, to prevent the least appearance of a return to
wild nature. Every winter the roses must be mulched afresh,

by the removal of the soil from above their roots, and the deposite of a layer of well-rotted dung immediately upon their fibres. Watering must be attended to in dry weather, and the several plants humoured according to their nature, to conserve their beauty till the latest moment; and then, so far from forcing any of the bedders into rapid winter growth, every means should be used to accumulate hard and healthy wood for another season, and the growth of most shrubby plants should be checked until quite the end of the year.

A season of rest is essential to every plant that has bloomed freely; and after the autumnal potting is completed, the plants should be watered sparingly, and kept at a moderate temperature, with full exposure to light till near February, when their growth may be gently hastened, till the advent of spring gives them a natural stimulus to the formation of new joints and trusses of bloom. Plants that come forward and begin to show bloom early should be stopped, no blooming should be allowed until near the time for planting out, and there are but few favoured spots where it is safe to bed out greenhouse plants before the second week in June. Previous to bedding them out they must be hardened gradually by exposure to the air, of course without disturbing their roots; and at night must be protected slightly against the ravages of late frosts. If brought forward rapidly in the house, and put out without undergoing some previous hardening, they are sure to go back and look wretched for weeks, in some cases not recovering till near the end of the season.

Cold frames will frequently be found useful for wintering tender bedders of shrubby growth. Calceolarias raised in dry elevated frames, usually make the finest plants for show in summer, and indeed most bedders except geraniums, do better in frames during winter than in the greenhouse, if proper precautions are taken to prevent the attacks of frost. With these hints this long chapter may now close;

the walls are not yet covered, the rosary has yet to be formed, the wilderness to be planned and planted, and the grounds everywhere embellished with works of art suited to the scene. Of these and other matters I shall discourse in the succeeding papers, and here quit the Flower Garden proper, sincerely hoping that I have done something towards increasing its gaiety, and its appropriateness as a fit adornment for a Home of Taste.

GARDEN AQUARIUM,
AND
WATER SCENERY.

"MILDLY and soft the western breeze
Just kissed the lake, just stirred the trees,
And the pleased lake like maiden coy,
Trembled but dimpled not for joy;
  * * * * *
The water-lily to the light,
Her chalice reared of silver bright."

THE Romans delighted in their fish-ponds, not so much as ornaments as preserves for epicurean delicacies. The lampreys were their water-gods, which, as in the case of Hortensius, they alternately petted and adored, and to whom they now and then sacrificed a human victim, not to appease the anger of the deities, but to satisfy their appetites, and improve them for the table. Our English fish-ponds and Aquaria bring suggestions of a more domesticating character, in unison with our national feeling and love of rural elegance. Water is the life and soul of a garden, whether on the ground-plot of a suburban cottage, or the embellished lawn of an extensive villa. It can be rendered appropriate to' any style of gardening, and is equally adaptable to the classic refinement of Italian terraces and gay parterres, as to the shrubby umbrage of a rustic wilderness.

The appearance of water is always pleasing; even if ever so clumsily shaped or planted, still it is water; it reflects the blue sky and the fleecy clouds like

> ———"Some dead lake
> That holds the shadow of a lark,
> Hung in the shadow of a heaven;"

and it gives a brighter verdure to the adjoining lawn, a sweeter fragrance to the neighbouring flower-border. It accommodates itself to every situation, is the most interesting object in a landscape, and the happiest circumstance in a retired recess; captivates the eye at a distance, invites approach, is delightful when near; it refreshes an open exposure, it animates a shade, cheers the dreariness of a waste, and enriches the most crowded view; in form, in style, in extent, may be made equal to the greatest compositions, or adapted to the least; it may be spread in a calm expanse to soothe the tranquility of a peaceful scene, or, hurrying along in its devious course, add splendour to a gay, and extravagance to a romantic situation.

In most suburban gardens there is sufficient room for a small Aquarium, which may very well be associated with a rockery, or made an ornament to the lawn. If a space of only eight or ten feet diameter can be spared for the purpose, it may be made very ornamental by the introduction of water, and improve the gaiety of the scene from the windows. A circular pond of five feet diameter may be surrounded with a border of rock-work of twelve or

fourteen inches, the dark stones being merely loosely laid
on an even surface, with no pyramids or ruggedness of
surface, and beyond this a ring of turf two feet wide.
The pond should be well puddled with clay, or a basin may
be constructed of Roman cement. The rock-work should
be formed wholly of dark stones of small size, the whole
of the upper surface even, and the edge next the pond
sloping down towards it. The spoilt bricks from a kiln,
which form large blocks of half-a-dozen bricks together, are
very suitable for edging a small fish-pond. Around this a
light fence of wire-work should be placed, and on the turf
about eight or ten standard roses should be planted so as
to form a ring. The stones should be planted with one
or two bushes of juniper, which form very handsome masses
of a rich green, when they overhang the pool. Common and
major periwinkle, several varieties of *Sedum*, rock-rose, *Semper
virens*, violets, *Gysophilla*, and some showy perennials may
be set in the crevices, and the pond furnished with a fountain
and gold fish. The beauty of this little collection would
far excel that of a parterre, or the most showy groupings
of flowers, while it would enhance the glory of the flowers
in an adjoining border, and stand out brightly against
evergreens beyond.

Perhaps but few of those who need the help of such a
work as the present, enjoy anything like a variety of water-
scenery. Torrents of splashing rills, chiming over mossy
stones, or gurgling under gnarled tree stumps, are not very
common adjuncts to garden scenes; yet there is no reason
why the suburban garden should not be beautified by
water-scenery—by the formal stone basin and fountain, the
circular pond shaded with rose arches, and stocked with
ornamental fish, or the mimic lake or river, broken in
outline and suited in its position, as an accompaniment to
a sylvan scene, and the illusion helped out by sloping
banks, massive shrubs, and a few water-fowl.

The style in which water-scenery is laid out must, of

course, correspond to the general style of the garden. If trim and orderly, the paths formally arranged, and the parterres vividly bright with shrubby exotics, the formal basin in the centre of the garden, within view of the principal windows, will be most appropriate. The Italian terrace demands a fountain of high-class art, ample in proportions, visible from every point of view, and surrounded by noble vases containing fuchsias, agapanthus, *Humea elegans*, and specimen greenhouse plants of full growth and showy character.

Let us imagine, or rather describe, a well-kept suburban garden of small extent, the hobby of a respected friend; the length is little more than one hundred and fifty feet, the breadth forty. From the drawing-room and study windows, we look down on the out-houses, auxiliary to the kitchen. These are covered with ivy and clematis of many years growth, and boil over at all corners with huge tangled masses of glossy foliage, and interlaced branches. On the right hand, starting from beneath the roof of clematis, runs a close mass of evergreens, which forms a border winding by a bold curve to a series of flower-borders and parterres. On the left, the garden-wall is covered with old jasmines, almonds, pyrus, clematis montana, ivy, and Virginian creeper. The border under this wall consists of a few small evergreens, many of them rhododendrons, and before these stands a row of dwarf roses, with shrubby perennials between them. In the centre runs an oblong parterre, studded with bright flowering perennials in large groups of contrasting colours. The path runs on each side of this centre-bed, bounded on the right by the border of evergreens, on the left by the roses and perennials. Where the paths meet at the further end of the central bed stands the fountain, the path encircling it, and then passing on down both sides of the garden, where the shrubs thicken and at last terminate in trees, with woody country scenery beyond the garden as a back-ground. I describe details

not because they are uncommon, but because the fountain
is the key-note to the whole, when placed and arranged as
this is, and the result is a complete picture.

The stone basin is about ten feet in diameter; around
it is a ring of rock-work, or, to speak more correctly, dark
stones, studded with the choicest collection of British plants
ever got together in so small a space; a fine mass of dark
green juniper forming a rich clump of overhanging verdure,
that serves to break the formality of the circle, and adds,
by contrast, to the beauty of the brighter foliage, and gay
mingling of colours in the succulent and trailing plants
with which the remainder of the ring is thickly studded.
A light wire fence surrounds this beautiful garland, for the
periwinkles and choice varieties of *sedum*, and the brook-
lime, and other plants of a bright fresh aspect, give it the
appearance of a garland woven there by fairy fingers; and
beyond this is a broad circle of the greenest sward, out of
which spring about a dozen noble standard roses, each of a
distinct and bold tint, some with several varieties grafted
on the same stock. In the centre a bold jet plays: it is
supplied by a cistern, elevated and hidden by trees. This
scene from the windows of the house has a charming aspect,
and every one of the many fine clusters of colour in the
surrounding borders, derives additional glory from the vivid
green of the zone of turf, and the sparkling freshness of
the water, with its groups of lilies, cape pond weed, and
the fine *Calla Æthiopica*, and its stock of lively gold
fishes.

A garden of the smallest dimensions affords facilities for
the introduction of water-scenery of this kind. A basin
of artificial stone is to be preferred where the dimensions
are small, and the formal arrangements of the flower-beds
such as to render a rustic pond out of keeping with the
scene. Such a tank must not be enclosed by shrubs or a
profusion of vegetation, but must offer its white rim in
contrast with a smooth turf, sloping gently up towards a

hillock, out of which the basin rises with its circle unbroken, or only broken in one or two places, by an elegant trailing plant or piece of appropriate statuary. In such cases the surrounding borders should be formally laid out with gay exotics, the box, or, still better, stone edgings kept in the neatest trim, the standard roses on the turf few but fine, and anything in the nature of a shrubbery or sylvan retreat, placed sufficiently far away as not to break the formality and brightness which should surround the basin. The fountain may be of a classical design, a mere jet on the surface of the water not having sufficient dignity, while the ornaments of the walks and grass-plots should be elegant vases crowded with gay plants, and light iron chairs, rather than rustic baskets and mossy seats.

In an extensive garden of formal arrangement, laid out in parterres, planted with exotic shrubs of sorts, the centre should be appropriated to an ornamental basin and bold jet. From the centre the paths may diverge, and form the radii of a circle, so as to afford approaches to the fountain and views of it from every part of the formally planned scene.

Another mode of introducing water is to place it at the base of a sloping bank or rockery, beyond which a mass of shrubs and trees secures shade and coolness for the lounger, and completes the picturesque character of the scene. But in this case the Aquarium must be removed some distance from the house; it is too wild in character, if properly arranged, for close propinquity with the straight lines and angles of a building, derives its chief beauty from repose, and the apparent absence of human dwellings: in such a scene, rustic arbours, rustic seats, old tree stumps, crowded with mosses and ferns, are suitable ornaments, while the rockery itself may be converted into a garden for alpine plants and ferns, the portions sloping towards the water being planted with marshy and aquatic plants, revelling in moisture under the shadow of alders and willows. An island or peninsula should not be attempted unless the water covers a large space, and has its dimensions somewhat concealed by trees.

Whether the small circular pond in the midst of gay parterres, or the imitation lake under a sloping bank, be the form adopted, it must be constructed according to correct principles to insure success. Unless a stone basin is used, and this is certainly the best for a fountain in an architectural scene, the best method is as follows:—A concave hollow must be dug of the necessary dimensions, sloping steadily from the outer rim to a depth of not less than four feet in the middle. Over the bottom must be placed a layer

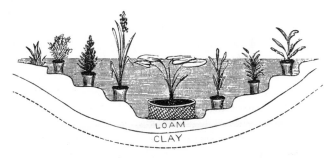

of puddled clay, of the thickness of from six to twelve inches; above the clay a layer of rich sandy loam, or well-tempered soil from the bottom of a pond, must be arranged in circular terraces, like the seats in an amphitheatre, so as to form a series of shelves of various depths, from the margin to near the centre. On these shelves may be planted the aquatics which are intended to be grown in the water. The advantage of a descent by a series of steps, instead of a regular slope, is that you may place pots with plants at various depths, so as to submerge each sufficiently, which you could not do on a slope; the pots being of course removable at any time, for renewal of plants, or during severe weather. This form of bottom also affords the best possible facilities for repairing or altering the arrangements of the plants; they are readily accessible, and exotic aquatics, grown in pots, may be immersed during summer at the several depths which they require, and removed back to the house during the severity of winter. In any case the bottom of the pond must be of well-puddled clay, and the mould above it a strong loam, with a surface of sand and pebbles. Our engraving gives a sectional view of such a construction.

In combination with a rockery, a regular outline is not desirable, but as the water must usually be *still*, it is not advisable to imitate river-scenery, nor, unless it be on a large scale, would it be well to make the boundary of the lake very irregular, a number of small bays and inlets looking as if the designer had attempted too much. The arrangement which I myself prefer in such a case, and which I think would generally be preferred by persons of taste, is that of a circular pool broken at only one part of its outline, where it is made to flow into a shallow inlet, from the edge of which a green dimple, or scooped-formed slope, runs up to the bank of ferns and alpines. In this inlet a number of choice marsh plants may be grown, such as yellow iris, *(Iris Pseudacorus,)* the beautiful grass, *(Poa aquatica,)* also *Primula farinosa, Cardamime amara, Lychnis flos cuculi, Saxifraga irrigata, Acorus calamus, Œnanthe globifera, Lythrum salicaria,* and the beautiful buttercup, *Ranunculus repens,* besides other showy plants that love moisture. To these may be added a number of the most elegant of British ferns. The slope from this inlet should be of the smoothest unbroken turf, shaded with one or two trees on its highest portion, and the slope itself as well as the inlet should be cut in the face of the rock-work, which latter should enclose, somewhat irregularly, two-thirds of the circumference of the pond, the open portion being towards the approach. On either side of the green hollow, the rocks should be studded with fragant alpines, such as lemon thyme, and others of gay but modest colour; some

of them planted so as to droop from the face of the cliff towards the water beneath them. The moist and shady portions of the bank may be stocked with ferns, and as most alpines thrive best in a cool, moist shadow, the aspect, of at least a considerable portion of the bank, should, if possible, be towards the north. Where it is not practicable to give it such an aspect, there is still an extensive choice open of suitable plants, and indeed of ordinary garden favourites, which may be made to flourish in full exposure to the sun. The water-scenery of a garden may also be embellished with the yellow iris, the noble water-gladiole or flowering rush, the fairy-like forget-me-not, the water-avens, the water-violet, and the buck-bean, all of them highly ornamental, and worthy the attention of all lovers of rural beauty who prize the productions of their native land.

In water-scenery of this kind, there should be no mingling of high-art ornaments. The fountain should be of a rustic design; tritons and dolphins, and even old Neptune himself, and all the water-gods, had better seek more congenial scenes. A fountain flowing easily down the face of a pile of rock-work, gently splashing and gurgling, will be more appropriate than a jet of any kind, for the mixture of incongruities betrays a want of taste, which no perfection of individual details will atone for.

In park scenery, and on well-wooded lawns, bold sheets of water very much increase the interests of the walks, though wholly unconnected with rock-work, or other rustic adjuncts. But unless a few leading principles are kept in view in the construction of such lakes, the pleasure to be derived from them will be materially lessened. Whoever plans or improves a piece of ground, should bear in mind that we should never *ascend* to water, or *descend* to rock-work; the first requires to be placed in a depression, the second on an elevation; and though it is not always possible to find sites eminently suitable, it is at all times better to do without water-scenery than have to view it on an elevation.

I could name not a few fine properties that in my opinion are completely spoiled by the neglect or subversion of this principle. If the view from the drawing-room windows embraces a lake on the top of a hill, the imagination will be perpetually haunted with anticipations of rheumatism, catarrh, ague, and other calamities incidental to damp dwellings and undrained soils; for a lake placed above the level of the house will convey the idea that the house is irremediably damp, though it may in fact be one of the dryest and healthiest in the world. Our chief pleasures, and many of our pains, arise out of associations, and to place water in a high level will assuredly beget many associations of an unpleasant nature, besides violating an important principle of gardening taste.

The shape and extent of an ornamental lake must of course depend on the position it is to occupy, and where there is sufficient space the boundary should be extensive, and formed of a few bold curves rather than any regular line. A large sweep of water broken in its outline, yet with the avoidance of anything like a number of minute coves, bays, and inlets, is always preferable to a merely circular pond; and though it may consume a large portion of ground which might be available for other purposes, it is too fine an object in itself to be stinted as to space. In the work of excavating a deep cutting would not be necessary, and it would in most cases prove a poverty of invention if a single load of earth had to be carted away. A couple of knolls rising from the water's edge could easily be constructed as the work went·on, and these knolls thrown into round masses, sloping down in easy curves to the general surface of the lawn, and with a wide space of hollowed valley between them, would, where there already existed an extent of open view, give a pleasing diversity to the landscape, especially if planted with deciduous trees.

The water itself should be liberally planted with willow, elm, ash, and alder, in huge clumps, not in lines or borders,

but so as to make landscape masses, with a wide sweep of
water visible between each clump, the willows so placed as,
from the principal points of view, to stand before the trees
of darker foliage.

Along the margins of lakes where the chief walks extend,
or in positions to which the eye is likely to wander in
"search of something," I can conceive nothing more ornamental than rich belts of rhododendrons, backed by shrubs
and trees; and as these showy shrubs flourish in the mud
from lakes, and even the soil at the water's edge, there is
no reason why they should not be as extensively planted
about water-scenery, as they are in the wilderness at Cob-
ham, along the Serpentine at Kensington, at Bushy, and
other places where they form a brushwood of oriental
magnificence.

The *Pinery* may very well be placed within the view
from one of the knolls above a lake, or as part of the
scenery of the lake itself, for the dark forms and bold outlines
of the conifers form good contrasts to the delicate lines and
graceful outlines of willows, and the placid smoothness of the
water itself. For special ornaments to the adjoining lawns,
Irish yew, huge Portugal laurels, hollies, arbor vitæ, the splendid *Araucaria imbricata*, the deodara, the cedar, the Chili
pine, groups of silver birch, and larch are suitable; the
difficulty indeed is not to find suitable shrubs and trees,
but to avoid *over-planting*, so that instead of open glades
and slopes, and sweeps of level turf broken at intervals by
bold masses of foliage, we get a confused mass of wood,
through which there is no escape for the eye, no repose
or relief anywhere.

The waters of lakes may be rendered still more ornamental
if *sparely* planted with aquatics in distinct masses, and in
some of the inlets and other suitable spots, the margin may
be adorned with a selection of amphibious plants from the
list given at the end of this section. For the deep water,
on a bottom of loam covered with gravel, the large white

lily, (*Nymphæa alba*,) and the yellow *Lotus*, or brandy bottle, (*Nuphar lutea*,) are indispensable ornaments. The *Calla Æthiopica* will bloom and flourish in the open air in this country in any except the most exposed districts; so will the known Cape pond-weed, (*Aponogeton distachyon*,) and those established Aquarium favourites, *Pontederia crassipes* and *Nymphæa cærulea* and *rubra;* the latter are rather delicate, and should be preserved in pots plunged to the rim in the greenhouse all winter, and planted out in April by immersing the pot according to the hints just given in the description of the section of a Garden Aquarium.

A few water-fowl would complete the scene, by adding the interest that always attaches to living objects. A good selection would be a pair of swans, half-a-dozen Aylesbury ducks, a pair of Canada geese, a pair of the docile and beautifully-coloured *Chenalopex*, or Egyptian geese, two pairs of summer ducks, which are easily domesticated, and will most probably build in an alder branch, and raise a brood every season, one ungainly Australian swan, for the sake of its colour, a *black* swan being always an object of interest. Here are thirteen birds, all of various forms and colours, and all easily attainable, and requiring but ordinary care to preserve them: the list might be extended by adding the bernacle goose, the sheldrake, the teal, the widgeon, and the coot, but these are all a trifle wilder than those in the preceding list, and, for the first season at least, it would be unsafe to turn them out without first denuding them of a pinion each. They would require more space, too, and some amount of seclusion for the first few months. For the walks in the vicinity of the wilderness, a few silver pheasants would be highly ornamental and interesting.

Returning once more to the home garden, a few words are necessary as to the fitting and construction of fountains. Rustic fountains are inappropriate to the terrace or the flower garden, and yet we do frequently see masses of rock-work in such positions looking so well that we should be sorry

to aid or sanction its removal; in fact, rocks may be
made ornamental and appropriate to an architectural scene,
but their arrangement must in that case be artistic, con-
veying the idea of strength wedded to beauty, and suggesting
the thousand forms of grace to which the chisel of the
sculptor might reduce them. So long as they are not
built up to imitate caves and cairns, they may very suitably
form accessories to a fountain on a large scale, as we have
good proof afforded us at the Crystal Palace.

Stone is unquestionably *the* material for fountains, but
its cost precludes any extensive use of it, and the best
substitutes claim a moment's consideration. There are
several kinds of artificial stone in use for garden embellishments; Austin, and Coade and Seeley have done very
much towards the revival of classic taste in gardening, by
placing within the reach of many who could not aspire to
the luxurious marble and porphyry of the old princely
fountains, a material in every way suitable by its durability
and cheapness, even when wrought to forms of high art
and its perfect resemblance to stone. The best designs
have been sought, and well worked out, for fountains,
statues, vases, and groups of objects of various kinds, and
these form valuable accessories to an ornamental garden.
Messrs. Cottam and Hallen, who exhibited that magnificent
set of park gates and bronzed fountain in the nave of the
Hyde Park Exhibition, have given a large share of their
attention to the production of fountains in iron and artificial
stone, and the result is all that could be desired for the
gratification of artistic taste, as well as for durability and
cheapness. Iron is not only more capable of assuming
graceful outlines when fused into well-designed moulds,
but has many other advantages over stone, or, indeed, any
other material. It bears exposure to the weather for any
number of years without deterioration; if painted once in
two or three years, it is not liable to chip, as most real
and some few artificial stones are, and generally the cost

is lower than artificial stone of any kind. Then we have the admirable invention known as Ransome's Patent Silicious Stone, respecting the excellence of which for durability, cheapness, and the ease with which it can be moulded to any required design, Professors Ansted, Faraday, and Phillips, Mr. Henry, and Sir H. De la Beche have given such high testimonials. This is prepared by an entirely

Fountain by Ransome.

new process, and in appearance bears a close resemblance to the celebrated Cragleith Stone, being, to all intents and purposes, a sandstone of very high quality produced by artificial means, the cost of sculpture being saved by the moulding of it to the required form in the process of its production. That it is cheap may be judged by the fact that the fountain here engraved by permission from one of

Mr. Ransome's designs is sold, exclusive of rock-work, at £8 18s. 6d., its entire height being five feet from the base. For basins and fountains, Cottam and Hallen's designs are to be highly commended, and the choice between the several makers I beg to leave to be determined by intending purchasers. Ransome's fine productions may be inspected at the Show Rooms, Cannon Row, Westminster; Cottam and Hallen's, Winsley Street, Oxford Street; and Austen's, in the New Road.

With regard to the practical fitting of a fountain, but few remarks need be made, because this is a work which must always be accomplished by efficient and experienced hands, who neither need nor will have suggestions "from a book." What I shall say respecting this department, therefore, will be for the guidance of those who may need a few hints as to the working requisites before determining on the position, extent, and character of their water-works.

In the gardens of suburban villas the fountains are of necessity on a small scale, and it will be found an easy matter to elevate the supply cistern, so that the bottom of it will be higher than the top of the jet, in which case the fountain will flow with full force as long as there is any water in the cistern at all. Should the house afford no suitable spot in which to place an elevated tank for supplying the fountain, it may be elevated on a timber platform, and concealed by trees. Where expense is not an object, a small tower for such a purpose might be built; the upper story would contain the tank, hidden from view by the walls of the tower, while the lower portion might be used as a summer-house, a summer retreat, a garden reading-room, or an appendage to the domestic offices of the house. Its use would determine its proper situation. The hydraulic ram would raise the water, where sufficient pressure is not to be obtained from the pipes which supply the house.

The length of pipe between the reservoir and the jet

has much to do with the height to which the jet will rise; every increase in the length of the pipe increases the friction, which impedes the movement of the current, and hence diminishes the height of the jet. M. François, in his work on fountains, "Art des Fontaines," estimates

Classic Fountain by Voyez.

the decrease in the height of the jet to be one foot below the level of the source for every hundred yards distance. This author considers the adjutage, or opening of the pipe, should be one-fourth the size of the pipe itself. Where pipes are already laid down, and the power of the head not very accurately known, it is well, by means of a leaden nozzle, the orifice of which may be readily increased or diminished, to test the amount of force, so that the adjutage may be adapted to throw the highest and fullest jet the head is capable of.

The annexed design for a fountain, consisting of a group of Tritons supported by dolphins, in a basin of the old French school, might very well be worked out in artificial stone. It should be produced on a somewhat large scale, to tell with effect in the scene, and is, of course, only adapted to the terrace of an Italian garden, or to form a centre to a series of brightly-coloured parterres, or grass-plots, broken by flowers. In a rustic scene it would be inappropriate. The artist has carried the outer jets too high; if they had but half the height given them in the engraving, the summits of the several jets would form a pyramid, and give much more grace to the *coup d'œil* than it has at present.

The instructions given as to the stocking of the Fresh-water tank, apply, with very few modifications, to the equipment of an ornamental pond, on the brink of which the same ferns will flourish as well as many other plants of large growth, which it would be impossible to accommodate in a glass receptacle.

No addition need be said on the subject of fishes, except that the smaller kinds, such as sticklebacks and minnows, are not wanted in Garden Aquaria, except as food for larger fish. They are amusing in the glass tank, but are too small to be worth attention as ornaments in gardens. Almost every kind of fresh-water fishes may be kept in open-air tanks, and it is advisable also to include frogs and water-snails among the stock, for the sake of the scavenger labours they perform, if not for intrinsic beauties of their own. A garden pond should be kept free of fresh-water algæ, and the minute plants recommended for the drawing-room tanks. We have here no means of examining

2 D

their growth, and they rapidly spoil the purity of the water.

In all water-scenery a prominent place should be given to the large white water-lily, or to one or two kinds of yellow water-lily. These may be transplanted from their native beds, or the roots purchased of the florists. The thick prostrate stem of a lily should be placed in a basket of very open wicker-work, and covered with earth; the basket should then be loaded with stones, and so sunk in the deep water. From February to May is the proper time to plant them. In due time the graceful foliage floats on the surface, and the gorgeous flower-cups form chalices of exquisite beauty.

The following is a list of plants suitable for the surrounding rock-work, and the pond itself. Any of the damp-loving ferns would grow in such positions, especially if enjoying a moderate amount of shade, and a regular sprinkling of water from a fountain.

The reader may consult the instructions on the formation of a Rockery and Fern Garden, for further hints on the management and culture of plants for the borders of an Aquarium. The list given below is confined exclusively to water-plants. The plants suitable for the rock-work will be found in the lists appended to the chapters on the Rockery and Fernery, which it would be unnecessary to repeat here, the rock border being a mere subsidiary to the Aquarium.

LIST OF
SELECT PLANTS FOR THE GARDEN AQUARIUM.

English Name.	Botanical Name.	Col. of Blossom.
Sweet Flag,	Acorus calamus,	Green.
Marsh Lychnis,	Lychnis Flos-cuculi,	Red.
Willow Herb,	Epilobium angustifolium,	Pink.
Spiked Water-milfoil,	Myriophyllum spicatum,	Red.
Water Villarsia,	Villarsia nymphæoides,	Yellow.
Heart-shaped Villarsia,	Villarsia cordata,	White.
Water Knot-grass,	Polygonum amphibium,	Pink.
Floating Pond-weed,	Potamogeton fluitans,	Red.

English Name.	Botanical Name.	Col. of Blossom.
Water Germander,	Tenerium scordium,	Purple.
Brooklime,	Veronica Beccabunga,	Sky-blue.
Floating Caltrop,	Trapa natans,	White.
White Water-lily,	Nymphæa alba,	White.
Yellow Water-lily,	Nuphar lutea,	Yellow.
Strange Water-lily,	Nuphar advena,	Yel. & red.
Flowering Rush,	Butomus umbellatus,	Pink.
Water Ranunculus,	Ranunculus aquatilis,	White.
Water Plantain,	Alisma Plantago,	Pink & white.
Ranunculus-like Do.	Alisma ranunculoides,	Purple.
Marsh Calla,	Calla palustris,	White.
Double Marsh Marigold,	Caltha palustris flore pleno,	Yellow.
Asarum-leaved Marigold,	Caltha asarifolia,	Yellow.
Water Violet,	Hottonia palustris,	Flesh.
Watercress,	Nasturtium officinalis,	White.
Water Arrow-head,	Sagittaria sagittifolia,	White.
Broad-leaved Arrow-head,	Sagittaria latifolia,	White.
Dortmann's Lobelia,	Lobelia Dortmanna,	Blue.
Bog Bean,	Menyanthes trifoliata,	Red.

LIST OF FERNS
FOR THE BORDERS OF GARDEN AQUARIA.

English Name.	Botanical Name.	Av. Hgt.	
Marsh Equisetum,	Equisetum palustre,	4 ft.	0 in
Beech Fern,	Polypodium Phegopteris,	2	0
Oak Fern,	Polypodium Dryopteris,	1	6
Withering's Fern,	Lastrea spinulosa,	3	6
Brittle Bladder Fern,	Cystopteris fragilis,	1	6
Alpine Bladder Fern,	Cystopteris Alpina,		8
Lady Fern,	Athyrium Filix-fæmina,	4	0
Marsh Fern,	Lastrea Thelypteris,	1	6
Crested Fern,	Lastrea cristata,	2	0
Male Fern,	Lastrea Filix-mas,	2	8
Hart's Tongue,	Scolopendrium vulgare,	1	6
True Maiden-hair,	Adiantum Capillus-Veneris,	1	0
Hard Fern,	Blechnum spicant,	1	6

These should have a shady aspect. Their root-stocks should be planted at the brink of the water, or on those portions of the bank where the soil is constantly moist. Peat soil is most suitable.

Most of the foregoing will flourish in any damp loamy soil, either away from water or with their roots constantly submerged. Many, as their names imply, are wholly water-plants, and must have a depth of from one foot, to two or three feet. They are mostly British plants, and must be sought in their native marshes, and by the sides of the clear streams that

"Go singing in fine lines."

The flowering rush should have a place on the shore of every ornamental water, its noble lance-like blades and tall stem surmounted with a head of crimson blossoms, making it "a picture in itself."

The following excellent plan of propagating marshy plants, is recommended by Mr. Jewite, in the "Floricultural Cabinet." —A stone-trough from six inches to one foot deep, and of any convenient length and breadth, and with a hole for a tap at one corner, is treated as if it were a flower-pot, the bottom being covered with small stones, and the trough filled up with a compost of peat and light loam. The top is then mulched with any description of light moss that can be got. The top being closed, the mould is then watered till it is saturated to the brim. Planting may be performed in March or April, or whenever the plants can be obtained from their native sites.

> ———— "The rill
> Thou haply may'st delight in, will I fill
> With fairy fishes from the mountain tarn,
> And thou shalt feed them from the squirrel's barn,
> Its bottom will I strew with amber shells,
> And pebbles blue from deep enchanted wells."   *Keats.*

"I KNOW a bank, whereon the wild thyme blows,
Where ox-lips and the nodding violet grows,
Quite over-canopied with luscious woodbine,
With sweet musk-roses, and with eglantine."

HE mere mention of rock-work is usually sufficient to raise a smile on the face of an enthusiast in gardening; for of all the mistakes that are made by amateurs, and even by professed gardeners and landscapists, the Rockery is but too frequently the most ridiculous. Most of the places of public resort near London have Rockeries—heaven bless the mark!—as appendages to the general scheme of out-door attractions; in fact, rock-work is vastly relished by the mass of pleasure-seekers who haunt such places; and as far as the cultivation of public taste through the medium of exhibitions is concerned, the sooner these so-called Rockeries are abolished the better. If we stroll through

one of the popular tavern gardens we are sure to see plenty
of raised banks; they abound in place and out of place, and
when they *are* appropriately placed it is after all a matter
of chance, because as they are sprinkled about everywhere,
some few, like seed scattered by the wind, are sure to fall
into suitable places. The same may in a certain sense be
said of the Rockeries in private grounds, and it really makes
one feel melancholy to reflect upon the waste of money,
time, and ingenuity involved in the construction of many
of these accessories.

Take a flower-garden, and in the midst of it make a
pyramid of vitrified bricks and flints, or throw up a hillock
of huge stones, and set upon the top of it a small plaster
statue, or a cast of Queen Elizabeth, or Shakspere, or
Jullien; daub the stones over with blue and green paint—
in fact, moss them and bronze them, and use plenty of
colour. Then stick in anywhere a geranium, a fern or two,
put a few shabby lilacs at the back, and make round the
whole a gravel-path, edged with white flints or brick-rubbish to correspond with the eminence, and you have one
of these "model Rockeries" that delight Londoners at Cre-
morne, Vauxhall, and elsewhere, and which some people
copy in arranging their own grounds. It is the best fun
in the world to visit a garden where there is plenty of
rock-work; you must smile at it if "on the sly," but if you
were to "up and out with it," that you thought every idea
of propriety was violated, you would at once be estimated
in the eyes of the proprietor as a person very devoid of
taste.

Now between *rock-work* and a *Rockery* there is the
greatest possible difference. Rock-work of a certain kind
is admissible almost anywhere—in a tank of marine fishes,
in a tank of river-fishes, in a fern-shade, in the basin of a
fountain, at the point where walks meet in flower-gardens,
and as objects on which the eye may rest in walks through
lawns, shrubberies, and wilderness scenery. But in every

case the material must be adapted to the work, and in all coloured and formal scenes, the rocks should be used in huge blocks in piles and mounds, not to imitate caverns and rude cairns, but strictly as ornaments to set off the beauties of other objects, or to give light or shadow as the case may be. This is rock-work, not Rockery, and it involves the disposal of rough blocks in symmetrical masses or groups, not in wild and fantastic outlines, and it conveys the idea of artistic repose, not natural and rugged sublimity. The two ideas must not be confounded, for while a *Rockery* may be a most fantastic, gloomy, romantic, or savage scene, according to the desire of those who construct it, and its fitness in this or that form to the scenes in which it occurs. Rock-*work* must be artistic and elegant, every puerile conceit banished from it; and the rough unhewn material used simply, because *that*, in the hands of an artist, may be made as appropriate and beautiful as the exquisitely sculptured forms which the chisel *might* have obtained from it.

There are many ways in which rock-work may be used to advantage, but it must ever have symmetry about it, however it may lack, as it should lack, a stern formality. Suppose you have a neat little flower-garden, with a wooded lawn adjoining. This lawn, especially if it has a border of fruits, will be as frequently resorted to as the walks through the parterres. Your long walks under embracing branches will be pleasant at all seasons, but much more pleasant both to you and your visitors if there are some few special arrangements made to please the eye. The gloom of green foliage is delightful, but how much is the joy of an avenue enhanced if light is seen at its termination. Now a border of shrubs, a bank of ferns, a shrubby corner, or walks diverging into other scenes, may form the vanishing point of your perspective, and the calm shade has no relief therein. Let the gardener get together a barrowful of white stones of any kind, the larger the better, and let these be thrown down "any how" at the end of such a walk, and

in an instant the entire aspect of the scene is changed. The eye wanders to the light

> "As the sunflower turns to her god when he sets
> The same look which she turned when he rose."

So far the object is accomplished; a bank of light stones is evidently just the thing to make the avenue charming. It is of course not to remain for ever a mere barrowful "flung into the void," but is to be built up neatly and properly planted, and on that matter I shall trouble you presently.

Many other uses for rock-work may be found, even in the immediate vicinity of the house and flower-garden, as I have already suggested in the preceding paper on Aquaria and Fountains. Wherever it is so used, it must be bright and artistic, pleasing the eye by contrast to the orderly lines that prevail around, yet harmonizing with such lines in its general restriction as to space, and its use made legitimate by a display of abronias, verbenas, rock-roses, choice sedums, and other plants that trail elegantly, or that look best when spread over raised surfaces, as most alpines do. Then where mounds are used—as they should be every where, for an everlasting flat betrays tameness of invention —there is no better mode of constructing them than to form the foundation of brick-rubbish, and cover the whole with huge dark stones, or with those conglomerated bricks which are cast from the kilns as refuse. Ivy grows slowly at first; it taxes one's patience when it is wanted as a distinct furnishing element, and while it is in progress the appearance of the mound, if tastefully built, is at least pleasing. Annuals of quiet colours and a few greenhouse perennials may be put out into the pile, and a clump of evergreens placed at the summit, and neatness and completeness may thus be attained at once, and the smaller aids dispensed with as the ivy makes its second spring growth, and promises to cover

the whole with its glossy wealth of green. In the planting of ivy in these mounds, a cutting should be put into every good crevice at not less than a foot apart, and around the whole of the base stout cuttings; well-rooted plants cut in close will of course be better, and April is the best season to plant in.

Now as to another sort of rock-work for the strictly ornamental ground, let us take even the smallest of suburban or town gardens, measuring say from sixty to ninety feet in length, by from twenty to thirty in breadth. The garden is bounded on three sides by walls, and on the fourth by the house. It is laid out with a central grass-plot, in which are one central oval, and two small circular beds. Around the walls runs a narrow border, separated from the grass-plot by a continuous path. The walls must be covered with ivy, clematis, jasmine, and other climbers; and if the evergreen shrubs are well disposed, and the flowers grouped in good masses of colour, the scene will be pleasing, and afford as much space for gardening labours as most people having but moderate leisure will be able to perform. Let the border under the rear wall be raised into a bank, with a facing of large burrs, such as are supplied for the purpose, the lower tier being sunk a few inches below the surface. A few large rough blocks of limestone, or any other grey or dark rock, may mingle well with the facing; and on the upper tier some large dark flints may be set. The mass of the bank is composed of rich sandy loam, and the rock-work is so arranged that there are plenty of interstices for the insertion of plants in the front. Now in one corner place a syringa or a holly, and in the other a few rhododendrons. A white poplar, birch, or tree of any kind, will be an improvement if planted towards one side. The bank should have either a concave or a convex outline, but there should be no "ins and outs" about it in so small a space, one good curve being quite sufficient. Towards the adjoining borders it should slope into the general level of the garden,

but the general level of the bank should not be uniform—
one side should rise higher than the other.

Now plant the wall behind it with ivy, virginian creeper,
white jasmin, or any thick, shrubby, and *dark* climber.
Fig tree, *Pyrus Japonica*, or even clematis would be hardly
suitable. The wall should be verdurous, but dark. The
surface of the bank may then be planted with showy flowering plants of almost any kind, and the front rock-work
with a few good alpines, or some bright verbenas, heliotropes,
hawkweeds, yellow and white alyssum, and in one corner
ivy, which should be trailed over the stone into a rich
knoll, so as to contrast with the flowers beside it. The
slopes adjoining the side borders should be studded with
crocus, snowdrop, narcissus, jonquil, crown imperial, gladiolus,
and other good bulbs, so that at all seasons they will glow
with colour, and be crowded with a gay pendant foliage.
On a few ledges in front of the bank one or two ornamental
grasses would look well, such as *Briza gracilis*, *Stipa pennata*,
and *Agrostis pulchella;* while, as a matter of course, the
several choice varieties of stonecrop, houseleek, and such
favourite alpines, will not be forgotten.

From the house such a bank would be at all seasons
beautiful. Its elevation and the mingling of various-coloured
foliage and flowers in the dark rock-work, which every year
would improve with weather stains, would render it a fine
back-ground, and prevent the eye from wandering beyond.
Yet this would not be a Rockery strictly, but a raised
bank, faced with stones and clinkers, and devoted to miscellaneous showy plants, rather than to alpines.

Now every ornamental pile or mound may be treated in
a manner similar to what I have just described for the bank
at the rear of a suburban garden. Wherever you want a
bit of rock-work build it up with one kind of material only
—no mixtures of colours, no shells, no gingerbread of any
kind. Let the mass be sufficiently bold, but subordinate to
the general scheme of the garden, for it is not in any case

to form a special object of attraction, but is intended only to diversify the colouring and character of the scene. Within a considerable distance of your house it ought to be impossible for you to say to a friend, "come and see my rock-work," because it should have no special importance at all. But in making it subsidiary it may still be beautiful. In a dark bowery spot, where light is wanted, it should be formed of white stones; in an open space where a dark mass would give relief, there use the refuse of the brick-kiln or furnace slag, using large blocks only outside; the small stuff will do for the foundation.

Where a few large blocks are used to adorn a terrace or a lawn, they ought to be handsome specimens of some interesting stone, such as two or three immense blocks of granite, or porphyry; they must have majesty of aspect and richness of colour; and to give them a perfect right to the place they occupy, the owner should have a story to tell about them—when and where quarried, the cubic measurement and weight of each block, the nature of the strata to which they belong, and whatever details of geological or geographical interest may attach to them. If a philosopher can give you a four hours lecture on a wayside pebble, surely your mineralogical ornaments must be capable of yielding some items of amusement and instruction.

About flower-gardens, and all bright orderly scenes, every bit of rough stone should be made beautiful with flowers. A very few plants will in such cases produce an effect, for there is no position in which flowers look more grateful to the eye than when springing from the clefts of a boulder, or the sides or summit of a dark mound. The eye is arrested at once, and art seems to have set a chaplet on the brow of nature. All creeping and trailing plants that flower gaily, and that endure a season, are suitable, except of course those of large growth; and where the bank does not offer a suitable soil for them, ten minutes labour with a trowel will suffice to remove a stone or two, or the soil from

between them, so as to make room for a little of the proper
compost into which to turn the plant from the pot without
breaking the ball, or disturbing its fibres. If sandy loam,
with a moderate admixture of leaf mould and well-rotted
dung, is used in the construction of the mound, six inches
deep all over its exterior, there is scarcely anything you
may wish to plant in it but is sure to flourish. Plants
that spread or trail, such as geraniums, verbenas, and petunias, will suit better than those of stiff growth, such as asters
or chrysanthemums. They should be gay ones too, and but
sparingly planted. Where banks and mounds are much
indulged in, I would plant one with the dark major Indian
cress to contrast against another covered with ivy—the effect
is delightful, and continues so till nearly Christmas; and if
spring bulbs are planted in October, the Indian cress will be
cleared off just in time for these to peep through—

> "Before the swallow dares, and take
> The winds of March with beauty."

Where similar artifices are used to embellish the walks
around lawns, or to diversify the sameness of an extent of
grass and shrubs, ferns will be found very appropriate additions; but in the immediate neighbourhood of a flower-
garden ferns are not appropriate, though the idea is very
prevalent that they may be planted anywhere. There are
plenty of gay pendant forms to be had where such are
wanted to adorn the flower-garden without having resort to
ferns; for lovely as most of these are in whatever position
or whatever scene they may be found, their own intrinsic
merits are not thoroughly discernible when the eye is en-
raptured by a fine display of colours. Ferns are too delicate,
too choice, too individual ever to be placed at a disadvantage,
and in the midst of gay borders and parterres they are so;
therefore adorn your banks and mounds that are near the
house with flowers, and if peculiarly graceful forms are
required there are such things as *Agapanthus*, lilies, *Humœa*

elegans, gladiolus, pavonias, irises, specimen fuchsias, and no end of trailing, twining, and drooping plants already specified in these chapters on the garden.

The real Rockery, though so distant from rock-work, may nevertheless have many distinct forms, and may be either artistic and beautiful, or truly rustic, and wedded to a rustic scene. A detached Rockery has the best effect in a well-wooded neighbourhood, and in a garden so arranged that it may form in itself a distinct feature in the scenery of the place. The bright parterres and trim gravel walks should not terminate abruptly in an imitation of wild nature, nor even in the design of the Rockery should too much ruggedness be aimed at, for it is after all an artificial structure, and can seldom be composed of such materials, and never in such a manner as Nature herself would form it. With water-scenery a Rockery is a charming ornament, and it may combine the attraction of the Fernery and the Garden Aquarium, or give character to a retired nook of the wilderness.

For a rocky bank or mound in connection with water, the outline should be curvelinear and bold; a few rugged peaks and wet hollows are quite allowable. The elevation should be various, and if possible it should slope down again on the other side of the pond by a smooth sward into a shrubbery, so as at every view to be grateful to the eye. The material should be dark rock, in large bold masses, and if these are not attainable, the large brick clinkers have almost as good, and sometimes a better appearance when mossed over by a season's exposure to the weather.

The soil of the bank should be chiefly peat, or poor sandy loam: any plants which this does not suit might have a compost prepared for them, and inserted at the time of planting in the spot they are to occupy.

If the pond can be supplied from above, so as to give opportunity for a rustic fountain, the supply-pipe may be concealed, and the water made to trickle slowly down a

few blocks of granite or grey limestone, which will soon
get beautifully stained, and beside this fountain a few suitable
plants, and especially some of the ferns, may be grown. An
inlet in the margin near the bank will serve for some other
ferns and marsh plants, as already described in the article
on the Garden Aquarium.

The elevation above the pool should be in the highest
portions ten or twelve feet, or even twenty or thirty feet,
if the site admits of it; but this and the general extent
will so depend on the local circumstances, that no general
directions can be given. One important matter is to vary
the surface, the elevation, the general outline, and the angle
of the face, which may generally have a slope of about 45°
to the horizon. The variations should be few, but bold, and
the colours of the rock as little varied as possible. If the
summit can be made to command a fine view, it will be a
good position for a rustic summer-house.

In districts where stone is abundant, such a scene as the
engraving represents might be produced on a very grand
and complete scale at a moderate expense; but if the real
material were not available, it might be built up of any
rubbish, or even of *bricks and mortar*. This may sound
odd to many readers, but I can assure those who may feel
inclined to smile that an artificer possessed of genuine taste
and judgment could erect a noble Rockery of any material
that could be stuck together with a common cement. Suppose that every one of the huge blocks that lie in planes
of stratification were built in ordinary brick-work, the
shattered face of the cliff being imitated by the workmen
as the work proceeded, care being taken to leave proper
interstices to enable the roots of the plants to find their
way into the soil forming the bulk and base of the construction. Then to convert the whole into stone, let it be
daubed over with Roman cement an eighth of an inch
thick, and, if well designed, it will assume as solid and
real an appearance, as if nature had herself heaved up the

mass ready modelled in adamant. Time would improve it
with many stains of green and grey, and if well planted
at the first, one season would suffice to destroy all traces
of its mean origin.

Where a considerable elevation can be attained, a dark
cave may be constructed, both for general effect and for
the growth of mosses and ferns, which may be made to
depend from the roof in rich beards of green, and grey,
and gold. Around the cave ivy, honeysuckle, *Calystegia*,
Virginian creeper, and Stauntonia may be thickly twined, and
the face of the rock-work and each side of the cave planted
with the gayest alpines, let into chinks in the blocks of
stone. The Scotch Thistle will be an appropriate and noble
addition, if planted in the most elevated spots. Willow,
birch, and mountain ash trees would add to the completeness
if judiciously placed with reference to their effect on the
water. A few birds might be domesticated in such a cave;
a pair of owls, for instance, whose hooting at night would
be no unpleasant music.

Nor is gaiety to be forgotten, though it be of a simpler
kind. The periwinkle, the rock-cress, the lovely tormentil,
and the still more lovely wall snap-dragon, or ivy-leaved
toadflax; the cinquefoil, linaria, sea-side thrift, fairy mul-
lein, Germander speedwell, mallows, wild convolvulus, rock-
rose, crane's-bills, willow herbs, hawkweeds, and musk
thistles, are friends with whom we cannot easily part; and
the author has some faith in the fair readers of this work,
that the suggestions will not be lost, but that many a
garden will have its raised bank devoted to these simple
children of our native wilds, whose traditional histories
sanctify them in our memory as associates in many of the
greatest scenes in our history, and embellishments of many
a glorious page of pastoral verse. Beside those mentioned
above, the brilliant bird's foot trefoil, which may be found
in any meadow or hedge-row, the pimpernel, the wild hearts-
ease, the yellow avens, the lovely oxalis, lithrum, orchises,

and the bladder campion, are all gay children of the fields, which easily adapt themselves to almost any soil and situation; and beside the pleasure of obtaining them in spring and summer rambles, there is the perennial pleasure of seeing them bloom year after year under the culture of our own hands.

In open districts remote from town smoke, the native varieties of heath, double furze, broom, bugloss, large bindweed, wild-briar rose, and squill, might be added to the collection, and would have a pleasing effect on the higher portions of the bank, if backed by dark sheets of ivy and evergreens. None of these plants require special modes of management; most of them will establish themselves readily in a sandy loam or peaty soil. The ferns may be judiciously mingled in the scene, and a very novel effect produced without the help of a single exotic. A collection of such plants will occupy but a small space, and their interesting, literary, and domestic associations, and even their individual beauty of foliage, and habit, and blossom, will enable them to rival successfully the showy borders where exotics have a proper and appropriate home.

A similar kind of Rockery may be adopted without water scenery, but it must be on a large scale if it is to form a special object of attraction, and the more secluded the better. In the depth of a wilderness, where mossed walks are chequered by the shadows of interlacing branches, and the light softened by masses of foliage and forests of grey stems and ancient tree boles, I would raise a mount of softest turf, which should lead the way through a heathery to a genuine grotto of ample dimensions and fantastic design. No parlour fancies of propriety should check me here, nor should any paltry conceits mar the wildness and picturesque solitude of the scene. The hill slope should look to the north, and break into rounded knolls covered with the choicest heaths; the hollows and slopes should be covered with ferns, and in whatever direction the eye should wander

it should catch sight of huge masses of lastrea and brake, and Royal Osmund springing like emblems of witchcraft from the mossy turf and the cushions of ling and marchantia, and harebells and orchises; and the distance should embrace a prospect of fine open country, or woods rising one above the other, till their neutral tints blended with the grey heaven and the rolling clouds; or if nature denied me such help, I would plant the shrubberies through which this "nest of coolness" was approached so as to hide every trace of the flowery lawns, and make the house and its surrounding parterres utterly invisible. There should be slopes below, dotted here and there with knolls of thorn, irregular masses of elm, ash, sycamore, beech, dogwood, service tree, hazel, oak, and pine, and a few lady birches standing alone should be somewhere visible. If ivy, bramble, honeysuckle, briony, and other of the strong-growing wild creepers took possession of these sylvan scenes, they should riot amongst them, so that no view was shut, or walk choked, or open space of lawn disfigured.

> "Paths there were many,
> Winding through palmy fern, and rushes fenny,
> And ivy banks; all leading pleasantly
> To a wide lawn, whence one could only see
> Stems thronging all around between the swell
> Of tuft and slanting branches: who could tell
> The freshness of the space of heaven above,
> Edged round with dark tree-tops? through which a dove
> Would often beat its wings, and often too
> A little cloud would move across the blue."
>
> *Keats.*

The orchises and heaths, and smaller tribes of wild thyme, harebell, ground ivy, and hound's tongue, which should dazzle the eye and perfume the air, and help me in the serene enjoyment of this nook, I would plant myself. The orchises should have a deep bed of strong maiden loam, with a plentiful admixture of chalk; they should be brought from their native meadows in April, each with its own soil about the roots, and set out on slopes facing the east, and with the partial shade of the trees surrounding the grotto. When planted every bloom should be nipped off, and I should then be sure that for many years to come, they would enamel the ground with their choice colours, and delight me with their quaint resemblances to bees, birds, butterflies, and lizards—the clever mimics of the vegetable world.

The heaths should dot the rising ground in clear patches, backed by the ferns and other plants of large growth. They should have a northern aspect, or at least be shaded from the full play of the meridian sun. The soil should be peat, turfy loam, and sand, in equal proportions, not a fragment of it sifted or broken, but intermingled rather with broken sandstone and harsh gritty refuse from banks and Rockeries elsewhere. The site should be naturally or artificially rocky; broken, jagged, and splintered masses should rise up amongst them; and the lower stratum should be of broken chalk, or some material that would convey away every drop of superfluous moisture, and keep their roots at all seasons as nearly dry as possible. The ling, and our own native ericas, should mingle with some of the choicest of the hardy heaths from the Cape, of which I would find at least thirty distinct kinds that would need no protection in winter.

Having thus planted my knoll with ferns, heaths, oxalis, violets, wild thyme, orchises, and the choicest wildings that nestle in hedge-rows and in the shadow of the wood-side, and adorned it with rough blocks and tree stumps, I would complete it by the erection of a grotto. It should be a bark house, backed by a huge wall of rock, round and past which it should be impossible to pass, or even to peep, owing to the thickness of the underwood for many square yards around, matted about the stems of the trees, which latter should be planted close as soldiers in file, yet as disorderly as an election mob. A Rockery or a grotto should

never be placed so as to admit of inspection on all sides.
The house should be rude in structure, most fantastic in
design, and of ample dimensions. A couple of huge oaks
on the summit of the mound, should stand on either side
as giant guardians, and between them should rise the pointed
roof of bark, with a sloping penthouse, supported by fantastic unbarked tree stems. Mosses, lichens, and masses of
stonecrop and periwinkle should dangle from the roof, and
honeysuckle and ivy should mantle over it and around the
guardian oaks, so as to festoon the whole.

A sun-dial should stand on the turf at the entrance,
and on one side of the grotto facing the east, there should
be a rustic alcove for a row of straw bee-hives, under
cover of the penthouse; but the hives should be outside
entirely, so that I could sit within and hear the music of
the band, without having even to brush one stray bee from
my face. A rustic table, a rustic bench, and a locker
would be useful, if ideas of pic-nicking came into one's head;
and to enhance my own solitary and selfish enjoyment, I
would have an inner chamber luxuriously furnished with a
couch, a locker for whatever I might choose to put into
it, such as a bottle of Burgundy and a box of cigars, and
a few of the choicest books, quaintly bound, and arranged
neatly in a recess; Jean Paul Richter should be there, along
with Tennyson, Keats, Robert Browning, Chaucer, Spenser,
and Shakspere. I would have "Undine" and Crignelle's "Le
Morvan," and Victor Hugo's poems, and a few Danish and
German poets, Oehlenschläger, and Körner, and good old
Goethe, with all the good English books of Natural History,
from Ray to Jesse, and Gilbert White should smile upon
them all.

A side window of stained glass, hidden outside by a
screen of ivy, would admit sufficient light, without betraying
to the eye of the curious this hidden and secret bower of
repose. As for the rest, I would make many additions
inside and out; curiosities of all kinds should be there, but

as individual fancy is to have way here, I shall say
no more about this rustic grotto, except that on one side
the entrance should be shaded by a mountain ash. One
thing, however, I may mention, that birds of all kinds
should be encouraged to build in the midst of every green
retreat. Magpies and daws are as amusing as nightingales
and thrushes. The latter are sure to come without invitation,
and you will not need to pine for Jenny Lind; but the
larger birds must be procured, clipped, and domesticated
near the spot, and allowed to recover the use of their
wings by degrees. A rookery may soon be formed where
the trees are high and thick, by sticking a few birch brooms
up in the trees, or by placing a few old rooks' nests anywhere among the branches. Here is a "cooling covert
'gainst the hot season," commanding the heavens to the
north, east, and west.

At midsummer Phœbus at his rising would splash some
gold from his chariot wheels upon the threshold of the
grotto and the slopes of the mount, and the glories of daybreak as seen thence, would at least be a temptation to
early rising. Sunsets would be as attractive when the day
"dies like the dolphin;" and in the depth of wintry frost,
what a superb spectacle would be the greater and lesser
bears, wheeling round the pole in the centre of a whole
hemisphere of glittering constellations:—

> "An endless fountain of immortal drink,
> Pouring unto us from the heaven's brink."

At any time except in a drenching rain or blinding sleet,
the mount might be worth a visit; in the season of rustic
strength and luxuriance,

> "When summer's hourly mellowing change
> Should blush with many roses sweet,
> Upon the thousand waves of wheat
> That ripple round the lonely grange,"

to the season of the year's maturity, when

"Autumn with a noise of rooks,
That gather in the waning woods,"

shall dash her fiery hand through the foliage, and leave
on the scorched and flaming boughs the concentrated glories
of the sunsets of a year.

"In this retreat,
Immantled in ambrosial dark,
To drink the cooler air, and mark
The landscape winking through the heat,"

would be to realize for an hour at least, the poetical idea
of "sweet dreams, health, and quiet breathing;" an enjoyment that never yet was found to unfit either man or woman
for the more serious duties which profitably engage so large
a portion of our lives.

There are so many circumstances to influence the site
and general design of a Rockery, that its success must
depend rather on the taste and judgment of the designer,
to make the best of the ground at his command. Fitness
must be first thought of, and all the details of a garden
must be in keeping one with another; and a Rockery staring
full in at the window, or rising abruptly from a series of
gay parterres, would be as inappropriate as if brought at
once within the house; though Rock-work artistically disposed,
may legitimately enter into the composition of polished
scenes.

The author of the "Poetry of Gardening" thus describes
a Rockery suited to grounds laid out in the modern style,
where the Italian terrace and garden leads off to shrubberies
and park-like scenery, where water can occupy a large
space, and every detail have its full development.

"At the right-hand corner of the lower terrace the ground
falls abruptly away, and the descent into the lawn, which
is overlooked from the high western terrace, is by two or
three steps at a time cut out in the native rock of red sandstone, which also forms the base of the terrace itself. Rock

plants of every description freely grow in the crevices of
the rustic battlement which flanks the path on either side;
the irregularity of the structure increases as you descend,
till, on arriving on the lawn below, large rude masses lie
scattered on the turf, and along the foundation of the
western terrace. A profusion of the most exquisite climbing
roses bloom over the very balustrades of the higher terrace,
or creep over the rough stones at the foot of the descent.
Here stretching to the south is the nosegay of the garden.
Mignionette, "the Frenchman's darling," and the musk
mimulus spring out of every fissure of the sandstone;
while beds of violets,

> "That strew the green lap of the new-come spring,"

and lilies of the valley scent the air below. Beds of heliotrope flourish around the isolated blocks of sandstone; the
fuchsia, alone inodorous, claims a place from its elegance;
and honeysuckles and clematis of all kinds trail along the
ground, or twine up the stands of rustic baskets filled with
more choice odoriferous plants of the greenhouse. The
scented heaths, the tuberose, and the rarer jasmines, have
each their place; while the sweet-briar and the wallflower,
the clove and stock gilliflower, are not too common to be
neglected. To bask upon the dry sunny rock on a bright
spring morning, in the midst of this "wilderness of sweets,"
or on a dewy summer's eve to lean over the balustrade
above, while every breath from beneath wafts up the
perfumed air,

> "Stealing and giving odour,"

is one of the greatest luxuries I have in life.

A little further on the lawn are the trunks and stumps
of old pollards hollowed out; and from the cavities, filled
with rich mould, climbers, creepers, trailers, and twiners,
of every hue and habit, form a singular and picturesque
group. The lophospermum, the eccremocarpus, the mau-

randya, the loasa, the rodokiton, verbenas, and petunias in all their varieties, festoon themselves over the rugged bark, and form the gayest and gracefulest garland imaginable; while the pretty wall snap-dragon weeps over the side, till its tiny pink threads are tangled among the feathery ferns that fringe the base of the stump."

Alpines proper are very suitable for Rockeries of all kinds; the showy sorts being of course best adapted for mounds in the home garden, and among the walks and lawns. Mr. C. Moore, in a paper read before the Regent's Park Gardener's Society, thus describes his own mode of cultivating rock plants:—"About the beginning of August they are shifted; those intended for specimens are put into pots four inches deep by six across; and those for stock in pots three inches across. I am principally guided as to what sort of soil I put them in by judging in what situation they naturally grow; for instance, those that are found in very exposed places, I put in a mixture of loam, peat, and sand, thoroughly incorporated with fine broken potsherds; while the more delicate sorts, and those which grow in moist damp situations, are potted in sandy peat; in some instances with a very small addition of loam, and where pure leaf-mould can be had, a small portion is beneficial in both mixtures. After being potted they are put in some shady situation, or into cradles, over which hoops are placed, so that they can be exposed, shaded, or protected, at pleasure. On the approach of winter they are plunged to the rim in coal-ashes, or some other coarse porous material, and protected from severe frosts by suitable coverings. In this state they require very little water during the winter months, and when given, it is but very sparingly. On the arrival of spring they are unplunged; if this is not done they are apt to root out of the pot, and when removed suffer a slight check. As the season advances they are shaded from the mid-day sun, and sprinkled night and morning with water, gradually diminishing this on the ap-

proach of winter. The plans generally adopted for their
propagation are by seed, which should be sown as soon
as ripe; and by division of the plant, which can be done
at the potting season."

Mr. James Lothian, in his pretty little work "Practical
Hints on the culture of Rock-Plants," advises growers of
these to pot one or two duplicates of every plant which
they have in the Rockery, "that they may with more
facility be covered or protected during severe or frosty
weather. This will afford the means of replacing any plants
that may have died during winter on the Rockery; it will
serve besides for giving a better acquaintance with the
names, and a general knowledge of each genus and species,
which, when in pots, can be more advantageously studied
and correctly tallied; and when in flower the seeds of some
which are annuals are more easily collected for general
propagation."

The situation in which these are kept should be sufficiently screened from summer sunshine to prevent the exhaustion of the plants by evaporation, yet not screened from
sun altogether. The best screen is a border of shrubs which
will admit the sunlight in gaps and patches, but defend the
plants from the constant blaze of the long summer days.
The place chosen for them should be paved with a stratum
of clay, coal-ashes, and a little lime, and beat down firmly;
then a coat of coal-ashes finely riddled can be laid on
previous to placing the plants on it: vermin will rarely
visit a spot so prepared. In winter the plants will need
the protection of a frame.

Should there be no convenience for the allotment of
a space for duplicate specimens of alpine plants, and a
large number will occupy but little room, a great many
may be kept in windows, cold frames, and on ordinary
greenhouse shelves. It should be remembered that these
are to supply the places of any that adverse circumstances
destroy in the Rockery, therefore they must be tended with

care, and excessive exposure to sun and frost avoided. On the latter point Mr. Moore says wisely, "It is a mistaken notion that because many of them grow upon the summits of mountains, and in other exposed situations, they are capable of enduring an intense degree of cold, and are therefore left unprotected during the winter."

When naturally placed, they are during the greater part of the winter season enveloped in snow, which is impervious to severe frosts, and forms a protecting screen much superior to any man can supply. Under this they are kept at one uniform temperature—just below the freezing-point; but in gardens, if unprotected, they are kept in an excited state for several weeks together by warm damp weather, and then cut off by a sudden frost of arctic intensity. Ordinary plants of the fields need no such winter treatment.

LIST OF PLANTS
SUITABLE FOR ROCKERIES AND RAISED BANKS, AND FOR RUSTIC WORK GENERALLY.

English Name.	Botanical Name.	Col. Blossom.
Barren Wort,	Epimedium alpinum,	Red.
Geneva Bugle,	Apiga genevensis,	Purple.
Rock Alyssum,	Alyssum saxatile,	Yellow.
Variegated Alyssum,	A. variegata.	
Rock Wallcress,	Arabis saxatile,	White.
Variegated Wallcress,	A. lucida variegata,	White.
Canadian Dogwood,	Cornus Canadensis,	White.
Rock Sweet William,	Dianthus alpestris,	White.
Creeping Gysophyllum,	Gysophylla prostrata,	White.
Wall Snap-dragon,	Linaria cymbalaria,	Purple.
White Toadflax,	L. alba alpina,	White.
Rosy Toadflax,	L. cymbalaria variegata,	Rose.
Rosy Oxalis,	Oxalis rosea,	Rose.
Early Sandwort,	Arenaria verna,	White.
White Shining Bell-Flower,	Campanula nitida alba,	White.
Dwarf Shining Bell-Flower,	C. pumilla alba,	White.
Vital's Aretia,	Aretia vitaliana,	Yellow.

English Name.	Botanical Name.	Col. Blossom.
Mountain Wallflower,	Chieranthus alpina,	Yellow.
Little Coronilla,	Coronilla minima,	Yellow.
Aizoon Whitlow-grass,	Draba aizoides,	Yellow.
Alpine Erinus,	Erinus alpinus,	Purple.
Heron's Bill,	Erodium Reichardii,	White.
Purple Primula,	Primula ciliata purpura,	Purple.
Bear's-ear Primrose.	P. auricula alpina,	Various.
Little Tormentil,	Potentilla reptans,	Yellow.
Double Cinquefoil,	P. reptans flore pleno,	Yellow.
Early Flame-Flower,	Phlox devaricata,	Blue.
White Flame-Flower,	P. nivalis,	White.
Creeping Flame-Flower,	P. procrumbeus,	Lilac.
Mossy Saxifrage,	Saxifraga muscoides,	Yellow.
Double-grain-rooted Saxifrage,	S. granulata pleno,	White.
Snowy-grain-rooted Saxifrage,	S. nivalis,	White.
Bird's-foot-grain-rooted Do.,	S. pedatifida,	Purple.
Starry-grain-rooted Do.,	S. stellaris,	White.
Azure Stonecrop,	Sedum azureum,	Blue.
White Stonecrop,	S. dasyphyllum,	White.
Great Stonecrop,	S. monstrosum,	White.
Common Stonecrop,	S. acre,	Yellow.
Mountain Houseleek,	Sempervirem montanum,	Red.
Spider Houseleek,	S. arachnoideum,	Red.
Globular Houseleek,	S. globiferum,	Red.
Tabular Houseleek,	S. tabularium,	Red.
Mountain Speedwell,	Veronica montanum,	Blue.
Rock Speedwell,	V. saxatile,	Blue.
Stemless Catchfly,	Silene acaulis,	Pink.
Alpine Soldanella,	Soldanella alpina,	Purple.
Little White Soldanella,	S. minima alba,	White.
Wild Thyme,	Thymus serpyllum,	Purple.
Azorian Thyme,	T. azorica,	Purple.
Double Periwinkle,	Vinca minor rubra pleno,	Red.
Great Bird's-foot Trefoil,	Orobranche majus,	Yellow.

Many showy border-flowers may be advantageously used, such as Phloxes, Delphiniums, Gentians, Abronias, Violas, ornamental Grasses, etc., etc.

THE FERNERY

"TO-MORROW, ere fresh morning streak the east
With first approach of light, we must be risen,
And at our pleasant labour to reform
Yon flowery arbours, yonder alleys green,
Our walk at noon, with branches overgrown,
That mock our scant manuring."

MILTON.

OUR first parents, if we credit Milton, (as we must,) were not wholly indebted to the spontaneous growths of their happy garden for their green bowers and mossy seats; but with delicate fingers wove the pliant branches into arches of umbrage, and set alleys of sweet-scented herbs

before their favourite retreats. Who knows but that a
Fernery was one of their choice delights? few rustic adornments would better have become their sylvan home, where
shade and coolness, fragrance and verdure, softened the
song of love and the hymn of praise.

The Fernery belongs to the truly rustic rather than the
rural department of gardening. Though ferns are beautiful
anywhere, and may suitably adorn the trim border, and
mingle with ornaments of formal design, they are more at
home, more befitting among tree-stumps, and in boldly
designed rock-work, or water-scenery, where they appear
in their proper character of wildness and simplicity. In
the preceding papers so much has been said on the landscape
uses of ferns, and their fitness for banks, rock mounds, and
the margins of pools, that I may now safely confine my
attention to the Fernery as a special contrivance—a garden
in itself; and the treatment described as necessary for the
several kinds will, of course, also apply to their culture
anywhere out of doors.

In forming rock-work expressly for ferns, it is best to
construct a round or square hillock, with a foundation of
lime and brick rubbish, and a surface of about a foot of
the proper soil, faced with stones or other material to
constitute a rock-work. The south border may be bounded
by a high wall or border of shrubs to insure the necessary
shade. One side, at least, should never see the sun, one
should have it winter and summer, while the other two
should but occasionally bask in its rays. The requisites of
an open-air Fernery are ample space, variety of sunshine
and shadow, plenty of moisture, an atmosphere comparatively pure, alternations of slopes, hollows, and acclivities
of surface, and good shelter from high winds and frost.

In town localities, it is difficult to establish ferns in
the open air, owing to their delicacy of constitution, and
impatience of a dry or smoky air. But in the suburbs of
London, any of the ferns that are ordinarily grown in

the open air will succeed, as we know by experience, and could name some very flourishing fern gardens at distances varying from two and a half to six miles from St. Paul's.

Ferns artificially grown, and tended with proper care and skill, exceed very much the beauty of those grown by nature. True, we cannot grow the scene as well as the fern—we cannot have the dark glen, the dank moss-grown cave, the decayed tree trunk, or the crumbling archway of the waterfall. The scenes amid which ferns grow, the lovely secluded spots which they seek out—shy wood-sprites that they are—are the chief charms of the associations they always suggest to us; for they do haunt the greenest and coolest nooks, the most mossy and ancient banks above water-brooks that trickle from unseen founts, in the deep recesses of wild rocky caverns, and under the branching arms of twisted grey-beard oaks and ancestral beeches—spots only discovered by the explorer of woodbine coverts and deep-hidden shades, where, searching for rare beauty, he finds it far excelling his anticipation, and checking his silent footsteps by sights that hold him breathless with surprise. Yet though we cannot have the mountain dells, and creeping thorns, and purple knolls of wild thyme, we may have the emblems of them in our little mural paradise, we may have the ferns to suggest such things, and to keep alive the remembrance of pleasures and of scenes which keeps a coolness in the brain and a freshness in the heart—breathings of fragrance from the green world that sweeten the resting-places in the march of life.

Where a garden-wall affords the necessary shade for one side of the Fernery, the rock-work should be so arranged that in summer a fourth part of the structure shall enjoy a full and deep shadow. The rock-work may either be adapted in its general configuration to the nature of the ground, and the view we wish to obtain of it, or thrown up in a square or rounded outline, slanting upwards from the base, and with a rugged or smooth surface, as may suit the taste of the planter.

The best material is dark rock or vitrified bricks, with some masses of grey limestone and granite, all sobered down in colour. The foundation should in some parts be of builders' rubbish, or a mixture of broken bricks, tiles, and old lime rubbish, and in others a stratum of clay on which the superstructure should rest. The builders' rubbish will insure dryness for those plants which naturally grow on rocks, walls, and other aspects, where they are exposed to much light and little moisture; and these usually delight to have their roots in fissures of limestone, old mortar, or crumbling rock. The clay will serve to retain the moisture about the roots of the more amphibious kinds; the marshy species requiring as close an imitation of their natural soil as can be accomplished.

Those ferns which grow beside waterfalls, and in dripping caves, require to have their fronds constantly wet, while others thrive best if kept comparatively dry. If a perforated pipe can be carried over one side, for the good of the water-sprites, such as *Scôlopendrium, Osmunda regalis,* and others of similar habit, they may be kept constantly drenched; and without some provision of this sort many kinds cannot be grown at all. In the absence of a permanent drip the garden engine must be worn out as quickly as possible, and the cultivator must not object to a daily exercise during the continuance of dry weather in spring and summer.

The soil should be varied to suit the various habits of the plants; but for general purposes of fern-growing, a compost of old mortar, sandy earth, peat, and broken charcoal, is the best. Some kinds will require composts made expressly for them, which we shall indicate in the lists of ferns for a fern garden. In planting these, the crevices or holes into which they are to be set, must be filled with the proper soil; but the root-stocks often penetrate to a

great distance beyond the range of the compost in which they were originally planted. A good supply of soft peaty earth, rotten wood, and leaf-mould is very essential in fern cultivation.

Where the cultivator would choose a still simpler plan, so as to avoid the necessity of preparing a special soil for some of his favourites, the whole may be built up with a foundation of sandy loam, old lime, and brick rubbish, and afterwards made up with a compost of two parts of heath-mould, two of rotten leaves, and one of potsherds or flower-pots broken into small pieces. Most ferns will thrive in such a compost if kept very moist. The exterior may be faced with rock-work, or may be smoothed round the sides of an angle of about forty-five degrees, and the summit made flat, or the form of a rounded hillock may be given it, care being taken to secure shade for at least one-third portion, and occasional sunshine only for the remainder, except on the south side, which may enjoy the full blaze of the summer's sun.

There is another and more picturesque mode of growing ferns in a collection by themselves, and this mode occurred to me a few years since through an accidental circumstance. I had, in a yard adjoining my garden, a large stock of faggots, tree loppings, bean-sticks, roots, and other forest refuse, and amongst them a number of old unbarked blocks, on which some fine ferns were rooted and flourishing. Setting to work one day to put the stack in order, and having a number of ferns for which I had no room in the garden, I placed several dead trees of large girth to form the outlines of a large space. Within this I placed the roots with no particular order, and at the back I piled up a mass of rotten wood and moss, which had been collected for cultural purposes. I roofed the whole with loppings and bean-sticks, so as to construct a sort of extemporaneous hermit's cell, or grotto of wood, into which no perpendicular light could fall, but the light entered freely at three of the sides. Here among the roots, on the ground, and on the bank of rubbish at the back, I planted my spare ferns, and left the rest to nature. Sufficient rain gained entrance through the interstices of the roof, the ferns flourished, and a number of pretty wildings sprung up from the moss and peat used in planting, and in this way I came into the possession of one of the prettiest Ferneries I have ever seen, though it was in a position quite unsuited to it, and at a distance had no more romance about it than belongs to any stack of faggots in a farmer's yard.

The space within measured about twelve feet by seven, and was about seven feet high, the roof resting on rough props and the stems of dead pollard alders. Its appearance inside was beautiful; groups of *Pteris* and *Filix mas* towered up among the dead branches, patches of *Polystichum* and *Polypody* covered the dark blocks and ungainly roots, the Royal Osmund spread out its leafy fronds beyond the boundary of timber to the open air, and all over the ground where smaller Ferns had even been thrown in and forgotten, new fronds broke out and covered the bank of the dusty floor with wooly croziers and bright green shepherd's crooks so completely and luxuriantly, that ever since I have regarded such an arrangement as just the one required for an ornamental Fernery. Instead of throwing the materials together pell-mell, I should now, were I laying out a Fernery, select a number of unbarked pollards, some large knotted loppings of old plum, or apple, or oak trees. With these I should construct a frame-work, setting the supports at the corners, and making a very light roof of rough trellis. Then I should plant it round with fast-growing hard-wood climbers, some of which should run up light posts midway between the corner pillars; and so I would construct green walks, with plenty of open spaces for the admission of full daylight, as also for the entrance and exit of the cultivator and his visitors. The roof would also be covered, and indeed to a great extent formed of greenery, and the knife and shears

would keep the trailers within bounds, so that they should not obstruct either daylight or rain, but effectually screen off the mid-day summer sun.

Then inside I would build a bank of fern compost, with a bottom of building rubbish; in one corner, where light came in plentifully, I would make a hollow, and puddle it with clay, and then spread in it a foot of peat for some

of the marsh ferns, such as the Royal Osmund, the lovely
Lady fern, and others that like moisture at their roots. A
little rock-work, formed of dark stones, or the burrs from a
brick-kiln, would round off the corners and slopes of the
bank; and about the ground I would place a few huge tree
roots, also to be planted with suitable ferns. I would in
such a space find room and proper positions for every one
of our native ferns, except such few as it is not possible
to cultivate out of doors, such as *Hymenophyllum* and *Trichomanes*. I would have at least ninety species and varieties
of British, and thirty or forty more of American and Exotic
ferns; and to add the variety of a few quiet colours, a
corner or two might be found for a few primroses, oxalis,
anemones, bird's-foot trefoil, and orchises. There would be
a Fernery and bower combined, green and cool, and dark
at all times, a charming place in summer, and not quite a
desolation in winter; for with the shelter afforded, especially
if the side towards the east were made pretty close with
rustic trellis, the majority of the plants would carry their
fronds through the winter; and by draining off superfluous
water by a mere slope and drain of crocks in a covered
trench, a warm air would prevail within, that would be just
sufficient to bring them on early in spring, without weakening
them so much in autumn as to risk their winter existence.

The shedding of the foliage of the trailing plants outside
would give freer access to the light in winter, and the strong
light of summer would be shaded off by the thickening of
the foliage then; but if at that bright season too deep a
gloom prevailed, it would be the fault of the pruning-knife,
not of the scheme itself. It would cost next to nothing,
for if you were tired of fern growing—and the attentions
requisite would in this case be reduced to a minimum—
you might pull down the structure, and get back the cost
of the timber by turning it into firewood; and as the
ferns and other plants would increase considerably, the
nursery stock would be worth more than it was at starting,

so that a Fernery of this description is cheap enough for the poorest lover of the beautiful, and choice enough for the most wealthy connossieur of taste in gardening.

But out-door Ferneries enable us to cultivate only the hardy ferns, and many of the finest varieties of exotic filices demand the shelter of the greenhouse, or the stove. Here, of course, the regular routine must be gone through.

A greenhouse cannot be extemporized; though expense need not stand greatly in the way of in-door fern culture, seeing that a very humble structure, heated from a kitchen fire, will do wonders with patience and skill, and that roomy and substantial buildings are not so costly as to be beyond the compass of ordinary incomes.

The above is a design for a lean-to house, suitable for

ferns, because they could be staged so as to present a regular arrangement from the ground to the roof, the whole front being of glass, and affording a beautiful view of the collection. Here also are designs for the stages on which the plants might be exhibited to best advantage, and which would be equally adaptable, with a little ingenuity, to either a lean-to or a span roof. This greenhouse differs from the ordinary form in the greater extent of glass, and hence more brilliant display without and within, and the amount of light so admitted, would prevent the spindling or drawing of such plants as were set back from the glass. The front sashes extend without interruption of timber or brick-work, from the roof to the ground; and an elegant cornice runs along the front, which serves as gutter and ornament at the same time. The heating arrangements would have to be on the ordinary plan, or a hot-water pipe might be carried through from an adjoining kitchen, and economy of building and fuel thus accomplished very satisfactorily. Of course such a house could be used for any of the purposes to which greenhouses are put, and many plants may be associated with ferns, and come to perfection under the same regulations of temperature and moisture which they require.

Mr. Newman says, in his delightful "History of British Ferns," "Whenever I found a fern which I thought would be worth removing, I invariably noticed the situation in which it grew—whether it was naturally exposed to the sun, rain, and wind; whether it grew on a horizontal or perpendicular surface, etc.; whether its fronds were erect, horizontal, or pendulous; whether its roots enjoyed depth of earth, or were 'simply moored in the rifted rock.' And having thus minutely observed every natural peculiarity, my next object, when the ferns had reached home, was to copy nature as closely as I could, not indeed to imitate rocks and mountains by a structure of Bath bricks or clinkers, but simply supplying to each, as far as possible, the

adjuncts which it naturally enjoyed. Thus some bog-lovers, as the *Osmunda regalis*, were placed in slight excavations, which I could readily flood with water; others, as the *Ceterach officinarum*, which almost deserting its natural station on rocks, has established itself on our mortared walls, I supplied with crumbled mortar, carefully introduced between the stones, and placed at the root, so that in all rains, and in the constant waterings in which the Ferneries rejoice, it should remain as dry as possible; for to the roots of some ferns wet is as injurious as it is needful to the well-being of others."

Mr. Newman's advice may be accepted as an epitome of fern-culture, though we must cross swords with him on the subjects of clinkers and rock-work; which we think infinitely preferable, for ferns never show to such good effect as when their emerald feathery fronds droop over masses of dark stones; besides which, rock-work, well built up— busts, shells, and gingerbread excluded—is an additional item in the imitation of the "adjuncts which the plants naturally enjoy." If built up in fantastic pyramids, and with pinnacles cleaving the air; if adorned with Triton's horns, and blocks of coral, and foreign shells and gleanings from curiosity shops, a Fernery becomes a pantomime; but there is no fear of such quaint fancies; it is impossible for any one to give much attention to ferns without attaining to very correct and chaste notions of taste: and we might say that the love of ferns is always an accompaniment of correct ideas of embellishment. It must be a pure and simple taste which finds pleasure in the culture of plants which have no gaudy blossoms to attract vulgar attention, which have no claims upon our attention beyond chaste simple outlines, rare shades of green and brown, and methods of growth neither noticed nor cared for by minds unschooled to simple elegance and exquisite delicacy of form.

To obtain ferns for your rockeries and fern banks, you will of course make an occasional excursion to some lone

glen or forest shade, some shady covert or rocky waterfall, and as you find them growing in their several sites, you will take a hint as to their future management. Then, if you are a novice in cryptogamous botany, you will consult some work of authority, such as Lowe's splendid "British and Exotic Ferns," the cheapest and most perfect of all the many fern books that have been lately published; or, if that sounds expensive, then you will take refuge in the pretty little "Handbook of British Ferns,' by Mr. Moore. In these works you will gain all the information that will enable you to name, group, and cultivate your fairy feathers accurately, and the culture will open the way to pleasure and to wisdom, while it will also prove the best of tonics for both body and mind.

Thus purified from low desire
Thy spirit shall but soar the higher.

But no one district will supply ferns in any great variety, and if actual collecting be depended on for the gathering together of the most desirable kinds, it may be many years ere the Fernery attain to anything like completeness. There is the need of a purveyor and professed cultivator of ferns, and it may assist many who wish to form collections, and who want ferns true to name at reasonable prices, to refer them to Mr. Robert Sim, of Foot's Cray, Kent, who is unquestionably the first of fern collectors and cultivators in the country. I have been supplied by Mr. Sim, and am more than satisfied as to quality and price, and largely indebted to that admirable catalogue of British and Foreign Ferns, which he sends out for six postage-stamps. It is an epitome in itself, most admirably arranged, full of practical hints on selection and culture, and contains descriptions of four hundred and forty ferns collected from all parts of the globe, and offered at prices varying from sixpence to a guinea each, according to the relative scarcity or character of the species, and to a lover of ferns is as interesting as a romance. Lovers of ferns, Mr. Sim is your guardian spirit!

In selecting plants for the hardy Fernery, the British species and their several varieties may be taken almost *ad lib;* but there are a few to be avoided, because they can be made to succeed only in the close damp air of a bell-glass or Wardian case. Those tender kinds are the *Adiantums, Hymenophyllums, Trichomanes radians,* and *Asplenium marinum,* which require damp air in a greenhouse or cool stove, or the confinement of a Wardian case. Among the Foreign ferns best adapted for the rockery and out-door culture generally, nearly all those that come from North America are suitable, but some few Asiatic species may also be located there, on account of their ready acceptance of the rigours of our climate.

Among the British ferns the *Polypodies* are all adaptable, and are so distinct in their beauty, as to stand apart from those that have finely-divided fronds, as they do also by their rich tints of darker green, and their showy masses of fructification. *P. calcareum* is the most troublesome of the tribe, and will only thrive in a compost of sandy peat and old mortar, and in a constant shade. The *Lastreas* come next in botanical order, and here we have the splendid *Cristata,* the delicate *Thelypteris* and *Oreopteris,* all requiring a boggy soil, and hence suitable to the dampest parts of the Fernery. The *Polystichums,* or holly and prickly ferns, give the relief of darker shades of green and stiff hirsute habits of growth; they are evergreen, easy of culture, and make fine contrasts against the more delicate and pendant forms.

But no collection can be worth much in which the lovely Lady fern has no place. She is the true empress of the woods, and when domiciled in the fern-garden, sits regally at the base of the bank, shaming meaner kinds by her superb form and colour. The fronds, very delicate in

texture, spring from the crown of the caudex in a large tuft, "the older plants of the larger varieties sometimes throwing up from twenty to thirty fronds, such examples being noble as well as lovely." During May, when the fronds first appear, they are beautifully coiled up, and by degrees the apex of the vernation gets liberated, and hooks downward in the form of a shepherd's crook. It is abundant in all parts of Britain and Ireland, frequenting warm moist woods and damp hedge-rows. It is the bracken of Ireland, and is used for packing fish. Mr. Lees, in the "Botanical Looker Out," has some very pretty lines on the Lady fern—

> "By the fountain I saw her just spring into sight,
> Her texture as frail as tho' shiv'ring with fright;
> To the water she shrinks—I can scarcely discern
> In the deep humid shadows, the soft lady fern.
>
> Where the water is pouring for ever she sits,
> And beside her the ouzel and kingfisher flits;
> There, supreme in her beauty, beside the full urn,
> In the shade of the rock, stands the tall lady fern."

Fortunately for the beauty of the suburban Fernery, the Lady fern bears civilization admirably. I have grown it in town in pure sand under the trickling of water, chancing on one occasion to have a suitable place in a damp back area beneath a cistern which supplied the drip. "If planted about rock-work," says Mr. Moore, "it should occupy a low boggy situation at the foot of the rock, being planted amongst turfy soil, kept well moistened, either naturally or artificially. It is far less beautiful if planted in dry exposed situations. No object about a piece of rock-work is so beautiful as a vigorous plant of the Lady fern placed just within the mouth of a dark cavernous recess, large enough to admit of its development, and just open enough that the light of day may gleam across the dark background of the cavern, revealing the drooping feathery fronds. In such a situation it will grow freely, provided there is a sufficient supply of moisture to its roots. For planting in shady woods, or on the margin of ornamental water, no fern can be more appropriate or beautiful."

A few other genera contain species worthy the labours of the cultivator. The hart's tongue, (*Scolopendrium vulgare,*) is an essential in the Fernery as much for its distinct rich character, as for the ease with which it may be grown. The glossy, leathery, and entire fronds, of from one to two feet in length, are so different to the finely-cut

pinnatifid fronds of other ferns, that it makes a striking object as it puts forth its long green pendant tongue from a crevice between the stones.

Among the ferns of smaller growth, the spleenworts, bladder and alpine ferns, and *Blechnum spicant* are valuable, but the magnificent brake is not to be neglected. There is but one British species of brake, *(Pteris aquilina,)* to the profusion of which we owe half the glories of our forest and moorland scenery. There are few finer scenes than an

amphitheatre of steep slopes rising from a glen, covered up
their sides with jungles of waving bracken, and crowned
with old oaks and thorns, forming cover for all sorts of
wild creatures—the joy of the sportsman and the naturalist.
The brake is a noble fern; the great height which its fronds
attain, and their erect arching, but not pendant attitude,
give them a majesty of character which assorts well with
the grandeur of old forest scenery. How admirably the
mere mention of the bracken gives reality to many of Scott's
romantic scenes, and perhaps to none more so than in that
vision of the Clan, which Roderick Dhu calls up within
sight of the astonished James.

> "He whistled shrill,
> And he was answered from the hill;
> Wild as the scream of the curlew,
> From crag to crag the signal flew.
> Instant through copse and heath arose
> Bonnets, and spears, and bended bows;
> On right, on left, above, below,
> Sprang up at once the lurking foe;
> From shingles grey their lances start,
> The bracken bush sends forth the dart;
> The rushes and the willow wand
> Are bristling into axe and brand,
> And every tuft of broom gives life
> To plaided warrior armed for strife."

Still more does the bracken give completeness to the
contrast of the peace of nature, the cold and quiet solitude
of the hill-side, when at the signal every bright plaid and
claymore vanishes from the sight.

> "Then waved his hand:
> Down sunk the disappearing band,
> Each warrior vanished where he stood,
> In broom or bracken, heath or wood;
> Sunk brand, and spear, and bended bow,
> In osiers pale, and copses low;
> It seemed as if their mother earth
> Had swallowed up her warlike birth.

> The wind's last breath had toss'd in air
> Pennon, and plaid, and plumage fair,—
> The next had swept a lone hill-side,
> Where heath and fern were waving wide;
> The sun's last glance was glinted back
> From spear and glaive, from targe and jack,—
> *The next, all unreflected, shone*
> *On bracken green, and cold grey stone.*"

The graphic power of the last two lines is vastly heightened by the "bracken green," a brave covert for the crouching foeman.

Fortunately the bracken is killed by the first frost, which leaves it brown and sere—a fine accompaniment to the rich colouring of our autumn wood-side scenery; but under cultivation the shelter preserves its greenness longer, and it waves bravely from the moist hollow, when the verdure of the garden begins rapidly to fade. Its scenic value, skirting hedge-rows and arching out from brushwood, is depreciated by culture, for it becomes stiffer in outline, especially in a dry aspect; but under the most adverse circumstances it is still a noble fern, and one of the necessities of the wilderness walk, or arched bank of an artificial pool.

The cultivation of the bracken is most easy; a mere fragment of the root-stock will establish itself, and throw out fine luxuriant fronds, while it endures many years, continually improving as its roots extend. It will thrive in any but a calcareous soil; and in planting it in rock-work, care should be taken to place it at some distance from compost containing lime-rubbish and old mortar: bog-earth or sandy peat forms the best soil, and, like most other ferns, it glories in shadow and moisture.

The prominent attractions of the British Fernery are the Lady fern, the Bracken, and the Osmund Royal, the three noblest members of this shy community of green shadow-haunting dryads. If the two former claim attention for the grandeur of their forms, the first exhibiting a rare grace, and the second a sylvan boldness, the last is un-

doubtedly the most stately of the tribe. It is well named, for it attains a great size; we have seen it tower above the head of the tallest Yorkshire yeoman, reaching far beyond that beau-ideal of perfect human stature, six feet, with a stem more trim and tree-like than any other of our British ferns; and in damp sheltered spots it frequently sends up its fronds in a rapid growth to a height of even ten and twelve feet. The fronds appear in May, and are destroyed by the first autumn frost.

It is not widely distributed; the Cumberland lakes reflect its green feathers on their glassy dimples; and on the margin of many a pool in Yorkshire and Lincolnshire it may be seen doing battle with huge rushes, over which it asserts its royalty and right to govern.

Touching the relation of this fine fern to many of the most romantic and classic scenes that poetry has hallowed, there is a passage in an article on Shelley, by De Quincey, which appeared in "Tait" in 1846, wherein this Titan denounces sundry innovations on the lonely quietude of Grassmere, and amongst them an "insane substruction" which was carried along the eastern margin of the lake as a basis for a coach-road. He says, "This infernal mass of solid masonry swept away the loveliest of sylvan recesses, and the most absolutely charmed against intrusive foot or angry echoes. It did worse; it swept away the stateliest of Flora's daughters, and swept away at the same time the birth-place of a well-known verse, describing that stately plant, which is perhaps (as a separate line) the most exquisite that the poetry of earth can shew. The plant was the *Osmunda regalis;*—

> 'Plant lovelier in its own recess
> Than Grecian naiad seen at earliest dawn
> Tending her fount, *or lady of the lake*
> *Sole sitting by the shores of old romance.*'

It is this last line and a half which some have held to ascend

in beauty as much beyond any single line known to literature, as the *Osmunda* ascends in luxury of splendour above other ferns."

The cultivation of this fine fern is attended with no difficulties; it prefers a peat soil and plenty of moisture, looks noble in rock-work, or about water-scenery. It is propagated by detaching and planting any lateral offshoots from the caudex.

Among the hardy exotic ferns a large proportion are in a certain sense counterparts of British species, and where the object of the cultivator is to secure variety rather than botanical completeness in his collections, it will be necessary to exercise some amount of caution in the selection of foreign ferns. Thus many of the American *Lastreas, Aspleniums, Osmundas, Pteris,* and *Polypodiums* are scarcely distinguishable from native species, except to experienced botanical eyes, though where the habit is distinct and striking such additions are to be highly prized.

Some of the more distinct kinds are eminently worthy of adoption, and of these I shall specify a few, referring the readers for the names of others to the complete lists at the end of this section.

Lastrea gives us at least three noble species, very readily distinguishable from any British kinds. The stately *L. cristata major* is one of the most desirable; it rises to a height of three or four feet, with twice-divided shining fronds. This fern has been generally sold under the name of *L. Goldieana,* but the true fern of that name is perfectly distinct from *cristata major,* and is perhaps the rarest hardy exotic fern ever introduced to an English garden. That *Lastrea* is indispensible; *L. noveboracensis* and *intermedia* are two others that may be used to advantage, the first especially, as a lovely object. Among the exotic *Osmundas* there are none that attain to the stately stature of our own *O. regalis,* but all are elegant in proportion and habit; *O. interrupta* and *spectabilis* are the most distinct and orna-

mental. *Polystichum acrostichoides,* a noble evergreen fern, *Pycnopteris Sieboldii,* and *Woodwardia angustifolia* may be further named as among the most distinct.

In a Fernery of the bower kind, such as I have described as formed of timber of trailing plants, a large number of greenhouse ferns would find sufficient shelter, especially if the bower was made close with a screen of ivy to the north, or sheltered by adjacent shrubberries or walls. Some of the pretty foreign species of *Adiantum,* especially *A. Moritzianum, assimile,* (so pretty when used in boquets,) and *formosum,* a splendid species, rising eighteen inches high. The well-known hare's-foot fern, *Davallia Canariensis;* the hardy Chinese fern, *Drynaria Fortunii;* and in warm shady nooks *Lastrea Canariensis, Lygodium palmatum,* which is a decided climber; *Polystichum æmulum* and *falcinellum,* the latter being one of those palm-like ferns that so notably represent the characteristics of the tropical jungle. To these many others might be added according to the space at disposal; and the means of shelter during winter, which would be brought into use, but the narrowness of my space precludes further specification, and a sufficient variety of kinds that are sure to succeed, has been already enumerated for the general purposes of the amateur.

In the greenhouse the rarer and more delicate forms would find a congenial home; the silver and gold ferns, *(Gymnogrammæ,)* would by contrast of habit and colour heighten the beauties of the rare climbing ferns, *(Lygodium,)* and the taller sorts of tree fern, such as *Aspidium Barometz,* (the Tartarian lamb of Darwin's "Botanic Garden,") *Dicksonia antartica,* which however requires an immense space for its full development, *Cyathea dealbata,* and *Marattia cicutæfolia,* the latter a most distinct tall fern, which soars above the dwarfer kinds to a height of five or six feet, but without crowding or incommoding its lowlier neighbours. Here however the species and varieties dawn upon me by hundreds; some aquatic, *(Meniscium, Ceratopteris,)* and requiring to be grown in pans plunged into water; others suitable for vases, and making magnificent objects when so grown apart from all other kinds, (*Asplenium præmorsum;*) others suitable for suspended baskets, mossed blocks, or to surface the pots around the roots of larger species, a use to which many forms of *Lycopodium* are adapted on account of their strange diversities of colour and habit, and their generally procumbent growth. In fact the fern-house may be very easily rendered a little palace of enchantment; its path edged with *Lycopodium denticulatum*, its roof adorned with suspended baskets and blocks of moss, from which the pendant fronds of foreign ferns would dangle in a variety of the most graceful tints and outlines, its well-staged pots, handsome vases, miniature rockeries for the smaller kinds of creeping ferns, and the Aquarium in the centre, with its splashing fountain and "fairy fishes from the mountain tarn," and there ferns again rising from, and dipping down to touch the sparkling water, would be in all seasons, and in winter especially, a cheerful retreat, and a source of delightful recreation eminently worthy of a Home of Taste.

Those who possess a collection of dried ferns in an herbarium, may readily propagate any of the kinds which have ripe seeds on the fronds. Turn back one of the ripest leaves, and gently rub off the clusters of capsules, and shake them on a plate; next crumble over them some sandy earth, shake all together, and the seeds will adhere to the earth; then spread this lightly over sandy or loamy soil in those portions of the rock-work where the ferns are wanted. Or, better still, sprinkle the seeds over crushed peat in pots in-doors, moistening each freely, and covering them with bell-glasses washed with mud to keep them opaque. The author has frequently used the empty flasks used for Florence oil for propagating ferns. These washed with potash, and with two or three inches of fine sandy heath mould at the bottom, with which the seed is mixed, have only to be corked and hung up in the dark at first,

and afterwards in a window. In a few weeks the surface
of the soil is studded with strange vegetable forms, which
develope into true ferns, mingled frequently with other
plants of a delicate and rare nature. When the ferns
reach the narrow neck the flask is broken, and the ferns
transplanted to their proper sites during wet weather.
The flasks are of no value, and the salad-bowl and fish-
pan supply a sufficiency of empty ones.

All those ferns which have a creeping caudex are easily
propagated. A portion of a moderate length bearing a
frond, if separated and planted at once in moist leaf mould,
or peat, or sandy heath, will soon establish itself and throw
up a succession of fronds. They improve vastly as they
get older, and every year adds to the glory of a well-
stocked Fernery.

In transplanting, the soil should be as little broken from
the roots as possible; each should have its little ball of
earth, and be handled gently. The herbarium, if fairly
supplied with fern specimens, will supply abundance of
seed; and a very fair stock may be obtained without the
necessity of a single purchase or collecting expedition. But
Heaven forfend we should lapse into such inanity. Let
the lover of ferns see his favourites in their native solitudes,
climbing up rocky passes, waving in wide seas of verdure
on forest borders, and broad shaggy tracks of wild wood,
which the plough has never desecrated, and where, ever
since the creation, the wild birds and creeping creatures
have had a home under the thick arching branches of the
bonny bracken. See them at the water-fall, where they
lean forward from giddy heights, and for mere sport hold
their fingers amongst the light spray, adding to the beauty
of the diamond sparkles and rainbow arches, rejoicing in
the rush and thunder of the fall. See them on the
boles of grey trees, and among the clefts of shattered rock,
beside the rill, drinking all day long from the fountain at
its source. Within the haunted cavern, where, like creatures

of necromantic power, they preserve beauty and silence where superstition seeks for monsters howling in despair. No; trust not too much to the withered ghosts of ferns, that hang about sheets of cartridge and brown paper, wretched spectres of the green living things that glad the eye everywhere, but seek them for yourself, by river and mountain sides, hedge-rows, meadow hollows, woodland slopes, and mossy cairns.

To keep a Fernery in a bright and luxurious condition, frequent drenching with water is necessary. In summer, during dry weather, water should be given twice a day, and if a fine shower is thrown over by means of a garden-engine, or a copious supply from the *fine rose* of a common watering-pot, the benefit will be very great. The plants will grow rapidly to their full luxuriance, and assume that fresh glossy sparkling greenness in which a Fernery is unmatched. When the fronds cease growing in autumn they should have rest, for ferns soon shew the effect of injurious forcing by prolonged waterings late in the season. Mosses and rock-plants that spread over the surface, and form moist carpetings of green, are of great service to ferns, by keeping their roots cool and moist; but grasses, except such as are grown for ornamental purposes, must be destroyed, or they will soon overspread and destroy them. Marchantia is useful about ferns as a preservative of moisture, and adds to the beauty of the scene by the softness and luxuriance of its spreading verdure.

Where there are no arrangements of pipes for keeping a constant drip on those ferns which require it, such as the delicate *Trichomanes speciosum, Polypodium phegopteris,* and *Cystopteris fragilis,* Mr. Newman's plan may be adopted. He suspends a vessel of water, in which a pierced cork is inserted. This is made to drip near the plants on a hard flat stone, so as to splash the fronds with a fine spray, and thus maintain the humidity essential to their growth.

ON THE CULTURE OF FERNS IN POTS.

WHAT has been already said as to the culture of ferns in the open air, applies, with but few variations, to their treatment in pots in the greenhouse or dwelling-rooms. One great advantage of in-door fern-growing is the facility afforded for the culture of several species that are scarcely manageable when exposed; when so close under our eye, we can render them attentions suited to their delicate habits, while they are removed from those influences which check their growth under exposure to the weather. The hardier sorts of exotic ferns may be set out under shelter on a layer of sifted coal-ashes or tan, but no potted (whether hardy or exotic) ferns should ever be exposed to frost. As they cease growing, watering should be suspended till April, when they may be brought forward again with moisture. The drip may be obtained by suspending over the plant a vessel of water, out of which a worsted thread should hang. This supplies a succession of water-drops, which should fall on a stone beside the plant.

The best soil for general use in the greenhouse and for ferns in pots, baskets and vases in rooms, is one of which *spongy* peat is the basis. It must be porous to facilitate a free drainage, and for large ferns it is advisable to add a little turfy loam and well-rotted dung, but the smaller kinds will do best in spongy peat alone. A liberal admixture of pieces of freestone or broken pots will be found beneficial, as allowing a circulation of air through the soil, and preventing stagnation of moisture. The soil for ferns should not be fine, indeed it is better never to sift it, but if it requires to be broken it may be loosened sufficiently with the hand when being used. A notion prevails that ferns cannot have too much water, but this is a serious mistake.

If not allowed a season of repose, the strongest growers eventually languish, and as the seasonal vigour of the plants subsides, watering must be gradually discontinued, and at any time, except in the case of the few aquatic ferns, a wet muddy state of the soil is destructive. When growing, the plants should never be allowed to flag for want of water, and their love of moisture may be gratified by an occasional syringing of the leaves, or by splashing water about the house, so that in hot dry weather they may enjoy a genial moist atmosphere. Several of the choicest species require special culture, as indicated in the notices of species in the preceding pages; other useful advices may be obtained by reference to the splendid works of Lowe, Moore, Lindley, and Sowerby, and valuable catalogue of Mr. Robert Sim, of Foot's Cray.

LIST OF BRITISH FERNS BEST SUITED FOR CULTURE IN POTS.

English Name.	Botanical Name.	Length of Frond.	Soil.	Remarks on General Treatment, etc.
Beech Fern	Polypodium phegopteris.	5 to 12 in.	Peat leaf, charcoal, & sand.	A delicate object when potted, requires the shelter of a cold frame in hot summer weather and the drip always while growing.
Smith's three-branched Polypody	P. calcareum	" "	Peat and old mortar ...	Likes exposure, but must have good drainage at the roots.
Rock Brake, or Mountain Parsley	Allosorus crispus	6 to 10 in.	Common ...	Requires good drainage. Grows best in shade, and is a famous Fern for pots.
Ray's Woodsia	Woodsia ilvensis	2 to 4 in.	Common ...	Small and rare, but not esteemed for elegance.
Bolton's Woodsia ...	W. alpina	" "	Common ...	The Woodsias succeed best in pots. They want shade, and but little moisture. During winter should have a shelf in the greenhouse, and in spring the tufts should be divided.

LIST OF BRITISH FERNS FOR POT CULTURE.

English Name.	Botanical Name.	Length of Frond.	Soil.	Remarks on General Treatment, etc.
				They are deciduous. In planting elevate the roots above the surface of the mould by means of three pieces of freestone, and then place the soil carefully about their roots. This will prevent injury from stagnant moisture.
Marsh Fern	Lastrea thelypteris ...	6 to 20 in.	Leaf mould and charcoal.	Requires plenty of room for its roots, and loves a boggy soil. Is elegant, and grows freely.
Mountain Fern	L. oreopteris	20 to 36 in.	Peat, sand, and charcoal.	Must be very moderately supplied with water, and well drained at the roots.
Crested Fern	L. cristata	15 to 26 in.	Peat, sand, and charcoal.	Requires plenty of root-room, and abundance of water : must have shelter in winter.
Rough Alpine Fern ...	Polystichum lonchitis ...	6 to 18 in.	Sandy loam, and broken freestone.	A rare and beautiful Fern, but not easily domesticated. It should be potted firmly, and well drained. A cool frame is the best situation for it.

LIST OF BRITISH FERNS FOR POT CULTURE.

English Name.	Botanical Name.	Length of Frond.	Soil.	Remarks on General Treatment, etc.
Brittle Bladder Fern ...	Cystopteris fragilis ...	4 to 12 in.	Common ...	This is one of the gems of the collection. It must be potted in a five-inch pot, and requires plenty of water and free drainage. It grows freely, and has a neat and elegant appearance.
Alpine Bladder Fern ...	C. alpina	4 to 8 in.	Common ...	May be propagated by separation of new crowns. The alpine species is a scarce one but very beautiful.
Lady Fern	Athyrium Filix fœmina.	6 to 30 in.	Common ...	The smaller varieties, such as *multifidum, molle,* and *crispum,* are the best for pot-culture. They require plenty of water and large pots. The soil should have a good mingling of broken charcoal and freestone.
Smooth Rock Spleenwort	Asplenium fontanum	3 to 6 in.	Common	An elegant tufted Fern, which thrives under cultivation. Must be well drained, and should be potted with its roots elevated on two or three pieces of sandstone. Requires a close shady frame.

LIST OF BRITISH FERNS FOR POT CULTURE.

English Name.	Botanical Name.	Length of Frond.	Soil.	Remarks on General Treatment, etc.
Hudson's Spleenwort	A. lanceolatum	5 to 12 in.	Common ...	A scarce species; requires shelter and warmth, a moist atmosphere and free drainage.
Black Spleenwort	A. adiantum-nigrum ...	4 to 20 in.	Common ...	A glossy evergreen, needs only shade and moisture. It is common on ruins and hedgerows.
Sea Spleenwort	A. marinum	6 to 14 in.	Peat, silver-sand, broken sandstone, & charcoal ...	Of vigorous habit, and ornamental, but established with difficulty. It requires a warm moist air, and does better in a greenhouse or close frame. A hand-glass should be put over the pot during winter.
Common Spleenwort	A. trichomanes	4 to 10 in.	Peat, sand, charcoal, & old mortar.	Grows freely in the shade with good drainage. May be propagated by the division of the crowns.
Green Spleenwort	A. viride	3 to 8 in.	Sandy peat and freestone.	Must be well drained, though fond of moisture. Grows most luxuriantly in the shade.

LIST OF BRITISH FERNS FOR POT CULTURE.

English Name.	Botanical Name.	Length of Frond.	Soil.	Remarks on General Treatment, etc.
Wall Rue	A. Ruta-muraria	1 to 6 in.	Sandy peat and freestone.	Requires similar treatment to the last.
Forked Spleenwort ...	A. septentrionale	2 to 4 in.	Turfy peat ...	A rare species, requires warmth and shade, and careful protection in winter.
Scaly Spleenwort	Ceterach officinarum ...	3 to 8 in.	Common ...	Requires a porous soil, and plenty of room. Grows finest in the shade.
Common Hart's Tongue	Scolopendrium vulgare.	6 to 24 in.	Common ...	This noble Fern will thrive in almost any situation, in pots it requires plenty of room for its roots.
Maidenhair	Adiantum capillus veneris	6 to 12 in.	Peat, sand, and charcoal ...	This is a tender shade-loving Fern. It is superlatively elegant, needs warmth and shelter, and does best in a Ward's case.
Hard Fern	Blechnum spicant... ...	18 to 24 in.	Peat, sand, and charcoal ...	Fond of moisture, is a splendid ornament, and of easy culture.

LIST OF BRITISH FERNS
SUITED FOR CULTURE IN CLOSED CASES.

English Name.	Botanical Name.	English Name.	Botanical Name.
Mountain Polypody,	P. phegopteris.	Common Spleenwort,	A. trichomanes.
Oak Fern,	P. dryopteris.	Wall Rue,	A. ruta-muraria.
Brittle Bladder Fern,	Cystopteris fragilis.	Wiess's Spleenwort,	A. Germanicum.
Alpine Bladder Fern,	C. alpina.	Hart's Tongue,	Scolopendrium vulgare.
Mountain Bladder Fern,	C. montana.	Maidenhair,	Adiantum capillus veneris.
Hudson's Spleenwort,	Asplenium lanceolatum.	Bristle Fern,	Trichomanes radicans.
Sea Spleenwort,	A. marinum.	Tunbridge Filmy Fern,	Hymenophyllum Tunbridgense.
Black Spleenwort,	A. adiantum-nigrum.	Wilson's Filmy Fern,	H. unilaterale.

LIST OF FERNS FOR ROCK-WORK.

WEST ASPECT.

Requiring much moisture, but must be well drained at the roots. Where no special soil is requisite, the common soil of which the bank is composed is sufficient.

English Name.	Botanical Name.	Length of Frond.	Soil.	Remarks on General Treatment, etc.
Beech Fern	Polypodium phegopteris.	5 to 12 in.	Common ...	Requires abundance of moisture and does best under a constant drip.
Crested Fern	Lastrea cristata	15 to 26 in.	Common ...	
Roth's Fern	L. dilatata	1 to 5 ft.	Common ...	This is a very noble Fern, and grows freely in moderate shade.
Common Prickly Fern ...	Polystichum aculeatum.	15 to 20 in.	Common ...	Common in hedge-banks, and grows freely under moderate exposure. It is green during winter.
Black Spleenwort	Asplenium adiantum-nigrum.	4 to 20 in.	Common ...	Neat and evergreen, and grows freely with moderate shade. The varieties of this species differ much in height.

WEST ASPECT.

English Name.	Botanical Name.	Length of Frond.	Soil.	Remarks on General Treatment, etc.
Common Spleenwort ...	A. trichomanes	4 to 10 in.	Common ...	An elegant evergreen Fern, should have a prominent position on account of its small size. Must have good drainage.
Green Spleenwort	A. viride	3 to 8 in.	Common ...	Requires the same treatment.
Scaly Spleenwort	Ceterach officinarum ...	3 to 8 in.	Common ...	Requires very porous soil, in which there is a good proportion of old mortar.
Moonwort	Botrychium lunaria ...	3 to 10 in.	Peat	This is rather a troublesome plant. It requires to be kept moderately dry, cool at the root, and in a free current of air. The moist warmth which suits Ferns generally is fatal to this curious member of the family.
Adder's Tongue	Ophioglossum vulgatum.	4 to 10 in.	Loam and leaf mould.	Requires coolness and moisture.

SOUTH AND EAST ASPECTS.

MODERATE WATERING, AND WELL-DRAINED AT THE ROOTS.

English Name.	Botanical Name.	Length of Frond.	Soil.	Remarks on General Treatment, etc.
Common Polypody ...	Polypodium vulgare ...	6 to 18 in.	Turfy peat or decayed wood and broken charcoal.	Of free growth, and suits any aspect. Finer in the shade, and hence it may be well to have a duplicate on the north bank.
Smith's Three-branched Polypody	P. calcareum	5 to 12 in.	Common, with broken lime rubbish.	Must be rather dry, and does not require much shade.
Rock Brakes, or Mountain Parsley	Allosorus crispus ...	6 to 10 in.	Common ...	Requires plenty of water on fronds. Shade improves it.
Withering's Fern	Lastrea spinulosa ...	15 to 30 in.	Common ...	Very elegant and of erect habit, should be moist at the roots.

SOUTH AND EAST ASPECTS.

English Name.	Botanical Name.	Length of Frond.	Soil.	Remarks on General Treatment, etc.
Bree's Prickly-toothed Fern,	L. Fœnisecii,...	10 to 30 in.	Common ...	Has graceful curved outlines. Bears exposure well, but grows to greater size in the shade.
Common Hart's Tongue,	Scolopendrium vulgare.	6 to 24 in.	Common ...	Thrives best in shady humid spots, but will bear exposure well. It is one of the choicest Ferns in the collection, on account of its distinct character and rich verdure.
Osmund Royal, ...	Osmunda regalis... ...	18 to 40 in.	Common ...	The noblest of Ferns for rockwork. Thrives best in moist shadow and a peat soil, but bears exposure, and is accommodating in habit.
Adder's Tongue, ...	Ophioglossum vulgatum.	4 to 10 in.	Common ...	Requires a prominent but moist position. Though it bears exposure it does better if shaded. It grows well in a cleft or hollow.

NORTH ASPECT.

REQUIRING MUCH MOISTURE AND LITTLE DRAINAGE.

English Name.	Botanical Name.	Length of Frond.	Soil.	Remarks on General Treatment, etc.
Oak Fern	Polypodium dryopteris.	4 to 14 in.	Common ...	A fine dwarf rock-fern, must be well drained at the roots. May be propagated by division of its caudex. Will also suit a west but not a south aspect.
Marsh Fern	Lastrea thelypteris ...	6 to 20 in.	Common ...	Grows freely in a boggy situation.
Mountain Fern	L. oreopteris...	20 to 36 in.	Common ...	Rather shy of cultivation, but grows freely when established; should be well drained. Grows freely from spores, or from lateral crowns detached from old plants.
Male Fern	L. Filix-mas.	20 to 30 in.	Rich sandy loam.	Very common, but a most elegant ornament for shady rock-work or dark walls.

English Name.	Botanical Name.	Length of Frond.	Soil.	Remarks on General Treatment, etc.
Willdenow's Fern ...	Polystichum angulare ...	24 to 50 in.	Rich sandy loam	Very ornamental, and from its great size, suits well for wilderness scenery.
Lady Fern	Athyrium Filix fæmina	6 in. to 5 ft.	Rich sandy loam	There are several varieties of this species, and they vary in stature and outline. The ordinary height is from two to four feet. It grows freely in a shady boggy situation. There is no Fern more appropriate for the margin of ornamental water.
Hard Fern	Blechnum spicant ...	18 to 24 in.	Rich sandy loam	Grows best in a boggy situation. It is one of the finest Ferns for rock-work.
Common Brake	Pteris aquilina	2 to 5 ft.	Peat	This noble and gigantic Fern is the easiest grown of any in the collection. It will not grow near lime, and does best in sandy peat. It loves shade and moisture. It does not attain its full height in artificial rock-work.

LIST OF SELECT HARDY EXOTIC FERNS.

THE Ferns in this list may be grown in the hardy Fernery, and will add to it many curious and interesting forms. A large number of the American species are so much like our own that they would hardly be desirable for purposes of effect merely; those in the list, however, are distinct in character, and are selected because of their special beauty and character.

Adiantum pedatum: North side, requiring shade and moisture. A very pretty Fern for pot-culture. Two feet.

A. assimile: Very neat spreading fronds; most desirable.

Asplenium angustifolium: A fine deciduous Fern. One foot and a half.

A. lucidum: Erect shining fronds, which rise in noble clusters.

Botrychium Fumarioides: A curious Fern, with but one triangular thrice-divided frond four inches high. It is easily cultivated in chopped moss and sand, or leaf-mould with a little sandy peat.

Cyrtomium falcatum: Dark green glossy fronds, handsome and distinct. Quite hardy. Two feet.

Camptosorus rhizophyllus: A very choice but minute Fern to crawl about the prominent parts of a sheltered rockery. It spreads by runners in a way similar to the strawberry.

Davallia Canariensis, the Hare's-foot Fern: Neat in habit, and bears exposure well.

Diplazium thelypteroides: Deciduous. One foot and a half.

Dicksonia piloriuscula: Very pretty, and will do on exposed parts of the Fernery. One foot and a half.

Drynaria Fortunii: A hardy Chinese Fern. Eight inches.

Lastrea Goldieana: This is considered the rarest hardy Exotic Fern in cultivation, but *Cristata major* is very generally sold for it. Mr. Sim, of Foot's Cray, has the true species. One foot and a half.

L. decurrens: A striking and distinct species; the fronds once divided, and of a lurid green. One foot

Lygodium palmatum: An elegant climbing Fern, very scarce, and highly prized.

Osmunda interrupta: Exquisitely delicate, the fronds spreading with much grace, and of a peculiar pale green. Three feet.

O. cinnamonea: The fertile fronds of this species rise very majestically above the foliage. Three feet.

O. spectabilis: This is like a miniature of our own *O. regalis,* and is very choice and delicate. One foot and a half.

The *Osmundas* like shade, shelter, and a moist peaty soil. They are all deciduous.

Onychium Japonicum: Curious and skeleton-like, creeping in habit. One foot.

Polypodium Virginianum: Very like the English *P. vulgare.* One foot.

Polystichum acrostichoides: A fine evergreen Fern, which bears exposure well. One foot and a half.

P. æmulum: Very striking; would need a little protection in winter. Two feet.

P. proliferum: Fronds spreading, triangular, and spiny-looking, bearing young plants near their points. One foot and a half.

P. falcinellum: Palm-like and elegant. Two feet.

Pycnopteris Sieboldii: Large spreading fronds of a dull green, very fine in character, and very hardy. One of the most desirable of hardy Ferns. One foot and a quarter.

Pteris serrulata: This is the only exotic *Pteris* that can be considered desirable for planting out, being very pretty and quite hardy.

Selaginella (Lycopodium) denticulatum: A very useful plant for surfacing, as it adapts itself to any soil or situation, and soon makes fine patches of rich verdure.

EMBELLISHMENTS
OF THE GARDEN.

THIS quiet garden's humble bound,
  This homely roof, this rustic fane,
With playful tendrils twining round,
  And woodbines peeping at the pane.

That tranquil, tender, sky of blue,
  Where clouds of golden radiance skim,
Those ranging trees of various hue,—
  These were the sights that solaced him.
                    TAYLOR'S Visit to Cowper's Arbour.

O embellish a garden well, needs a discriminating and in some cases, a severe taste. Whatever errors may be committed in the laying out, the planting, and the disposition of colours, will more readily escape the eye or meet with forgiveness from the critic, than the injudicious adoption of any kind of special embellishment. Yet if the leading principles of gardening taste are kept in view, the smallest plot may be so ornamented as to convey an idea of luxurious completeness, and present at all seasons a wealthy fullness that shall prove its owner to be an artist in the work; and the garden of ample dimensions and varied features, will have its several beauties enhanced and brought out by exactly similar means. We do not value a picture for the extent of its canvas, but for the perfect development of its story through the medium of form and colour, light and shade; and though artifices for concealing the dimensions of a piece of ground are, in most cases, illegitimate and unworthy, the more that ground, whether large or small, is embellished with special ornaments adapted to it and tastefully disposed, the more will its extent be really enlarged, because it will offer more and more to interest the eye, and occasion pleasurable emotions in the mind.

In this, as in other things, ornament may be carried to excess, yet in the higher and architectural departments excess is not so much to be feared, when we remember how lavishly the gardens of ancient times were adorned with colonnades, terraces, statues, fountains, and other productions of the quarry and the chisel; and how that same fullness of expression was sustained in the princely gardens which were the models of Italian art in landscape, and which remain to us on canvas and in books as examples of taste worthy of being copied at the present time. Excess in this department is the less dangerous, because architectural forms of all kinds suggest wealth and ease; and it is one of the tendencies of wealth to multiply these sources of pleasure, and with an unsparing hand heap up on all sides the evidences of an enthusiasm in the refining arts. Indeed when we meet with examples of excessive embellishment, it is usually of the strictly rustic class, which may certainly be most easily overdone; and an excess of rustic work anywhere betrays more of eccentricity and littleness than it does of a cultivated mind.

The first and fatal objection to elaborate ornamentation

in gardens, arises out of the fashion in which the houses themselves are built; for the garden begins at the garden door, the house is an integral portion of the whole scene, and except the princely mansions that melt by degrees into lawns and shrubberies, through the medium of terraces and gay parterres, the spectacle out of doors is ruined by the fact that *there* we have but a "back view of the premises."

Whatever builders may say about usage, and expense, and doing as their fathers did before them, it must be admitted that a fundamental principle of taste is violated when we give our houses handsome frontages to the public, and reserve for our own daily contemplation from the garden, nothing but bare walls and plain windows, and oblique chimneys rising from a basement of ugliness. Why should the stranger see a fair exterior, and we ourselves in our privacy and home life, have to stare perpetually at outhouses, pantries, shapeless lobbies, and kitchen windows? Turn the house round then, and expose our domestic offices with the odour of our daily dinner to the streets? No;—let the rear wall and attached offices have as much symmetry as the portico, and flight of steps, and handsome windows in the front. It is as bad as for a man to appear in society with a showy vest and faultless collar, but with soiled fustian at his back, because, forsooth, you are not expected to address him from behind, or because "a front view of the elephant" is all that is seemly.

Where architectural beauty is fully developed, as it is in most of the mansions of our nobility and landed gentry, the construction of terraces and geometric gardens may be definitely proceeded with, but these hump-backed houses admit of artistic embellishments very unkindly indeed. What is to be done for them? Sometimes the builder, for an additional outlay, will construct a balcony terrace, opening from the drawing-room window by a glass door, and leading down to the lawn by a flight of iron or stone steps. When you can have a handsome iron trellis of ornamental design, over which to carry a vine or a small collection of miscel-

laneous climbers, and with a few improvements above and below, taste and ease may be satisfactorily gratified, and the house fitted for the acceptance of what may be termed terrace ornaments. If the situation and character of the house does not admit of the builder's aid, refuge may be found in trellis-work, which certainly has a transforming power, as effectual as Harlequin's wand, and in a manner at once simple and inexpensive.

An example of this mode of using trellis-work, is seen in the annexed sketches. The first presents us with a cluster of ugly buildings:—A is the larder, adjoining the kitchen,

B a scullery, C a dog-house, D a back wall with door leading to a lane, E a pony stable, and F an open space littered with straw and the results of frequent traffic between the several offices.

To change the scene, the only necessary alteration of the buildings, is to remove the front of the larder, so that the scullery shall form a line parallel with the window of the stable. Then throw across the space formerly occupied by the window of the larder, a wooden lattice with pediment and roof, so that the space within may still be used for domestic purposes, A. Before the stable B, place a lattice and pediment to correspond with A, and across the

yard, at the rear of the two side lattices, place another
lattice, with a gate in the centre. A border of flowers and
grass may then be made on each side, and continued back
to the rear lattice, and the whole scene is altered from one
of extreme ugliness to one moderately graceful and pleasing;
and the domestic offices remain intact. A few climbers might
be judiciously disposed over the trellises, but without them
the great object is served, that is, the abolition of ugliness.

In many cases a plain neatness is to be preferred to
verdurous luxuriance, yet the occasions will be few indeed
where walls and trellises will not need to be covered. A

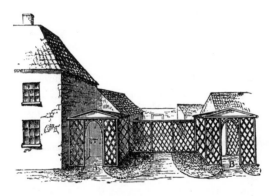

neat little country box embowered in jasmine, honeysuckle,
pyrus, and Virginian creeper, conveys an idea of warmth,
hospitality, and homely comfort; and where a dwelling-
house has not a decidedly architectural aspect, it is all the
better as to beauty and the dryness of its walls, to be well
ivied and screened with greenness. Garden walls, outhouses,
porticos, trellises, and arbours, all need the touch of floral
grace to make them complete; and a judicious selection of
such is another legitimate mode of extending your growing
space and your round of pleasures.

For the fronts of houses those two commonest of screens,
ivy and Virginian creeper, are for general purposes the best

that can be had. They train themselves; they may be cut trim, square, and sharp, or left to festoon the gables and chimneys at their own free will, and in any way are beautiful. The deep ruddy glare of the Virginian creeper in autumn, is scarcely equalled by any tint of earth or sky—it is a sunset photographed. But as the coverings of walls and trellises constitute a very special and important department of ornamental gardening, I will here enumerate the plants most suitable for the various positions in which creepers may be required, and with these general remarks, that evergreens are of most value, in consequence of their unchangeable cheerfulness, even though they may not produce visible blossoms; that where an extent of wall is to be covered, and variety is desired, evergreens may very well alternate with deciduous sorts; that in selecting flowering climbers it will be found advisable to introduce between them liberal breadths of fig, ivy, Stauntonia, or Virginian creeper, as relief agents, or, in the absence of such an arrangement, any of those which bloom nearly at the same time should be so placed as to contrast favourably. A *Pyrus Japonica* does not look so well when it adjoins a *Ribes sanguinea*, as when a mass of rich green stands between them for relief.

For south and west walls the best hardy climbers are *Jasminum revolutum*, yellow; *officinale*, white; and *nudiflorum*, yellow. *Cotoneaster microphylla*, red berries and deep green foliage; *Ceanothus rigidus*, *dentatus*, *intermedius*, and *azureus*, blue, and *Americanus*, white. *Clematis vitalba*, white, and *montana*, white. *Pyrus Japonica* and *Ribes sanguinea*, crimson. *Wistaria chinensis*, the most superb hardy climber we possess. *Cratægus pyracantha*, red; *Escallonia rubra*, pink; *Magnolia grandiflora*, white. *Berberis* of any species, especially *Asiatica*. The majority of these are evergreen; they are all hardy, the *Escallonia* less so than the others, and in severe winters the slight protection of an evergreen branch may be afforded it. They will all flourish in a border made up of sandy loam and peat. The

Magnolia and *Ceanothus* must be planted in fresh heath soil, but may extend their roots beyond it into the general soil of the border. The hawthorn will flourish better if, when it is planted, a barrow-full of building rubbish is mixed with the soil where it is to stand. Strong plants should be obtained in the first instance, and planted out in October or the end of February, and the only one that will require any special pruning beyond what may be necessary for neatness is the *Ceanothus*, which, when it once begins to bloom freely, must have the young shoots of the last season's growth cut back to one or two buds, and the new wood from those buds will produce flowers abundantly.

A few chapters might here be written on roses for walls; for south and west walls are just the places for the climbing sorts, but as the Rosary will fall into its place presently, I must refer the reader forward for such hints as I have space for, and to the remarks on roses in the chapter on the Flower Garden, page 351.

For trellises in good positions many of those just named would be suitable, but the quickest growing kinds are *Passiflora ceruloea*, which is half-hardy, and would need protection by means of mulching at the root, and matting round the stem in winter; and would have to be cut hard back before frost set in. *Lophospermum scandens*, *Eccremocarpus scaber*, and *Maurandya Barclayana*, are three quick-growing trailers that will flower the first year, but if left out during winter will inevitably be lost. The selection of trellis-plants may be extended by reference to the paper on Window Gardening, and the remarks presently to be made on roses.

For *low* walls and trellises facing the south or west, the most suitable are *Jasminum nudiflorum*, a lovely object in winter; *Jasminum revolutum* and *officinalis* already noticed. *Berberis Darwinii*, which is rather tender, and needs a sheltered position and a west aspect. *Clematis montana* and *Sieboldii*, the latter a most lovely thing; *Ceanothus azurea*. Clematis and passion-flowers should be cut down close at

the end of April, for the first three years. *Coronilla glauca,* which is very beautiful and quite hardy; *Veronica* and myrtle; the latter will not stand the winter in exposed situations, but in a mild climate, and on a light limestone soil, it will sometimes take a firm hold and become quite hardy, and with careful training will, in the course of a few years, make a glossy, cheerful, fragrant, and free-flowering trellis or wall plant. A new myrtle, (*Myrtus microphylla,*) exhibited at the June show, at the Crystal Palace, in 1856; promises to take its place as the most elegant of evergreen shrubs we possess. It throws out long, feathery, palm-like branches, with alternate leaves. If this proves to be moderately hardy, it will be the choicest thing for a wall or trellis that could be had, as it is already a lovely thing as a standard for the conservatory or lawn. It should be planted of good size originally.

For a wall within view of any of the principal windows, tall rhododendrons of common sorts might be trained close and nailed, and with a border before them of shrubby kinds of the same plant, selected as to sorts, a splendid back-ground might be made, and the wall effectually hidden. In autumn this rich green mass of foliage would greatly enhance the beauty of the borders and parterres by contrast to the lighter forms and gayer colours. They would thrive if planted in a deep soil of fresh peat or hazelly loam, and in autumn they require mulching with well-rotted dung.

As the climbers come on, bare spaces may be covered with *Cobea scandens,* old fuchsias, and geraniums, that have been trained up for a few years; with sweet pea, convolvulus, gourds, and even runner kidneybeans, the Dutch being the most ornamental, and making a quick and handsome screen if planted alternately white and scarlet, two seeds of each. The old *giant* scarlet geranium does admirably to put out against a wall or trellis during summer, but it must be carried back to the house early in October, and shortened in a little and kept as dry as possible, and well secured against frost. There are plenty of hardy fuchsias that may remain as permanent occupants of a trellis, a liberal mulching of the root being sufficient to carry them safely through the winter, if shortened in as soon as they cease blooming.

The east and north aspects are not the most difficult to cover, but where there is anything like ordinary exposure to the bitter winds that prevail in spring, the selection is narrowed to a few of the oldest and hardiest climbers, and choice flowering kinds must be to some extent dispensed with. The common ivy, Virginian creeper, and the new *Stauntonia latifolia* will flourish in any soil or situation, so that here are three strong-growing and luxuriant climbers, on which the eye may always dwell with pleasure, and which may be used to cover almost any extent of space in the bleakest situation. The last does not train itself as the other two do, but must be led along. Neither of these produce conspicuous blossoms, but if ivy is allowed to mantle over a roof or stack of chimneys, or any place where it can make a foamy head, and escape the shears, it blooms freely in October, and is beautiful and fragrant. Then for similar aspects where there is moderate shelter from the cutting east winds of March, the common fig, a fresh and healthy object; the common jasmine, the *Felicite perpetuelle*, and Ayrshire roses, *Cotoneaster microphylla*, very suitable for trellises or walls on either side of a door; *Chimonanthus fragrans* and *grandiflora*, and that fast-growing, free-blooming, frost-defying beauty the renowned *Clematis montana* may be planted. Northward it would be impossible to preserve the lovely *Escallonia macrantha* without some covering during frost, but to the south and west it would do out of doors, in any position except due north. Though not truly a climber it readily adjusts itself to a flat surface if trained in the ordinary manner of an espalier fruit tree. Cuttings of half-ripe wood struck in June, and wintered in a cool frame, might go to their final

quarters in May, and remain there safely, if not exposed
to the severest spring weather, especially if started in a
little peat.

The transition from walls and trellises to arbours, arches,
and rustic work generally, would be easy enough, but it
would be impolitic to pass at one bound from the house
to the remote grounds, where rustic-work may be supposed to prevail. The house itself claims more adornment,
and there are many accessories that demand each a word.

The first of these is vases, because though statuary and
fountains may be dispensed with, vases are so thoroughly
gardenish, and whether planted well or ill, or not planted
at all, there is ever a tone about them that commands
respect.

Wherever there is terrace work, or architectural lines,
or ornamental masonry, or formal gravel, parterre, and lawn,
vases are appropriate embellishments. They refuse to
mingle with rustic work, and they look lost in large spaces
of wood where flowers are not freely mingled; but in all
artistic scenes they produce rich and finished effects.

In some remarks on vases in a former portion of this
work I have laid stress on the beauty of vases of elaborate design and rich ornamentation; but here, considering
what vases are most suitable for out-door embellishment,
I should, as a rule, give preference to those of bold and
classic outline, but of quite plain exterior, except where
a single vase or pair would have to stand alone, and then
I would have the grandest examples that the positions
would admit of.

The Crystal Palace has done as much for vases perhaps
as it has for suspended baskets; nothing in the way of
Garden Embellishments can be more magnificent than the
large vases filled with geraniums, which all the summer
long stand at regular distances along the balustrades and
the flights of steps that connect the terraces together.
Here is a lesson in colour that an amateur may profit by.

The general colour of the building is blue and white; the balustrading is a dark stone; there is also an immense breadth of gravel visible, and the vases themselves are light, and arrest the eye as much from their colour as their majesty of outline. Were they planted with anything less brilliant than those monster geraniums with their intense lustre of scarlet and extraordinary profusion of bloom, the vastness of the terrace space would itself produce a langour, and there would be a tone of emptiness or of ostentation not supported by dignity.

Scarlet and blue are always the best colours to relieve a great breadth of stone work, and where a dwelling has a commanding position and the architectural accessories of terraces, fountains, and broad gravel paths; one long blaze of scarlet along the garden front will produce a simple and grand effect, where a miscellaneous colouring would appear ridiculous.

Wherever the occasion will admit of large vases of very simple design, a few of such will be preferable to any number of smaller examples, even if the latter are ornamented in the most costly manner. The best terrace plants we have are humea elegans, agapanthus, yucca, hydrangia, fuchsia, and geranium. Variety is never so telling as sameness, or rather repetition, in architectural scenes, especially as to the colours of the flowers exhibited, and a simple line of vases planted all alike, or with two colours only, as scarlet geranium and agapanthus alternating, will produce the chasteness of classic severity with the warmth of hospitality added, provided all the elements of the scene are in keeping one with the other.

If vases arc planted with a variety of plants, as they may be when there are few of them, or in the case of a pair, the plants should be arranged in well-contrasted colours. The verbenas, mixed in colours, trail over and produce a charming effect. Petunias, heliotropes, and other low-growing half-creeping exotics are best suited.

The dark nasturtium also looks well when partially covering the base with pendant stems and rich crimson blossoms. Geranium, cineraria, calceolaria, Noisette roses, orange and lemon trees, collinsia, nemophila, schizanthus, balsam, coxcomb, anemone, and all kinds of bulbs, especially hyacinths, are suitable. The plants should all be grown in pots, none of them on any account planted in the vases. The pots can be lifted in or out as occasion requires, and a succession kept up during all seasons. The space between the pot and the inner side of the vase should be filled with moss to prevent exhaustion of the

roots by the heat of the sun. *Bonapartea gracilis* is another graceful thing for a vase in summer, and *Hibbertias* tell well in small vases if allowed to crawl over the edges.

Among the various productions of the Messrs. Seeley, Messrs. Cottam and Hallen, and Mr. Ransome, of Ipswich, a selection of vases might be made to suit any purpose, or conform to any class or style of design. I should always advocate simple forms for the garden, and highly elaborate ones for the house. In the latter position, the size should be determined by the use they were to be put to; but for the garden I would have them as large as the scene would admit, so that while they should not compete for importance

with the house itself, they should still be grand in outlines
and proportions. A poverty of ornament is as miserable as
an excess is ostentatious.

I have a favourite walk which I prize because it leads
me through a splendid "alley of limes," and gives me as
great a variety of views as I ever knew to be compassed
within so short a space of travelling. This walk leads me
past a very princely mansion on the summit of a wooded
hill. The frontage of the house is very plain but enormous
in its dimensions, and in the centre is a plain doorway,
large enough to admit the family carriage without even gra-
zing the paint of the lintels. The forecourt comprises rather
more than a quarter of an acre of ground, enclosed in an
iron railing and gates, laid out in one semicircular grass-
plot. The view from this frontage is magnificent, and hence
I do not wonder that the grass-plot is left so bare, not a
single shrub lending grace to its wide surface; but I do
wonder that in front of such a breadth of brick-work and
windows, in front of such a doorway too, there should be
a pair of vases just large enough for the doorway of a toll-
house; compared with the house they are meant to embellish,
they appear as if dropped there by accident by some wandering Italian, but they are meant to embellish it, for each
vase has in it *one* small Tom Thumb geranium. But there
is more ornament in the centre of the grass-plot, and hence
in view of all the windows stands a tree-stump just as
large as the two vases would be if they were melted into
one. This is decorated with one verbena, one geranium,
and a central handful of mignionette. Could anything be
more miserable, more poverty-struck, than such things in
front of a mansion whence an earl *might* issue?

To me it always conveys the idea of shabby gentility
lost in empty rooms, and seeking refuge from rats and ghosts
in a servants' attic, and it would seem quite appropriate
to the meagre tastelessness of the whole exterior, if a "small
servant" were suddenly to emerge on a ragged errand to a

chandler's shop. The absence of shrubs gives the whole affair a bald appearance, for tower as they might they could not shut out the view from that noble hill, but the vases and the *rustic* adornment compel one to find relief in a hearty "ha! ha!" This I call embellishment *underdone*.

Walks, beds, and lawns, offer their several points for ornamentation; and if the style of ornament is suited to the character of the scene, the interest is greatly enhanced, because there is not only more to see as to mere multiplicity of forms, but that impression of fullness is conveyed to the eye, which is always so graceful in garden scenery. Arches and arbours are among the ornaments that are suitable every-where if not carried to excess, and to fit them to the gardenesque of gravel and lawn, or the picturesque of woody hills and vales, it is only necessary to give them a proper individuality of character—art should prevail in the first case, nature in the second.

Handsome wire structures are now prepared at low prices by manufactures of horticultural ornaments, and these, when made to span paths, break angles, or heighten the interest of an object seen through them, are extremely useful. There are all sorts of climbers suitable for these arches, indeed any of the soft-wooded climbers referred to in con-nection with the walls and trellises would do upon them, but for special purposes I might add *Aristolochia sipho*, which produces a superb foliage of light green cordate leaves, and which grows profusely into rich arcadian masses and graceful festoons. Then there is the somewhat new but very choice bind-weed, *Calystegia pubescens*, which adds to the curiosities of the flower-garden the novelty of a double convolvulus. It is unique in its way, though not a very showy plant. The blossoms are as large as those of a double anemone, of a delicate pink colour, and remain expanded for several days. It flowers freely in July and August, and has all the habit of a hedge trumpet-flower, and is as hardy. Another suitable plant of this same family is the *Calboa*

globosa, a handsome and free-growing bindweed which produces a flower of a rich deep red. It is one of the best
of the family for an arch, but will not endure exposure to
a low temperature, and hence must in autumn be cut down
and transferred to the house. It grows freely in any loamy
soil, and is easily increased by cuttings of the young shoots.

Lapageria rosea and *Bomarea acutifolia* are two other
novel and beautiful plants suited for arches and parasols,
both of them being sufficiently hardy to endure the winter

out of doors, if first mulched, and then covered with a deep
stratum of coal ashes in October; neither of these latter
however are of such rapid growth as to be suitable for
entirely covering an arch of any great size. A parasol or
wire design of such special kind would be the best for them;
and for such wire designs a good selection of plants may
be made from the lists given in the chapter on Window
Gardening, and in the remarks on walls in this chapter.

2 I

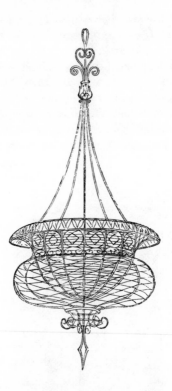

Here however we come naturally into the region of roses, for an arch of roses, or a fine arcade of considerable length, formed of a light but substantial frame-work, and well covered with these royal flowers, may very properly lead the way to the Rosary itself; which forms a good connecting link between the formal garden and the picturesque garden; in fact between art in her full dress, formal, proper, and august, and art humbled in her own esteem through close observance of the freedom of nature.

Where will you plant your rosary? How will you plant it? Will you make it rich in free and flowing outlines, suggestive of the luxuriance of the lands in which the rose attains its highest glory; or will you give your attention so much to sorts, new and old, as to lose sight of the beautiful in a search for technical perfection?

A rosary near a house will be in a position that will preclude its full development, for it may be made quite a curiosity—fanciful, quaint, exuberant in varied attractions for the eye, and at the same time unique in its beauty and completeness. It must be intricate, and therefore should be removed from the house, and placed in some part of the grounds where it will have prominence, or, at least, speciality of position. A low hollow which can be shut in by verdure is a good position, and one too that will suit roses, for they like moisture and shelter. A fanciful gate may lead the way to it from the main path, and the gate may open through a noble wire arch, covered with a dark green climber, but not a rose. This would be the garden entrance, and at the other side of the rosary another walk leading off to the shrubbery and wilderness, would open the way for true rustic work, and prepare the mind for the Rockery, the root-house, and such other objects of interest as were scattered about the wilder parts of the ground. Between these two walks I would lay out a space for a pavilion, which should form the centre of the rosary. This pavilion should be in a most fantastic but artificial design; it should be Chinese or Italian, fancifully gilt and garnished with as much elaborate ornament as could be crowded upon it, and the colour should be very light throughout, relieved by mouldings, carvings, and gilt-work, rather than by gaudy colours. Blue and amber might be picked out in some of the ornamental tracings, but no shade of red or pink should anywhere be seen. If of Chinese pattern the roof would be tent-like, hung with bells; the windows would be oval, for such is the Chinese style, and the whole affair very dandyish and artificial.

Then around this pavilion I would have a gravelled space of four or five feet wide, and from this gravelled space a

number of small paths of silver-sand should radiate, and between each two paths should be a border of dwarf roses, one sort only in each border; and in the centre of each of these beds there should be three standards close together, their heads brought into one mass by means of a copper wire passed through a hole in the stem of each, close under the grafting. In this way large masses would be formed, and the trees would be self-supporting. The standards in each bed should be different in colour from the dwarf roses in the same bed.

There would now be a central pavilion, a gravelled space around it, two main walks on opposite sides the pavilion, leading to and from the rosary, and such other paths radiating from the same central space of gravel, but formed only as divisions to the rosary itself. Let us suppose that to obviate a harsh formality, the main walk leading to the shrubberies proceeds at an angle to the direction of the chief entrance. Then between these main walks you will have room for two paths and three borders on one side, and four paths and five borders on the other side.

Now let all these minor paths terminate in another circular gravel path, bounded within by the beds of dwarf and standard roses, and without by a smooth lawn, which loses itself in a back-ground of shrub borders, formed of evergreen cypress, tree box, holly, arbor vitæ, rhododendron, Irish yew, or other rich massive evergreens, arranged in bold sweeping outlines. Every one of the minor paths, where it meets the outer circular one, may be spanned by an arch of climbing or weeping roses; and the two main walks spanned by similar arches on a grand scale, composed of mixed sorts framing over in festoons of odorous beauty. The lawn bounding the whole might be broken into a symmetrical arrangement of beds for dwarf and standard roses again, and the tallest and boldest of the standards should stand above at regular distances, away from the borders and paths on the midway of the lawn, so as to show up their colours against the boldly-defined back-ground of shrubs.

Such a plan could be modified in a hundred ways, according to the taste of the planter. One would prefer a rustic arbour, covered all over with climbing roses; and another would have a basket or a group of statuary, such as some of the copies of the antique which Brucciani, of Little Russell Street, has brought to such perfection, as centres; and indeed any arrangement might be adopted, so long as the general style did not clash with that of the ground in general. But in any case an air of profusion and luxuriance should prevail in a rosary; it may be placed on a hill to command a view, be made an adjunct to water-scenery, or may consist of a simple display upon the flat surface of a lawn. But whatever it is, whether large or small, simple or complex, in design let it be full and rich; nothing scanty or meagre about it, for the rose is the symbol of pride, power, beauty, and cultivated grace; it is oriental in its suggestions, and must have the help of a liberal disposition of gardening elements to make the ground it beautifies worthy of its name and fame.

> ———"Never yet by night or day,
> In dew of spring or summer's ray,
> Did the sweet valley shine so gay
> As now it shines--all love and light,
> Visions by day and feasts by night
> A happier smile illumes each brow,
> With quicker spread each heart uncloses,
> And all is ecstacy,--for now
> The valley holds its feast of roses."
>
> *Moore.*

To grow roses well you must have shelter from cutting east winds, and if the position is not sheltered it must be made so by means of a wall, a fence of yew, borders of evergreens, or some other plan that will enhance rather than mar the beauty of the scene. Then there must be good drainage to carry off excess of moisture. My own

way of growing roses in borders, is to take out the soil
three feet deep, then lay down a foot of brick rubbish,
then two feet of strong loam, into which an abundance of
well-rotted sweet dung has been worked. If the space
covered by roses is too extensive for this plan, drainage
must be secured by means of drain pipes, if the soil itself
does not serve as a natural filter. In any case the soil
must be rich, but none of the old-fashioned exciting composts
of bullocks' blood, new pigs' dung, or such killing stuff
must be used. Then in planting let them go to their final
quarters from the middle of October to the middle of
November, being first shortened in, and, if possible, none
should be used, especially of worked standards, that have
been grown to any size in pots. Once a year dress the
roots with rotted dung, as described at page 352.

During dry weather when roses are in bloom, they must
have plenty of water, not cold and hard from a well, but
tepid through exposure to the sun, and occasionally strengthened by the admixture of a little guano. Whatever insects
appear water is the remedy, it must be played over them
from an engine, and continued till all the pests disappear.

Pruning must be performed in March, but not severely
unless special circumstances require it, for there is scarcely
any rose that will bear close cutting with impunity. On
this head see the notes on rose fences at page 360. With
such management you may insure roses in abundance,
whether you live in the north or the south, the main requisites being liberality of food and water, moderate shelter,
good exposure to the south, and the roots to be disturbed
as little as possible.

As to sorts, it is scarcely within the compass of this
work even to mention the most noted ones. Mr. Alphonse
Karr, a distinguished amateur of roses, and author of that
curious and entertaining work, "A Tour round my Garden,"
contributed to the "L' Illustration," some time ago, a
paper on roses, in which he enumerated a hundred and

forty choice varieties, severally selected by eminent growers, and classed by himself, with the addition of many interesting historical and cultural particulars. An able analysis of this communication was given in the "Cottage Gardener" of August 5th. and 12th., 1856, and to that or the original I gladly refer those lovers of roses who may desire to improve their old collections, or make new ones.

To give a full list here would be impossible, but the subject cannot be allowed to pass without at least a suggestion of the varieties that would be found most valuable for the several positions that roses would have to occupy in the rosary and elsewhere.

First, as to climbers and standards of full height. Among the old and noted sorts, the finest white climbing rose is undoubtedly *Lamarque*, which grows rapidly, flowers freely, has splendid foliage, and blooms a great size, with exquisite fragrance. It does well either on arches, trellises, or as standards for the lawn, but it demands a good exposure to the south and very judicious pruning. The head of the old red climbers is *Madame Desprez*, a vigorous-growing and very hardy climber. The foliage is splendid, but the blooms are not equal in size or fragrance to those of *Lamarque*. For lattice and arbour work *Ruga* is a capital sort, on account of the rapidity of its growth, the profusion and fragrance of its flowers, and the ease with which it may be trained to any design that may be required. For large spaces, especially walls, where a mass of *green* is required, *Bracteata odorata alba* is a useful rose, on account of its rapid growth and evergreen foliage, but the blooms are worth little, though there are usually plenty of them. The old climbing roses that are most highly coloured are *Brennus, Fulgens,* and *Billiard;* and for general uses the next best are *Felicite Perpetuelle, Lilac Noisette, Bougainville Noisette, Common Noisette, Princess Nassau, Princess Hélène, Boursault Amadis, Dr. Roake, Prince Nassau,* and *Ariel.* All of these may be used as climbers, most of them train well, and they are all showy, fragrant, and free-blooming kinds except the *Bracteata*.

To train as weeping roses the Ayrshires, multifloras, and sempervirens, are the best, and as the Ayrshires prosper in any aspect, the north side of the rosary, if exposed, may be covered with a selection of them, with *Felicite Perpetuelle*, to add variety, and to work other sorts upon. The best of the Ayrshires for weeping roses are *Ruga*, *Bennet's seedling*, *Queen of the Belgians*, *Dundee Rambler*, and *Ayrshire Queen*. The best multifloras for a similar use are *Alba*, *Rubra elegans*, and the famous *Multiflora var. Grevellii*, which will flourish in a northeast aspect, and produce enormous trusses of roses of all colours, light blush, deep blush, crimson, purple, and many shades of red. It is an extraordinary grower, and should only be planted where it can have plenty of room to spread. I have seen this rose make shoots of fifteen feet in four weeks. But for bowers, arches, and most kinds of rustic work the evergreens bear the palm, and of these *Princess Maria*, *Princess Louisa*, *Myrianthus*, *Ranuncule*, *Rampante*, *Donna Maria*, *Spectabile*, *Felicite Perpetuelle*, and *La Biche*, are admirable sorts to work for weeping roses.

Among the new sorts of climbing roses the *Duchess of Norfolk* may be named as a fine one for a pillar in a conservatory, or the pilasters or trellis-work of a pavilion; it is a fine crimson shaded with pink, and has magnificent foliage. *Mathurin Requier* is a large-flowering perpetual that trains well on a low trellis.

There are several curiously-coloured climbers that may be used for variety; the most useful of them are *Jeaune Desprez*, a flesh yellow, not a free bloomer, nor yet very hardy; the other is the very singular *Bouton Nankin*, the buds nankeen coloured, quite a curiosity. Both these may be worked as standards, but they do not themselves take other sorts well.

For working on full standards and dwarfs the *Hybrid Perpetuals* take precedence; they offer us the finest colours and richest scents, and bloom freely and continuously. The best of the leading sorts of hybrid perpetuals are, for crimson and pink, *Geant des Batailles*, an old rose of magnificent colour, now somewhat eclipsed by *Jaqueminot*, which is perfect in form and colour; Mr. Lane's splendid *Bacchus, Baron Laray, Comte de Nanteuil, Evêque de Meaux, Gloire de France, La Fontaine, Lord Raglan, Madame de Cambaceres, Madame de Trottaire, Madame Masson, Duchess of Sutherland, Madame Laffay, Lady Alice Peel, Baronne Prevost, Dr. Marx, Mrs. Elliot,* the last being a shy bloomer in most soils, *Paul Ricaut* and *Leon des Combats,* are all of high character, free bloomers, requiring no special culture, and all obtainable at moderate prices. The newest sorts of crimson and red perpetuals are of course expensive; the best of them are *General Simpson, Madame Desire, Giraud, Mathurin Requier,* a robust and splendid rose, *Pæonia, Souvenir de la Reine,* very large and double, a bold and brightly-coloured rose; and the finest of all the new roses, *Triomphe de L' Exposition,* bright foliage and dazzling crimson, large bloom, and very strong habit.

The hybrids of the darkest colours are *Arthur de Sansalles,* the only purple hybrid with *double* flowers; *Triomphe d' Avranches, Deuil de François Willermoz,* the *darkest* perpetual known, the petals velvetty crimson, but *single* and of fine shape.

Among the light kinds the most desirable are *Belle Lyonnaise,* pale flesh; *Marquis de Murat,* lilac; *General Pellissier,* lilac; *Louise Magnan,* pure white with blush centre; and *Maiden's Blush,* one of the older sorts.

Among the Bourbons *Malmaison* must stand first as a decided beauty, the colour a pale flesh tinted with fawn; *Grand Capitane* is a fine dwarf-growing Bourbon, suitable for an edging, very brilliant crimson; *Great Western,* crimson, strong habit; *Hortensia*, bright pink, very striking; *Charles Duval*, bright rose, large and double; *Paul Perras*, shaded rose, extraordinary vigour; *Elise Mercœur*, fine foliage, strong habit, large rose-coloured blooms; *Chenedolé*, a very vigorous grower, equal to any of the preceding. To these may be added a few of the newer hybrid Bourbons, the most desirable of which are *Aurora de Guide*, bright crimson, one of the finest Bourbons ever raised; *Omar Pacha*, crimson pink; *Charles Lawson*, large, vivid crimson bloom; and *Impératrice Eugenie*, which is reported as the finest of the new roses. It certainly produces a large flower of a rosy blush with deep centre, but has scarcely yet established itself, though it promises to become an acquisition.

For dwarfs and standards, and for growing on their own roots, there are the briars, the Provence roses, the Noisettes, the tea roses, the moss and China roses, and intermediate kinds again, that unite the qualities of several.

Amongst the earliest roses are the *Rose de Meaux*, dwarf; the *Mossy Pompone*, the *Persian Yellow*, bright gold colour; *Chinese Sweet Briar*, very sweet scented, pink bloom; *Burgundy*, double pink, very suitable for an edging; these are all small-sized roses. The earliest large roses are the Chinese hybrids, *George the Fourth*, *Fulgens*, *Blairii No. Two*, a very showy sort; *Magna Rosa*, and *Triomphe d' Angers*, all old favourites.

The choicest of the new kinds of moss-roses are *Impératrice Eugenie*, rosy pink perpetual, distinct from the rose of the same name just referred to; *Salet* and *Madame Edward Ory*, bright pink perpetuals; *Madame de Blois*, *Gloire des Mousseuses*, and *William Lobb*. These are all of various shades of rose and pink, with the exception of the last, which is a fine rose for specimen growth in pots; it is of a deep velvetty crimson, shaded with dove-colour: the French call it a "*blue* moss-rose," a thing we are as likely to have as a blue dahlia.

The Noisettes and tea roses are very numerous, and a rosary affords a proper site for a selection of them in compartments. There are many hundreds of kinds of every one of the sections, but the number of really desirable sorts does not greatly exceed those just named. A visit to any of the noted rose growers would enable an amateur to judge what sorts he would want, better than volumes of description, and the list is here given, not to render such visits unnecessary, but to indicate the kinds that should first be sought, and seen in flower, because they are proved as to excellence, and quite distinct from each other. Lane, of Great Berkhampstead; Rivers, of Sawbridgeworth; and Paul, of Cheshunt, are the greatest rose growers in the country, and to one of these an amateur in need of a collection true to name, and grown to perfection, should apply. There are hundreds of worthy nurserymen who can supply *well*-grown and high-class roses, but these three names carry all before them for novelties, extensive variety, and successful production of the newest and oldest sorts. The arts of budding and grafting, and the various other operations connected with rose culture, are all so interesting both as to the artistic nature of the operations themselves, and the fine results that flow from them, that I should recommend every amateur in gardening to give the rose some special attention.* With the gardening gauntlet introduced by Mrs. Loudon, and a basket on wheels, in place of a wheelbarrow, there can be no reason why ladies should not take to rose budding and other departments of rose culture; indeed a rosary stocked with plants raised wholly by one fair hand, would be a triumph, not of strong-mindedness and blue stocking-ism, but of feminine patience and ingenuity, applied to a work of artistic taste and high ornament.

When you have laid out your rosary, you may turn

* I may here refer the reader to my epitome of Rose Culture in "Garden Favourites," where the methods of budding and grafting are practically treated.

your eyes elsewhere, and while the roses gain strength to
sustain perennial beauty, you may busy yourself in finding
good sites for many choice things, to enrich your lawns
and increase the beauty and interest of the walks. You
are now getting into the region of the truly rustic, rough
outlines and dark masses begin to be more appropriate
than angles and curves, and graceful minglings of form and
colour—you are getting into the thick of the shadows,
where the Dryads have a leafy pleasure.

> The solemn shade,
> Verdure and gloom, where many branches meet;
> So grateful, when the noon of summer made
> The valleys sick with heat.

Here you may sprinkle about all kinds of rustic work,
arches, arcades, arbours of trellis and branch-work, cool
grottoes and moss-houses, and baskets and knolls of flowers.
Where paths diverge, or where the lawn is too open, or
where some distant object requires a framing as the eye
falls upon it, an arch or arcade is often of great value.
An embellishment of this kind may be very speedily made
by means of a few stout tree loppings, the rougher and
more gnarled the better; or where a couple of limes or
alders stand in a position ready for the work, the saw and
bill might be set to work to give them the required form,
and one season's growth will obliterate any stiffness of
outline which might result from a want of skill in the
operation. It would be worth while in laying out grounds
to plant a few trees along the margins of walks, expressly
to cultivate in this way, so as to construct natural arches,
or long alleys, some object of interest being placed at the
remote end, to engage the eye and entice the rambler to
an inspection of it. A bank of light stones, thinly planted
with choice ferns and alpines would do well for such a
purpose, and as a termination to an alley would assist in
creating a picturesque and poetical scene. Indeed artificial

arbours might in most cases be replaced by natural ones, a little judicious pruning and leading of the trees being all that is necessary to give them any outline we may desire, though that outline should always be as simple and natural as possible. Maples, elms, chesnuts, alders, and limes, are the most suitable for such work; but you must keep watch over yourself that you do not too readily yield to the popular love for avenues, for though these are often effective when formed of weeping limes or hornbeam, they generally consume more space than can be afforded for such formal effects.

There are many ways of leading and pruning to compel trees to space a walk, or form a leafy roof to cover a rustic seat. Who does not prefer a seat under a tree,

> Shaking its million leaflets in the sun,

to one in the confined air of a timber box, yclept a Summer House? Here are four examples of this mode of planting and lopping in the construction of natural arbours when, by the shortening of the leaders, a vigorous sidegrowth of the laterals is induced, a roof of greenery is soon formed, that not only excludes the "sun's perpendicular rays," but gives shelter during the heaviest of July showers, so that in changeable weather the enjoyment of the garden is not cut short by a flight to the house, or made irksome by the carrying of umbrellas.

These arcadian shades are more appropriate positions for rustic seats and resting-places than open lawns or orderly paths. Not but that a seat may often be well placed as an ornament in any spot where it may prove useful as a place of rest and gossip, and sometimes as an invitation to the enjoyment of a view; yet as a rule a rustic shade is the best position for a rustic seat; it looks useful and appropriate there, and may be embellished with a few rough stones, planted with ferns or other plants that like shade, or a couple may be placed one on either side of the bole of a large tree, and the spaces between them filled up with large root stumps, profusely planted with ivy, periwinkle, toadflax, orchises, and ferns, and a truly rustic and beautiful retreat will be formed without the introduc-

tion of a single element that would interfere with the general tone of the landscape, as a summer-house or grotto frequently will do.

Another kind of arch is that formed of dead timber, the materials being unbarked stems selected as to shape, or

brought together so as to form a symmetrical span by a little judicious carpentry. An arch of this kind is here represented; the construction is very simple, but produces an agreeable effect by means of a few accessories. The

base on each side of the walk is flanked by a rough
lattice of selected tree loppings, and the walk leads to a
lawn, in the centre of which stands a fine root ornament,
covered with a profusion of trailing plants. This and the
shrubberies beyond form a picture, to which the arch acts
as framework, and the eye is gratified by a judicious disposal
of a few very simple elements.

This sort of work leads the way naturally enough to the
consideration of arbours and summer-houses generally.
Where shady trees invite the wanderer to a seat, how
pleasant is it to find the means of rest and shelter in a
garden. What more delightful when the sun burns in Leo,
or when the Virgin holds empire in the meridian, than to
lounge in a cool shady recess, with a favourite volume and

a canister of that seductive, sedative weed, which wafts us
on its thin blue wreaths of smoke to the highest region of
the most dreamy Elysium. The bees hum about full of
business, reproaching us for the listless mood in which we
watch their earnestness—everything but the bee is sleepy;
the flowers nod as if napping, the air hums itself to sleep,
and lo! when we thought we were fast anchored to that
favourite book, we too have drifted, like a weed upon the
wave, into that tropical region where sleep, the "comfortable
bird," broods "over the troubled sea of mind, till it is
hushed and smooth." There is no better vindication of a
summer-house than the opportunity it affords for the quiet
enjoyment of a book, or an afternoon nap. There are some
books which seem to have been written for such reading.
You could not read Herrick with such pleasure in the
presence of a lamp and curtains, nor Earl Surrey, nor Jean
Paul, no, nor Tennyson. Did Alexander Smith write his
"Life Drama" in such a spot; I think he could hardly
have produced it with his feet on a carpet hassock,
cramping his chest to a vile mahogany table.

Judging from the tactics of publishers, no one is supposed to read now-a-days, except when in a railway train.
The quiet of a garden disposing the mind to tranquil
thought, and hushing that agitation of spirit which compels
us to be ever hurrying somewhere, as if we were endea-
vouring to escape from ourselves;—the genial tone of mind
which rural scenes so happily induce, is ignored by the whole
corporation of bibliopolists, and against the million of books
provided for river, rail, and road, there is not the balance
of one professedly for the garden or the summer-house.
O age of commercial fever, railway collision, and rotten
banks; forty miles an hour is the pace of reading and
travelling alike! You may plunge into a brown study while
the iron wheels rattle and jar, and the engine roars you
into stupidity and deafness; you may wanton in a comic
novel at the very moment that a shunting coal-train is

about to break your neck; but your daft purveyors of
literature will not offer you one precious volume to beguile
a peaceful hour amid the calm of a leafy and flowery shade.
But the prodigality of printers in providing literature for

travellers, will not prevent the consignment of a few choice
volumes to the garden-house, *there* they may have a chance
of being "devoured wholly," which is more than can be said
for at least ninety per cent of the red, green, blue, and

2 K

harlequin sandwiches intended to render us oblivious of elbows,
noisy babies, garlic, tooth-ache, cramp, danger, and official
insolence.

As to summer-houses and arbours generally, there never
was so much ugliness scattered about the world as of late
years has been sprinkled over suburban gardens under the
vain pretence of ornament and use. The majority are like
toll-houses, or beer-shops, or sweet-meat stalls, destitute of
elegance, use, and propriety. A summer-house need not
be utterly hidden, but it ought not to stare straight out
upon us from a back wall, its ugly lattice-work without
one creeping tendril to cool and comfort it, and its interior
visible to every gazer, as if it were anything but a place
of shade and rest. Though you never use it, it must appear fit for use or it is no ornament. It should be well
shrouded with greenery, be easy of access, sufficiently inviting to attract a stranger, yet quiet in tone, and of a
chaste pleasing outline. Some of these suburban retreats
look very much like the little cabins of the fly-boats on
the junction canal; and one always expects to see a head
pop up above them to take hold of the rudder and steer
them into port. Arbours indeed! what a perversion of language, they are *h*arbours for earwigs, cats, and other vermin,
not tree bowers and trellis shelters, as their philology
imports.

Where it is possible to make an ornament useful, or at
least appear useful, it is always much more appropriate.
Thus the summer-house or arbour offers shade and a place
of rest, and hence should be placed in a spot where rest
will be most agreeable: a good view is often appropriately
chosen as the site for an invitation to halt.

Summer-houses in the Chinese style have a fantastic and
pleasing effect if well placed. The construction is thoroughly
artificial—rural, but certainly not rustic; and if such building
be associated with moss mounds, rustic chairs, tree-stumps,
and rock-work, the effect will be anything but pleasant to

a cultivated eye. The approach to a pagoda should be by a clean winding walk, with a well-cut box-edging, and a bright display of the finest flowers and evergreens. One or two fine aucubas, some rhododendrons, tree box, and laurel, may be grouped to support the scene, and give a welcome shade; but deciduous trees and shrubs, with the exception of lilacs, acacias, and jasmines, are scarcely appropriate in the immediate neighbourhood of such an edifice. The construction itself cannot be too elaborately decorated; quaint carving, geometrical ornaments, and filigree-work, the whole gaily painted and kept fresh, all give it an appropriate character; for if Chinese at all, it should be so all over in its design and adjuncts. Fanciful gates and trellises are often used in connection with such edifices, but rustic work is always inappropriate.

A well-kept patch of turf, with some gaily-disposed exotics, will complete the scene. Rose, jasminum, or clematis arches may lead off to the less artificial walks, so as to form a transition from the highly artificial tone of the house and its surrounding ornaments.

The genuine rustic arbour must be of a totally different character. It must be in the midst of shrubby and rustic scenery, on a mound well sprinkled with ferns, with perhaps a rill of water below, and a mossy walk leading from it to dark wilderness scenery.

Now though there are many modes of constructing garden-houses, one feature is common to them, and that is that they are usually permanent structures. It is this permanency that has brought them into ridicule, and has caused a pretty general exclusion of them as *retreats* from most modern gardens. But the beauty of our short summers is so welcome, there is such a recurring desire as the season opens in its fullness, for occasional escape from the house to a bower of some kind, that it has frequently surprised me that rustic architects do not provide for gardening folks a kind of structure that might be put together by an amateur

in a few hours, and as quickly taken to pieces, and removed altogether at the end of the season. Yet, if such bowers were once fairly introduced to the gardening world, I feel assured they would be gladly used as agreeable resorts for the younger members of families, where Master Tommy would read Robinson Crusoe, and Miss Lucy would work in wool or lace, while other brothers and sisters would keep the flowers in trim, and so find an interest in gardening that would develope ingenuity, and furnish young minds and hands with pleasurable and educational employment.

To make a structure of this kind, the only materials necessary are a few frames of wood, and some breadths of cheap wire netting. Let there be six frames constructed of deal, each being made after the fashion of a picture-frame, but with a piece across its centre to add to its strength. The frames should be of inch-deal, three inches wide, mitred at the corners, and with the centre-bar mitred into the two lengths. Then make seven similar frames of a triangular shape, of similar materials. The measurement might be for the larger frames six feet by three feet, and for the smaller ones three feet for each side of the triangle. Then let a double frame-work be constructed, each of seven strips of one-inch deal, four inches wide, one frame-work fitting loosely within the other, so that the six larger frames can be let into the spaces between them.

These frames will have to be made so that the strips of deal are placed on edge, leaving a slit between them, into which the inch-deal of the larger frames will fall easily. You have only to cover the six large, and seven triangular frames with wire netting, and paint the whole of a cheerful green or brown, and you have all the materials for a garden-house. Lay down the double frame-work where the house is to stand, drop into each diagonal slit one of the large frames, and when all are inserted between the frames of the base, fix them by means of a few bolts at the bottom. You will now find that you have a seven-sided erection, firmly welded together by the bolts that pass through the three thicknesses of wood at the base, the outer and inner base framing forming a beading as well as a support. Now place the triangular pieces to form the roof, fasten them and the side pieces with a few screws, and place on the summit some kind of suitable ornament.

It will look very thin and bare for a few weeks, but that is to be remedied by planting round it an abundance of quick-growing climbers; but as the house is to be removed from the scene in autumn, it will be best to use annuals only, though a clematis, which may be cut down close at the end of every season, may be planted to cover it annually. Dutch runner beans, major convolvulus, dark major nasturtium, sweet peas, *Tropæolum Canariensis*. Of course a border must be made for the plants, and any choice half-hardy climbers in pots may be added, such as *Cobeas, Lapagerias, Calystegias, Maurandya*, etc., a class of plants of which sufficient has been said already. Ornaments of many kinds might be added, such as a rough lattice of barked apple-tree branches over the entrance, and around some portions of the sides, a rustic mound or tree-stump, with flowers or ferns near the doorway, or any other objects that would increase the beauty and add to the interest of such a garden retreat. A structure of this kind would be far preferable in hot weather to any timber structure, because it would form a sufficient screen against the heat of the sun, and at the same time allow the air to circulate freely within through the meshes of the wire, and the light screen of tendrils; indeed a bark or moss house ought always to have an open space around the base of the roof, for the admission of a current of air, otherwise it becomes as hot as an oven within, after an hour's sun, and is only comfortable in seasons when no such resort is needed.

A few other miscellaneous ornaments require a few words and my task will be completed. Rustic baskets, seats, and tree-stumps have been referred to pretty frequently, and they certainly deserve to be liberally used where their appearance will be appropriate. It is a common thing enough to see in the forecourts of substantial suburban villas, a very brave display of such things, but such a position is the very worst that can be found for them. In front of a rustic cottage, where the eglantine climbs over an old porch, and the grape-vines and cluster-roses festoon a rough timber trellis, and mingle their green and purple tints with the orange lichens on the roof, giving shadow to the mud cabins of homely swallows, and darkening the pavement of clean red tiles, rustic baskets and roots may find a place, but in the front garden of a trim citizen's box, all such things are out of place, and a mockery to the stone-facings, the broad steps, and the white-curtained windows.

I have just noted two such houses during a short walk; they are near each other, and the several proprietors seem to vie with each other in exhibitions of rustic tables and seats, sprinkled about profusely on the grass-plots, and under the shade of well-grown chesnuts. The appearance of each of these houses is exactly that of a suburban tavern, with "Tea Gardens" inscribed above the gateway; and if any weary wight were to saunter in, and like the hero in "She stoops to conquer," rudely call for "a pint of porter and a crust," it would be an act of gross injustice were he not at once supplied with the refreshment. Nor would it be any excuse to quote Longfellow, and say, "things are not what they seem;" in worldly matters things ought to seem what they are, and it is not in good taste to decorate a private residence so that it shall seem a beer-shop.

Proper sites being found for all such things, the next thing is to plant the stumps and baskets judiciously. Rough roots look admirable when planted with ferns, and the best ferns for such work are *Lastreas, Brakes, Polypodies, Polystichum angulare* and *aculeatum;* hartstongues, the English and American species of *Athyrium*, the splendid *Pycnopteris Siboldii*, and indeed numerous others, of which particulars

will be found in the article on "the Fernery." To these
may be added a selection of trailing plants, and many pretty
alpines, each of which may be planted in a soil congenial
to it by filling in the hollows with proper composts, and
giving such care as the several plants require. Groups of
ferns have the finest and most appropriate appearance, and
render such ornaments highly attractive.

Baskets admit of great variety, and most of the choice
greenhouse bedders are admirable stock for them. Fuchsias,
calceolarias, geraniums, hydrangeas, petunias, cinerarias, verbenas, nemophilas, jacobeas, œnotheras, of procumbent
growth, hawkweeds, *Hibbertia grossularifolia*, a yellow-
flowered free-growing trailer, *Entoca viscida*, *Nolana paradoxa*, and many annuals may be used; and if well
assorted, and not too much crowded, a very gay effect
may be produced, of which more specific remarks will occur
presently.

The makers of rustic furniture, who are too often as
ignorant of flower-culture as they are destitute of ideas of
taste, have a very queer fashion of filling these baskets;
and since it is the fashion never to question the *modus
operandi* of any man who works according to his trade, the
general opinion being that he at leasts understands his own
business, I must caution my readers never to purchase
rustic baskets filled with plants, without first ascertaining
whether or not they are properly planted. Just thrust a
finger through the moss which covers the surface round
the roots of the plants, and if the smallest trace of *sawdust*
be visible have nothing to do with it, unless it be charged
at the price of an empty basket, for you may rest assured
that before the season is half out it will require to be
re-stocked. These *ouvireus* have a quick method of making
a basket tempting to the eye, and hence of setting it at
a good price. A neighbouring florist sends in a cart-load
of greenhouse plants in pots, generally the refuse of the
greenhouse. There is always plenty of sawdust at hand,

and the basket is half-filled with it, the pots plunged into the sawdust, the basket filled up with the same material, and a layer of moss put over the top to make all fair and tempting. When purchased and sent home it looks beautiful, but the first heavy rain soddens the sawdust into a sort of granular paste, the drainage of the pots is stopped, and the plants having had no proper hardening, and perhaps put out a fortnight too soon, succumb to the several evil influences that combine against them, and before the summer is at its height, the whole affair looks wretched, and folks say "such things dont answer." Now they do answer to perfection if first filled with friable mould, previously compounded with sheep droppings of a month old, or well-decayed stable dung, and the whole made light and porous by an admixture of sharp sand and small crocks, the roots of the plants being confined; for there should never be more than from nine to twelve inches of soil in even the largest basket: good drainage should be secured, by placing over each hole in the bottom of the basket a large crock or oyster shell.

The plants are to be hardened off as for bedding, turned out of their pots and carefully planted in the soil of the basket, watered and shaded for a day or two, and thereafter watered liberally every evening in dry hot weather. Of course one or two holes for drainage should be pierced in the bottom of the basket, and the inside should be well pitched to preserve the wood from the effects of moisture. The best timber for every kind of rustic work that is not to be denuded of its bark, is that of the false acacia, (*Robinia pseudoacacia;*) it will last at least as long as the term of an ordinary lease—ninety-nine years—and the bark never peels off. Mr. Curry, of Clapton, has a very ingenious mode of stripping the bark from wood for rustic work, by which it acquires a fine tint and a durable hardness; but it would be unfair to Mr. Curry were I to explain a process which I believe to be an invention of his own. Wood that does

not hold its bark well when exposed to the weather is better stripped and prepared, and in this work Mr. Curry excels, as he does, indeed, in every department of his rustic craft.

As to the arrangement of the plants in a rustic basket, those of stiff shrubby growth, such as roses, calceolarias, and geraniums, must occupy the centre, and those of pendulous habit, such as verbenas, petunias, *Nolana paradoxa,* and *Hibbertia grossularifolia,* should be planted so as to hang over the sides, and the whole should be so assorted as to make a massive and rounded head of foliage, and blossom spreading convexly from the centre to the sides.

Any plants that stand high above the rest will give a stiffness to the whole, very detrimental to its beauty. Hound's tongue, variegated mint, ground ivy, speedwell, toadflax, and pimpernel, may be used in some cases to vary the pendant forms, and a shrubby plant of ivy-leaf geranium, the *Peltatum violaceum* being best of all, will greatly enhance the beauty of the green fringing of the edges.

Some taste and knowledge of the plants used will be necessary to secure a tasteful arrangement that shall not lapse into a general confusion before the end of the season; but in this and in other matters experience is the best teacher, and if your heart is in your work you will improve your baskets every season, till they equal those at the Crystal Palace, which of course you have seen and admired. Mr. Beaton, in the "Cottage Gardener," gives a very effective arrangement for a basket, which I here transcribe, in the hope that many of my readers will adopt it in preference to the mixture of colours that are so generally used. He says "keep the planting to three kinds of plants; two of them to be of most distinct colours—scarlet and yellow; and the third a half-distinct colour—a pale blue; and plant them in this wise. Take first a pale running *Lobelia* of the *Erinus* breed, but avoid *Ramosoides*, it is too upright, and

too dark a blue next the wood-work. Nothing suits so well as a pale blue. The plants are in sixty-sized pots; turn one out and *flatten the ball gently* between your hands, till it is nearly as flat as a pancake, but do not hurt a root. Open the side at the very edge of your basket, and *lay down* the flattened ball, with the root end of the plant as near the rim as possible; the herb part will then point out horizontally over the edge of the basket, and so on, making nearly a continuous hedge all round. Smooth the surface of the basket now, and plant a row of young Tom Thumbs, with the heads slanting. After the lobelias then another row of old Tom Thumbs quite upright, and fill the middle with yellow bedding calceolarias, quite full; and the plants

must be old ones, and higher than the last row of geraniums. Water well through a rose, and the thing is done for this season."

A few distinct colours artistically arranged, is infinitely better in any display of flowers, to such multifarious assemblages as we meet with in beds, borders, and baskets, and which too often emulate the hedge-rows for wildness, and make a burlesque of the art of gardening.

There are many makers of rustic furniture, but unfortunately, not being florists, they do not avail themselves of all the opportunities which present themselves for a display of rustic taste in such things. Mr. Curry, of Brook Street, Upper Clapton, has gone far in advance of his craft, in

all the details of design and adaptation, through the help of his skill as a florist, and perhaps still more from his intense love of ferns and mosses. Mr. Curry's rustic chairs and baskets are as superior to the majority of such productions as might be expected from one whose hobby and passion is fern-growing, and who devotes as much enthusiasm to the stocking of stumps and baskets with rare and beautiful plants, as he does to the mere carpentry of their formation. His rustic arbours and bark-houses are of admirable designs, and he fits up bark-baskets and tree-stumps in a manner most tasteful and bewitching.

Once more I must impress upon my readers that incongruities should be studiously avoided in the adornment of the garden, and indeed in all that pertains to the Home of Taste. The artistic and the rustic have each their place. Let the house be surrounded by elegance of form and colour, the truly rustic should have its place elsewhere, we should go to it, not have it come to us; for nothing can be more absurd than to imitate eastern luxury in carpets and furniture, and by one step pass from mirrors and gilt cornices, and rich tapestry, to honeysuckle hedges, hermits' huts, and bogs covered with toad-stools. A really rustic cottage may have rustic ornaments, even at the threshold, but a villa of formal design must have its garden in keeping at least in proximity to its walls. Propriety, unity,

congruity—these are the words that should be remembered
at every step. Secure fitness of style, and the individual
taste may roam at pleasure through all the regions of
statuary and fancy-work, till it finds pleasure in the smallest

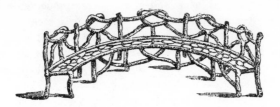

and humblest ornament that ever decked the threshold of
an English home.

Where a rustic tone prevails, as it does in the good old
English gardens, where the digitalis and the hollyhock still
assert their claims to admiration, there are no better ornaments than rustic baskets and tree-stumps. In such a

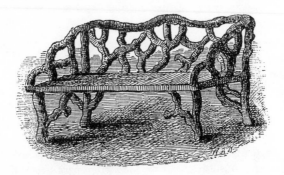

garden the summer-house should be of simple design, with
an elliptic arch, or domed roof of bark or thatch, the front
opening to a rill of water on a green slope, beyond which
the eye catches avenues of stately flowers, while on the

other hand, the garden loses itself in a maze of verdurous branches. In such scenes, rock banks and ferneries, aquaria shadowed with willows, and stocked with water-lilies and British fish, are appropriate, while the fancy too may sport with ivy mounds, mossy tree-trunks covered with polypodies,

bark baskets filled with British wildings or gay flowers— every separate detail helping towards the production of a scene of enchantment, or at least one of homeliness, of comfort, and of taste.

> "Look on this beautiful world, and read the truths
> In her fair page; see, every season brings
> New change to her, of everlasting youth;
> Still the green soil, with joyous living things
> Swarms, the wide air is full of joyous wings,
> And myriads still are happy in the sleep
> Of ocean's azure gulfs, and where he flings
> The restless surge. Eternal Love doth keep
> In His complacent arms the earth, the air, the deep."
>
> *Bryant.*

MY DEAR READER,—The household gods require no further vindication at my hands; you and I are agreed as to the homage they are entitled to, and the mission they are to perform in our behalf. May your hours of rustic recreation profit you in body and soul. May your flowers flourish, your bees prosper, your birds love you, and your pet fishes live for ever. May the blight never visit the tendrils that make your arbours and porches leafy, your borders gay, or your fern-banks verdurous; and may you find in every little thing that lives and grows a pleasure for the present hour, and a suggestion of things higher and brighter for contemplation in the future. I herein reach my hand towards you with an affectionate FAREWELL!